Maximum Performance:
The Dow Jones-Irwin
Complete Guide to Practical
Business Management

Maximum Performance: The Dow Jones-Irwin Complete Guide to Practical Business Management

Volume I

Joseph Shetzen

DOW JONES-IRWIN
Homewood, IL 60430
Boston, MA 02116

TO MY MOTHER, Alichen Shetzen, who instilled in me
decency, diligence, optimism, and the desire to help others.

TO MY FATHER, Benno Shetzen, who taught me that in order to succeed,
one needs to persevere and remain strong and calm.

This publication is designed to provide accurate and
authoritative information in regard to the subject matter
covered. It is sold with the understanding that neither the
author nor the publisher is engaged in rendering legal, accounting,
or other professional service. If legal advice or other expert
assistance is required, the services of a competent
professional person should be sought.

*From a Declaration of Principles jointly adopted by a Committee
of the American Bar Association and a Committee of Publishers.*

Sponsoring editor: Jim Childs
Project editor: Joan A. Hopkins
Production manager: Diane Palmer
Compositor: Publication Services
Typeface: 11/13 Times Roman
Printer: The Maple-Vail Book Manufacturing Group

Library of Congress Cataloging-in-Publication Data
Shetzen, Joseph.
    Maximum performance: The Dow Jones-Irwin
    complete guide to practical business
    management, Volumes I and II
    1. Industrial management. I. Dow Jones-Irwin.
II. Title.
HD31.S453 1990   658   89–25848
ISBN 1–55623–111–3 (v. 1)
ISBN 1–55623–112–1 (v. 2)

Printed in the United States of America

1 2 3 4 5 6 7 8 9 0 MP 7 6 5 4 3 2 1 0

Preface

If you are a business owner, accountant, or management consultant, this book is definitely for you. The primary purpose of this book (Volumes I and II) is to provide you with essential, practical knowledge and the ability to solve problems in business management. Although numerous books have been written by various experts on this subject, most are designed to meet the needs of students and therefore present complex theoretical concepts coupled with little practical knowledge.

This book, however, contains substantial practical information and is designed as a highly effective business management tool. Just like a builder who uses tools in erecting a house, you need tools to plan, develop, and manage your business or to provide sound professional advice to your clients. Your task is particularly difficult since your success or failure depends primarily upon your personal knowledge and experience in various areas of business management.

As a co-owner of a small manufacturing company and later as a management consultant, I have engaged in an extensive search for the "magic formula" for successful business management. While gaining experience, I found that many business owners have limited management skills and fail to see the "big picture." Some employ experts in various management areas but then cannot coordinate the activities of their management teams effectively.

This brings to mind the story about Swan, Pike, and Crayfish written by a Russian fabulist, Ivan Krilov. These three friends wanted to move a cart together. They tried very hard but could not succeed because Swan wanted to fly, Pike wanted to swim, and Crayfish wanted to crawl. In the end they failed in their efforts, and the cart was never moved. In business terms this is called "mismanagement."

A business owner's inability to see the "big picture" and the resulting mismanagement are among the major causes of failure for thousands of businesses every year. This is particularly unfortunate because starting a new business requires tremendous internal strength and motivation, significant financial resources and sacrifices, and a total commitment to working 25 hours a day to become the master of one's destiny.

Since lack of managerial knowledge and experience is so widespread in the business community, I felt compelled to continue the search for the "magic formula" for successful business management. The discovery took place unexpectedly one evening during a symphony concert. While I was listening to the beautiful music and watching the conductor leading his orchestra, something struck me. I suddenly realized that every business should operate precisely like an orchestra; the conductor knows what each musician should play and when it should be played. In business terms this means that every entrepreneur, company president, or CEO must know what each member of the management team should do and when it should be done. Only then will the business produce "beautiful music" or perform to the satisfaction of its shareholders and employees.

This simple discovery led me to devise a new business management method, which I hope will break the vicious cycle of incompetence, ignorance, mismanagement, and ultimate failure. The method represents a "be-your-own-management-consultant" guide for business owners. It is designed to enable entrepreneurs, company presidents, and CEOs to identify, analyze, and solve various management problems. This method also teaches business people to delegate effectively a wide range of responsibilities to subordinates and to control their performances. Finally, it is designed to help accountants and management consultants render effective management advice to their clients.

I termed it the "Business Engineering Method" because it is based on an integrated multidisciplinary approach to business management and it uses engineering principles of solving problems. The six parts to this method are described in two volumes as follows:

Volume I

Part 1   General Management Guide
Part 2   Personnel Management Guide
Part 3   Financial Management Guide

Volume II

Part 4   Production and Operations Management Guide
Part 5   Marketing and Sales Management Guide
Part 6   Business Analysis and Action Guide

Each part is written in simple language, and, together they highlight all the major elements of practical business management. In addition, each part contains a detailed set of working instructions and self-explanatory standard forms. These have been designed for and successfully used in various small and medium-sized companies.

When you complete the management tasks according to the guidelines in both volumes, you should be able to:

1. Understand all major elements of operational business management.
2. Assess personal knowledge and evaluate your company's performance in each management area.
3. Evaluate your company's financial performance, interpret results, and prepare a consolidated plan of action.
4. Implement the most effective business solutions by following the prescribed guidelines.
5. Assess action taken and adjust such action where necessary.

Business Management Club

If you experience difficulty in accomplishing any of these tasks, additional management assistance can be yours through membership in Business Management Club. This organization represents a network of licensed and highly skilled business experts who are professors in various business schools, accountants, and management consultants. Since Business Management Club is being developed on a countrywide basis, you will soon have an opportunity to obtain additional assistance locally.

Business Management Club has a number of important purposes:

• To provide business owners with a wide range of practical management methods, systems, and solutions.

- To enable business owners to act as management consultants to their own organizations.
- To enable business owners to coordinate the work of their management teams in the most efficient manner.
- To keep business owners abreast of all the latest developments in operational business management.
- To provide business owners with low-cost management consulting service when necessary.
- To provide training for business owners, accountants, and management consultants in various areas of operational business management.

Business Management Club is totally committed to the promotion of interests of all small and medium-sized organizations. This commitment will always remain the most important single factor in the process of development, distribution, and implementation of sound, effective management solutions on a do-it-yourself basis or through low-cost services of licensed management consultants.

Since additional management assistance is provided solely to members of Business Management Club, you are invited to apply for your free membership. Once your application is accepted, you will be contacted by the local representative of Business Management Club's network, who will then give you additional details about the management assistance you can expect in the future. Hopefully, this will be the beginning of a most productive and mutually beneficial association.

Joseph Shetzen

Santa Monica, California
April 1, 1990

Acknowledgements

Just as a long distance runner feels tremendous appreciation of his supporters, I am filled with deep gratitude to a few very special people who helped me complete this project.

First, I want to thank my parents, Alichen and Benno Shetzen, for their devotion and continual support throughout my life and particularly during the tought times we endured together. They served as a constant source of inspiration to me from the very beginning of the project.

I also want to thank Dr. Bruce A. Samuelson, Chairman of Accounting, Law and Finance at the School of Business and Management, Pepperdine University. Dr. Samuelson's generous contribution of knowledge, time, and moral support played a significant role in the completion of this project.

Further, thanks go to the following contributing editors for their valuable input to this project:

- Dr. Richard E. Gunther, Professor of Management Science at California State University, Northridge
- Dr. Charles W. Fojtik, Associate Professor of Marketing at the School of Business and Management, Pepperdine University
- Dr. Barry R. Nathan, Assistant Professor of Management and Organization at the School of Business Administration, University of Southern California

In addition, I am grateful to the following persons for their generous assistance and cooperation during the development of this project:

- Mr. Anthony Southall, management consultant
- Mr. Brian C. Schiff, partner at Price Waterhouse Associates
- Dr. Zvi Livne, Professor at the Graduate School of Business, Columbia University
- Dr. Richard H. Buskirk, Professor of Marketing and Director of the Entrepreneur Program, University of Southern California
- Dr. William A. Cohen, Professor of Marketing, California State University, Los Angeles

Moreover, I want to thank Jim Childs, Senior Editor with Dow Jones-Irwin, and the staffs of Dow Jones-Irwin, Richard D. Irwin, Inc., and Publication Services, Inc., who worked so hard to make this book a reality. My special thanks go to Shirley Sunn for her support and superb proofreading of my manuscripts. She certainly helped me overcome the fact that English in not my mother tongue. My thanks also to Jeanette Udwin and David D'Albany for their efficiency and patience in typing the manuscripts.

Finally, I would like to express my appreciation to all my clients, who provided me with a variety of management problems and the ultimate challenge of finding the right solutions.

J. S.

About the Author

Joseph Shetzen is the founder and president of the Business Management Club, Inc., a nationwide organization that is committed to promoting self-education of entrepreneurs and professionals in the area of business management. Mr. Shetzen is constantly engaged in developing practical management solutions for organizations in such areas as general administration, human resources, finance and accounting, production and operations, marketing, and sales. One of his major accomplishments is the development of the unique "business engineering" method. This method is designed to enable business owners to become management consultants to their organizations and to solve a broad range of managerial problems on a "do-it-yourself" basis.

Mr. Shetzen is a professional engineer with extensive business management experience. He previously ran a successful management consulting practice and co-owned a small manufacturing company. Mr. Shetzen received his B.S. in engineering from Ben-Gurion University in Israel and is a member of the American Production and Inventory Control Society.

About the Contributing Editors

BRUCE A. SAMUELSON
B.S., M.B.A., Washington State University; C.P.A., State of Washington;
D.B.A., University of Southern California

B. Samuelson is a Professor of Accounting and Chairman of the Department of Accounting, Law and Finance at School of Business and Management, Pepperdine University. Prior to that he served for five years as a Director of the Small Business Institute at the University of California and in that capacity provided a management consutling service to small businesses in Orange County. Dr. Samuelson is also an executive officer of several corporations. Previously he served as an audit supervisor in the U.S. General Accounting Office, an auditor for a public accounting firm, and an accountant for a manufacturing firm. He also taught at University of Southern California, California State University in Long Beach, and the University of California at Irvine. Furthermore, he is an author of several articles that have appeared in *The Accounting Review, The Journal of Accountancy*, and *Organization Studies*.

RICHARD E. GUNTHER
Ph.D. in Operations Management, UCLA

R. Gunther is a Professor of Management Science at California State University in Northridge. His research interests are in production and inventory control. Dr. Gunther also has an extensive management consulting experience providing service to various small and medium-sized companies in California. In addition, he serves as executive officer of several organizations. Dr. Gunther has also taught a number of courses for the Ventura and San Fernando Valley Chapters of the American Production and Inventory Control Society (APICS). He has also published several articles in such professional publications as *Management Science, Decision Sciences*, and the *Journal of Operations Management*.

CHARLES W. FOJTIK
B.A., Northwestern University; M.B.A. and D.B.A., University of Southern California

C. Fojtik is an Associate Professor of Marketing at the School of Business and Management, Pepperdine University. His research interests are in various areas of marketing management. In addition, Dr. Fojtik heads the Delphi Bureau, a consulting operation specializing in forecasting and research for new products and services. He provided management consulting service to numerous small and medium-sized companies in such areas as assessment of sales potential and development of marketing plans.

BARRY R. NATHAN
B.S., University of Maryland; M.A. and Ph.D., University of Akron

B. Nathan is an Assistant Professor of Management and Orgainzation in the School of Business Administration, University of Southern California. He specializes in various areas of human resource management such as employee selection, compensation, performance appraisal, and training. Dr. Nathan is the author of many professional publications—the latest include *Legal and Technical Standards for Performance Assessment* and *Behavior Modeling: Training Principles and Applications*. Furthermore, he is a member of the Academy of Management and the Society of Industrial/Organizational Psychology.

Contents for Volume I

Contents for Volume II

Part 1

General Management Guide

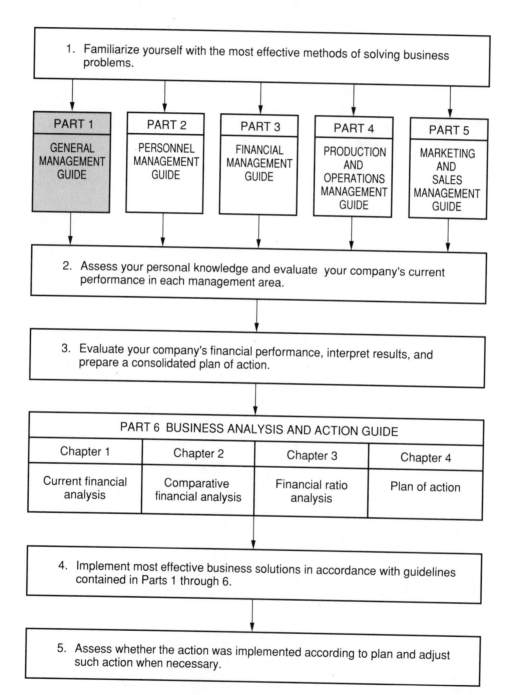

1. Familiarize yourself with the most effective methods of solving business problems.

PART 1	PART 2	PART 3	PART 4	PART 5
GENERAL MANAGEMENT GUIDE	PERSONNEL MANAGEMENT GUIDE	FINANCIAL MANAGEMENT GUIDE	PRODUCTION AND OPERATIONS MANAGEMENT GUIDE	MARKETING AND SALES MANAGEMENT GUIDE

2. Assess your personal knowledge and evaluate your company's current performance in each management area.

3. Evaluate your company's financial performance, interpret results, and prepare a consolidated plan of action.

PART 6 BUSINESS ANALYSIS AND ACTION GUIDE			
Chapter 1	Chapter 2	Chapter 3	Chapter 4
Current financial analysis	Comparative financial analysis	Financial ratio analysis	Plan of action

4. Implement most effective business solutions in accordance with guidelines contained in Parts 1 through 6.

5. Assess whether the action was implemented according to plan and adjust such action when necessary.

- *The 20 elements of practical general management*
- *Working instructions and forms for evaluating your company's general management*
- *Guidelines for implementing effective general management strategies and much more*

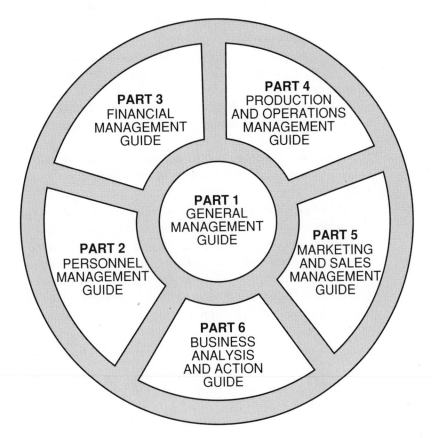

Contents

1.00 Introduction

The prime purpose of the **general management guide** is to identify business problems and implement the most effective solutions in the area of general management. This guide highlights a variety of issues, such as:

- How to develop strategic and operational plans
- How to implement management by objectives as a part of the overall management process
- How to formulate a set of strategies, policies, and rules
- How to structure and departmentalize the company in the most appropriate manner
- How to develop leadership within the organization
- How to maintain continuous control over the company's activities

These and other related issues are addressed in the general management guide. All issues are described in **20 checkpoints** presented in **Sections 1.01–1.20.**

To develop the most suitable solutions in the area of general management, it is necessary to understand the issues discussed in this part. Thorough self-assessment by company executives and evaluation of company performance in the aforementioned area will indicate the effectiveness of current general management principles. This, in turn, will help to formulate a sound plan of action and to implement the most effective solutions in accordance with the **work program** presented in Exhibit 1–1.

Exhibit 1-1

Work Program for Part 1

Work Program	
Planned Action	**Objective**
1. Study of general management principles	To attain an adequate level of knowledge in the area of general management
2. Self-evaluation of knowledge by members of the management team in the area of general management	To identify individual strengths and weaknesses of members of the management team in the area of general management
3. Evaluation of company performance in the area of general management	To identify the level of company performance in the area of general management and to establish the average evaluation level
4. Formulation of a plan of action in the area of general management	To summarize the range of activities that must be undertaken in the area of general management
5. Implementation of the most effective business solutions in the area of general management	To develop a set of the most suitable solutions in accordance with guidelines presented in this part
6. Evaluation and control of actions in the area of general management	To assess whether the action was implemented according to plan and to adjust such action when necessary

Note: Please familiarize yourself with relevant working instructions prior to completing forms at the end of this part. Additional information on these forms is available from Business Management Club, Inc., upon request.

1.01 The Basic Management Process

Management is frequently called "the art of getting things done through people." This definition, by Mary Parker Follet, suggests that one category of people, known as **managers,** should achieve their organizational objectives by arranging for others, known as **subordinates,** to carry out the necessary tasks instead of performing those tasks themselves. Thus, the prime purpose of management is to create a suitable environment in which people can perform productively and coordinate individual efforts toward achieving organizational goals. The most important managerial functions are summarized in Exhibit 1–2. They are

1. **Planning** the development of specific organizational objectives and the appropriate actions to achieve those objectives. This enables management to pursue its goals in a systematic manner instead of relying on chance.
2. **Organizing** the company's human and material resources into a workable structure to ensure effective organizational performance. This entails coordinating all working activities into an integrated operational framework, creating functional positions, and staffing them with appropriate personnel.
3. **Leading** the company's personnel toward accomplishment of organizational objectives. This entails directing and influencing subordinates in performing their designated duties in the most efficient manner.
4. **Controlling** the performance of company personnel and ensuring that the organization is progressing toward its goals. This entails establishing standards of performance, measuring actual performance, comparing it against established standards, and taking action to correct significant deviations.

In addition to planning, organizing, leading, and controlling organizational activities, managers play other important roles within a company. These roles were investigated in the late 1960s by Henry Mintzberg, who examined performance of several managers on the job. According to Mintzberg, managers perform 10 different but highly interrelated management roles. A **management role** is defined as "an organized set of behaviors belonging to an identifiable office or position."[1] As illustrated in Exhibit 1–3, all management roles can be summarized into three major categories:

Exhibit 1–2

The Basic Management Process

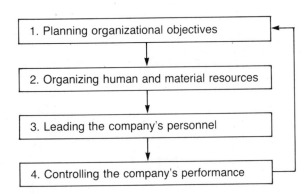

Exhibit 1-3

Summary of 10 Managerial Roles as Identified by Mintzberg

Role	Description	Identifiable Activities from Study of Chief Executives
Interpersonal		
Figurehead	Symbolic head; obliged to perform a number of routing duties of a legal or social nature	Ceremony, status requests, solicitations
Leader	Responsible for the motivation and activation of subordinates; responsible for staffing, training, and associated duties	Virtually all managerial activities involving subordinates
Liaison	Maintains self-developed network of outside contacts and informers who provide favors and information	Acknowledgments of mail; external board work; other activities involving outsiders
Informational		
Monitor	Seeks and receives wide variety of special information (much of it current) to develop thorough understanding of organization and environment; emerges as nerve center of internal and external information of the organization	Handling all mail and contacts categorized as concerned primarily with receiving information (e.g., periodical news, observational tours)
Disseminator	Transmits information received from outsiders or from other subordinates to members of the organization; some information factual, some involving interpretation and integration of diverse value positions of organizational influencers	Forwarding mail into organization for informational purposes; verbal contacts involving information flow to subordinates (e.g., review sessions, instant communication flows)
Spokesperson	Transmits information to outsiders on organization's plans, policies, actions, results, etc.; serves as expert on organization's industry	Board meetings; handling mail and contacts involving transmission of information to outsiders
Decisional		
Entrepreneur	Searches organization and its environment for opportunities and initiates "improvement projects" to bring about change; supervises design of certain projects as well	Strategy and review sessions involving initiation or design of improvement projects
Disturbance handler	Responsible for corrective action when organization faces important, unexpected disturbances	Strategy and review sessions involving disturbances and crises
Resource allocator	Responsible for the allocation of organizational resources of all kinds—in effect the making or approval of all significant organizational decisions	Scheduling; requests for authorization; any activity involving budgeting and the programming of subordinates' work
Negotiator	Responsible for representing the organization at major negotiations	Negotiation

- **Interpersonal roles.** All managers frequently perform duties that are ceremonial and symbolic in nature, thus acting as a *figurehead* on behalf of their company. In addition, managers assume the role of *leader* and are constantly involved in hiring, training, motivating, and disciplining subordinates. Furthermore, managers perform a *liaison* role by dealing with various individuals and groups inside and outside the organization.
- **Informational roles.** All managers constantly *monitor* information obtained from various external sources (e.g., reading newspapers or studying reports about competition). In addition, managers act as *disseminators* by transmitting information to other members of their organization. Moreover, managers often act as *spokespersons* by transmitting information to individuals and groups outside the organization.
- **Decisional roles.** All managers are constantly faced with a need to make decisions. By acting as *entrepreneurs,* managers develop and implement new projects to improve organizational performance. Managers also identify problems and take corrective action, thus acting as *disturbance handlers*. In addition, managers act as *resource allocators* by planning the use and allocation of human, physical, and financial resources. Finally, managers act as *negotiators* by representing their organizations in the negotiating process with other individuals and groups.

Although all managers perform common roles in various organizations, the nature of their work depends upon the size of the organization and type of operation—manufacturing, service-oriented, wholesaling, retailing, projects, or contracting. Various types of operations are discussed in detail in Part 4 (Volume II) and are summarized in Exhibit 4–3.

Size of the organization is a particularly important factor in developing different managerial roles. Thus, for example, an owner-manager in a small business usually "wears several hats," performing a broad range of duties and playing a variety of managerial and nonmanagerial roles. **Small business** may be defined as an independently owned and profit-oriented organization with fewer than 100 employees, annual sales of less than $5 million, and a limited geographical area in which it offers products or services.[2] However, when an organization grows in size and employs more people, management's role usually becomes more specialized in terms of duties and responsibilities. Thus, in larger organizations, managers may operate on several levels, as follows:

- **Top managers.** These include company president and vice presidents.
- **Middle managers.** These include heads of departments.
- **First-level managers.** These include supervisors and foremen.

Irrespective of their functional designation within the organization, all three types of managers are constantly required to plan, organize, lead, and control various aspects of organizational activities. However, the distribution of time spent on each activity differs, depending on the manager's level in the organization. This is illustrated in Exhibit 1–4.

The question is frequently asked whether management is an art or science. Some experts consider management to be an art since there are very few established laws—unlike such sciences as engineering, mathematics, or physics. During recent decades, however, a number of principles have been summarized in various areas of business management and condensed into five major disciplines:

Exhibit 1-4

Distribution of Time per Function by Organizational Level

Top Managers	Middle Managers	First-Level Managers
Planning—28%	Planning—18%	Planning—15%
Organizing—36%	Organizing—33%	Organizing—24%
Leading—22%	Leading—36%	Leading—51%
Controlling—14%	Controlling—13%	Controlling—10%

SOURCE: James A. F. Stoner, *Management*, 2e, ©1982, p. 10. Adapted by permission of Prentice Hall, Inc., Englewood Cliffs, New Jersey.

1. General management
2. Personnel management
3. Financial management
4. Production and operations management
5. Marketing and sales management

General management is concerned with the administrative aspect of running a company; developing strategic and operational plans; and formulating strategies, policies, and rules. In addition, general management entails organizing human and material resources into a workable departmental structure, establishing lines of communication, and leading the company toward achieving its goals. The ultimate task of general management entails controlling the company's performance, monitoring results, and taking corrective action in all areas of its activities.

Personnel management is based on equal employment opportunity laws and entails analyzing various jobs, preparing job descriptions and job specifications, planning and forecasting personnel requirements, and recruiting and hiring employees. Moreover, personnel management is concerned with screening and testing of applicants; conducting employment interviews; and personnel orientation, training, development, motivation, compensation, performance appraisal, and career management. Finally, personnel management deals with establishing sound labor-management relations, managing interpersonal conflicts, and ensuring safety and health of employees.

Financial management entails gathering of accounting information, maintaining a bookkeeping system, collaborating with accountants in preparing financial statements, and evaluating the company's financial performance. In addition, financial management entails preparing operating, capital expenditure, and cash budgets; formulating tax strategies; identifying suitable sources of finance; and maintaining cash, credit, and expenditure control. Finally, financial management is concerned with inventory and capital assets management, costing of products or services, developing pricing methods, preparing management accounting reports, and managing computerized accounting systems.

Production and operations management is concerned with facility design, location, and organization; product selection, design, and standardization; process design; and drafting office supervision. Furthermore, production and operations management entails equipment evaluation and selection, plant layout, equipment maintenance and replacement, tool control, cost estimating, and production planning and control. Finally, production and operations management deals with material requirements planning and purchasing, quality control, inventory control, and storage and dispatch.

Marketing and sales management entails gathering marketing information, measuring and forecasting market potential, and formulating appropriate marketing strategies. In addition, marketing and sales management deals with developing product, pricing, promotional, and distribution strategies; summarizing marketing plans; and initiating the sales management process. This process is concerned with sales planning and budgeting; developing a sales organization; and recruiting, training, compensating, motivating, allocating, and controlling the sales force.

In order to ensure successful organizational performance, managers must be familiar with various elements of the aforementioned disciplines and be able to implement relevant principles within their organizations. Large and medium-sized companies normally employ a number of managers who specialize in a particular field of business management and are expected to provide a professional service. Smaller companies, on the other hand, usually cannot afford the services of highly paid professional managers, thus forcing their owners to adopt a generalistic or multidisciplinary approach to management.

Since most principles of business management apply to all companies irrespective of their size, this subject is becoming more of a science rather than an art. This trend has been further confirmed by the development of *Master of Business Administration (MBA)* programs. These programs, introduced in the 1960s, became particularly popular in the last decade.

Unfortunately, the majority of small business owners cannot afford to spend time in universities to study business management. They continue to manage their businesses using entrepreneurial skills and often achieve significant success. The term **entrepreneur** was introduced in the eighteenth century by French economist Richard Cantillon. This term is used to describe people who are innovators and are prepared to take risks in developing and introducing new ideas, products, or services to society. The majority of new businesses throughout the entire world have been founded by entrepreneurs. Some of these businesses grew to become the largest corporations in the twentieth century. Among the most well-known entrepreneurs are J. Paul Getty, Howard Hughes, John D. Rockefeller, J.P. Morgan, Henry Ford, Andrew Mellon, Harry Oppenheimer, and Aristotle Onassis.

It is essential that entrepreneurs, or entrepreneurial managers, study all elements of business operations and understand management principles discussed in this volume. Doing so will enable them to evaluate the performance of their organizations and to plan, organize, lead, and control future activities in the most efficient manner possible.

1.02 Evolution of Management Theory

The first principles of management theory were introduced several thousand years ago. Since then, management theory has evolved, and new principles have been developed by different nations. Numerous examples prove the existence of early management principles. These principles were successfully employed by the ancient Greeks to build the Acropolis, by the Egyptians to build pyramids, by the Chinese to build the Great Wall, by the Roman Empire, and by many others. However, the real development of management theory got its momentum only at the end of the last century.

The first significant development of management theory was initiated by Frederick W. Taylor (1856–1915), who is considered the father of *scientific management*. Taylor studied various jobs and searched for the most efficient ways to accomplish them. According to Taylor, each task had to be divided into a number of smaller tasks, or subtasks, and each subtask had to be properly designed to achieve maximum efficiency. The design of subtasks had to be carried out by a specialist known as a *management scientist*. Once the design of each subtask was completed, it was given to a particular worker, who had to complete the job in "one right way." The process of dividing the task into smaller tasks was termed by Taylor as *job fractionation,* and each subtask has been termed the *basic work unit* of the job.

Throughout his research, Taylor observed the work of different types of workers and made substantial use of *time and motion* studies. In addition, he used a system known as *piece rate,* whereby each worker was compensated according to the amount of work produced. By introducing incentives, Taylor managed to increase the production output and improve overall worker efficiency. In 1911, he summarized various findings of his research and published *Principles of Scientific Management*.[3] That year is considered, therefore, the beginning of scientific management.

Frank B. (1868–1924) and Lillian M. Gilbreth (1878–1972) are also considered pioneers of scientific management. This husband and wife team, in fact, was the innovator of the time and motion studies.[4] As a result of their work, the Gilbreths developed and introduced a *job simplification* process. This process aimed at reducing the number of subtasks, thereby simplifying the job and ensuring improved efficiency of performance.

In 1912, Lillian Gilbreth published her research in *Industrial Engineering Magazine* and subsequently authored a book titled *The Psychology of Management*. Although Lillian Gilbreth collaborated with her husband in the area of time and motion studies, she was also preoccupied with the welfare of workers. As far as she was concerned, the main aim of management is to help workers reach their full potential and obtain the benefits of their performance.

The Gilbreths also developed a *three-position plan* of promotion, which aimed at stimulating employee development and boosting morale. According to that plan, each employee was expected not only to do his or her job, but also to train a successor and be prepared for promotion. Thus, every employee would become a performer, a pupil, and a teacher at the same time.

Henry L. Gantt (1861–1919) is considered another pioneer of scientific management. He made significant contributions in the areas of production and operations scheduling and control, as well as compensating workers for their performance. Gantt believed that one of the major reasons for workers' poor efficiency was management's inability to establish realistic standards of performance. During the course of his work Gantt observed and measured the production performance of various working groups and established appropriate standards of work. Once the nature and the amount of work to be completed was established, Gantt proceeded with the scheduling of work. This led to the development of the well-known Gantt Chart, illustrated in Exhibit 1–5.

A typical Gantt Chart lists various tasks that have to be accomplished and summarizes specific periods when the work should take place. Gantt Charts are frequently used nowadays in planning and scheduling production and other related activities.

Another important contribution made by Gantt was introduction of a *production bonus*. Gantt maintained that such an incentive motivates workers to perform better and subsequently increases production efficiency within the organization. Production bonuses developed by Gantt are still used by many companies.

Mary Parker Follet (1868–1933) was one of the first management researchers who recognized the importance of the team approach to work. She studied individual and group performance of workers and concluded that management

Exhibit 1-5

Gantt Chart

Task	Production Department—Week No.				
	1	2	3	4	5
Order materials	X				
Inspect materials	X				
Manufacture parts		X	X		
Assemble parts			X	X	
Final inspection				X	
Packaging					X
Shipping					X

should stimulate teamwork in the organization and a spirit of cooperation among employees. Follet went further to suggest that one of the most important managerial duties is to harmonize and coordinate group efforts. Managers and workers, she continued, should view each other as partners who work for the same goal. Follet's humanistic approach influenced many other researchers who developed new ideas in the field of leadership and personnel motivation. Many Japanese management principles, for example, incorporate ideas developed by Follet many years ago.

Henry Fayol (1841–1925) made a substantial contribution to the development of scientific management. Trained as a mining engineer, Fayol spent his entire working life with a large coal and iron corporation in France. Throughout his career he developed a set of management principles based on his belief that "with scientific forecasting and proper methods of management, satisfactory results were inevitable." Fayol focused his efforts in the direction of collating management information into an integrated set of principles, thus attempting to apply an "engineering" approach to business management.

Fayol conducted an intensive investigation of various activities within a business and analyzed functions of managers. In 1929 he published his famous book, *Administratim Industrielle et Generale,* which has been translated subsequently as *General and Industrial Management.* In this still-popular book, Fayol made several important contributions to management theory.

First, Fayol divided business operations and identified six closely related activities, illustrated in Exhibit 1–6, as follows:

1. *Technical activities.* These include manufacturing of products.
2. *Commercial activities.* These include purchasing raw materials and selling finished products.
3. *Financial activities.* These include acquiring and utilizing capital.
4. *Security activities.* These include protecting employees and business property.
5. *Accounting activities.* These include recording financial transactions; determining assets, liabilities, and profit; preparing balance sheets; and compiling management reports.
6. *Managerial activities.* These include planning, organizing, commanding, coordinating, and controlling all business activities.

Exhibit 1–6

The Operations of a Business and the Functions of a Manager (after Fayol)

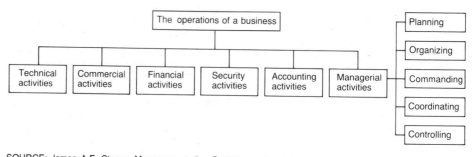

SOURCE: James A.F. Stoner, Management, 2e, ©1982, p. 40. Adapted by permission of Prentice Hall, Inc., Englewood Cliffs, New Jersey.

Fayol, concentrating particular attention on the sixth business activity, defined five prime managerial functions as follows:

- *Planning.* This means devising a course of action that will enable the organization to meet its goals.
- *Organizing.* This means mobilizing the material and human resources of the organization to put the plans into effect.
- *Commanding.* This means providing direction for employees and getting them to do their work.
- *Coordinating.* This means making sure that the resources and activities of the organization are working harmoniously to achieve the desired goals.
- *Controlling.* This means monitoring the plans to ensure that they are being carried out properly.[5]

This classification of managerial functions is very similar to the modern version of four prime functions described in Exhibit 1-2. Thus, Fayol's model of management, which includes a number of key functions, provides the foundation of modern management theory.

Another important contribution made by Fayol was his definition of management principles. Fayol carefully selected the term "principles of management" rather than "rules" or "laws" because he believed that principles would provide more flexibility in management matters. Fayol developed **14 principles of management** that he "most frequently had to apply." These principles are as follows:

1. *Division of labor.* The more people specialize, the more efficiently they can perform their work. This principle is epitomized by the modern assembly line.
2. *Authority.* Managers must give orders so that they can get things done. Although their formal authority gives them the right to command, managers will not always compel obedience unless they also have personal authority (such as relevant expertise).
3. *Discipline.* Members of an organization need to respect the rules and agreements that govern the organization. To Fayol, discipline will result from good leadership at all levels of the organization, fair agreements (such as provisions for rewarding superior performance), and judiciously enforced penalties for infractions.

4. *Unity of command.* Each employee must receive instructions about a particular operation from only one person. Fayol believed that when an employee reported to more than one superior, conflicts in instructions and confusion of authority would result.

5. *Unity of direction.* Those operations within the organization that have the same objective should be directed by only one manager using one plan. For example, the personnel department in a company should not have two directors, each with a different hiring policy.

6. *Subordination of individual interest to the common good.* In any undertaking, the interests of employees should not take precedence over the interests of the organization as a whole.

7. *Remuneration.* Compensation for work done should be fair to both employees and employers.

8. *Centralization.* Decreasing the role of subordinates in decision making is centralization; increasing their role is decentralization. Fayol believed that managers should retain final responsibility but also need to give their subordinates enough authority to do their jobs properly. The problem is to find the best amount of centralization in each case.

9. *The hierarchy.* The line of authority in an organization—often represented today by the neat boxes and lines of the organization chart—runs in order of rank from top management to the lowest level of the enterprise.

10. *Order.* Materials and people should be in the right place at the right time. People in particular should be in the jobs or positions best suited for them.

11. *Equity.* Managers should be both friendly and fair to their subordinates.

12. *Stability of staff.* A high employee turnover rate is not good for the efficient functioning of an organization.

13. *Initiative.* Subordinates should be given the freedom to conceive and carry out their plans, even though some mistakes may result.

14. *Esprit de corps.* Promoting team spirit will give the organization a sense of unity. To Fayol, even small factors could help to develop this spirit. He suggested, for example, the use of verbal communication instead of formal, written communication whenever possible.[6]

As a result of his work, Fayol developed the **process approach** to management. According to this approach, illustrated in Exhibit 1–2, the management process can be viewed as the continuous task of planning, organizing, leading, and controlling a group of employees to accomplish organizational goals. The majority of authors, educators, managers, and entrepreneurs consider the process approach as the fundamental guide to business management.

Elton Mayo (1880–1949) was an Australian social scientist who investigated human behavior and conducted the famous *Hawthorne experiments.* The original purpose of these experiments, carried out at the Hawthorne (Chicago) Works of the Western Electric Company from 1927 to 1932, was to determine the influence of illumination on performance of workers in the facility. At the start, all workers were informed of their participation in these experiments. While conducting the study, Mayo and his associates from the Harvard University School of Business Administration created two groups of workers. The first group worked under a constant level of lighting, while the second one worked under changing light conditions. It was expected that the fluctuating level of illumination would influence the efficiency of employees. However, it was found that workers in both groups performed better than usual throughout the experience, irrespective of the level of illumination.

In the next experiment, Mayo and his Harvard associates again created two groups, such that workers in the first group remained working under unchanging conditions while several variables were introduced into the second group. These variables included increased salary, shorter working days, and varying lengths of rest periods. Researchers acted as supervisors to both teams, and established a relaxed working atmosphere throughout the experiment. Once again, production performance improved in both groups, irrespective of financial incentives, and of lengths of working and rest periods.

Both experiments led Mayo and his team to an important discovery, which has been summarized as follows:

- Workers perform better if they get a feeling of being participants in a meaningful event.
- Workers perform better if they are observed by supervisors and their results are monitored (*the Hawthorne Effect*).
- Workers perform better if supervisors create a relaxed atmosphere and an increased sense of belonging to a team.

Mayo and his colleagues concluded that apart from physical aspects of work, such as good illumination, higher salary, longer rest periods, and shorter working days, there are *human relations factors* that may influence the efficiency of workers' performance. These factors, as outlined above, represent the prime result of the Hawthorne experiments.

Douglas M. McGregor (1906–1964) made an important contribution by observing different aspects of human behavior in the workplace. He investigated Taylor's approach to management, which incorporated a relatively pessimistic view of workers, and developed a *Theory X*. In addition, McGregor investigated Mayo's approach to management, which included a more optimistic view of workers, and developed *Theory Y*. Although the two theories, summarized in Exhibit 1–7, are quite contradictory, they provide better insight in understanding workers and people in general.

Exhibit 1-7

Theory X and Theory Y

Theory X	Theory Y
People do not like work and will try to steer away from it whenever they can.	People do not really dislike work. They are prepared to work provided working conditions and attitudes are positive.
Since people do not like work, they must be forced into it.	Provided people are personally committed, they will show self-direction toward organizational goals.
People are generally unambitious, avoid responsibility, and seek security in the workplace. They have to be led and actually prefer this.	Responsibility can generally be taught to people and they subsequently are willing to accept it.
People generally lack imagination and creativity.	People are generally imaginative and creative.
Due to their intellectual limitation, people are generally not able to meet the growing challenges in the workplace.	People's talents are not completely utilized in the workplace.

SOURCE: Adapted from Douglas M. McGregor, *The Human Side of Enterprise* (New York: McGraw-Hill, 1960, 1988). Reprinted with permission.

McGregor presented his observations in *The Human Side of Enterprise,* published in 1960. In this book, McGregor suggested that managers take a more positive approach toward employees, based on Theory Y, by doing such things as

- Delegating authority to lower levels in the organization, thereby challenging workers to make decisions and expressing faith in their abilities.
- Making jobs more interesting for the worker.
- Increasing the level of responsibility inherent in each job.
- Innovating new rewards for worker performance that relate to a variety of worker psychological needs, not just money.
- Treating workers with respect and increasing the share of information regarding work content, design, and results.[7]

Observations and conclusions derived by Follet, Mayo, and McGregor represented an important contribution to the development of the **behavioral approach** to management. This approach focuses on understanding human behavior and evaluating factors that influence workers' performance and productivity. The behavioral approach caused the development of managerial skills in the area of human resources, or personnel, management and provided basic guidance in dealing with employees.

In the mid-1960s another management theory was introduced. This theory, based on a **systems approach,** suggests that an organization is a set of interrelated parts—such as people, materials, and equipment—that are arranged in one structure but pursue diverse objectives in a changing environment. The environment includes suppliers, customers, financial institutions, government organizations, and other external bodies. A typical systems approach is presented in Exhibit 1–8.

The most recent approach to business management, developed in the late 1960s, is the step-by-step methodology known as the **contingency approach**. According to this approach, there is no universal solution to management problems. Managers, therefore, need to familiarize themselves with various management techniques and apply these as needed in solving their specific problems. According to Patrick Montana and Bruce Charnov, the contingency approach can be summarized as follows:

1. Perform a situational analysis, consisting of
   1.1 analysis of the current internal condition of the organization:

Exhibit 1–8

The Systems Approach

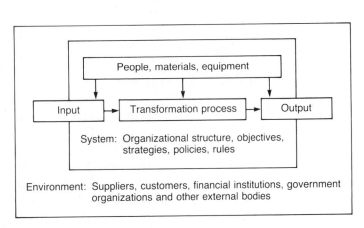

        1.1.1 internal organizational strengths

        1.1.2 internal organizational weaknesses

   1.2 projection of the future external condition of the organization:

        1.2.1 external opportunities for the organization

        1.2.2 external threats to the organization

2. Based on the situational analysis, formulate a statement of the problem.

3. State the performance standards that meet the following requirements and the completion of which indicates that the problem has been solved. Performance standards are stated in a form of behavior that is

   3.1 observable

   3.2 measurable

   3.3 relevant to the goal

4. Generate alternative solutions to the problem.

5. Evaluate the possible solutions in terms of their consequences to the organization.

6. Select the best alternative solution that solves the problem and causes the least number of detrimental side effects in the organization.

7. Implement a pilot test of the proposed solution and revise as indicated from practical experience.

8. Implement the solution.

9. Evaluate the solution.

10. Revise the process as necessary.[8]

The contingency approach takes into consideration various limitations under which the organization has to operate. These may include the existing skills of management and employees, available resources, level of technology, and general conditions in the marketplace. It is important, therefore, that managers identify specific limitations of their organizations and seek the most appropriate set of solutions.

Although the contingency approach enables the manager to remain flexible during the problem-seeking and problem-solving process, it has certain drawbacks in its implementation. One of the prime drawbacks is the absence of clear guidelines pertaining to different operational matters. Thus, managers must generally rely on their own knowledge and experience while evaluating the performance of their organizations and implementing new solutions.

1.03 Business Engineering Method

Hundreds of thousands of people start new businesses each year. All these people are considered entrepreneurs, and they play an important role in the U.S. economy. Unfortunately, a high proportion of new businesses fail during the first few years of their existence. Some, however, survive the initial difficulties and find their niche in the marketplace. According to recent statistics, there are approximately 11 million businesses in the United States, out of which 10.8 million, or over 98 percent, are small. These businesses employ about 60 percent of the total workforce in the country, and the number of entrepreneurs increases every year.[9]

The vast majority of small and medium-sized companies are managed by entrepreneurs who are usually extradesmen and who do not have formal professional or business management education. Some of the typical facts about entrepreneurs are summarized as follows:

- Many entrepreneurs who manage small and medium-sized companies often overestimate their abilities and are unaware of personal inefficiencies in the field of business management.
- Those entrepreneurs who are aware of their inefficiencies still prefer to solve their management problems by themselves either to avoid exposure and possible embarrassment as a result of any mismanagement in the past or in order to protect their "trading secrets."
- Most entrepreneurs who manage small and medium-sized companies are usually skeptical toward any advice about business management given by outsiders, particularly management consultants, and they often cannot afford such professional services.
- Many entrepreneurs are usually not overly enthusiastic about business management education or literature and do not really know how to select suitable material. They have the time neither to shop around for needed information nor to absorb it.
- Those entrepreneurs who do read business literature or attend specialized courses and seminars still do not receive sufficient information to enable them to cover all aspects of business management effectively.

On the other hand, many professionals specialize in various aspects of business management such as general administration, personnel, finance and accounting, production and operations, or marketing and sales. Facts about professionals and organizations which render professional services are gathered below:

- The majority of all professionals, including specialists in business management, do not practice entrepreneurship and are usually employed by various organizations, teach students, or render professional consulting services.
- Accountants probably are the only category of professionals whose services are widely accepted by entrepreneurs in the field of small and medium-sized business management. However, accountants spend most of their time verifying financial statements and dealing with tax issues. They are neither trained nor geared to provide management consulting service to their clients.
- Large accounting firms (the Big Eight and a few others) have management consulting service (MCS) departments. However, these firms, as well as independent management consulting organizations, prefer to deal with larger companies which have the necessary funds and may require consulting services over a reasonably long period of time.
- Most management consulting firms have a variety of specialists in different fields of business management but do not have sufficient numbers of experienced generalists who know all aspects of small and medium-sized business management.

Obviously, a very large army of entrepreneurs manage small and medium-sized companies without having suitable business management education. The lack of such education causes a high level of ignorance among many entrepreneurs, particularly those who have been successful in the past. These entrepreneurs usually do not appreciate the significance of business management education, literature, seminars, or management consulting services. They often manage their businesses utilizing primitive and outdated methods, show poor ability to delegate functional responsibilities, and sometimes become the biggest stumbling blocks within their own organizations.

Furthermore, there is no evidence that professionals and their institutions, audit houses, and management consulting firms succeed in promoting a broad range of business management techniques to small and medium-sized companies. Probably one of the major reasons is that entrepreneurs indeed represent a highly complex market to penetrate from the educational point of view.

Hence, the successful performance of small and medium-sized companies depends upon owners' knowledge and experience in various areas of business management and their ability to act as entrepreneurial managers. Since small business management is based on an integrated and multidisciplinary approach, the entrepreneurial managers must become *business engineers* and learn to apply appropriate elements of the business engineering method.

Business engineering method entails a comprehensive study of various management disciplines by entrepreneurs, self-assessment of their knowledge, evaluation of their company's operational and financial performance, preparation of a plan of action, and implementation of the most effective solutions. The prime purpose of the business engineering method is to enable entrepreneurs, business owners, and managers to act as management consultants to their own organizations while performing a range of routine executive duties.

Business engineering method has been developed by the author over the period of the last 10 years. This method incorporates a broad range of management principles and represents a logical continuation of different approaches to management discussed earlier in this volume. The main focus of the business engineering method, as presented in Exhibit 1–9, is on the practical application of various management theories, principles, and methods developed during this century.

The business engineering method consists of six major parts:

1. General management guide (Volume I)
2. Personnel management guide (Volume I)
3. Financial management guide (Volume I)
4. Production and operations management guide (Volume II)
5. Marketing and sales management guide (Volume II)
6. Business analysis and action guide (Volume II)

General management guide explains how to identify business problems and implement the most effective solutions in the area of administration and general management. This guide deals with such issues as evolution of management, business engineering method, environment and organizational culture, principles of decision making, the planning process, strategic planning and its implementation, management by objectives, operational planning, plan of management, the organizing process, organizational departmentation, management structure, organizational development, the leading process, principles of communication, the controlling process, managerial ethics, and Theory Z.

Personnel management guide explains how to identify business problems and implement the most effective solutions in the area of personnel management. This guide deals with such issues as equal employment opportunity laws, job analysis, job descriptions and job specifications, personnel planning and forecasting, personnel recruitment and hiring, screening and testing of applicants, employment interviews, personnel orientation, personnel training, management development, personnel motivation, personnel compensation laws, basic job compensation, financial incentives, fringe benefits, personnel perfor-

Exhibit 1–9

Introduction of the Business Engineering Method

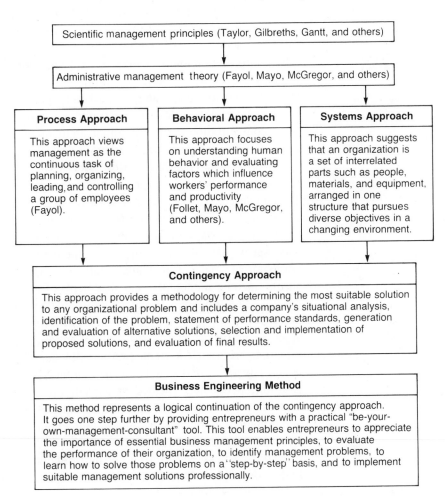

mance appraisal, personnel career management, labor-management relations, collective bargaining and conflict management, and personnel safety and health.

Financial management guide explains how to identify business problems and implement the most effective solutions in the area of accounting and financial management. This guide deals with such issues as accounting information, bookkeeping system, financial statements, financial performance evaluation, operating budget, capital expenditure budget, cash budget, tax strategies, sources of finance, internal control and cash management, control of purchases and disbursements, credit control, inventory management, capital assets management, payroll accounting system, cost accounting system, pricing methods, management accounting system, and computerized system.

Production and operations management guide explains how to identify business problems and implement the most effective solutions in the area of production and operations management. This guide deals with such issues as classification of operational activities, facility design and location, product selection, design and standardization, process design, the drafting office, equipment evaluation and selection, plant layout, equipment maintenance and replacement, tool control, cost estimating, production planning, material requirements planning, production control, planning and control of services and projects, quality control, material purchasing, material control, storage and dispatch, and Just-In-Time (JIT) manufacturing philosophy.

Marketing and sales management guide explains how to identify business problems and implement the most effective solutions in the area of marketing and sales management. This guide deals with such issues as buying behavior, marketing information and research, market segmentation, market measurement and forecasting, marketing strategy, product strategy, pricing strategy, promotional strategy, distribution strategy, marketing plan, sales planning and budgeting, sales organization, sales force recruitment and training, personal selling, sales force compensation, sales force management and motivation, sales performance evaluation and control, and marketing audit.

Business analysis and action guide explains how to conduct financial performance evaluation, interpret results, and develop an effective plan of action. This guide consists of four parts: current financial analysis, comparative financial analysis, financial ratio analysis, and plan of action. The first part, current financial analysis, entails a comprehensive examination of the most recent balance sheet, income statement, and statement of cash flows. The second part, comparative financial analysis, entails a comprehensive examination of balance sheets, income statements, and statements of cash flow for three preceding fiscal periods. The third part, financial ratio analysis, entails a comprehensive evaluation of the company's liquidity, solvency, profitability, and ability to manage assets. Finally, the fourth part, plan of action, explains how to develop the most effective program for implementing practical business solutions. The plan of action covers all major areas of the company's activities such as general administration, personnel, finance and accounting, production and operations, and marketing and sales. This part also contains consolidated financial statements and comments, conclusions and recommendations pertinent to the financial performance evaluation.

The business engineering method entails a number of steps as described in Exhibit 1–10. This method serves several important purposes, which are summarized as follows:

- To present basic management principles and to outline fundamental business strategies related to five major operational areas—general administration, personnel, finance and accounting, production and operations, marketing and sales
- To provide entrepreneurs and their management teams with a simple and practical method for conducting a situational business analysis on a do-it-yourself basis
- To enable members of the company's management team to assess their personal level of knowledge and to evaluate the subsequent performance of the organization in all operational areas of business activities
- To identify personal strengths and weaknesses of each member of the management team and to highlight various problematic areas within the range of the company's activities
- To enable the company's financial executive to conduct a comprehensive financial analysis pertinent to current and past performance results attained by the organization
- To facilitate development of a comprehensive plan of action aimed at improving overall performance of the organization
- To provide effective guidance to members of the management team throughout the implementation of the most effective business solutions by their organization

Exhibit 1–10

Business Engineering Method

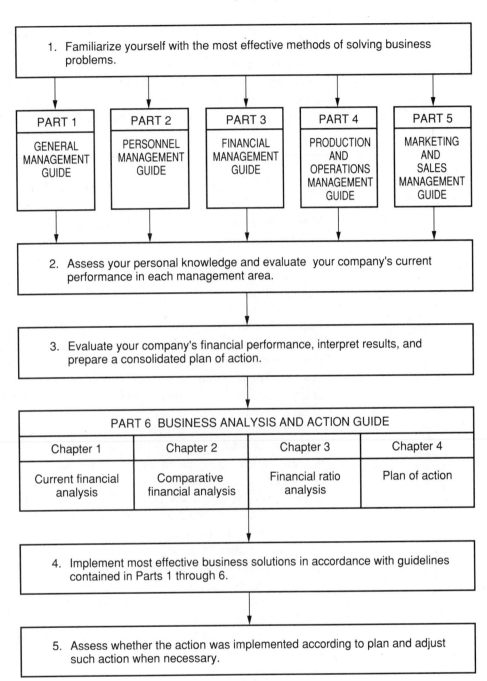

1. Familiarize yourself with the most effective methods of solving business problems.

PART 1	PART 2	PART 3	PART 4	PART 5
GENERAL MANAGEMENT GUIDE	PERSONNEL MANAGEMENT GUIDE	FINANCIAL MANAGEMENT GUIDE	PRODUCTION AND OPERATIONS MANAGEMENT GUIDE	MARKETING AND SALES MANAGEMENT GUIDE

2. Assess your personal knowledge and evaluate your company's current performance in each management area.

3. Evaluate your company's financial performance, interpret results, and prepare a consolidated plan of action.

PART 6 BUSINESS ANALYSIS AND ACTION GUIDE

Chapter 1	Chapter 2	Chapter 3	Chapter 4
Current financial analysis	Comparative financial analysis	Financial ratio analysis	Plan of action

4. Implement most effective business solutions in accordance with guidelines contained in Parts 1 through 6.

5. Assess whether the action was implemented according to plan and adjust such action when necessary.

Each part contains a detailed set of working instructions and self-explanatory standard forms. These have been designed and successfully used in various small and medium-sized commercial organizations.

The main principles adopted in the development of the business engineering method are as follows:

- High quality of information
- Simplicity of documentation
- Practicability in application

- Logical approach
- Common sense

Business engineering provides a condensed, comprehensive, practical, and simple method of teaching entrepreneurs how to be management consultants to their own small and medium-sized companies and how to identify, analyze, and solve various business problems. It further teaches entrepreneurs how to delegate effectively a wide range of important functional responsibilities to other members of their organizations to ensure a profitable performance.

1.04 Environment and Organizational Culture

Various environmental factors influence the way in which entrepreneurs develop their organizations. These factors constitute two basic types of environments:

- External environment
- Internal environment

External environment consists of several elements outside of an organization which influence its development and behavior in the marketplace. These elements, presented in Exhibit 1–11, include customers, suppliers, banks, competitors, labor unions, and government agencies. Additional elements of the external environment which strongly influence organizational development are of an economic, political, social and technological nature.

Customers represent one of the most important factors in the external environment which influence the development of an organization. According to well-known management expert, Peter F. Drucker, the only valid purpose of a business is to create and satisfy a customer. Drucker further suggests that identification of customers and their needs is the first step toward survival of the organization. Customers are the ones who generate the need for products and services, thus initiating business interaction in the marketplace. Since their needs change over time, customers represent uncertainty to an organization. It is important, therefore, to ensure timely identification of customers' needs in order to exploit the opportunity of satisfying their demands at a profit.

Suppliers represent another important factor in the external environment which influences the development of an organization. Managers must constantly make decisions pertinent to the purchase of raw materials, components, and parts

Exhibit 1–11

The External Environment of Organization

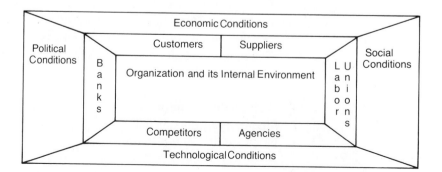

in order to manufacture specific products or to provide services to customers. Thus, the development of an organization depends upon establishing sound relations with reliable suppliers to obtain required materials at the right price and in the right time. Effective liaison with suppliers is of particular importance to the organization if it aims to minimize its level of inventory and ensure timely supply of goods and services to customers.

Banks and other financial institutions play a significant role in the development of an organization by providing lines of credit, loans, and other financial services. Once sufficient capital is obtained, the organization can activate the business process and proceed with its regular operational activities. Hence, managers and entrepreneurs need to understand how to negotiate with various financial institutions in order to secure availability of capital for organizational growth. Development of sound relations with banks is of paramount importance to small and medium-sized companies, which often experience shortages of funds and difficulty in obtaining additional finance.

Competitors constantly influence a broad range of managerial decisions pertinent to routine business activities and to the development of an organization. If the marketplace is highly competitive, managers must ensure that the organization remains competitive and provides products or services to customers at the right price. Competitors represent a significant factor in formulating the organization's marketing plans and in adopting suitable product development, price setting, promotion, and distribution strategies. It is important, therefore, that managers monitor relevant trends in the marketplace in relation to competition in order to secure the company's survival and growth in a highly competitive environment.

Labor unions also play an important role in the process of organizational development. Labor unions were established to protect the interests of specific categories of employees and to regulate the negotiating process between employers and workers. Organizations constantly need employees with different skills and experience who usually belong to specific labor organizations. Several laws which relate to employment procedures and labor unions have been passed in the United States since the 1930s. In accordance with the National Labor Relations Act of 1935, for example, every organization must recognize and negotiate with a particular labor union selected by its employees. Managers and entrepreneurs, therefore, need to be familiar with the labor legislation which regulates employment procedures, collective bargaining processes, and other labor-related issues.

Government agencies also have a strong impact on the development of an organization. Federal, state, and local governments have introduced a broad range of laws and regulations which stipulate what organizations can or cannot do. The Sherman Anti-Trust Act of 1890, for example, was designed to stop monopolistic practices, thus resulting in restraint of trade. The Social Security Act of 1935, on the other hand, prescribed that employers and employees must contribute equal payments to a special fund in order to provide for unemployment compensation to jobless workers. In addition, the Civil Rights Act of 1964 forbids any form of discrimination with respect to hiring and to compensating employees because of race, color, sex, religion, or national origin. Thus, managers and entrepreneurs need to be familiar with a variety of laws which may affect the activities of their organizations.

Economic, political, social, and technological conditions also have an impact on the development of the organization. **Economic conditions**, for example, depend upon interest rates, inflation rates, stock market indexes, the trend of the gross national product (GNP), and other related factors. Improved economic conditions naturally stimulate an increased demand for products and services, thus creating additional opportunities for organizational growth.

Political conditions, on the other hand, are stimulated by general stability within a country and specific policies of government officials. In the United States, organizations generally enjoy substantial benefits and continuous encouragement of new business ventures as a result of the free enterprise system. The ever-changing **social conditions** must also be taken into consideration by managers and entrepreneurs. These are particularly important since values, tastes, and needs of customers change in accordance with their specific lifestyles. Finally, **technological conditions** need to be examined on a regular basis in order to secure continuation of organizational development and growth in a highly competitive environment.

In addition to the external environmental factors, organizational development depends upon the availability of certain elements within the company. These elements constitute the **internal environment** of the organization and include human, financial, physical, and marketing resources. Each element of the company's internal environment plays a critical role in its performance and development.

Human resources are of paramount importance to any organization. In fact, most managers and entrepreneurs agree that skilled, experienced, and loyal employees represent the biggest asset and provide security for successful organizational performance. Managers, therefore, need to understand the fundamental principles of human resources, or personnel, management and acquire the necessary skills to conduct an efficient operation. The prime elements of personnel management include obtaining suitable employees and ensuring their training, compensation, and integration within the organization. These and other related activities are discussed in detail in Part 2 (Volume I).

Financial resources are required by all organizations to provide for continuous operations and to fund growth. The prime sources of capital utilized by organizations include their own retained earnings, equity capital provided by shareholders, and debt capital provided by banks and other financial institutions. Availability of sufficient capital is of prime importance since it enables the organization to offer more favorable payment terms to its customers and to obtain maximum discounts from suppliers. In addition, sufficient capital enables the organization to offer competitive salaries, wages, and fringe benefits, thereby attracting a higher caliber of employees. Furthermore, sufficient capital enables the organization to purchase modern equipment, thus ensuring higher operational efficiency and productivity. Hence, managers need to understand the basic principles of financial management which are outlined in detail in Part 3 (Volume I).

Physical resources of an organization include manufacturing equipment and tools, inventories, and assembly, storage, and distribution facilities. These resources are of particular importance to a manufacturing organization and usually require a substantial investment of capital. Acquisition, maintenance, and development of physical resources represents an integral part of production and operational activities. Managers and entrepreneurs, therefore, need to be familiar with the underlying principles of production and operations management to ensure efficient organizational performance. Various elements of production and operations management are highlighted in detail in Part 4 (Volume II).

Marketing resources of an organization include a well-prepared marketing plan and the company's goodwill in the marketplace. Every organization requires a detailed marketing plan which outlines its strategy with regard to product development, price setting, promotion, and distribution. An accurate marketing plan plays a critical role throughout the budgeting process and helps to secure effective utilization of all company resources. The development of a marketing plan is influenced by the company's overall position in the marketplace, relations with customers, behavior of competitors, and government agencies. Thus, the marketing plan represents a fundamental link between the company's internal and external environments. The company's goodwill also plays a significant role in attaining organizational objectives and should, therefore, be utilized to its highest potential. A comprehensive marketing plan and strong goodwill are expected to help the organization to promote its products and services to customers in the most efficient manner. Managers and entrepreneurs, therefore, need to improve their skills in the area of marketing and sales to ensure sound functioning of the organization. Various elements of marketing and sales management are described in detail in Part 5 (Volume II).

Another important element of the organization's internal environment is its **corporate culture**. Corporate culture refers to the character of the organization and is comprised of its unique values, traditions, and attitudes. Corporate culture is developed throughout the company's existence and embodies the values, mentality, views, and aspirations of its owners. Ethical standards of managers and employees are constantly affected by the corporate culture, thus influencing behavior both within and outside the organization. Although the corporate culture cannot be properly measured, preliminary research suggests that it can be assessed in terms of the following ten characteristics:

1. *Individual initiative:* the degree of responsibility, freedom, and independence that individuals have
2. *Risk tolerance:* the degree to which employees are encouraged to be aggressive, innovative, and risk-seeking
3. *Direction:* the degree to which the organization creates clear objectives and performance expectations
4. *Integration:* the degree to which units within the organization are encouraged to operate in a coordinated manner
5. *Management support:* the degree to which managers provide clear communication, assistance, and support to their subordinates
6. *Control:* the number of rules and regulations, and the amount of direct supervision that is used to oversee and control employee behavior
7. *Identity:* the degree to which members identify with the organization as a whole rather than with their particular work group or field of professional expertise
8. *Reward system:* the degree to which reward allocations (i.e., salary increases, promotions) are based on employee performance criteria in contrast to seniority, favoritism, and so on
9. *Conflict tolerance:* the degree to which employees are encouraged to air conflicts and criticisms openly
10. *Communication patterns:* the degree to which organizational communications are restricted to the formal hierarchy of authority[10]

Depending upon a particular corporate culture, the organization may or may not impose certain rules and regulations on its personnel. In addition, corporate culture plays an important role in the formation of labor-management relations as well as compensation, development, and integration of employees. Adoption of a specific managerial style and selection of a particular set of strategies is also strongly influenced by the company's corporate culture.

1.05 Principles of Decision Making

Management is constantly required to make decisions throughout the process of planning, organizing, leading, and controlling the company. The more important decisions deal with the strategic issues of the organization and involve finding out the existing situation and how to change it. Other managerial decisions relate to operational activities and necessitate evaluation of the existing resources and their most effective application within the organization. Hence, it is apparent that managers and entrepreneurs should be familiar with the basic **principles of decision making**, thus ensuring efficient performance of their organization.

The importance of the decision-making process is generally recognized and identified as a critical factor in overall managerial activity. This process concerns the development and selection of a suitable course of action toward organizational objectives. The most common error in management decisions is the emphasis on finding the correct answers rather than the correct questions. An illustration of typical questions which managers should be asking themselves and other members of their management team is summarized in Exhibit 1–12.

There are no universal rules in the decision-making process. However, those managers who use a systematic, intelligent, and rational approach have a better chance to reach the right decision and solve their specific problems. A rational decision-making process consists of six distinct steps, as illustrated in Exhibit 1–13.

Analysis of the existing situation represents the first step in the decision-making process. Managers and entrepreneurs, therefore, need to conduct a

Exhibit 1-12

A Summary of Typical Managerial Questions

Planning

1. What is our basic mission or the nature of our business?
2. What should our objectives be?
3. What changes are occurring in our external environment and how will they affect us now and in the future?
4. What strategies and tactics should we use to attain our objectives?

Organizing

1. How should the work of the organization be divided? How should we group work into larger units?
2. How can we coordinate these units so they work in harmony with, not against, one another?
3. What decisions should personnel, especially managers, at each level of the organization be allowed to make?
4. Do we need to change our structure because of changes in the external environment?

Leading

1. What needs do my subordinates have?
2. To what degree are these needs being satisfied through working toward the organization's objectives?
3. If my subordinates' satisfaction and productivity have decreased, why?
4. What can we do to increase the satisfaction and productivity of subordinates?

Controlling

1. How should we measure performance?
2. How often should we measure performance?
3. How well have we succeeded in attaining our objectives?
4. If we have not made sufficient progress toward our objectives, why and what corrective action should we take?

SOURCE: From *Management*, 3/ed. by Michael H. Mescon, Michael Albert, and Franklin Khedouri. Copyright © by Harper & Row, Publishers, Inc. Reprinted by permission of the publisher.

Exhibit 1–13

The Decision-Making Process

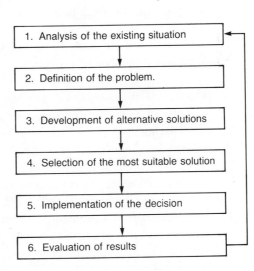

1. Analysis of the existing situation

2. Definition of the problem.

3. Development of alternative solutions

4. Selection of the most suitable solution

5. Implementation of the decision

6. Evaluation of results

situational analysis by using various data at their disposal. Situational analysis relates to any aspect of the company's activities and answers the following questions:

- What is the existing situation?
- What happened in the past?
- What has been the trend so far?
- What may happen in the future if the same trend continues?

For example, consider Mr. President, who examines the performance of his company. Information provided by the financial department indicates that the company earned net income equal to $70,000 during 1989. Thereafter, Mr. President turns to previous financial statements in order to establish the company's earnings during the preceding three fiscal periods. Appropriate records indicate that the company produced the following net income: $100,000 in 1986, $90,000 in 1987, and $80,000 in 1988.

The trend analysis of the company's net income indicates an average 10 to 12 percent deterioration of performance during the last four years. Hence, if the same trend continues, the company's net income in 1990 may drop again by about 10 percent. This obviously constitutes an undesirable condition and presents a potential problem which should be prevented.

In order to avoid any undesirable conditions, it is essential to get to the root of a particular problem. Definition of the problem represents, therefore, the next step in the rational decision-making process. Complete identification of a problem often represents a difficult task, since all parts of organizational activities are closely interrelated. It is helpful, therefore, to break the overall problem into smaller segments and to identify and subsequently solve each segment separately. This type of approach is frequently used by engineers and usually provides effective results.

Continuing with the decision-making process, Mr. President proceeds with identification of reasons which may have caused the deterioration of his company's earnings. This entails detailed examination of the company's performance in such areas as general administration, personnel, finance and accounting, production and operations, marketing and sales. In addition, Mr. President needs to be familiar with relevant management principles and set appropriate standards of performance in the aforementioned areas. Subsequently, the company's existing situation can be examined in terms of the corresponding standards of performance.

As a result of detailed examination of all operational activities, Mr. President identifies a number of problems in the following areas:

- General management. Unclear delegation of duties, responsibilities, and authority; inefficient operational planning; poor communication between departments
- Personnel management. Absence of job descriptions and job specifications, inefficient personnel performance, high turnover of employees
- Financial management. Absence of a budgeting procedure, poor credit control, inaccurate management accounting reports
- Production management. Inefficient plant layout, inaccurate cost estimating, irregular production scheduling, poor inventory control
- Marketing and sales management. Absence of a clear marketing plan, ineffective coverage of sales territories, poor product knowledge by salespeople

Once a specific problem is identified, it is necessary to determine what kind of action is required to rectify the problem. Thus, the third step in the rational decision-making process entails development of alternative solutions. These solutions may be generated by one individual or by a group of employees within an organization, depending on the nature of a particular problem. Sometimes managers use brainstorming techniques by inviting several employees to participate in the process of generating alternative solutions.

Mr. President, from the previous example, continues with the decision-making process. This entails a search for alternative solutions to improve the company's level of earnings. It is apparent from the problem identification stage that there are several interrelated problems which have to be solved in order to upgrade the company's performance. Hence, it is necessary to select alternative courses of action in various areas of the company's activities and evaluate each option in terms of its consequences. In performing the evaluation of consequences, the manager must provide answers to such questions as:

- Does the alternative action help the company to achieve its objective?
- Does the alternative action carry any undesirable consequences or negative side effects?
- Can the company afford a particular alternative action?

If the answer to any of these questions is unsatisfactory, there is a strong indication that a particular course of action is unacceptable. Hence, alternatives need to be found to secure an effective solution in a specific area of the company's activities. This leads to the next step in the decision-making process: selection of the most suitable solution.

If the manager succeeds to define a particular problem, to develop a set of alternative courses of action, and to evaluate consequences of each option, then the decision itself becomes a relatively easy task. Managers usually consider a number of factors and often consult with other members of the management team prior to reaching a final decision. Selection of the most suitable solution is often based on a "trade off" between various positive and negative consequences in relation to future activities of the organization. This, in turn, requires a delicate balancing of the proposed solution and a "diplomatic" approach by the manager to the decision-making process.

The next step in the decision-making process requires Mr. President to evaluate a number of alternative solutions in collaboration with his management team. Each alternative course of action is examined in detail in terms of its consequences and influence on the company's overall performance. Finally, Mr. President selects the most suitable solutions and prepares the following **plan of action:**

- General management. Revision of the organizational chart; accurate formulation of duties, responsibilities, and authority for each position; preparation of detailed operational plans; development of effective communication between departments
- Personnel management. Preparation of job descriptions and job specifications; execution of regular personnel performance appraisal; introduction of new personnel training and development methods
- Financial management. Preparation of a company budget; introduction of new credit control methods; development of new management accounting reporting procedures
- Production management. Revision of plant layout; development of new cost estimating procedures; preparation of regular production schedules; maintenance of an effective inventory control
- Marketing and sales management. Development of a clear marketing plan; redesign of sales territories; introduction of new training programs for salespeople

The next step in the decision-making process entails thorough implementation of decisions undertaken by management. It is essential, therefore, that managers "sell" their plans of action to each member of the management team in order to ensure effective implementation. Acceptance by subordinates of a particular plan of action enhances its chances for a successful implementation and improves cooperation among employees.

In accordance with information from the previous example, Mr. President proceeds with the implementation of the newly developed plan of action. This entails allocation of the following responsibilities within the organization:

- General management. Responsibility of the president
- Personnel management. Responsibility of the president or the vice president, personnel
- Financial management. Responsibility of the vice president, finance
- Production management. Responsibility of the vice president, production and operations
- Marketing and sales management. Responsibility of the vice president, marketing

The final stage of the rational decision-making process entails evaluation of results obtained during and after the implementation of previously selected decisions. Managers, therefore, need to collect data pertinent to the company's activities in a particular area, to evaluate actual results, and to compare these results with the corresponding projections. The evaluation of results represents a prime element of the management control function, which is discussed later in this volume.

Returning to the previous example, Mr. President proceeds with the evaluation of his company's performance and implementation of the plan of action. Provided that all members of the management team carry out their individual responsibilities, significant improvement in the company's performance may be expected. This, in turn, may lead to an effective solution to the original problem and subsequently generate higher net income.

1.06 The Planning Process

Regardless of its size, every business organization comprises a group of individuals working in unison toward the common purpose of earning a living. How good that living may be, both for the organization and the individual, is determined by the effective performance of individuals within the group. This can only be accomplished if management ensures that every member of a particular group understands its purpose, objectives, and methods of attaining such objectives. Satisfactory results can only be achieved by people who know and understand what is expected of them. Thus, the **planning process** on all levels is concerned with deciding on a course of action in advance and answering such questions as:

* What to do?
* When to do it?
* How to do it?
* Why to do it?
* Who should do it?
* How much will it cost?

Proper planning is the cornerstone of good management. Whether it is the chief executive, who is concerned with the best return on the shareholders' funds invested, or the foreman, who is concerned with the most efficient use of the labor force under his control, managers can only achieve success in their area of activities by planning the steps necessary to achieve their respective goals. There are several reasons why managers should engage in planning, some of which are as follows:

* Planning helps to establish a coordinated effort and provides general direction to managers and non-managers alike. When they know their organization's goals and expectations, employees begin to cooperate with each other and coordinate their activities toward reaching common objectives. Absence of planning usually causes "running in circles" and contributes to deterioration in organizational performance.
* Planning helps to reduce uncertainty by anticipating change. As a result of planning, managers are forced to look ahead, to examine the future, to anticipate change, to consider the impact of change, and to develop a suitable plan of action. Furthermore, planning helps to anticipate consequences of specific actions which might be undertaken in the future.
* Planning helps to reduce overlapping and wasteful activities. As a result of planning, managers are expected to evaluate the situation within their areas of responsibility prior to the implementation of a specific plan of action. If all managers work as a team, they can develop an overall plan by which all actions effectively complement each other.

- Planning helps to establish standards of performance and formulate objectives. As a result of a planning effort, managers are forced to develop certain performance parameters, which are subsequently used as a compass or travelling map. Availability of clear objectives enables managers to compare actual and planned results, thus facilitating management control.[11]

The planning process must be initiated and carried out as an integral part of managerial responsibility, thereby making a sound contribution to the desired efficiency of the total business operation. The *efficiency* of the planning effort in the business operation is the contribution value of the plan as measured against input costs. A plan may be effective in attaining desired objectives, but it would certainly not be efficient if the cost is excessively high. In the measurement of cost, not only must time and money be considered, but also the degree of individual and group satisfaction. There is little merit in a plan to cut costs if, in its implementation, the morale of employees is so depressed as to negate the objective of the plan.

The overall planning activity comprises two different types of plans:

- Strategic plans
- Operational plans

Strategic plans are prepared on an organization-wide basis and include establishment of overall objectives, development of strategies, and formulation of policies, rules, and procedures necessary to achieve specific objectives. Preparation of strategic plans represents one of the prime responsibilities of the company's top management.

Operational plans specify details about how and when overall objectives are to be achieved in various areas of company activities. These plans are usually prepared in areas such as general administration, personnel, finance and accounting, production and operations, and marketing and sales.

The planning process has to accommodate various time spans, which are generally grouped into short-, medium-, and long-term periods. Hence, all plans can be classified as follows:

- Short-term plans
- Medium-term plans
- Long-term plans

Short-term plans are prepared for a period of less than one year. Strategic plans for small organizations are usually prepared for such a period. Also most operational plans for small, medium-sized, and even large organizations are generally prepared for a short-term period. This period may vary from one day to one year, depending upon the specific type of organization and at what level of management planning is taking place.

Medium-term plans are prepared for a period of between one and five years. Strategic plans for medium-sized companies, for example, are generally prepared for several years. In addition, managers frequently prepare financial plans for medium-sized and large organizations in accordance with specific policy requirements.

Long-term plans are prepared for a period in excess of five years. Strategic plans for large organizations are normally prepared for extended periods. In addition, management of large organizations often prepares long-term financial plans in accordance with specific organizational requirements.

An ordinary planning process usually entails a number of steps illustrated in Exhibit 1–14, whether or not it is concerned with strategic planning for a large multi-national organization or operational planning for a small company. Since it represents a simpler task, planning for a small organization will require less time and effort on the part of management. Although none of the steps should be ignored, managers are not expected to spend half a day to produce a decision worth $10. On the other hand, managers should prevent spending only five minutes on making important planning decisions concerning millions of dollars.

The major steps in the planning process are as follows:

1. *Being aware of opportunities.* This step, in fact, precedes the planning process and is concerned with the search and identification of problems (i.e., situational analysis). Understanding of strengths and weaknesses helps to solve uncertainties and to take advantage of new opportunities in a specific area of company activities.

Exhibit 1–14

Steps In the Planning Process

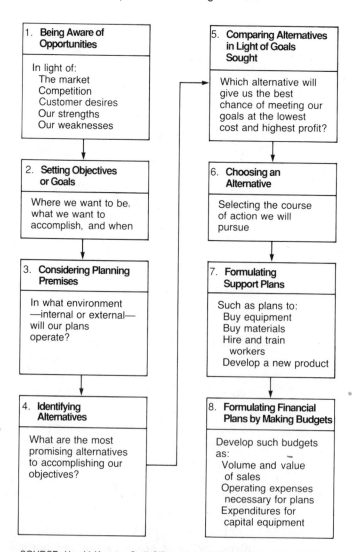

SOURCE: Harold Koontz, Cyril O'Donnel, and Heinz Weinrich, *Essentials of Management*, 3rd ed. (N.Y.: McGraw-Hill, 1982), p. 76. Reprinted with permission.

2. *Establishing objectives.* Once situational analysis is completed and strengths and weaknesses identified, appropriate objectives need to be established. Initially, such objectives are established for the whole organization and, thereafter, for each department and subordinate work unit. Objectives specify the goals which need to be accomplished by the company or by a particular work unit.

3. *Developing premises.* Upon establishing the company's objectives, management must ensure that all individuals engaged in the planning process become familiar with the organization's existing situation and its current strategies, policies, and plans. In addition, these individuals need to be familiar with external environmental factors such as customers, suppliers, competitors, and government agencies.

4. *Determining alternative courses.* Once individuals engaged in the planning process are familiar with what is happening within the organization and the surrounding environment, alternative courses of action need to be established. The prime purpose of such action should be to meet previously established objectives, taking into consideration the strengths and weaknesses of the organization.

5. *Evaluating alternative courses.* Upon establishing a number of alternative plans of action in a particular area of organizational activities, it becomes necessary to evaluate each plan separately. Evaluation of a plan may be carried out in terms of its efficiency (e.g., personnel planning), profitability (e.g., financial planning), productivity (e.g., production planning), or market penetration (e.g., marketing and sales planning).

6. *Selecting a course of action.* Once each alternative course of action has been properly evaluated, the next logical step is to select the most efficient, profitable, and productive course. The final decision about the most suitable course of action may be made by one individual or by a group, depending upon the nature of the plan (strategic or operating) and level of its application (company-wide, departmental, or individual).

7. *Formulating supporting plans.* Selection of a specific course of action would be incomplete without the development of a set of secondary plans to support the main course. Thus, it is necessary to identify a broad range of possible minor problems or needs which may be encountered en route to the implementation of the main course and to develop appropriate supporting plans.

8. *Formulating financial plans by budgeting.* The final step of the planning process entails providing numerical meaning to a plan and preparing a budget. A *budget* represents a quantitative expression of a specific plan of action and provides a summary of anticipated revenue, expenditure, and income as a result of implementing such a plan.[12]

One of the key elements of the planning function is preparation of financial projections, or budgets, for the organization. Budgets play a critical role in the effective planning and controlling of activities and are commonly used by management as financial performance standards. All top managers, therefore, are expected to participate in the budgeting process and formulate accurate financial projections in accordance with strategic and operational planning. These projections represent a set of statements of financial resources allocated for specific organizational tasks which need to be accomplished during a particular period of time. The scope of information provided by budgets depends upon the type of activity they support. Financial budgets, for example, summarize the planned level of the company's revenues, expenses, and income, while production budgets itemize elements of the projected manufacturing expenditure. More details about the budgeting process are provided in Part 3.

Once a particular plan of action has been selected, managers must commit all the necessary resources in order to ensure efficient implementation. In addition, managers must decide upon a specific period of time necessary to accomplish a particular plan. Thus, according to a **commitment principle,** logical planning encompasses a series of actions decided on today to meet future needs.[13]

Another important element which should be considered by managers who are engaged in the planning process is flexibility. According to the **flexibility principle:** "The more flexibility can be built into plans, the less the danger of losses that will be incurred by unexpected events; but the cost of flexibility should be weighed against the risks involved in making future commitments."[14]

Flexibility by itself does not guarantee successful implementation of a specific plan of action. Managers, therefore, need to act as navigators, continually checking the course and redrawing the plan in order to accomplish a predetermined objective. This is consistent with the **principle of navigational change:** "The more planning decisions a company commits for the future, the more important it is that a manager periodically checks on events and expectations and redraws plans as necessary to maintain a course toward a desired goal."[15]

1.07 Strategic Planning

Strategic planning is the process of defining the organization's mission and objectives, examining the existing situation, identifying opportunities and threats, developing and selecting strategies, and establishing the methods necessary to achieve specific objectives. In simplified terms, strategic planning represents a long-term planning process which aims at defining and achieving organizational goals.

The basic principles of the strategic planning process apply to large, medium-sized, and small organizations alike. Although managers in small organizations take a less formal approach and spend less time on the strategic planning activity, the basic issues remain the same. Some managers and owners of small organizations assume that strategic planning is an expensive and time-consuming exercise designed only for large organizations. Such an assumption, however, is incorrect. Several studies conducted recently throughout the United States indicate that strategic planning helps many small and medium-sized organizations to attain a higher growth rate and improve profitability. Strategic planning, thus, plays a critical role in successful organizational development and offers the following advantages:

- It leads management toward understanding the corporate mission of the organization.
- It serves to formulate organizational objectives and create unity of purpose among employees.
- It guides management in conducting a situational analysis and creates awareness of opportunities and threats in the marketplace.
- It results in development of strategies, policies, rules, and regulations essen-

tial for achieving organizational objectives.

- It provides a framework for effective decision making about various strategic and operational issues.
- It reduces the risk of making incorrect managerial decisions, thus ensuring effective organizational performance and favorable results.

The background of the strategic planning process is of a military nature. The word "strategy" derives from the Greek word *strategos*, which can be translated as "the art of the general." In business terms, **strategy** represents a detailed, comprehensive, and integrated plan designed to assure that the mission and objectives of the organization are met.[16]

A strategic plan must be formulated by the owner or chief executive of the organization at least once a year. Other members of the company's executive management team are also expected to participate in the strategic planning process by providing relevant information and by helping to select an appropriate course of action. Moreover, a strategic plan is designed to provide guidance to the management team for a long period and must remain clear and flexible at all times. Clarity and flexibility are particularly important since every organization operates in competitive and constantly changing business and social environments.

The formal strategic management process is illustrated in Exhibit 1–15. This process includes nine steps discussed below.

The first step in strategic planning involves the definition of the organization's mission. Many managers and entrepreneurs never really bother to define their missions. They simply believe that their only mission is to make as much profit as possible. This kind of attitude is particularly popular among those individuals who are driven by greed and selfishness. It appears, however, from examples produced by many hundreds of thousands of failed businesses, that such an attitude is incorrect and usually short-lived.

Managers should remember that, although making a profit is an integral part of **internal objectives**, the organization does not operate in isolation from the external environment. In fact, no organization can survive alone. It is essential, therefore, that managers turn their attention to the external environment and develop appropriate **external objectives**. As Peter F. Drucker suggests, "There is only one valid definition of business purpose: to create a customer."[17] Hence, it should be apparent that *the prime mission of any organization is to create a satisfied customer*. In order to achieve this, management must ensure that

- Products and services offered to customers are of high quality and competitive price.
- Products, services, and aftersales services are available in accordance with customers' requirements.
- Professional and ethical standards of all employees are maintained on a high level.
- Shareholders earn a fair and adequate return on their investments.
- All employees receive fair treatment and compensation for their work.

The process of defining the organization's mission is also influenced by the specific values, aspirations, education, experiences, and socioeconomic backgrounds of its top management. It is essential, therefore, to examine these factors and to ensure their positive effect on the statement of the organization's mission. Generally, such a statement should convey the following:

Exhibit 1–15

Strategic Management Process Including Strategic Planning (Steps 1–7)

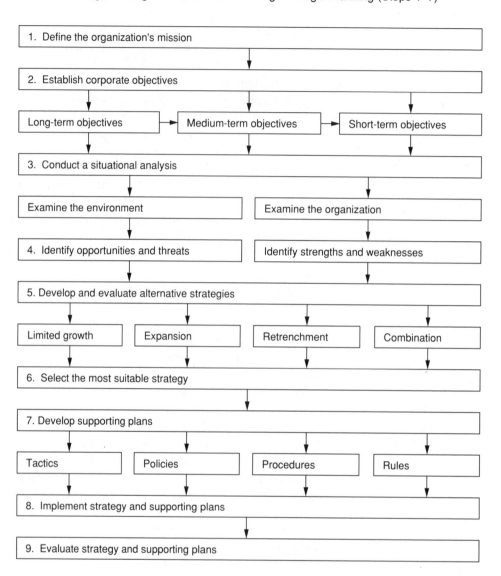

1. The purpose of the company in terms of its basic products or services, its primary markets, and its major technologies. What business is the company in?
2. The nature of the external environment that determines the operating philosophies of the company. Who are the customers and what are their needs?
3. The organizational culture. What type of working climate exists within the company? What type of people does this climate attract?[18]

Once the organization's mission is stated, management can proceed with establishment of overall company objectives. These objectives, known as **corporate objectives**, represent the end toward which various organizational activities are aimed. Corporate objectives are essential in every area of the company's operation where performance and results directly affect the existence and success of the organization. Peter F. Drucker suggests that the company's objectives of performance should be set in the following areas:

- Market standing
- Innovation
- Productivity
- Physical and financial resources
- Profitability
- Manager performance and development
- Worker performance and attitude
- Public responsibility[19]

In order to remain effective, corporate objectives should specify not only *what* management plans to accomplish but also *when* the results should be attained. For this reason, all objectives are classified as follows:

- Long-term objectives (five years and over)
- Medium-term objectives (one to five years)
- Short-term objectives (not exceeding one year)

Furthermore, it is essential to ensure that all corporate objectives remain *attainable* and take into consideration specific resources available to the company at a particular point in time. As George Steiner and John Miner point out, attainable objectives "are important motivators of people in organizations because, generally, people like to try to achieve the objectives set for the organization."[20] Hence, if they are set beyond the company's means, corporate objectives can have disastrous consequences, can increase frustration, and can reduce motivation among employees.

Corporate objectives represent not only the final destination of the planning process, but also the final phase in organizing, leading, and controlling activities. These objectives should always remain feasible, clear, and consistent to provide the organization with an attainable set of goals.

Once the organization's mission is defined and corporate objectives are established, management can begin a situational analysis. Such an analysis consists of two prime elements:

- Environmental analysis
- Management audit

Environmental analysis is the process of evaluating the influence of factors external to the organization in terms of opportunities and threats to the company. The three basic questions which should be answered by management as a result of the environmental analysis are:

- Where is our company now?
- Where do we want our company to be in the near and the distant future?
- What must we do to get our company from where it is now to where we want it to be?

The prime elements of environmental analysis for small and medium-sized companies relate to external factors such as:

1. *Customers*
   - Who are our current customers?
   - What kind of customers do we want to attract in the future?
   - What opportunities can we expect from current and potential customers?

2. *Suppliers*
   - Who are our current suppliers?
   - Where should we look for new suppliers in the future?
   - How can current and potential suppliers help us in taking advantage of the marketplace?
3. *Competitors*
   - Who are our current competitors?
   - What kind of threat is presented to us by our competitors?
   - What can we do to overcome the competitors' threat?
4. *Banks and financial institutions*
   - How effective is the service obtained from out current bank?
   - Where should we look for additional sources of finance in the future?
5. *Labor unions*
   - What effect does the labor union have on our company at present?
   - How do our employees feel about unionization?
   - What should our policy be toward labor unions in the future?
6. *Government agencies*
   - What effect do government agencies have on our company at present?
   - How can we minimize the effect of the government agencies in the future?

While conducting the environmental analysis, management also needs to consider prevailing economic, political, social, and technological conditions. This may enhance management's understanding about current and future opportunities and threats in the marketplace.

The second part of situational analysis includes a management audit of the organization. A **management audit** is a methodical evaluation of the organization's operational activities and financial performance, designed to identify its strengths, weaknesses, and potential. This audit is based on the business engineering method previously described and illustrated in Exhibit 1–10. The prime elements of the management audit are:

- Evaluation of a company's operational performance
- Evaluation of a company's financial performance
- Consolidation of evaluation results

Evaluation of a company's operational performance deals with a broad range of questions which focus on the company's ability to take advantage of environmental opportunities and to combat external threats. Some of these questions are as follows:

1. **General management analysis**
   - Do we have a sound plan of management to ensure successful performance of our company in the future?
   - How effective is our company's organizational structure in terms of meeting corporate objectives?
2. **Personnel management analysis**
   - How effective are members of our management team in terms of leading the organization into the future?
   - Do we have a sufficient number of motivated and skilled employees to ensure organizational success in a highly competitive environment?
3. **Financial management analysis**
   - Do we have sound internal financial control within our organization?

- How accurate are our company's budgets in terms of current opportunities and threats in the marketplace?

4. **Production and operations management analysis**
   - How effective is our production department in terms of designing and manufacturing high quality products at competitive prices?
   - Do we have sufficient manufacturing capacity to meet anticipated demands in the marketplace?

5. **Marketing and sales management analysis**
   - Do we have a sound marketing plan to enable the organization to take advantage of current opportunities in the marketplace?
   - How effective is our sales force in covering the current sales territories?

The second part of the management audit entails evaluation of the company's financial performance. This includes the following:

- **Current financial analysis** (i.e., what is the company's most recent position in terms of its assets, liabilities, revenues, expenditures, income, and cash flow?)
- **Comparative financial analysis** (i.e., what has been the company's position during the last three fiscal years in terms of its assets, liabilities, revenues, expenditures, income, and cash flow?)
- **Financial ratio analysis** (i.e., what has been the company's position during the last three to four fiscal years in terms of its liquidity, solvency, profitability, and ability to manage assets?)

The final part of the management audit entails consolidation of the evaluation results and determination of the company's internal strengths and weaknesses. By combining this information with the environmental analysis results, management should be able to identify real opportunities and threats presented to their organization in the marketplace.

The next step in the strategic planning process is development and evaluation of strategic alternatives available to the organization. The four basic strategies considered part of this stage are as follows:

1. Limited growth strategy
2. Expansion strategy
3. Retrenchment strategy
4. Combination strategy[21]

A **limited growth strategy** is frequently used by small and medium-sized companies and is particularly popular in mature industries with a static technology. Managers normally select this strategy if they are satisfied with their company's performance and do not wish to adopt a risky course of action. Accordingly, managers develop a set of objectives which suggest marginal improvement in comparison with the previous year's sales, expenditures, and profitability. In addition, the trend of the organization's results during the last three years and the inflation factor are taken into consideration.

An **expansion strategy** represents another option which is particularly suitable for developing industries with a dynamic technology. Managers usually select this strategy if they see substantial opportunities for their products or services in the marketplace. In other instances, managers feel that their organization needs to expand in order to survive in a highly competitive environment. This is particularly important since no growth may mean loss of market, profits, and subsequent failure. In accordance with the expansion strategy, managers inject additional capital into their organization to increase product or service lines, to broaden production facilities, and to develop new markets. Alternatively, management may decide to merge with another organization, thereby creating an instant corporate expansion.

A **retrenchment strategy** is used least frequently by small and medium-sized companies and is often referred to as the "last option." Managers usually select this strategy if their company's performance and results continue to deteriorate, if the economy is declining, or if the company needs to be saved. In accordance with this strategy, managers develop a set of objectives which are generally aimed below the previous year's results. A retrenchment strategy enables management to achieve the following:

- **Consolidation.** If the company's performance and results are deteriorating, but there is a good chance of saving the organization, management should reduce the scale of operations and cut expenditures. This hopefully will lead to the consolidation and to the subsequent turnaround of the company's performance in the future.
- **Divestment.** If the company's performance and results are affected by constantly unprofitable product or service lines, or subsidiaries, management should take drastic measures and dispose of loss-causing operations. This will help management to generate additional cash, which could be reinvested into the healthy part of the company's operations.
- **Liquidation.** If the company continues to incur substantial losses over an extended period of time, and management believes that consolidation of operations or divestment of assets will not be effective, the next "best" option is to liquidate the company's assets. Based on the principle, "do not throw away good money after bad," liquidation will at least help to preserve the remaining portion of the shareholders' equity invested in the company.

A **combination strategy** is frequently used by larger organizations which may be active in different industries. Thus, upon identifying the organization's strengths and weaknesses in the marketplace, management may decide to apply the three aforementioned strategies to its various parts on an individual basis.

Once it is aware of all strategic alternatives, management must select the most appropriate option and develop supporting plans. These plans include formulation of tactics, policies, procedures, and rules and are discussed next in this volume.

1.08 Implementation of Strategic Plans

The selection of an effective strategy is one of the most critical responsibilities of top management. To remain effective, such a strategy must be clear in terms of its corporate objectives. Furthermore, it is necessary that each member of the management team gives total support and a firm commitment toward the implementation of the strategic plan.

Every strategic plan must be supported by a set of corporate objectives which specify *what* the organization wants to accomplish and *when* results are expected. To ensure that the selected strategic plan is implemented and objectives are met, management must determine *how* the organization should accomplish its mission. It is necessary, therefore, to develop specific guidelines to avoid misunderstandings among employees and misdirection of organizational efforts.

The prime purpose of these guidelines is to ensure the coordination and cohesion of all planned activities within the organization. These guidelines include several components:

- Tactics
- Policies
- Procedures
- Rules

Tactics are short-term strategic plans formulated by management to accomplish defined short-term corporate objectives. Some characteristics of these plans, illustrated in Exhibit 1–16, are as follows:

1. Tactics are formulated in pursuit of strategy.
2. Whereas strategy is almost always formulated at the highest levels of management, tactics often are developed and implemented at middle-management levels.
3. Tactics cover a shorter time period than strategies.
4. Whereas the results of strategies may not be fully seen for several years, tactical results tend to be quickly evident and easily related to specific actions.[22]

Once long-term (strategic) plans and short-term (tactical) plans are developed, it is necessary to formulate a set of additional guidelines, or policies, to ensure efficient execution of such plans. A **policy** is a clear and complete statement related to the day-to-day running of the organization. Policies can be viewed as a preliminary set of instructions, or general rules, which state the established procedure required for a repetitive situation. Policies are specified within defined, functional areas of organizational activities and provide consistent guidance throughout the decision-making process. Furthermore, sound policies help to resolve various operational issues before they turn into problematic areas within the organization.

Exhibit 1-16

Development of a Company's Tactics

Strategy	Tactics (Short-Term Strategy)
Limited growth	Develop and implement marginally improved operational plans in such areas as general administration, personnel, finance and accounting, production and operations, marketing and sales.
Expansion	Seek and obtain additional capital; develop and implement improved operational plans, or find, purchase, and absorb another company.
	Search for the possibility of merging with another company, and implement the merger.
Retrenchment	Consolidation: Develop and implement marginally reduced operational plans and cut expenditure. Prepare plans for a turnaround at a later stage.
	Divestment: Identify unprofitable product or service lines, or subsidiaries and try to dispose of same. Prepare marginally improved operational plans for the profitable part of the company.
	Liquidation: Develop and implement a plan aimed at liquidating all company assets and paying off creditors.
Combination	Identify whether limited growth, expansion, or retrenchment represents the most suitable strategy for an individual subsidiary of the organization. Develop and implement appropriate tactics as described above.

Policies usually exist on all levels of company activities and cover a wide range of organizational and operational issues. A typical list of such policies in a small or medium-sized company may include the following:

1. **General management policies**
   - To conduct situational analysis and to review strategic plans on an annual basis
   - To apply management by objectives (MBO) procedures to the operational planning process on a regular basis
   - To ensure strict adherence to the overall plan of management

2. **Personnel management policies**
   - To recruit employees in accordance with equal employment opportunity laws
   - To revise job descriptions and job specifications on an annual basis
   - To review the level of personnel compensation on an annual basis

3. **Financial management policies**
   - To maintain strict control over the bookkeeping system on a continuous basis
   - To ensure that all financial statements are prepared on an annual basis
   - To prepare detailed operating budgets on an annual basis

4. **Production and operations management policies**
   - To standardize the range of products and services offered to customers
   - To revise performance of equipment on an annual basis and to replace equipment when it becomes obsolete
   - To ensure that production planning and control are implemented on a continuous basis

5. **Marketing and sales management policies**
   - To review the marketing-mix strategy (i.e., product, price, promotion, and distribution) on an annual basis
   - To ensure strict adherence to the marketing plan
   - To review sales force performance on a monthly basis

Formulation of the company's policies represents an important task of the executive management team. Since they serve to direct the decision-making process, these policies must be sufficiently flexible to accommodate the constantly changing conditions in the marketplace. Sometimes policies alone do not provide sufficient clarity in the decision-making process and must be supplemented by a range of specific procedures.

A **procedure** represents a plan that provides the necessary method of implementing company policies. Procedures generally specify the particular sequence of steps required to ensure the most efficient manner of accomplishing certain objectives undertaken by the company.

Procedures are found on every level of operational activities within the organization. Such procedures may range from prescribing the method of conducting the board meeting to company directors to giving operational instructions to workers. Procedures frequently cut across organizational lines and consist of numerous operating instructions issued to various departments within the company.

The main purpose of maintaining procedures is to provide a set of simple, clear, and comprehensive instructions to all employees to ensure efficient implementation of the company's objectives in accordance with the previously developed strategies and policies. Formulation of procedures represents, therefore, an important task of the management team and requires sound experience, suitable skills, and a methodical approach.

Another important element which needs to be specified by executive management is a set of rules that relate to the conduct of employees within and outside the organization. A **rule**, not to be confused with a policy or procedure, spells out a required action or non-action by an employee and does not allow for any discretion in its application. Rules are designed to provide a set of specific orders and prescribe what to do and what not to do within and outside the company. The basic difference between rules and policies is that rules are designed to enforce required regulations, while policies serve to guide management through the decision-making process.

A set of rules typical for a small or medium-sized company may include the following:

- Every employee is required to work during normal employment hours prescribed by the company and to take breaks only during the intervals allotted by management.
- Every hourly paid employee is required to punch "in" his or her own timecard when coming on duty, "out" and "in" for the meal period, and "out" again when going off duty.
- Every employee is required to obtain special permission from his or her supervisor in order to work overtime.
- Every employee is required to obtain an authorization from his or her supervisor prior to leaving the company's premises during normal working hours, unless pursuing company business.
- Every employee is entitled to receive the usual range of benefits offered by the company upon successfully completing a 90-day probation period.
- Every employee is entitled to paid annual leave equal to 10 days after one full year of employment and one additional day for every subsequent year thereafter.
- Every employee is entitled to 10 paid public holidays and five paid days of sick leave during one full year of employment.
- Every employee is allowed to smoke only during nonworking hours in specially assigned locations.
- The use of alcohol or drugs is prohibited.
- Private telephone calls are allowed only during nonworking hours, except emergencies.
- Every employee is expected to observe good taste in selection of clothes worn during working hours.
- Every employee is prohibited from accepting gifts and gratuities of any kind from the company's suppliers, customers, or fellow employees.
- Every employee is expected to demonstrate professionalism and courtesy while dealing on the company's behalf with customers, suppliers, and other people and organizations.

The main purpose of company rules is to enforce the implementation of various procedures, policies, and tactics developed in accordance with the specific strategic plans. Hence, the formulation of rules represents another important function of the company's executive management team, which serves to ensure effective implementation of strategic plans.

1.09 Management by Objectives

One of the most important techniques for implementing strategic planning is management by objectives. The term **management by objectives (MBO)** was popularized by Peter F. Drucker in 1954 and soon thereafter became a useful approach to planning.[23] According to Drucker, all managers within the organization must have a clear set of objectives which are aimed at supporting those of their superiors. By adhering to this approach, all managers will have a better understanding of what the organization expects of them, of the organization's objectives, and of specific objectives of their superiors.

The management by objectives approach has also been promoted by Douglas McGregor and used in the application of his Theory Y. According to this theory, presented earlier in Exhibit 1–7, individuals are prepared to work under suitable conditions, are keen to derive work satisfaction, and are willing to take responsibility for their performance. Thus, the prime purpose of the MBO approach is to take advantage of positive attitudes of employees and to create a suitable atmosphere through establishing joint objectives between managers and their subordinates. This approach, in turn, will enable managers and subordinates to evaluate their performance and compare actual results with established objectives.

According to Anthony Raia, another expert on the MBO approach, "the emphasis (of MBO) is on trying to predict and influence the future rather than on responding and reacting by the seat of the pants. It is also a 'results-oriented' philosophy of management, one which emphasizes accomplishments and results. The focus is generally on change and on improving both individual and organizational effectiveness."[24]

There are several requirements which must be met to ensure effective implementation of the MBO approach:

- Commitment of senior managers to the MBO process
- Joint setting of objectives by managers and their subordinates
- Autonomy during the process of program implementation
- Frequent review of program performance and preliminary results[25]

The implementation of the MBO process entails four interdependent and interrelated elements, outlined in Exhibit 1–17.

The first step, formulation of clear and concise objectives, is consistent with the overall planning process. Once long-, medium-, and short-term objectives are formulated by top management for the organization and their own work,

Exhibit 1–17

The Management by Objectives Process

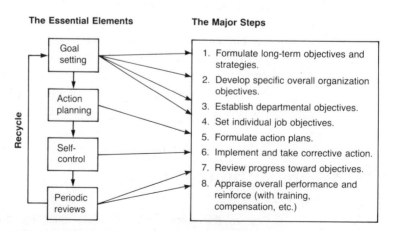

SOURCE: Stephen P. Robbins, *Management*, 2e, ©1988, p. 144. Adapted by permission of Prentice Hall, Inc., Englewood Cliffs, New Jersey.

it becomes necessary to establish detailed objectives for subordinates. Each subordinate is required to participate with his or her immediate superior in the individual goal-setting process. Joint setting of objectives by subordinates and their superiors helps to secure the firm commitment and active participation of each employee in the MBO implementation process. Setting of objectives in a small or medium-sized company is illustrated in Exhibit 1–18.

According to Drucker, the objectives of all managers' jobs must be defined by the contribution they have to make to the success of the larger unit of which they are a part. The district sales managers' objectives should be defined by the contribution they and their district sales force have to make to the sales department, the project engineers' objectives by the contribution they, their engineers, and their draftspeople make to the engineering department.[26]

To ensure that the company's objectives are clearly formulated, it is necessary to establish effective two-way communication between management and subordinates. Doing so will stimulate a continuous exchange of information between employees and help to clarify what is expected of each individual within the organization.

A typical statement of job objectives for a manager participating in the MBO program is illustrated in Exhibit 1–19.

Once specific objectives are formulated for the company and each employee within the organization, it is necessary to develop an effective plan of action. According to Raia:

> While a clear set of objectives reflects the "ends" of managerial performance, well-conceived action plans provide the "means" for their attainment. Action planning involves determining what, who, when, where, and how much is needed to achieve a given objective. It is a practical way of providing a connecting link between the statement of an objective and a more complete program of implementation.[27]

A clearly defined plan of action provides managers with a number of important advantages. Some of these advantages are as follows:

- A better understanding whether or not certain objectives are attainable
- Identification of potential problem areas and unexpected consequences
- Utilization of improved problem solving methods
- Preparation of a framework for budget development, cost estimating, and work scheduling

Exhibit 1–18

MBO Process: Setting of Objectives

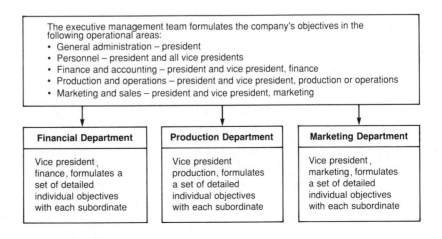

Exhibit 1–19

Management by Objectives Program

Management By Objectives Program For 1989/1990			
Objective	**Priority**	**Date**	**Result**
1. Reduce bank overdraft by $20,000	A	11-1-89	
2. Collect 80 percent of accounts receivable over 30 days	A	11-1-89	
3. Prepare new budget based on 10 percent revenue increase	A	1-1-90	
4. Hire additional clerk	B	1-1-90	
Prepared: A. Jones	Approved: A. Boss		Date: 9-1-89
Position: V.P. Finance	Position: President		

- Identification of the required level of relationships within the organization
- Identification of contingencies which should be taken into account for objectives to be attained[28]

The action planning stage of the MBO process entails six basic steps, outlined in Exhibit 1–20.

Each manager must follow these steps to ensure effective implementation of the MBO process. Once the plans of action are prepared for each department, the executive management team must verify the detailed cost estimates and deadlines in terms of the company's overall requirements and objectives.

The next stage of the MBO process entails review and evaluation of results achieved by each department and by the company as a whole. The prime purpose of this stage is:

- To determine the degree to which objectives were attained.
- To identify any problems and obstacles encountered during the MBO process.
- To determine the causes of problems which have occurred.
- To identify personal development needs for each employee.
- To ensure that effective performance of every employee is rewarded.[30]

This step is particularly important since it enables all managers within the organization to evaluate their own performance, to assess results attained by their subordinates, to evaluate the overall performance of their sections or departments, and to prepare concise reports for their superiors. In addition, such an evaluation promotes self-control in each employee and provides guidance for taking corrective action.

Exhibit 1–20

MBO Process: Action Planning

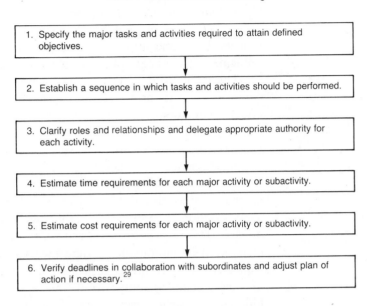

1. Specify the major tasks and activities required to attain defined objectives.

2. Establish a sequence in which tasks and activities should be performed.

3. Clarify roles and relationships and delegate appropriate authority for each activity.

4. Estimate time requirements for each major activity or subactivity.

5. Estimate cost requirements for each major activity or subactivity.

6. Verify deadlines in collaboration with subordinates and adjust plan of action if necessary.[29]

A typical process of reviewing and evaluating performance in a small or medium-sized company is illustrated in Exhibit 1–21.

Once the review and evaluation of results are available, each manager must take necessary corrective action in order to complete the MBO process. Taking corrective action is similar to the last step of the controlling process, which is discussed later in this part.

Consider, for example, that certain objectives of the company have not been accomplished during a predetermined period of time. In this case, each manager is required to identify such occurrences and to measure differences between actual results and predetermined objectives. A thorough analysis of reasons which may have caused the deviation between the actual results and planned objectives will help managers to readjust their plans of action. Furthermore, managers will be able to provide effective guidance to their subordinates in correcting their individual performance. This, in turn, will help to ensure successful implementation of the MBO procedures and subsequently to initiate an effective operational planning effort within the organization.

Exhibit 1–21

MBO Process Evaluation of Results

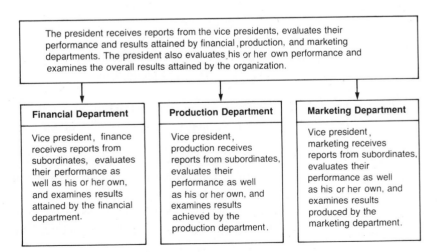

The president receives reports from the vice presidents, evaluates their performance and results attained by financial, production, and marketing departments. The president also evaluates his or her own performance and examines the overall results attained by the organization.

Financial Department	**Production Department**	**Marketing Department**
Vice president, finance receives reports from subordinates, evaluates their performance as well as his or her own, and examines results attained by the financial department.	Vice president, production receives reports from subordinates, evaluates their performance as well as his or her own, and examines results achieved by the production department.	Vice president, marketing receives reports from subordinates, evaluates their performance as well as his or her own, and examines results produced by the marketing department.

1.10 Operational Planning

Upon completing the development of the company's strategic plan and formulating appropriate objectives, management must initiate the operational planning process. The prime purpose of this process is to determine *how* the company should implement its strategic plan in order to ensure that overall objectives are met.

The main focus of operational planning is on the present activities of the company, and its prime concern is efficiency (doing things right) rather than effectiveness (doing the right things). Since strategic planning provides direction and boundaries for operational management, the two types of planning overlap. However, both are essential in ensuring effective management of the organization and must operate continuously on a day-to-day level to achieve it.

The nature of planning responsibilities depends upon the size and specific objectives of a particular organization. Executive management needs to commit itself to action in accordance with the ultimate objectives set out by the planning process. This process does not end when the objectives are selected. Operational plans must be thoroughly implemented and remain flexible at all times. Plans sometimes may require modification during the process of their implementation; thus the replanning abilities of the management team usually hold the key to the ultimate successful performance of the company.

The basic planning steps outlined previously can be condensed into four fundamental stages and adopted to all planning activities within the organization:

1. Establishment of an objective or a set of objectives. Planning starts with decisions about relevant needs and wants of the company.
2. Definition of the present situation. How far is the company from its objectives? What resources are available for achieving objectives?
3. Identification of operational methods. What internal and external environmental factors can help the company achieve its objectives? What factors may cause a problem?
4. Development of a plan or a set of actions to achieve the company's objectives.

Operational plans are generally prepared for periods of time not exceeding one year. These plans are developed by top and middle-level managers and serve to provide guidance to the company's employees on a daily basis. Operational planning activities in small and medium-sized companies normally include five interrelated elements, as illustrated in Exhibit 1–22. These elements are as follows:

- General administration planning
- Personnel planning
- Financial planning
- Production and operations planning
- Marketing and sales planning

General administration planning is a function of the company's president. This function entails a number of important activities such as:

- Preparation of a plan of management. This plan is based on a consolidated plan of action, which is summarized in Part 6 (Volume II).
- Development of an organizational chart. This chart is prepared in accordance with the specific nature and needs of the company.
- Development of a management structure. This structure is reviewed and

Exhibit 1–22
Elements of Operational Planning

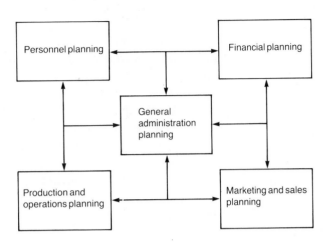

modified in accordance with the results of the situational analysis and needs of the company.

Personnel planning in small and many medium-sized organizations is also a function of the company's president, unless a personnel manager is employed. This function entails a broad range of planning activities which involve all departments within the organization. Some of these activities are as follows:

- Preparation of job descriptions and job specifications. Existing job descriptions and job specifications are reviewed and modified in accordance with the specific requirements of the company.
- Personnel planning and forecasting. Personnel requirements are identified and summarized in accordance with the company's needs.
- Preparation of personnel recruitment plans. New employees are recruited and hired in accordance with the personnel planning requirements.
- Personnel training and management development. Appropriate training and development plans are prepared for employees in accordance with the company's specific needs.
- Preparation of personnel compensation budget. The total cost of basic compensation, fringe benefits, and the company's contributions is summarized in accordance with the personnel planning requirements.
- Personnel appraisal planning. The performance of every employee is appraised on a preplanned basis in accordance with the company's specific requirements.

Financial planning is a function of the company's vice president, finance, or financial manager. This function is of particular importance to the whole organization and entails a number of activities. Among these activities are:

- Preparation of a new bookkeeping system. The existing system is reviewed and modified in accordance with the specific needs of the company.
- Preparation of an operating budget. This budget represents a numerical plan and provides a description of future operating results. It includes a sales (revenues) budget, production (cost of sales) budget, operating expenses budget, and budgeted income statement.
- Preparation of a financial budget. This budget provides a description of future financial conditions and includes capital expenditure budget, cash budget, and budgeted balance sheet.

- Development of new internal control procedures. The existing procedures relating to cash management and control, credit control, and control of purchases and disbursements are reviewed and modified in accordance with the specific needs of the company.
- Planning of inventory levels. The current level of inventories is identified, and future adjustments are planned in accordance with operating budget requirements.
- Development of new cost recovery rates. Current cost recovery rates are reviewed and adjusted in accordance with operating budget requirements.
- Development of new management accounting reports. The current set of reports is reviewed and redesigned in accordance with the specific needs of the company.
- Development of new computerized systems. Current computerized systems are evaluated, and new computerization plans are prepared in accordance with the specific needs of the company.

Production and operations planning is a function of the company's vice president, production/operations, or production/operations manager. This function exists in all manufacturing and some nonmanufacturing organizations and entails a broad range of activities. Some of these activities are as follows:

- Facility design and development. The current facility is reviewed and reorganized in accordance with the specific needs of the company.
- Development of a new product range. The current product range is examined, and new products are developed in accordance with the overall marketing plan requirements.
- Development of new manufacturing processes. The current manufacturing processes are evaluated, and new ones are developed in accordance with the specific needs of the company.
- Development of a production management plan. This plan includes evaluation and selection of new equipment, examination and redesign of plant layout, and preparation of equipment maintenance and replacement schedules.
- Development of new cost estimating methods. Current cost estimating methods are evaluated and readjusted in accordance with the specific needs of the company.
- Preparation of production plans. These plans include annual forecasts of production output, or aggregate plans, and short-term master production schedules.
- Material requirements planning (MRP). This entails preparation of a detailed list of materials needed to fulfil master production schedule requirements.
- Operational capacity requirements plannings. This entails planning of operational capacity needed to fulfil master production schedule requirements.
- Shop floor planning. This entails preparation of drawings, tools, operational and manpower capacity needed to fulfil specific production scheduling requirements in each shop.
- Materials purchasing planning. This entails preparation of a detailed list of optional suppliers, materials, prices, and delivery dates.
- Quality control planning. This entails examination of current quality control methods and development of new methods in accordance with the specific needs of the company.
- Material dispatch planning. This entails examination of the current methods of material dispatch and development of new methods in accordance with the specific needs of the company.

Marketing and sales planning is a function of the company's vice president, marketing/sales, or marketing/sales manager. This function entails a number of important activities such as

- Development of a new marketing information system (MIS). The current marketing information system is reviewed and modified in accordance with strategic marketing requirements.
- Market segmentation, measurement, and forecasting. This entails identification of new market segments, measurement of the market potential, and forecasting of future sales.
- Development of new marketing mix strategies. The current strategies relating to product, price, promotion, and distribution are reviewed and adjusted in accordance with the strategic marketing requirements.
- Preparation of a marketing plan. This plan includes a new product plan and the revised annual marketing plan. Both plans are developed in accordance with strategic marketing requirements.
- Preparation of a sales plan. This plan includes a detailed revenue budget which is developed in accordance with sales forecasts. This plan also includes marketing and selling costs budgets developed in accordance with marketing planning requirements.
- Development of a sales organization. The current sales organization is examined and redesigned in accordance with the sales planning requirements.
- Preparation of sales force recruitment plans. New salespeople are recruited and hired in accordance with the sales planning requirements.
- Sales force training and development. Appropriate training and development plans for salespeople are prepared in accordance with the company's specific needs.
- Preparation of sales force compensation plans. The current level of basic compensation, incentives, and fringe benefits for salespeople is reviewed and adjusted in accordance with the company's personnel compensation program.
- Sales force appraisal planning. The performance of every salesperson is appraised on a preplanned basis in accordance with the company personnel appraisal program.

All elements of operational planning require careful consideration by the company's management team to ensure efficient organizational performance. Without proper planning, individuals within the organization tend to react in an aimless manner and leave events to chance.

1.11 Plan of Management

The ultimate objective of strategic and operational planning activities is to develop and to formulate a suitable plan of management to ensure smooth functioning of the organization. This plan provides the company with a comprehensive guideline and presents an important source of business information.

The plan of management must be developed on an annual basis and reviewed every year thereafter. This plan incorporates consolidated results derived from strategic planning, management by objectives, and operational planning efforts. The fundamental issues summarized by the plan of management are illustrated in Exhibit 1–23.

The plan of management may include a broad range of issues, depending upon the size and specific needs of the organization. It is important, however,

Exhibit 1–23

Plan of Management

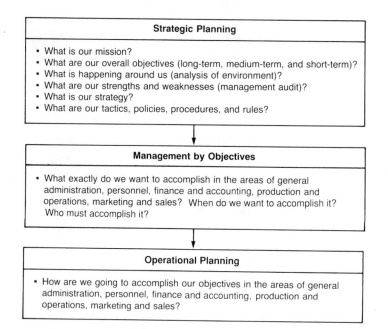

that all basic elements pertinent to strategic planning, management by objectives, and operational planning are included in such a plan. These elements are as follows:

1. Company's values and mission
2. Company's objectives:
    2.1 Long-term objectives
    2.2 Medium-term objectives
    2.3 Short-term objectives
3. Situational analysis:
    3.1 Environmental analysis
    3.2 Management audit
4. Opportunities and threats
5. Company's strategy
6. Company's supporting plans:
    6.1 Tactics
    6.2 Policies
    6.3 Procedures
    6.4 Rules
7. Company's plan of action:
    7.1 General management plan
    7.2 Personnel management plan
    7.3 Financial management plan
    7.4 Production and operations management plan
    7.5 Marketing and sales management plan
8. Company's budgets:
    8.1 Operating budget
    8.2 Financial budget

The plan of management starts with a brief statement defining the company's values and mission in the marketplace and describing its products or services.

Exhibit 1-24

Statement of Organizational Values and Mission

Apple's Values and Mission

Empathy for customers/users

We offer superior products that fill real needs and provide lasting value . . . . We are genuinely interested in solving customer problems and will not compromise our ethics or integrity in the name of profit.

Achievement/aggressiveness

We set aggressive goals and drive ourselves to achieve them. We recognize that this is a unique time, when our products will change the way people work and live. It's an adventure and we're in it together.

Positive social contribution

As a corporate citizen, we wish to be an economic, intellectual, and social asset in communities where we operate. But beyond that, we expect to make this world a better place to live. We build products that extend human capability, freeing people from drudgery and helping them achieve more than they could alone.

Individual performance

We expect individual commitment and performance above the standard for our industry. Only thus will we make the profits that permit us to seek our other corporate objectives.

Team spirit

Team work is essential to Apple's success, for the job is too big to be done by any one person. Individuals are encouraged to interact with all levels of management, sharing ideas and suggestions to improve Apple's effectiveness and quality of life. It takes all of us to win. We support each other and share the victories and rewards together.

Quality/excellence

We care about what we do. We build into Apple products a level of quality, performance, and value that will earn the respect and loyalty of our customers.

Individual reward

We recognize each person's contribution that flows from high performance. We recognize also that rewards must be psychological as well as financial, so we strive for an atmosphere where each individual can share the adventure and excitement of working at Apple.

Good management

The attitudes of managers toward their people are of primary importance. Employees should be able to trust the motives and integrity of their supervisors. It is the responsibility of management to create a productive environment where Apple's values flourish.

SOURCE: From *Management* 3/e by Michael H. Mescon, Michael Albert and Franklin Khedouri. Copyright ©1988 by Harper & Row, Publishers, Inc. Reprinted by permission of the publisher.

A typical statement is presented in Exhibit 1–24. This statement may clarify the nature of the market and describe the type of customers pursued by the organization.

The second element of the plan of management presents a summary of the company's strategic objectives. These objectives are classified as long-term objectives (over five years), medium-term objectives (between one to five years), and short-term objectives (not exceeding one year).

The third element of the plan of management contains summarized results of the situational analysis and includes the following:

- Results of the environmental analysis. These results describe the influence of customers, suppliers, competitors, banks, labor unions, and government agencies on the company's performance.

- Consolidated results of the management audit. These results describe the company's strengths and weaknesses in the areas of general administration, personnel, finance and accounting, production and operations, and marketing and sales. In addition, these results relate to the company's financial performance analysis.

The fourth element of the plan of management presents a summary of opportunities and threats that exist in the marketplace. All opportunities are expressed in terms of customer needs so that the company may have a trading advantage. All threats, on the other hand, are expressed in terms of possible adverse conditions that might be created by the company's competitors in the marketplace.

The fifth element of the plan of management specifies the overall strategy adopted by the company's management team. This strategy is selected on the basis of the following:

- Limited growth strategy
- Expansion strategy
- Retrenchment strategy
- Combination strategy

The sixth element of the plan of management outlines the specific supporting plans, which may include the following:

- Short-term tactics
- Revised policies
- Updated procedures
- Revised rules

The seventh element of the plan of management contains a detailed plan of action developed by the executive management team. The prime purpose of this plan is to maximize the company's strengths and to minimize its weaknesses in the following areas of activities:

- General administration
- Personnel
- Finance and accounting
- Production and operations
- Marketing and sales

The last element of the plan of management presents a summary of the company's budgets and includes the following:

- Operating budget. This budget includes a sales budget, production (cost of sales) budget, operating expenses budget, and budgeted income statement.
- Financial budget. This budget includes capital expenditure budget, cash budget, and budgeted balance sheet.

Since the future holds no certainty, any plan of management must remain flexible and incorporate alternative methods of achieving planned objectives. For this reason, more thought and consideration should be given by the company's management team to every component of the plan. The development of a flexible and effective plan of management represents the ultimate task of the executive management team and serves to ensure sound performance of the organization in the future.

1.12 The Organizing Process

Once the executive management team has identified the company's objectives and developed strategic and operational plans, the organizing process must begin. The prime purpose of the organizing process is to develop an effective organizational structure that will enable the company to attain specific objectives by utilizing its resources in the existing environment. An **organizational structure**, in turn, can be defined as the arrangement and interrelationship of the component parts and positions of a company.[31]

The organizing process is essentially similar for all types of businesses. The complexity of the organizing process, however, depends upon the size and type of the company and the nature of its activities in the marketplace. Since the prime purpose of any company is to create customers and to satisfy their needs, the organizing process must be geared to the same goals. Thus, the main questions that need to be answered during the organizing process are:

- How should we arrange our company in order to supply products or to provide services to customers in the most efficient manner?
- In what type of activities do we have to engage ourselves?
- What kind of functions need to be developed within the organization?
- How should these functions interrelate with each other?

Proper organizing represents an integral part of the overall management process. Whether it is the company's president, who is concerned with the most efficient performance of the organization, or the quality controller, who is responsible for the quality of components and finished goods, employees can only achieve success in their areas of responsibility if their jobs are organized in advance. Organizing is important for several reasons:

- Organizing helps management to utilize the company's physical, financial, and human resources in the most efficient and economical manner.
- Organizing helps management to direct all operational activities toward meeting the company's objectives.
- Organizing helps to develop a structure of specialized or standardized activities in accordance with the company's planning requirements.
- Organizing helps to create a clear framework of relationships among employees within the company.
- Organizing helps to specify the level of responsibility, authority, and accountability among employees within the company.
- Organizing helps to create an orderly environment within the organization, thereby reducing overlapping of work and minimizing confusion among employees.
- Organizing helps to streamline operational activities and to minimize running costs, thereby contributing to an increased level in company profitability.

The organizing process must be initiated and carried out as an integral part of management responsibility. This process entails six basic steps, outlined in Exhibit 1–25.

The organizing process starts by identifying and classifying a broad range of activities which must be carried out in order to accomplish the company's objectives. In general terms, such activities may include the following:

- **General management activities.** These activities include all administrative aspects of running a company; formulating and implementing strategic and

Exhibit 1–25

The Organizing Process

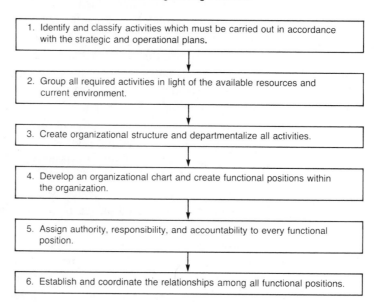

1. Identify and classify activities which must be carried out in accordance with the strategic and operational plans.

2. Group all required activities in light of the available resources and current environment.

3. Create organizational structure and departmentalize all activities.

4. Develop an organizational chart and create functional positions within the organization.

5. Assign authority, responsibility, and accountability to every functional position.

6. Establish and coordinate the relationships among all functional positions.

operational plans; organizing human and material resources into an effective functional structure; establishing lines of communication within the organization; leading the company toward achieving its objectives; controlling the company's performance, monitoring results, and taking corrective actions in all areas of its activities.

- **Personnel management activities.** These activities include analyzing various jobs; preparing job descriptions and job specifications; planning and forecasting personnel requirements; recruiting and hiring employees; screening, interviewing, and testing applicants; developing personnel orientation, training, motivation, compensation, and career management programs; appraising personnel performance; establishing sound labor-management relations; managing interpersonal conflicts; and ensuring safety and health of employees within the organization.

- **Financial management activities.** These activities include gathering of accounting information; maintaining an updated bookkeeping system; collaborating with accountants in preparing financial statements; evaluating the company's financial performance; preparing operating, capital expenditure and cash budgets; formulating tax strategies; identifying suitable sources of finance; maintaining effective cash, credit, expenditure, inventory, and capital assets control; costing of products and services; developing pricing methods; preparing management accounting reports and managing computerized accounting systems.

- **Production and operations management activities.** These activities include designing, locating, and organizing the operational facility; selecting and designing products or services; supervising the drafting office; evaluating, selecting, maintaining, and replacing equipment and tools; estimating manufacturing costs; planning and controlling production and operational activities; maintaining quality control; planning material requirements and purchasing materials; controlling inventories and dispatching finished goods to customers.

- **Marketing and sales management activities.** These activities include gathering marketing information; measuring and forecasting market potential; formulating product, pricing, promotion, and distribution strategies; developing marketing and sales plans and budgets; developing a sales organization; recruiting, training, compensating, motivating, allocating, and controlling the sales force.

Once all specific activities pertinent to the company's operations are identified, these activities must be grouped in order to initiate the development of an organizational structure. In developing the organizational structure, top management must realize that no individual can be an expert in every aspect of the company's activities. It is essential, therefore, to take into consideration the strengths and weaknesses of the members of the management team and other employees within the organization. The experience, competence, and talent of each employee must be identified and subsequently utilized in building efficient working teams.

The organizing process is also influenced by several factors related to the external environment which surrounds the company. These factors include customers, suppliers, financial institutions, labor unions, and various governmental agencies. Customers, for example, play an important role in the organizational departmentation process discussed later in this part. Suppliers, financial institutions, labor unions, and governmental agencies sometimes impose additional requirements which need to be considered throughout the development of the company's organizational structure.

James Stoner suggests that the organizational structure can be analyzed in terms of the following five elements:

1. Specialization of activities
2. Standardization of activities
3. Coordination of activities
4. Centralization and decentralization of decision making
5. Size of the work unit[32]

Specialization of activities concerns the specification of individual and group work tasks within an organization (division of work) and consolidation of these tasks into work units (departmentation). In a small or medium-sized company, for example, such tasks may be consolidated into five major areas of activities: general administration, personnel, finance and accounting, production and operations, and marketing and sales. This, in turn, leads to appropriate departmentation of the organizational structure, initiating the development of separate departments.

Standardization of activities concerns the development of uniform and consistent procedures within the organization. Such procedures are developed by formalizing the activities of individuals or groups and specifying their relationships within each department and the whole organization. One of the most effective methods of standardizing activities within the company is the development of its organizational chart, as discussed later in this part. Standardization of activities also includes formulation of operating procedures and rules and preparation of job descriptions for subordinates.

Coordination of activities concerns the integration of work carried out by individuals and groups within the organization. This action, in fact, is similar to the task of an orchestra conductor, who aims to create beautiful music. To succeed in his or her efforts, the conductor needs to know what individual musicians should play and when they should play it. Similarly, the company's president and every manager needs to know what functions should be performed by subordinates and when appropriate tasks should be carried out. Such knowledge

Exhibit 1-26

Organization Structures with Narrow and Wide Spans

Organizations with Narrow Spans

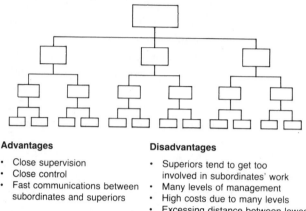

Advantages

- Close supervision
- Close control
- Fast communications between subordinates and superiors

Disadvantages

- Superiors tend to get too involved in subordinates' work
- Many levels of management
- High costs due to many levels
- Excessing distance between lowest level and top level

Organizations with Wide Spans

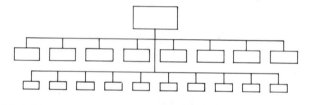

Advantages

- Superiors are forced to delegate
- Clear policies must be made
- Subordinates must be carefully selected

Disadvantages

- Tendency of overloaded superiors to become decision bottlenecks
- Danger of superior's loss of control
- Requires exceptional quality of managers

SOURCE: Harold Koontz, Cyril O'Donnel, and Heinz Weihrich, *Essentials of Management,* 3rd ed. (New York: McGraw-Hill, 1982), p. 185. Reprinted with permission.

will ensure effective coordination of activities within each working group and the whole organization.

Centralization or decentralization of decision making refers to the location of the decision-making authority within the organization. The majority of small and medium-sized companies are usually managed on a centralized basis, so all important decisions are taken by top management or even single individuals. Thereafter, all managerial decisions are passed to lower-level managers and subsequently dispersed among all employees. Minor operational decisions usually do not concern top management and are left in the hands of supervisors and their subordinates. In larger organizations, conversely, decision making is often decentralized by delegating additional authority to middle-level managers.

Size of the work unit refers to the number of employees engaged within a particular working group. Determination of the specific number of employees within a department, section, or working team depends upon the nature of the company's activities and skills of its management team. Well-known British consultant Lyndall Urwick suggests that the ideal number of subordinates for all executive management positions is four, while the number of subordinates at lower managerial and operative levels may vary from 8 to 12. Other experts found that a skilled middle-level manager may effectively control between 20 and 30 subordinates.

The ultimate size of the work unit depends upon the **span of management**, or number of subordinates who could be effectively managed by one superior. A small number of subordinates for every manager is represented by a **narrow management span**, while a larger number of subordinates relates to a **wide management span**. Both types have certain advantages and disadvantages, as illustrated in Exhibit 1–26.

Once an organizational chart is developed and functional positions are created, it is essential to assign authority, responsibility, and accountability to every position within the organization. Delegation of authority, responsibility, and accountability will be discussed later in this part. Finally, once these tasks are accomplished, managers must establish and coordinate the relationships between all functional positions, thereby completing the organizing process.

1.13 Organizational Departmentation

One of the main elements of the organizing process is the subdivision of a company into a number of specialized working groups. This task is known as **organizational departmentation**. The prime purpose of organizational departmentation is to group people and activities into departments to allow orderly functioning of the enterprise. The complexity of departmentation methods depends upon the nature, size, and objectives of a particular organization. Some commonly used departmentation methods are:

- Departmentation by function
- Departmentation by product or service
- Departmentation by market or customer
- Departmentation by territory

Departmentation by function is commonly used by most small and medium-sized companies that offer a limited range of products or services to customers. This method facilitates development of a **functional structure** and provides a basis for separating various functions within the organization. Such functions include general administration, personnel, finance and accounting, production and operations, marketing and sales. A typical functional structure in a manufacturing company is illustrated in Exhibit 1–27.

The illustration represents an example of functional departmentation in a small or medium-sized manufacturing organization. Functional departmentation in a nonmanufacturing organization can be carried out in a similar manner, although the production management function is replaced by the operations (service, contract, or project) or merchandising (wholesaling or retailing) management function.

Every executive manager within a functional organization is in charge of a specific range of operational activities on a company-wide basis. Thus,

- President is in charge of all general management activities.
- Vice president, personnel is in charge of all personnel management activities. In most smaller organizations, however, this function is carried out by the president.

Exhibit 1–27

Functional Departmentation In a Manufacturing Company

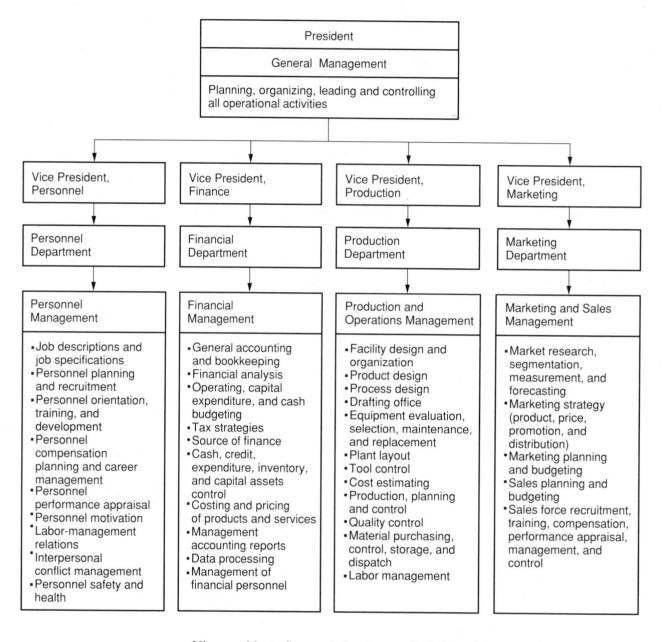

- Vice president, finance is in charge of all financial management activities.
- Vice president, production is in charge of all production and operations management activities. In most larger manufacturing organizations, this function is divided into engineering management (design work) and manufacturing management activities. In nonmanufacturing organizations, the title "vice president, production" is removed or replaced with another appropriate title (e.g., vice president, operations).
- Vice president, marketing is in charge of all marketing and sales management activities.

The main advantage of functional departmentation is that it provides a logical, effective, and time-proven method of planning and controlling the performance of each functional activity. Another advantage of this method is that it ensures the most efficient utilization of employees, following the **principle of occupational specialization** within the organization. In addition, functional departmentation simplifies the process of recruiting, training, and managing employees within each department. Finally, this method facilitates a centralized decision-making process and enables executive managers to maintain tight control at the top.

As an organization grows, it develops new product or service lines, increases a number of customers, and expands into new territories. As a result, a simple functional structure may become less effective, thus creating apparent problems in planning and managing operational activities. This represents a prime disadvantage for growing organizations that operate in a rapidly changing consumer and technological environment and that offer a broad range of products or services to a large number of customers. For this reason additional types of organizational departmentation are frequently used by larger companies. These types of departmentation facilitate development of a **divisional structure** and are described below.

Departmentation by product or service is particularly useful for organizations which handle diversified types of products or services. The majority of large multiproduct or multiservice companies, therefore, are departmentalized according to a product or service organizational structure. In this structure various product or service lines are grouped into separate divisions, as illustrated in Exhibit 1–28.

In organizational departmentation by product or service, divisional managers are in charge of all operational activities within their divisions such as general administration, personnel, finance and accounting, production and operations, marketing and sales. In addition, divisional managers are personally accountable to the company's president for the profitability of their divisions. Functional vice presidents, in turn, supervise and coordinate all operational activities within their areas of responsibility and provide support to divisional managers.

Departmentation by product or service has several advantages and disadvantages. Since all activities, skills, and resources required for a line of products or services are grouped within one division under one person, the whole task can be accomplished in a more efficient manner. In addition, this type of departmentation gives divisional managers more authority and enhances the quality and speed of their decisions. Moreover, the overall performance of each division can be effectively measured in terms of its profit or loss.

One of the prime disadvantages of the organizational departmentation by product or service is that it requires more persons with general management

Exhibit 1–28

Product or Service Departmentation

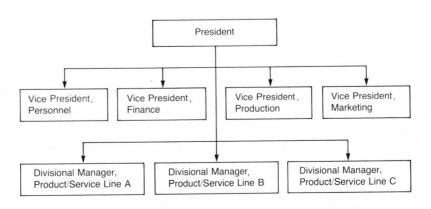

skills. Some of the operating functions may also be duplicated in various divisions, thus creating the need for an additional number of employees and higher overhead costs. Moreover, the decentralization of decision making may create conflicts between certain tasks and priorities within the organization.

Departmentation by market or customer represents another method of grouping employees and activities within an organization. This method is particularly useful for larger companies that operate in diversified markets and deal with a substantial number of customers. A large manufacturing company, for example, might have separate divisions for different types of markets (e.g., industrial or consumer); or for customers in different industries (e.g., chemical or engineering). Typical departmentation by market or customer is illustrated in Exhibit 1–29.

In organizational departmentation by market or customer, divisional managers carry full authority and responsibility within their divisions and are accountable to the president for their performance. In addition, each functional vice president is responsible for supervision and coordination of all operational activities within a defined area and provision of support to divisional managers. This arrangement, in fact, is similar to organizational departmentation by product or service.

Departmentation by market or customer also has a number of advantages and disadvantages. The prime advantage of this method of departmentation is that it enables the organization to serve diversified markets or types of customers in the most efficient manner. Other advantages and disadvantages are similar to the ones pertinent to departmentation by product or service.

Departmentation by territory represents an additional method of grouping employees and activities within an organization. This method is particularly useful for larger companies that conduct their business in different geographic regions. A large manufacturing company, for example, might have separate divisions in East Coast and West Coast regions or in different countries. Typical departmentation by territory is illustrated in Exhibit 1–30.

In organizational departmentation by territory, divisional managers carry full authority and responsibility within their divisions and are accountable to the president for their performance. Functional vice presidents, in turn, are responsible for supervision and coordination of all operational activities within defined areas and provision of support to divisional managers. This arrangement is also similar to organizational departmentation by product or service.

Departmentation by territory has a number of advantages and disadvantages. The prime advantage of this method of departmentation is that it enables the

Exhibit 1–29

Market or Customer Departmentation

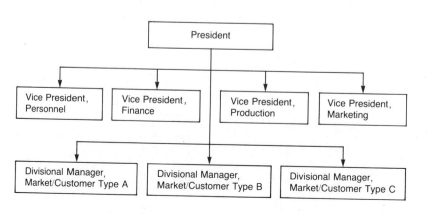

Exhibit 1–30

Departmentation by Territory

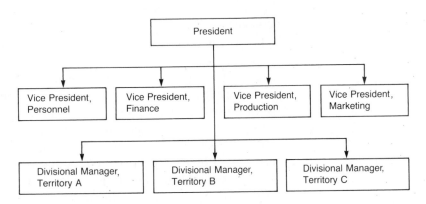

organization to serve local markets in a more efficient manner. Other advantages and disadvantages are similar to the ones prevailing in departmentation by product or service.

These methods of departmentation enable management to develop two basic organizational structures: functional and divisional structures. Functional structure facilitates effective specialization and control of operational activities and is particularly suitable for most small and medium-sized companies. The divisional structure, on the other hand, provides effective specialization by product or service, market or customer, and territory and is more suitable for large organizations. There is, however, a third type of organizational structure which combines the advantages of both functional and divisional structures. It is known as the **matrix structure** and is frequently applied to specialized product or project organizations. A typical matrix structure is illustrated in Exhibit 1–31.

In a matrix structure the team members in every group have two superiors—the functional vice president and the product or project manager. This creates a dual chain of command, contradicting the classical principle of unity of command within the organization. Thus, for example, each member in Accounting Group A

Exhibit 1–31

Matrix Structure in a Specialized Product/Project Company

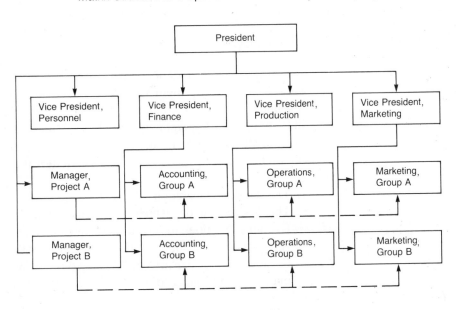

is simultaneously accountable to vice president, finance and to the manager of Project A.

Each executive manager within a matrix organization is in charge of specific functional activities on a company-wide basis. This is similar to the arrangement which exists in a functional organization. Thus, for example:

- President is in charge of all general management activities.
- Vice president, personnel is in charge of all personnel management activities.
- Vice president, finance is in charge of all financial management activities carried out by Accounting Groups A and B.
- Vice president, operations is in charge of all operations management activities carried out by Operations Groups A and B.
- Vice president, marketing is in charge of all marketing management activities carried out by Marketing Groups A and B.

Executive managers have authority over employees within their department with respect to coordination of functional activities, promotions, and salary recommendations. Project managers, on the other hand, have authority over respective members of their teams relative to the project's execution. Thus, for example

- Manager, Project A, is in charge of operational activities carried out by all Groups A (accounting, operations, and marketing).
- Manager, Project B, is in charge of operational activities carried out by all Groups B (accounting, operations, and marketing).

Project managers are accountable to the company's president for the profitability of their projects. This is similar to the relationship which exists between the divisional manager and the president in a divisional structure.

The matrix structure provides the organization with the advantages of both functional and divisional methods of departmentation. One of the prime disadvantages of this structure, however, is frequent confusion among employees as a result of receiving instructions from two superiors. In order to ensure effective performance of the matrix organization, it is essential to coordinate all efforts between functional and project managers on a continuous basis.

1.14 Management Structure

One of the most important elements of the organizing process is development of a company's **management structure** and creation of key management positions. A sound management structure plays a critical role in ensuring effective planning and control of all operational activities within the organization.

The development of the company's management structure necessitates a comprehensive analysis and the formulation of the following issues:

- The nature of operational activities
- The functions under which these activities are to be carried out
- Positions and titles to which these functions are assigned
- Personnel who occupy positions indicated by the titles
- Coordination of the activities for a common purpose and timing the performances of personnel to whom they have been assigned

The management structure of small and medium-sized companies may have several managerial levels, depending on the size of the organization. Department heads, for example, are accountable to executive management for the overall performance of their respective departments. The level of managerial authority, responsibility, and accountability is usually defined in advance in accordance with the requirements of the organizational structure. Details related to the degree of authority, responsibility, and accountability are specified by relevant job descriptions and serve to contribute toward effective overall control and sound performance of the organization.

Authority represents a specified degree of discretion delegated to individuals to enable them to use their judgment, to have power in making decisions, and to issue instructions to subordinates. The authority within the company starts with the shareholders, passes to the elected board of directors, and is further delegated to the management personnel and their subordinates. Authority is usually classified as either direct or delegated. **Direct authority** can be exercised by one person on another if there is a direct functional relationship between them. If such a relationship does not exist, then the superior may apply **delegated authority** over a particular employee.

Organizational authority is also described by means of the following factors:

- It may be formal (i.e., prescribed by the company's policy).
- It may be functional because it is based on particular professional knowledge or skill.
- It may be personal because it is based on seniority or any other outstanding quality of a particular manager.

Although authority implies the managerial right to request performance of duties by subordinates, its strength rests upon the extent of acceptance of instructions by employees. Authority is usually delegated in direct proportion to the level of responsibilities assigned to personnel within a particular organizational structure.

Responsibility represents a specified number of tasks assigned to individuals who are answerable for their duties and the performance of their subordinates. Responsibility commonly implies fulfilment of a particular objective, function, or obligation in accordance with orders issued or promises made. The process of organizational development requires detailed formulation of responsibility and its limitations for each activity and function; otherwise the performance of individuals cannot be judged objectively. Management with weakly defined responsibilities is usually neither able to carry the burden of simultaneous obligations nor to reach correct decisions throughout the company's operations.

Accountability represents an integral part of the process of delegation of authority and responsibility within the company. Accountability means being held responsible for results or outcome of a particular assignment. By accepting authority and responsibility, employees in the organization should also accept credit for good performance or blame for unacceptable results.

One of the essential principles of effective delegation, namely the **unity of command principle**, suggests that each individual in the organization should be accountable to only one superior. Reporting to more than one superior usually confuses employees, subsequently reducing the overall effectiveness of organizational performance.

Following the selection of a suitable organizational structure (functional, divisional, or matrix), it is necessary to establish an appropriate set of relationships between various positions within the company. These relationships are developed in accordance with the **scalar principle**:

> The clearer the line of authority from the ultimate management position to each subordinate position, the more likely there will be responsible decision making and organizational communication within a company.

Irrespective of the company's size, all positions are generally classified as:

- Line positions
- Staff positions

Line positions are all those which are directly responsible for achieving company objectives. Line positions carry **line authority** within the simplest form of organization—**line organization**. Here responsibilities are delegated from the chief executive to first-level subordinates (vice presidents or department managers), who, in turn, delegate responsibilities to second-level subordinates and so on. Each employee in a line organization is assigned a particular responsibility and reports to only one supervisor. This organization does not have employees in advisory capacities or specialists, and its planning is carried out on a centralized basis. Typical line organization for a small or medium-sized company has been illustrated in Exhibit 1–27.

Staff positions are defined as those whose main functions are to provide service, advice, or counsel to the line positions or to perform an auditing or monitoring function.[33] Staff positions neither carry responsibility for achieving company objectives nor have formal authority over the employees. Staff positions in **line and staff organization** merely provide line managers with advice in areas such as legal, personnel, finance and accounting, production and operations, marketing and sales. Moreover, staff members may be required to audit the company's performance in various areas of operational activities or to perform any additional duties upon request of line managers. A typical line and staff organization, based on a functional structure, is presented in Exhibit 1–32.

The example illustrates a number of potential reporting relationships. Thus, the relationship which exists between line positions is known as a **line relationship**. This type of relationship, for example, exists between the company's president and all vice presidents. An integral part of this relationship is line authority, which the president has over each vice president. The vice president, finance, in turn, has line authority over the bookkeeper and credit controller; the vice president, production has similar authority over design manager, production manager, and the buyer; and, finally, the vice president, marketing has the same authority over the sales manager. The line relationship also exists between the design manager and drafting staff, production manager and laborers, and sales manager and salespeople.

Another type of relationship exists between any line manager and staff member and is known as a **staff relationship**. Each staff member acts in an advisory capacity to his or her line manager and does not carry functional responsibility. Thus, for example, a staff relationship exists between the president and his or her assistant; between the vice president, marketing and market research manager; and between sales manager and sales analyst.

In most small organizations with limited financial resources, line managers often perform dual duties, acting as staff members while carrying out their routine responsibilities. In large organizations, however, the distinction between line and staff members becomes more visible. Staff members are generally classified

Exhibit 1–32

Line and Staff Positions In a Functional Structure

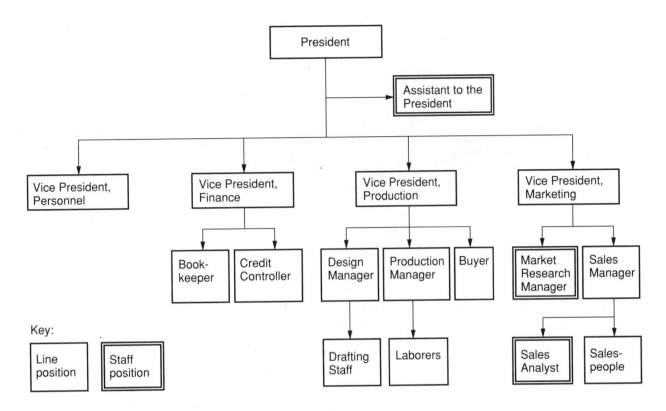

as personal staff and specialized staff. The **personal staff** reports to the line manager and provides assistance in carrying out a broad range of duties. The line manager carries full responsibility for performance of those duties despite assistance by the personal staff. The **specialized staff**, on the other hand, is engaged in activities which may require special working skills that the line manager does not possess. Thus, certain duties that cannot be performed by line managers are totally delegated to specialized staff, who carry full responsibility for accomplishing their work. In this instance, specialized staff carry **functional authority** over line managers within the limits of their functions. A typical example of this arrangement, based on a divisional structure, is presented in Exhibit 1–33. The example illustrates the three types of positions:

- **Line positions.** President, general managers of Divisions A, B and C, and line managers (finance, production, and marketing)
- **Personal staff positions.** Assistant to president and assistants to divisional managers
- **Specialized staff positions.** Vice presidents, personnel, finance, production, and marketing

In this organizational structure, the president holds line authority over all vice presidents and divisional managers. Each divisional manager, in turn, exercises line authority over all line managers within the division. However, all vice presidents who occupy specialized staff positions wield functional authority over each line manager within the limits of their function. Thus, for example, the financial manager in Division A reports to the general manager of that division and, in addition, is responsible to the vice president, finance at the corporate level.

Exhibit 1–33

Line and Staff Management Positions In a Divisional Structure

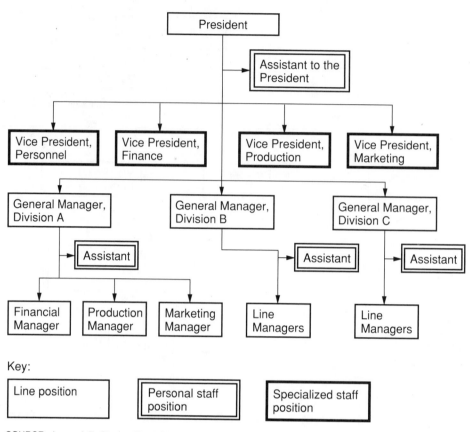

Key:

| Line position | Personal staff position | Specialized staff position |

SOURCE: James A.F. Stoner, *Management*, 2e, ©1982, p. 311. Adapted by permission of Prentice Hall, Inc., Englewood Cliffs, New Jersey.

The need for functional authority is very real in many organizations. This need arises from the necessity to ensure uniform application of expertise in carrying out various organizational tasks. One of the prime disadvantages of functional authority is the creation of dual accountability, similar to the arrangement that exists in a matrix structure. It is essential to ensure, therefore, that the extent of functional authority is clearly spelled out to managers who use it and to subordinates who are subjected to it.

1.15 Organizational Design and Development

Development of a management structure and creation of functional positions are the basic elements of **organizational design**. For a number of years, experts tried to develop the best method of designing an organization. They concluded, however, that such a method may lead to the creation of a bureaucratic and inflexible structure wherein human and environmental factors are often neglected. Hence, it is apparent that there is no single way to design an organization.

According to James Stoner, the key variables that affect the organization and its structure are its strategy, its environment, its technology, and its members' characteristics. The prime objective of the executive management team, therefore, is to establish an effective "fit" between the organization's structure and those variables. Stoner further clarifies the impact which a company's strategy has on its management structure:

1. Strategy determines organizational tasks, which are the ultimate basis for design of the organization (highly technical and creative tasks, for example, may require a matrix-type organizational design).
2. Strategy influences the choice of technology and personnel appropriate for the accomplishment of those tasks. These, in turn, influence the appropriate structure.
3. Strategy determines the specific environment within which the organization will operate; this too influences structure.[34]

External environment plays a significant role in the process of organizational design and development of an effective structure. There are three types of environments which should be considered by managers:

- Stable environment
- Changing environment
- Turbulent environment[35]

In a **stable environment**, an organization does not face an unexpected or drastic change of conditions in the marketplace. Customers' needs are identified well in advance and remain steady and predictable. Laws that affect activities of a particular organization or that relate to the development of a specific product have not changed much during the recent years and are not expected to change suddenly. New technological developments occur very slowly, thereby imposing a minimal burden on research budgets.

In a **changing environment**, on the other hand, an organization must be prepared for new conditions in the marketplace and for frequent change of customers' needs. New technological developments are expected to occur at a faster rate, thus imposing additional requirements on a company's research efforts. Furthermore, a number of new laws that affect organizational activities or product development may be introduced at a more frequent rate.

Finally, in a **turbulent environment**, an organization must be prepared for sudden changes of conditions in the market place. This may be caused by a drastic change in laws regulating a company's activities or product development, by new technological developments, or by the launching of new products by competitors. A turbulent environment exists in several industries, such as high-tech products, fashion, and computers.

Organizational design also depends on the nature of the company's operational activities. These activities, discussed in detail in Part 4 (Volume II) and illustrated in Exhibit 4–3, can be classified as follows:

- **Manufacturing activities.** These activities entail the process of converting raw materials into finished products through the use of equipment, tools, labor, and other production facilities.
- **Nonmanufacturing activities.** These activities include a broad range of service and merchandising operations. *Service operations* entail rendition of trade and professional service aimed at satisfying customers' needs. *Merchandising operations*, on the other hand, entail buying and selling of products at a profit.
- **Contractors and special projects.** These projects include a broad range of activities which are performed in accordance with specific contractual obligations undertaken by companies or individuals.

Joan Woodward and her colleagues examined 100 manufacturing firms in the mid-1960s in order to establish a relationship between technological processes and organizational structure. All firms have subsequently been classified into three groups according to their manufacturing activities:

1. *Unit and small batch production.*   Unit production entails the manufacture of custom designed items, while small batch production refers to the manufacture of small quantities of similar products.
2. *Large batch and mass production.*   This refers to the manufacture of large quantities of similar items, sometimes using an assembly line (e.g., appliances, automobiles).
3. *Process production.*   This refers to manufacture of large quantities of materials which are subsequently sold by volume or weight (e.g., chemicals, brewery).

As a result of her study, Woodward concluded that

1. The more complex the technology—from unit to process production—the greater the number of managers and management levels. In other words, complex technologies lead to tall organizational structures and require a greater degree of supervision and coordination.
2. The span of management of first-line managers increases from unit to mass production and then decreases from mass to process production. Lower-level employees in both unit and process production firms tend to do highly skilled work. As a result, they tend to form small work groups, making a narrow span inevitable. Assembly line workers, on the other hand, usually perform similar types of unskilled tasks. Large numbers of such workers can be supervised by one manager.
3. The greater the technological complexity of the firm, the larger the clerical and administrative staffs. The larger number of managers in technologically complex firms requires supportive services—to do the additional paperwork, for example, or to handle nonproduction-related work such as personnel administration. In addition, complex equipment requires more attention in terms of maintenance and production scheduling to keep it in operation a high proportion of the time.[36]

The significance of this conclusion is that "for each type of technology there were specific aspects of organizational structure that were associated with more successful performance." Hence, successful companies were those with the most suitable organizational structures for their type of technology.

The skills, experiences, and attitudes of employees also play an important role in the process of organizational design. Top managers, for example, have the opportunity to select specific strategies and to develop the organization in accordance with their personal aspirations, values, and abilities. Lower-level managers and other employees may also contribute to an effective organizational design through the use of their skills, education, and talent.

Most top managers are aware that the organizational design must be geared toward the continuous growth of their companies. This is particularly important since a no-growth situation leads to stagnation and signifies deterioration in a company's condition within a competitive environment. Larry E. Greiner studied a number of growing companies and developed a model to describe how organizations change over time and how these changes affect organizational design and general management practices.

According to Greiner, every growing organization undergoes five distinct phases over a certain period of time.[37] Each phase, in turn, consists of two stages termed "evolution" and "revolution." **Evolution** relates to an extended period of steady growth during which no drastic changes take place. **Revolution**, conversely, relates to a predictable period of a company's life during which major changes may occur. Greiner suggests that each evolutionary stage causes its own revolution which, in turn, leads the company into the next phase. The five phases of growth identified by Greiner are illustrated in Exhibit 1–34.

Phase 1: Creativity. In the beginning, an organization usually focuses on the development of products or services and on penetration in the marketplace. The organization starts to grow mainly as a result of the creative abilities of its owners and top managers. Since the organization is still small, the relationships between managers and subordinates are informal, and the communication is frequent. However, as the organization grows, it becomes increasingly difficult to control employees by applying informal management methods. Top managers become overloaded and their performance gets less efficient. This situation presents a *crisis of leadership*, thus causing the first revolution within the organization. In order to overcome the leadership crisis, top managers must be prepared to change their management style, to redirect the activities of their organization, and to develop a sound management structure.

Phase 2: Direction. Once an effective management structure is developed and operational activities are redirected, a period of sustained growth may be expected. During this period, a functional organizational structure is introduced and all operational activities are departmentalized. The company's top managers

Exhibit 1–34

The Five Phases of Growth

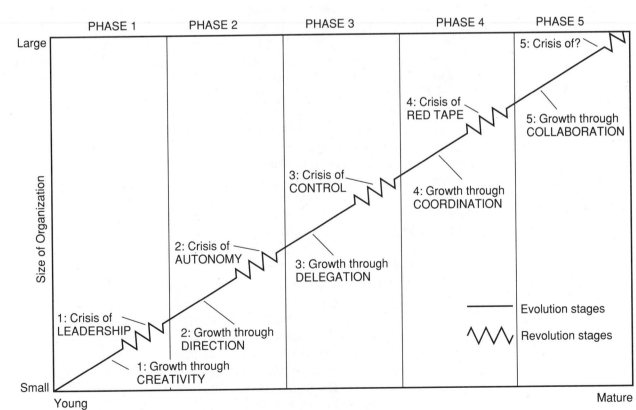

adopt sound management practices, develop budgets, and establish new work standards. As the company continues to grow, its managers become more divided between higher-level policy makers and lower-level functional experts. Communication between top managers and lower-level managers becomes more formal, thus leading to increased frustration and demands for more autonomy in the decision-making process. Top managers, however, are reluctant to give up authority in favor of lower-level managers and prefer to manage the organization using existing methods. This situation presents a *crisis of autonomy*, thus causing the second revolution within the organization. In order to overcome the autonomy crisis, top managers must be prepared to give up a part of their authority and delegate additional responsibilities to their subordinates.

Phase 3: Delegation. This phase is characterized by installation of an effective decentralization program within the organization. A broad range of routine managerial duties are delegated to lower-level managers. Top managers, on the other hand, do not interfere with the day-to-day operations and, instead, concentrate on the expansion of the organization and the search for new acquisitions. Eventually, lower-level managers succeed in penetrating into local markets and provide more efficient service to customers. As the organization continues to grow, however, top managers experience an increased sense of loss of control and try to return to a centralized organizational structure. This attempt usually fails and subsequently creates a **crisis of control**, causing the third revolution within the organization. In order to overcome the control crisis, top managers must develop new solutions and improve coordination between all departments and employees.

Phase 4: Coordination. This phase is characterized by restructuring the organization and by implementing a coordinated system of control. Decentralized work units are merged into larger groups as part of a new restructuring process. Depending upon the nature of its activities, the company is departmentalized by product, by territory, by industry, or in another appropriate manner. Each department or division is managed separately and is expected to produce a healthy return on invested capital. The restructuring process also entails employment of new staff who are given specific responsibilities within the organization. During this phase, top managers have the opportunity to stabilize the company's performance, while lower level managers are encouraged to utilize the company's resources in a more efficient manner. During the company's growth, however, tension increases between top managers and lower-level managers and between the headquarters and various divisions. Moreover, formal rules and procedures begin to interfere with the routine management process. If not resolved at this stage, this situation may lead to a *crisis of red tape*, causing the fourth revolution within the organization. To overcome the red tape crisis, top managers must develop more appropriate management systems and improve collaboration between all departments and employees.

Phase 5: Collaboration. This phase is characterized by a more flexible approach to management and by the creation of effective working teams. Existing teams are regrouped in order to improve the overall management process and to maximize the efficiency of the company's performance. This regrouping entails transfer of several staff members from the headquarters to individual departments or divisions, while other staff members are expected to continue to act as advisors to divisional managers. The main concern at this stage is to ensure collaboration between all divisions and to improve behavioral skills of managers. As a result of this effort, the company's performance as a group is expected to become more effective. During the company's growth, however, managers will experience additional problems in various areas of operational activities. These problems may relate to the psychological conditioning of employees, labor-management relations, labor unions, and other factors.

Greiner's model of organizational growth and development suggests that the organization grows out of its structure despite the structure's initial suitability. An important factor which managers should keep in mind, therefore, is that no management structure is suitable forever. Hence, it is essential to identify the present phase of the company's development, to create an appropriate management structure, and to evaluate its suitability on a regular basis.

1.16 The Leading Process

Leadership is essential for effective management in any organization. The **leading process** is generally defined as the art or process of influencing people so that they will strive willingly and enthusiastically toward the achievement of organizational goals.[38] The leading process entails guiding, conducting, directing, and motivating subordinates to accomplish specific corporate objectives. One of the basic principles of leadership suggests that

> Since people tend to follow those whom they see as a means of satisfying their own personal goals, the more managers understand what motivates their subordinates and how these motivations operate, and the more they reflect this understanding in carrying out their managerial actions, the more effective leaders they are likely to be.[39]

Some people often confuse the term **manager** with the term **leader**. It is important to understand that both terms are not necessarily the same. Managers are appointed to occupy certain positions within an organization. They have specific authority, responsibilities, and accountability and are expected to perform in accordance with their organization's requirements. Leaders, on the other hand, usually do not expect a formal appointment. They simply emerge from within a group and take initiative when an appropriate need arises. Leaders often demonstrate the ability to influence others to perform far beyond the actions dictated by formal authority.

Some researchers believe that leaders are born, not trained. Thus, leaders are those individuals who show a predisposition to be more aggressive, more courageous, more decisive, and more articulate than other people. Other researchers have tried to identify measurable leadership qualities. The search for such qualities has enabled researchers to develop two prime aspects of leadership behavior:

- Leadership function
- Leadership style[40]

Leadership function represents specific actions that must be carried out in successful organizations. Researchers have concluded that someone is expected to perform two important functions: problem-solving and group maintenance. The *problem-solving* or *task-related function* refers to the leader's responsibility to identify and to solve effectively a broad range of problems. The *group maintenance* or *social function*, on the other hand, relates to the leader's responsibility to communicate with other employees, to motivate them, and to develop a healthy working environment.

Leadership style involves a leader's general attitude in dealing with subordinates. Researchers have identified two basic leadership styles: a task-oriented style and an employee-oriented style. The *task-oriented style* is based on an autocratic approach and entails the completion of a job in the most efficient manner. This style emphasizes the leader's power, minimizes misdirection of subordinates, and increases efficiency of organizational performance. The *employee-oriented style*, conversely, is based on a human relations approach and involves motivating subordinates to perform in the most efficient manner rather than dictating their actions. This style is based on a more democratic attitude and, if successful, yields high productivity, increased employee satisfaction, and friendly relationships within the organization.

Robert Tannenbaum and Warren H. Schmidt were among the first researchers to study various factors that influence managers in selecting specific leadership styles. Although they preferred the employee-oriented style, both experts suggested that managers need to consider specific conditions in their organization. Moreover, managers should identify three important factors before selecting an appropriate leadership style. These factors are:

1. Individual strengths and weaknesses of the manager (knowledge, experience, values)
2. Strengths and weaknesses of subordinates (skills, performance, interests)
3. Specific situation within the organization (phase of development, external environment, profitability, productivity)

Once the manager identifies and examines all relevant factors, the selection of a suitable leadership style can be accomplished. Such selection, in turn, will determine the extent to which subordinates are allowed to participate in the decision-making process and to enjoy freedom within the organization, as illustrated in Exhibit 1–35.

Exhibit 1–35

Continuum of Leadership Behavior

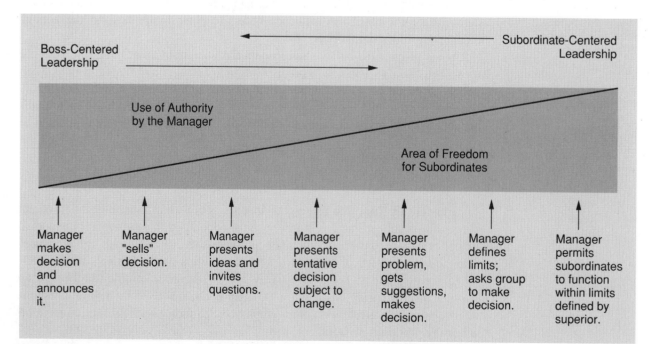

According to Tannenbaum and Schmidt, a manager can allow greater participation in the decision-making process and extend more freedom to subordinates if they

- Crave independence and freedom of action.
- Want to have decision-making responsibility.
- Identify with the organization's goals.
- Are knowledgeable and experienced enough to deal with the problem efficiently.
- Have experience with previous managers that leads them to expect participative management.[41]

If, on the other hand, such conditions are lacking, the manager is expected to adopt a more autocratic approach and to select the task-oriented leadership style. Irrespective of the selection of a particular style, the manager should remain flexible and demonstrate an open-minded approach to accommodate future changes.

Identification of factors that influence the selection of a particular leadership style is often insufficient in ensuring successful performance of the organization. This fact motivated experts to develop a contingency approach to leadership in order to identify the following:

- Which factors are most important in a particular set of conditions?
- Which leadership style will be most effective under those conditions?

One of the major studies in this regard was conducted by Fred E. Fiedler. Fiedler assumed that most managers would experience difficulty in changing their existing leadership styles. Furthermore, he believed that trying to change a manager's leadership style to fit specific conditions could not be accomplished effectively. Fiedler concluded that the effective performance of a group depends upon a proper match between a manager's leadership style and the degree to which the situation allows for managerial control and influence.

A special questionnaire, developed by Fiedler, helps to identify leadership style by indicating "the degree to which a man described favorably or unfavorably his **least preferred co-worker (LPC)**." The prime purpose of this questionnaire, illustrated in Exhibit 1–36, is to enable the manager to rate the employee with whom he could work least well. The rating is done on a scale 1 to 8 for each of the 16 sets of variables.

According to Fiedler's findings, "A person who describes his least preferred co-worker in a relatively favorable manner tends to be permissive, human relations-oriented and considerate of the feelings of his men. But a person who describes his least preferred co-worker in an unfavorable manner—who has what we have come to call a low LPC rating—tends to be managing, task-controlling, and less concerned with the human relations aspects of the job."[42]

It has been found that most managers fall into one of these two categories and only a small proportion fall in between. Hence, managers with high LPC have an employee-oriented leadership style and are expected to pursue warm personal relationships with co-workers. These managers believe in maintaining close ties with subordinates as part of an effective organizational performance. Managers with low LPC display a task-oriented leadership style and are expected to focus on getting the job done. These managers pay less attention to developing relationships with co-workers. Their major priority is effective performance and high productivity within the organization.

Exhibit 1-36

Fiedler's LPC Scale

Pleasant	8	7	6	5	4	3	2	1	Unpleasant
Friendly	8	7	6	5	4	3	2	1	Unfriendly
Rejecting	1	2	3	4	5	6	7	8	Accepting
Helpful	8	7	6	5	4	3	2	1	Frustrating
Unenthusiastic	1	2	3	4	5	6	7	8	Enthusiastic
Tense	1	2	3	4	5	6	7	8	Relaxed
Distant	1	2	3	4	5	6	7	8	Close
Cold	1	2	3	4	5	6	7	8	Warm
Cooperative	8	7	6	5	4	3	2	1	Uncooperative
Supportive	8	7	6	5	4	3	2	1	Hostile
Boring	1	2	3	4	5	6	7	8	Interesting
Quarrelsome	1	2	3	4	5	6	7	8	Harmonious
Self-assured	8	7	6	5	4	3	2	1	Hesitant
Efficient	8	7	6	5	4	3	2	1	Inefficient
Gloomy	1	2	3	4	5	6	7	8	Cheerful
Open	8	7	6	5	4	3	2	1	Guarded

SOURCE: Fred E. Fiedler and Martin M. Chemers, *Leadership and Effective Management* (Glenview, Ill: Scott, Foresman, 1974). Copyright © 1974 by Scott, Foresman & Co. Reprinted with permission.

By summarizing his findings, Fiedler identified three elements that prevail in the workplace and help to determine the most effective leadership style. These elements are as follows:

- *Leader-member relations* refers to the status of relations between the manager and subordinates. This element also relates to the degree of trust, confidence, and respect subordinates have in or for their leader.
- *Task structure* refers to the level at which various jobs are structured and formalized within the organization. In a well-structured environment, employees generally have a much better idea of what they are supposed to do.
- *Leader's position of power* refers to the degree of influence that managers have over their subordinates. This element also takes into consideration whether the manager has the authority to hire, promote, demote, discipline, and discharge subordinates.

As a result of his study of over 800 groups, Fiedler developed a model that helps to determine the most effective type of leadership in different situations.

This model, illustrated in Exhibit 1–37, specifies eight possible combinations that may exist in the workplace.

Fiedler found that task-oriented managers (with low LPC) performed most effectively in extreme situations where the leader either had a strong position of power and influence or, on the contrary, a weak position of power and influence. The employee-oriented managers (with high LPC) performed most effectively in situations where the leader had a moderate position of power and influence.

Other researchers also have conducted several studies and have tried to identify additional factors that influence the leadership process. Robert J. House, for example, has suggested that "personal characteristics of subordinates" and the "environmental pressures and demands in the workplace" also influence the effectiveness of managers and their leadership styles.[43] Paul Hersey and Kenneth H. Blanchard, on the other hand, have developed a "life cycle theory," which implies that the most effective leadership style varies with the maturity of subordinates.[44] This is illustrated in Exhibit 1–38.

According to Hersey and Blanchard, a manager's leadership style may undergo the following evolution:

1. Low maturity of subordinates (M1) forces a manager to adopt a *"telling"* leadership style (S1). At this stage subordinates are either unwilling or

Exhibit 1–37

Fiedler's Model of Effective Leadership

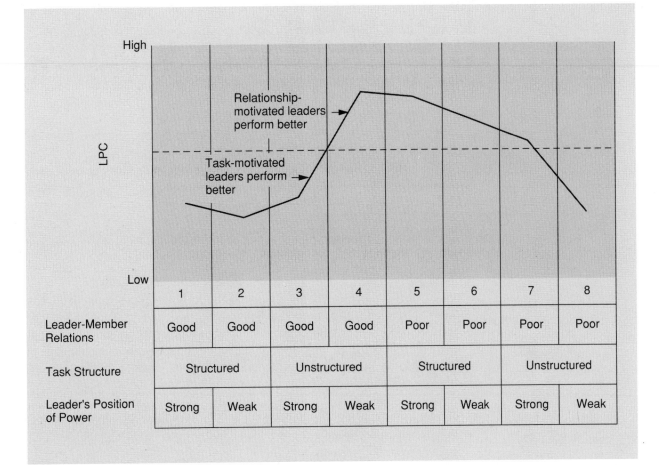

SOURCE: Fred E. Fiedler and Martin M. Chemers, *Leadership and Effective Management* (Glenview, Ill.: Scott, Foresman, 1974). Reprinted with permission.

Exhibit 1–38

The Life Cycle Theory of Leadership

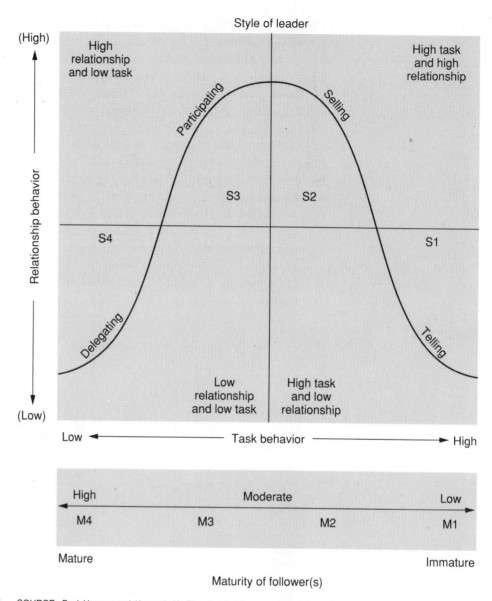

SOURCE: Paul Hersey and Kenneth H. Blanchard, *Management of Organizational Behavior: Utilizing Human Resources*, 4th ed. (Englewood Cliffs, N.J.: Prentice Hall, 1982), p. 52. Copyrighted Material from Leadership Studies, Inc. All Rights Reserved. Used by Permission.

    unable to take responsibility for a particular task and need to be instructed, directed, and closely supervised by the manager.

2. Slightly moderated maturity of subordinates (M2) permits the manager to adopt a *"selling"* leadership style (S2). At this stage subordinates are willing but unable to take responsibility and need to be instructed, directed and motivated by the manager.

3. Highly moderated maturity of subordinates (M3) permits the manager to adopt a *"participating"* leadership style (S3). At this stage subordinates are able but unwilling to take responsibility and need to be directed, motivated, and involved by the manager.

4. High maturity of subordinates (M4) permits the manager to adopt a *"delegating"* leadership style (S4). At this stage subordinates are able and willing

to take responsibility and need to be given support and the opportunity to perform independently by the manager.

Like other experts on the leadership process, Hersey and Blanchard recommend a flexible and adaptive leadership approach. Such an approach helps to ensure effective organizational performance and high motivation of employees over a long period of time.

1.17 Principles of Communication

One of the most important managerial responsibilities is to ensure effective communication between employees. For this reason, managers must be familiar with principles of communication and initiate the communication process in all areas of the company's activities.

Communication can be defined as the exchange of information between two or more individuals. The process of communication enables executives to carry out the essential managerial functions of planning, organizing, leading, and controlling the company. The main purpose of communication is to link personnel within the organization, to coordinate their group activities, and to provide sources of relevant information. Communication is necessary for the internal functioning of the company for the following reasons:

- To establish and to communicate the organizational objectives
- To develop functional plans for their accomplishment
- To select, develop, and appraise human resources
- To lead, motivate, and control the performance of personnel
- To arrange and to utilize available physical resources in the most efficient way

Furthermore, communication relates to the external environment and provides management with knowledge of customers' requirements, suppliers' offerings, and the government's regulations. Hence, communication represents a valuable management tool that facilitates the creation of a suitable working environment.

An ordinary communication process is described in Exhibit 1–39. This process consists of six basic elements:

Exhibit 1–39

An Ordinary Communication Process

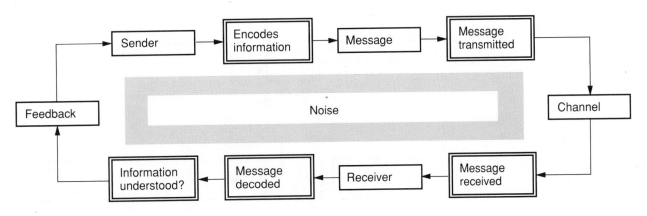

1. A **sender**, or a **source**, is an individual who initiates the communication process. In an organization, for example, any employee who needs to pass information to another employee can become a sender.
2. A **message** is the information that is encoded by the sender. Information can be encoded into various forms (e.g., speaking, writing, demonstrating, acting).
3. A **channel** is the communication medium that enables an individual or a group to transmit a message to another individual or a group.
4. A **receiver** is an individual who receives the message from the sender through the communication channel. The receiver is expected to decode the message and understand information contained therein.
5. **Feedback** is a basic response by the receiver to information obtained from the sender. Feedback ensures effective two-way communication by clarifying the degree to which the information has been understood and accepted by the receiver.
6. **Noise** is anything that may distort the meaning of message transmitted from the sender to receiver (and back) through the communication channel.

In order to ensure effective functioning of the organization, managers need to develop and to maintain a smooth communication process. This process permits managers to carry out their functional responsibilities by communicating information and instructions in the following directions, as illustrated in Exhibit 1–40:

*   **Vertical communication** consists of two types—downward and upward. *Downward communication* flows from employees at higher levels to those at lower levels. *Upward communication* flows from subordinates to their superiors.
*   **Horizontal communication** flows between employees who occupy similar-level positions within an organization.
*   **Diagonal communication** flows between employees at various levels of the organizations hierarchy. This kind of communication usually occurs between members of different departments.

Exhibit 1–40

Communication Flow in an Organization

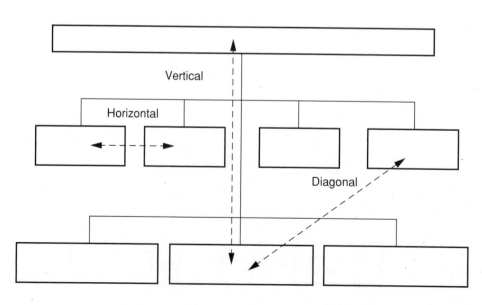

Some managers often do not appreciate the importance of an effective communication process. They simply assume that subordinates constantly listen to instructions and understand their intentions. Unfortunately, managers frequently issue unclear instructions, thus causing a communication breakdown within the organization. A typical illustration of the communication breakdown is presented in Exhibit 1–41.

It is apparent that effective communication cannot happen by accident. On the contrary, managers must be aware of possible communication breakdowns and become familiar with sound communication practices. The American Management Association (AMA) has developed a number of communication principles which became part of the Ten Commandments of Good Communication. The prime objective of these principles, summarized in Exhibit 1–42, is to improve the effectiveness of organizational communication between employees.

Effective communication is a two-way process. This means that, when an exchange of information takes place between two individuals or groups, one party does the talking, while the other party is expected to listen. Subsequently, the listening party is expected to understand the correct meaning of a specific message and to provide appropriate feedback to the sender. Unfortunately, the poor listening ability of many people stands in the way of an effective communication. Frequent misunderstandings between employees arise resulting in breakdown of communication within the organization. In order to maintain sound communication within the organization, it is necessary that each employee develops effective listening skills. A guide that contains 10 important instructions for effective listening has been developed by Keith Davis, and is presented in Exhibit 1–43.

Another type of communication that recently has gained popularity in many industries is a **suggestion system**. This system is designed to facilitate effective upward communication within an organization. By installing a suggestion system, managers encourage subordinates to exercise independent thinking and to

Exhibit 1–41

How Communications Break Down

What the Manager Said	What the Manager Meant	What the Subordinate Understood
I am tied up at a meeting right now. Let's meet later.	I can not see you for the next hour. Let's meet after lunch.	I am too busy right now. Talk to me next week.
I am not satisfied with your performance.	You must get 10 percent more sales to meet the budget.	If you don't improve your performance you are fired.
Mr. Jones will be transferred to our new office and his position will be vacant.	We will have to advertise for a new sales manager.	You may get the job of a sales manager if you want it.
I need the latest sales figures as soon as possible.	Prepare a detailed sales report within the next few days.	I need the sales report today.
A few customers complained about the quality of our Product A.	Quality control of Product A needs to be improved immediately.	We will probably discontinue production of Product A.
I plan to go the New York on a business trip next week.	Book me an air ticket and accomodation in New York today.	Since I will be away you can cancel all my meetings here.
I need to meet with you at 2:00 pm today.	I want to review sales figures with you.	I need to reprimand you for your poor performance.

SOURCE: Adapted from Steven Altman, Enzo Valenzi, and Richard M. Hodgetts, *Organizational Behavior: Theory and Practice* (Orlando, FL: Harcourt Brace Jovanovich, 1985), p. 532.

Exhibit 1–42

Ten Commandments of Good Communication

1. *Seek to clarify your ideas before communicating.* The more systematically we analyze the problem or idea to be communicated, the clearer it becomes . . . . Good [communication] planning must [also] consider the goals and attitudes of those who will receive the communication and those who will be affected by it.

2. *Examine the true purpose of each communication.* Before you communicate, ask yourself what you really want to accomplish with your message—obtain information, initiate action, change another person's attitude? Identify your most important goal and then adapt your language, tone, and total approach to serve that specific objective.

3. *Consider the total physical and human setting whenever you communicate.* Meaning and intent are conveyed by more than words alone. . . . Consider, for example, your *sense of timing*—i.e., the circumstances under which you make an announcement or render a decision; *the physical setting*—whether you communicate in private, for example, or otherwise; *the social climate* that pervades work relationships within the company or a department and sets the tone of its communications; *custom and past practice*—the degree to which your communication conforms to, or departs from, the expectations of your audience . . . .

4. *Consult with others, where appropriate, in planning communications.* . . . Such consultation often helps to lend additional insight and objectivity to your message. Moreover, those who have helped you plan your communication will give it their active support.

5. *Be mindful, while you communicate, of the overtones as well as the basic content of your message.* Your tone of voice, your expression, your apparent receptiveness to the responses of others—all have tremendous impact on those you wish to reach. Frequently overlooked, these subtleties of communication often affect a listener's reaction to a message even more than its basic content. . . .

6. *Take the opportunity, when it arises, to convey something of help or value to the receiver.* Consideration of the other person's interests and needs—the habit of trying to look at things from his point of view—will frequently point up opportunities to convey something of immediate benefit or long-range value to him.

7. *Follow up your communication.* This you can do by asking questions, by encouraging the receiver to express his reactions, by follow-up contacts, by subsequent review of performance. Make certain that every important communication has a "feedback" so that complete understanding and appropriate action result.

8. *Communicate for tomorrow as well as today.* While communications may be aimed primarily at meeting the demands of an immediate situation, they must be planned with the past in mind if they are to maintain consistency in the receiver's view; but, most important of all, they must be consistent with long-range interests and goals. For example, it is not easy to communicate frankly on such matters as poor performance or the shortcomings of a loyal subordinate—but postponing disagreeable communications makes them more difficult in the long run and is actually unfair to your subordinates and your company.

9. *Be sure your actions support your communications.* In the final analysis, the most persuasive kind of communication is not what you say but what you do . . . . For every manager this means that good supervisory practices—such as clear assignment of responsibility and authority, fair rewards for effort, and sound policy enforcement—serve to communicate more than all the gifts of oratory.

10. *Seek not only to be understood but to understand*—be a good listener. When we start talking we often cease to listen—in that larger sense of being attuned to the other person's unspoken reactions and attitudes . . . . [Listening] demands that we concentrate not only on the explicit meanings another person is expressing, but on the implicit meanings, unspoken words, and undertones that may be far more significant.

Exhibit 1–43

Guide for Effective Listening

1. **Stop talking!**
    You cannot listen if you are talking.
    As Polonius (*Hamlet*) says, "Give every man thine ear, but few thy voice."
2. **Put the talker at ease.**
    Help a person feel free to talk.
    This is often called a permissive environment.
3. **Show a talker that you want to listen.**
    Look and act interested. Do not read your mail while someone talks.
    Listen to understand rather than to oppose.
4. **Remove distractions.**
    Don't doodle, tap, or shuffle papers.
    Will it be quieter if you shut the door?
5. **Empathize with talkers.**
    Try to help yourself see the other person's point of view.
6. **Be patient.**
    Allow plenty of time. Do not interrupt a talker.
    Don't start for the door or walk away.
7. **Hold your temper.**
    An angry person takes the wrong meaning from words.
8. **Go easy on argument and criticism.**
    These put people on the defensive, and they may "clam up" or become angry.
    Do not argue. Even if you win, you lose.
9. **Ask questions.**
    This encourages a talker and shows that you are listening.
    It helps to develop points further.
10. **Stop talking!**
    This is first and last, because all other guides depend on it.
    You cannot do an effective listening job while you are talking.

- Nature gave people two ears but only one tongue, which is a gentle hint
  that they should listen more than they talk.
- Listening requires two ears: one for meaning and one for feeling.
- Decision makers who do not listen have less information for making sound decisions.

SOURCE: Keith Davis and John W. Newstrom, *Human Behavior at Work: Organizational Behavior*, 7th ed. (New York: McGraw-Hill, 1985). Reprinted with permission.

provide suggestions for improving organizational performance. Although this system is particularly popular among large organizations, small and medium-sized companies may also derive substantial benefits from it.

1.18 The Controlling Process

The ultimate responsibility of top management is to develop and maintain effective controlling procedures within an organization. These procedures are an integral part of the **controlling process,** which, according to Robert J. Mockler, is a systematic effort to set performance standards with planning objectives, to design information feedback systems, to compare actual performance with these predetermined standards, to determine whether there are any deviations and to measure their significance, and to take any action required to assure that all corporate resources are being used in the most effective way possible in achieving corporate objectives.[45]

Basic questions that relate to the controlling process are as follows:

- Is a particular task clearly defined?
- Who is responsible for accomplishing a task?

- Was the task completed on time?
- Was there any deviation between planned and actual results?
- What corrective action needs to be taken to eliminate the deviation and rectify the results?

Controlling procedures and methods are similar in their application for all operational activities within the organization. The basic controlling process includes the four fundamental steps presented in Exhibit 1–44.

The first step entails establishing the required standards and methods for measuring performance in the following areas of the company's activities:

- General administration
- Personnel
- Finance and accounting
- Production and operations
- Marketing and sales

For this step to be effective, standards and methods for measuring performance must be determined in meaningful terms and accepted by the employees involved. The establishment of required standards of performance is, in fact, an integral part of the MBO process, discussed earlier and presented in Exhibit 1–17.

The second step in the controlling process entails measuring actual performance in each department or division. Like all elements of control, this step has to be carried out with a frequency specific to the type of activity being measured. The prime responsibility for carrying out this task lies with respective departmental or divisional managers. A typical illustration of measuring actual performance and reviewing results in a small or medium-sized company has been presented in Exhibit 1–21.

The third step in the controlling process entails comparing actual performance with required standards and measuring variation. This step enables top management to examine whether actual performance matches the projected stan-

Exhibit 1–44

The Controlling Process

1. Establish the required standards and methods for measuring performance.

2. Measure actual performance.

3. Compare actual performance with the required standards and measure the variation.

4. Take corrective action if there is variation and repeat the process (absence of variation signifies that the performance is acceptable).

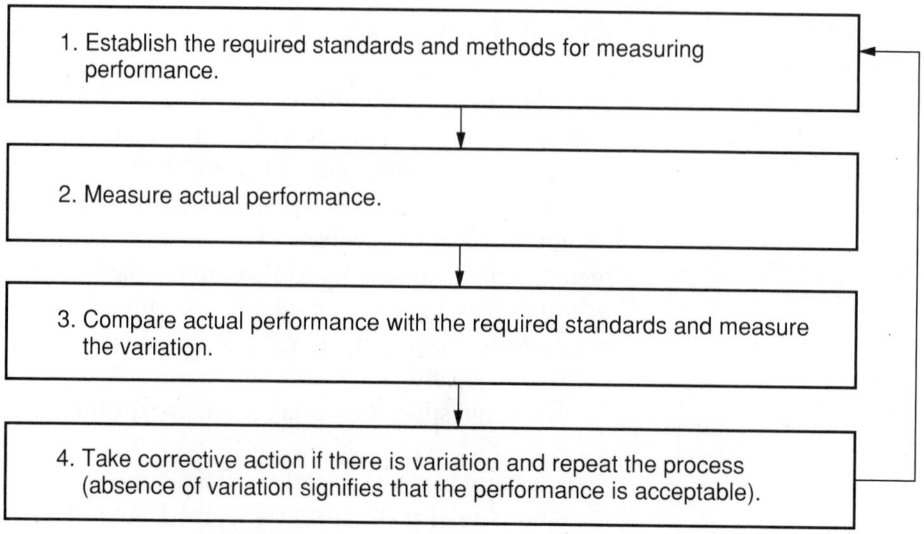

dards and to identify specific areas of inefficiency. Absence of variation between actual and projected results signifies that the performance is acceptable. Hence, managers may assume that "everything is under control" and the operation can continue without any additional changes. However, if variations are found, it is essential to identify the specific areas of operational activities in which such variations occur. Moreover, it is necessary to establish whether such variations are *favorable* (i.e., actual results are better than the projected ones) or, conversely, *unfavorable* (i.e., actual results are worse than the projected ones).

The final step in the controlling process entails taking corrective action if there is unfavorable variation between actual and projected performance. Such action often involves a change in one or more operational activities and a reassessment of employees' performances within the organization. The prime purpose of corrective action is not merely to rectify past inefficiencies but to develop constructive methods to maintain an acceptable performance level. A favorable variation, on the other hand, helps top management to identify those operational activities in which actual results exceed corresponding projections. This, in turn, enables managers to encourage and to promote those employees who contribute to improved organizational performance.

The controlling function must be carried out by every manager in accordance with the degree of authority, responsibility, and accountability vested in the employee. Typical elements of a controlling function in a small or medium-sized company are illustrated in Exhibit 1–45.

Controlling procedures usually cause unavoidable delays during the process of identifying and measuring performance variations, developing and implementing corrective action, and monitoring corrected results. Reliable and effective control is, therefore, particularly important to ensure successful performance of the organization. There are three types of control frequently used by managers:

- Feedforward control
- Concurrent control
- Feedback control[46]

Feedforward control is designed to prevent anticipated problems. This is the most desirable type of control since it helps managers avoid problems rather than rectify them later. In order to develop and to maintain effective feedforward control, managers need to have access continually to the most updated information. Feedforward control, in turn, enables managers to examine the situation in a specific area of the company's activities, to identify potential problems, and to take appropriate steps to prevent them.

Concurrent control occurs while a particular activity is in progress and enables managers to identify and to rectify problems before they cause excessive damage. One of the best forms of concurrent control is direct supervision. Thus, when they directly oversee the actions of their subordinates, managers are able to concurrently monitor specific actions of employees, identify, and rectify problems as they arise. Although there is a time delay between the activity and problem rectification, such a delay is usually minimized if concurrent control is carried out effectively. The majority of modern equipment and computers, for example, have built-in concurrent control, which enables operators to minimize delays and to rectify problems without causing further damage.

Feedback control is imposed after the action has occurred. The most common type of control used in industry, it enables managers to identify problems

Exhibit 1–45

Elements of the Controlling Function in a Small or Medium-sized Company

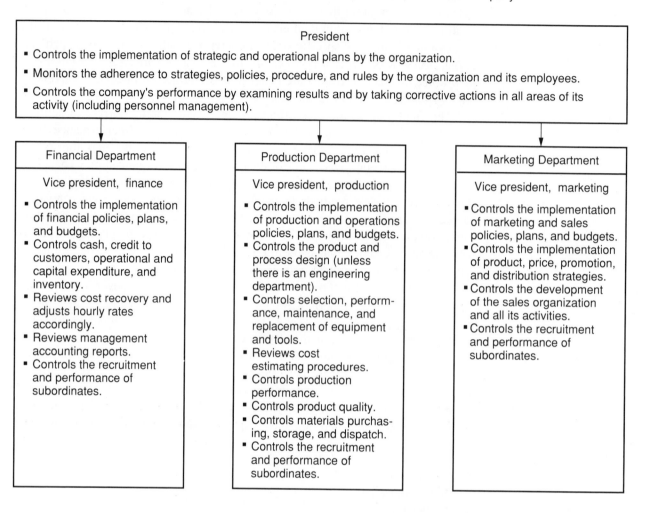

through regular examination of various management reports submitted by subordinates. These reports are prepared at different intervals depending upon specific operational requirements. Management accounting reports, for example, are usually prepared on a monthly basis, while inventory status reports may be prepared every day. Since they contain a broad range of information, management reports enable managers to exercise different levels of control. Thus, management accounting reports provide managers with a comparison between actual and budgeted financial results, while the inventory status reports help to monitor the availability of materials.

Feedback control has two distinct advantages over the feedforward and concurrent types of control.[47] First, feedback provides information that enables managers to evaluate the effectiveness of their planning efforts. If feedback indicates small variance between projected and actual results, the performance was generally on target. If, conversely, the variance is substantial, feedback reflects poor performance and helps to direct future planning efforts. Moreover, feedback control helps managers to evaluate the quality of performance by subordinates and enhances employee motivation.

To ensure effective overall performance, top management must design appropriate control systems, taking into consideration the specific nature of the company's activities and its organizational structure. Moreover, it is necessary to consider particular functions, abilities, and personalities of individual managers. Management control systems must ensure high accuracy and timely availability of information, be flexible and inexpensive, and focus on all strategic and operational aspects of the company's activities. It is essential that management information is coordinated with the overall flow of work within the organization and remains effective on a continuous basis. It is equally important to ensure that management control systems are organizationally realistic, are acceptable to employees, and provide sufficient autonomy in individual performance.

1.19 Managerial Ethics

The issue of managerial ethics and ethical behavior has become increasingly important in recent years. **Ethics** commonly refers to "the rules or principles that define right and wrong conduct."[48] It is often complicated, however, to determine *"what is right"* and *"what is wrong"* since such determination depends upon the specific standards acceptable to society. Moreover, managerial ethics are influenced by the several factors presented in Exhibit 1–46.

Government regulations certainly play an important part in molding the ethics of all law-abiding people. Moreover, there is a variety of laws specifically regulating behavior in the business sector. Equal employment opportunity laws, for example, prohibit discrimination of employees or applicants on the basis of race, color, religion, sex, or national origin. Other laws prohibit use of certain materials in various manufacturing processes or define deceptive advertising as illegal. Many laws clearly specify the boundaries of what is allowed and what is prohibited in business, thus leaving potential violators with the risk of paying substantial fines or of being penalized in other ways.

Industry ethical codes exist in many business sectors. These codes are usually developed by various trading and professional associations such as Direct Marketing Association, National Wholesale Hardware Association, or American Electric Association. Each association develops its own set of codes of conduct which clarify a broad range of ethical issues. These codes apply to companies that belong to a particular association on an industry-wide basis. Managers and other employees are expected, therefore, to observe specific codes of behavior and to convey these codes to others.

Exhibit 1–46

Factors Affecting Ethical or Unethical Behavior

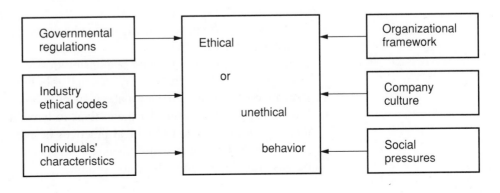

Individual characteristics of every person play a dominant role in ethical or unethical behavior. Each person starts to develop a set of values from the early stage of his or her life. The value development process is strongly influenced by parents, teachers, friends, and society. Once the person matures, he or she learns to distinguish between "right" and "wrong" and subsequently adopt a set of values. These values, however, may differ from one individual to another, depending on the influence of the aforementioned factors.

Organizational framework is another important factor that influences ethical or unethical behavior. Members of a particular organization are expected to behave in the manner prescribed by that organization. This process is regulated by various rules, job descriptions, and written codes of behavior stipulated by management. All employees, therefore, must be committed to act within and outside an organization in accordance with such rules, to perform their duties as prescribed by a job description, and to obey other written codes of behavior. Moreover, a clear organizational structure provides employees with additional guidance in the workplace. It helps to determine lines of authority, responsibility, and accountability in the context of ethical behavior within the organization.

Company culture also contributes to developing and to maintaining sound managerial ethics. As Stephen P. Robbins suggests:

> A culture that is likely to shape high ethical standards is one that is high in risk tolerance, direction, and conflict tolerance. Managers in such a culture will be encouraged to be aggressive and innovative, will have clear objectives and performance expectations to guide them, and will feel free to openly challenge demands or expectations they consider to be unrealistic or personally distasteful.
>
> A strong culture will exert more influence on managers than a weak one. Therefore, if the culture is strong and supports high ethical standards, it should have a very powerful and positive influence on a manager's ethical behavior. In a weak culture, managers are more likely to rely on subculture norms as a behavioral guide. Thus work groups and departmental standards will strongly influence ethical behavior in organizations that have weak overall cultures.[49]

Social pressures often influence ethical or unethical behavior. Since the modern society emphasizes the pursuit of money and its purchasing power, some people conveniently forget about issues of "right" and "wrong". There is strong evidence in today's business world to suggest, for example, that greed is becoming an important factor in managerial ethics. Unfortunately, this factor applies not only to Wall Street but also to many small and medium-sized companies operating in various industrial sectors.

In a study conducted in the early 1960s, Raymond Baumhart questioned 1,700 managers and examined their attitudes toward ethical behavior. Baumhart concluded that

- Top managers must lead the way to improve ethical standards within an organization.
- Top managers who have a clearly defined personal code of behavior are likely to match actions to ethics.
- Executives are aware of social responsibilities of business in general terms, although they believe that it plays a small role in the total society.
- Executives differ in their views about specific business practices.
- Executives generally consider themselves to have high ethical standards, but they hold a low opinion of ethical practices of average managers.
- Executives believe that many unethical practices exist in various industries because economics and ethics do not mix.

- Many executives relate positively to a written code of ethics for their organizations and industries, provided that such a code is rigidly enforced.[50]

Saul Gellerman has identified four common rationalizations frequently used by managers and their subordinates. These rationalizations indicate why some people adopt poor ethical standards and what can be done to reduce unethical practices.

1. *"It is not 'really' illegal or immoral."* Sometimes the line between "right" and "wrong" is not drawn clearly. In this instance, managers and their subordinates should use common sense and act in accordance with acceptable standards of ethics. It is important to remember that ultimately every person is answerable to his or her own conscience.

2. *"It's in my (or the organization's) best interest."* Managers and other employees often experience conflicts between personal values and professional goals. For example, a sales manager may be expected to offer a bribe to secure a new contract. Sometimes it may be effective, but often it leads to negative results. And it is certainly immoral.

3. *"No one will find out."* This type of rationalization is frequently used by people with weak ethical standards. However, it does not prove to be effective over a long period of time. Managers, therefore, should remember that only ethical behavior and decency pay true dividends in the end.

4. *"Since it helps the organization, the organization will condone it and will protect me."* Some managers justify bribery, kickbacks, cost duplication, product substitution, mishandling of employees, and other abuses as an essential part of doing business. While managers are expected to remain loyal to their organizations, there can be no justification for unethical conduct.[51]

An interesting test developed by Lowell G. Rein helps to evaluate the ethical standards of individual employees. This test, presented in Exhibit 1–47, requires an honest self-assessment by the person concerned.

Top managers should take various actions to improve the ethical standards of their employees. These actions include the following:

- To formulate clear policies, rules, and codes of conduct that encourage ethical behavior of all employees
- To maintain high managerial ethics in order to set an example for subordinates
- To define tangible objectives without making unrealistic demands on employees
- To initiate ethical training programs for all employees
- To maintain comprehensive performance appraisal of employees including evaluation of ethical standards
- To assume responsibility for disciplining wrongdoers
- To develop a mechanism that encourages employees to observe and to report the wrongdoing of their co-workers
- To conduct independent social audits by outside consultants

Improvement of ethical standards within an organization cannot happen overnight. It is important, however, that top managers pay serious attention to this issue and invest time and effort in upgrading ethical performance of employees. Although lengthy, the process should be started as soon as possible.

Exhibit 1–47

An Ethics Test

Many situations in day-to-day business are not simple right-or-wrong questions, but rather fall into a gray area. To demonstrate the perplexing array of moral dilemmas faced by 20th-century Americans, here is a "nonscientific" test for slippage .... Don't expect to score high. That is not the purpose. But give it a try and see how you stack up.

Put your value system to the test in the following situations:

Scoring Code: Strongly agree   = SA   Disagree   = D
                 Agree   = A   Strongly disagree = SD

	SA	A	D	SD
1. Employees should not be expected to inform on their peers for wrongdoings.	—	—	—	—
2. There are times when a manager must overlook contract and safety violations in order to get on with the job.	—	—	—	—
3. It is not always possible to keep accurate expense account records; therefore, it is sometimes necessary to give approximate figures.	—	—	—	—
4. There are times when it is necessary to withhold embarrassing information from one's superior.	—	—	—	—
5. We should do what our managers suggest, though we may have doubts about its being the right thing to do.	—	—	—	—
6. It is sometimes necessary to conduct personal business on company time.	—	—	—	—
7. Sometimes it is good psychology to set goals somewhat above normal if it will help to obtain a greater effort from the sales force.	—	—	—	—
8. I would quote a "hopeful" shipping date in order to get the order.	—	—	—	—
9. It is proper to use the company WATS line for personal calls as long as it's not in company use.	—	—	—	—
10. Management must be goal-oriented; therefore, the end usually justifies the means.	—	—	—	—
11. If it takes heavy entertainment and twisting a bit of company policy to win a large contract, I would authorize it.	—	—	—	—
12. Exceptions to company policy and procedures are a way of life.	—	—	—	—
13. Inventory controls should be designed to report "underages" rather than "overages" in goods received. [The ethical issue here is the same as that faced by someone who receives too much change from a store cashier.]	—	—	—	—
14. Occasional use of the company's copier for personal or community activities is acceptable.	—	—	—	—
15. Taking home company property (pencils, paper, tape, etc.) for personal use is an accepted fringe benefit.	—	—	—	—

Score Key: (0) for Strongly Disagree (1) for Disagree (2) for Agree (3) for Strongly Agree

If your score is:

0	Prepare for canonization ceremony	11–15	Good ethical values	36–44	Slipping fast
1– 5	Bishop material	16–25	Average ethical values	45	Leave valuables
6–10	High ethical values	26–35	Need moral development		with warden

SOURCE: "Is Your Ethical Slippage Showing?" by Lowell G. Rein. Reprinted with permission from *Personnel Journal*, Costa Mesa, California; Copyright September, 1980. All rights reserved.

1.20 Theory Z

Theoretically, the same principles of business management should be applicable to companies worldwide. In reality, however, this is not the case. One of the clearest illustrations of this disparity is the difference between American and Japanese business methods. These differences have been investigated by various experts in the United States and abroad.

One of the most significant studies of Japanese business practices was conducted by William G. Ouchi. His bestselling book, *Theory Z*, describes the basic elements of the Japanese approach to management and explains what American businessmen can learn from their Japanese counterparts. According to Ouchi,

Americans sense the value of technology; however, people are often taken for granted.[52] Thus, millions of dollars are spent on technological developments, but almost no funds go to the development of managerial skills. Hence, the first important lesson to be learned from the Japanese is how to manage and to organize people at work. Ouchi states that the problem of productivity in U.S. companies will not be solved solely with new financial policies nor through additional investment in research and development. One of the key elements that needs to be improved is mutual trust between managers and their subordinates. Only through mutual trust can managers motivate employees to work harder and be prepared for sacrifices that will be repaid in the future.

Theory Z also suggests that it is essential to develop subtle relationships between managers and their subordinates and to create a "family" feeling within the organization. Moreover, productivity, trust, and subtlety are not isolated elements. Not only do trust and subtlety yield higher productivity through more effective coordination, they are inextricably linked to each other.[53]

The central elements of the Japanese lifestyle include intimacy, caring for others, continuous support, and disciplined unselfishness. Thus, American managers should try to replace the common principle that "personal feelings have no place at work" with a more Japanese-like approach. To identify additional principles of Japanese management style that could be adopted by American companies, it may be useful to examine typical differences between management systems in both countries. Some of these differences are presented in Exhibit 1–48.

Lifetime employment is one of the most important characteristics of the Japanese organization.[54] Approximately one third of the workforce in Japan is under contract for lifetime employment in large companies and governmental organizations. All employees are promoted entirely from within and are retained by the organization until the mandatory retirement age of 55. Employees are guaranteed their jobs unless they are incriminated in a major criminal offense. Loss of job is considered a very harsh punishment in Japan and those who are fired have considerable difficulty in finding another job. Upon reaching retirement age, all employees, except a few top executives, must retire. All retirees receive a lump sum from their employer amounting to an average of five or six years' salary. No additional pension or social security is paid to Japanese retirees. As a result of the lifetime employment, managers and workers develop a strong sense of trust, loyalty, and commitment toward their organization. These elements are the foundation of Theory Z and play an integral part in successful recovery of Japanese businesses.

Slow evaluation and promotion is another typical feature of many Japanese organizations. Once young employees start their careers, they are encour-

Exhibit 1–48

Major Differences between Japanese and American Companies

Japanese Companies (Type J)	American Companies (Type A)
• Lifetime employment	• Short-term employment
• Slow evaluation and promotion	• Rapid evaluation and promotion
• Nonspecialized career development	• Specialized career development
• Implicit control mechanisms	• Explicit control mechanisms
• Collective decision making	• Individual decision making
• Collective resonsibility	• Individual responsibility
• Collective values	• Individual values
• Wholistic concern for employees	• Partial concern for employees

SOURCE: William G. Ouchi, *Theory Z* ©1981, Addison-Wesley Publishing Co., Inc., Reading, Massachusetts. Reprinted with permission of the publisher.

aged to cooperate with co-workers and to gain working experience in various departments. Employees are not "threatened" with a quick evaluation of their performance. On the contrary, they are prepared for frequent rotations to different positions and for slow evaluation and promotion within the organization. Since most Japanese companies hire only young people who still undergo life transitions, frequent rotation, slow evaluation, and promotion help to develop a teamwork spirit among employees. This element also plays an important role in successful performance of many Japanese companies.

Nonspecialized career development is a direct result of frequent rotations of employees within a Japanese organization. As a result of such rotations, employees acquire better knowledge and experience concerning people, tasks, procedures, and problems on a company-wide basis. Rotations further enhance the spirit of cooperation and teamwork among employees. An additional feature of nonspecialized career development is that most employees usually have vague job descriptions and their positions are often not defined clearly. According to recent research conducted at M.I.T. and Columbia University, employees rotated to different positions demonstrate improved vitality, productivity, and satisfaction with their work in comparison with those who stay on the same job. As the saying goes: "A change is as good as a holiday."

Implicit control mechanisms are an integral part of the Japanese management style. The basic mechanism of management control in a Japanese organization is very subtle and may appear non-existent to an outsider. Such an impression, however, is erroneous since controlling mechanisms are developed thoroughly on every organizational level. Unlike the Western approach to management and wide use of formal planning and controlling procedures, the basic mechanism of control in a Japanese company is embodied in the philosophy of management. According to Ouchi, this philosophy, an implicit theory of the organization, describes the objectives and the procedures required for accomplishment of organizational goals. Company objectives are formulated in accordance with the values of owners, employees, customers, and government regulations. Progress toward meeting objectives is regulated by a set of beliefs concerning the most appropriate solutions for the organization in the marketplace. Such beliefs help management to decide who should be doing what in a specific situation. This, in turn, greatly facilitates a teamwork approach and collective decision making within the organization.

Collective decision making is one of the best known features of a Japanese organization. Ouchi suggests that when an important decision needs to be made in a Japanese company, everyone who will feel its impact will participate in the decision-making process. Usually a team of three employees will be assigned the duty of talking to all employees who may be affected by a particular decision. Employees will have the opportunity of expressing their opinions and subsequently a final decision will be reached. If a particular issue involves modification, the questioning of employees will continue until the best solution is found. Subsequently, the decision-making process in a Japanese organization often takes a long time. For this reason, experienced American managers often advise that "if you are going to Japan to make a sale or close a deal and you think it will take two days, allow two weeks and if you are lucky you will get a 'maybe'. It takes the Japanese forever to make a decision." Japanese business people, on the other hand, often say that "Americans are quick to sign a contract or make a decision, but try to get them to implement it—it takes them forever!"[55]

Collective responsibility is another key feature of the Japanese management style. According to Ouchi, there is intentional ambiguity about who is responsible for a particular decision. This ambiguity often frustrates American business people, who complain that "if only they would tell me who is really in charge, we could make some progress." In fact, Ouchi continues, in Japan no one individual carries responsibility for a particular decision or assignment. Instead, a team of employees assumes joint responsibility for a set of tasks. Although an outsider may wonder at their comfort in not knowing who is responsible for what, the Japanese know quite clearly that each of them is entirely responsible for all tasks and that they share that responsibility jointly.[56]

Collective values are shared by the majority of employees in Japanese companies. This enhances the efficiency of collective decision making and facilitates a strong sense of collective responsibility among employees. In addition, collective values stimulate a more coordinated teamwork approach instead of focusing on individual performance of employees. When it comes to improvements in the workplace, Japanese workers maintain that "no one can come up with a work improvement idea alone. We work together, and any ideas that one of us may have are actually developed by watching others and talking to others. If one of us was singled out for being responsible for such an idea, it would embarrass all of us."[57] For this reason, Japanese managers neither impose responsibilities on nor pay bonuses to employees on an individual basis. Instead, specific tasks are given and bonuses paid to teams of employees. This collective approach has motivated people to work well together and to encourage one another toward better efforts. Moreover, this approach is economically viable in the context of Japanese culture.

Wholistic concern for employees is an underlying element of Japanese management practice. Ouchi suggests that the wholistic orientation of Japanese organizations stems from both a historical accident and underlying social and cultural forces. The historical accident is that Japan became an industrial nation after being ruled for decades by a feudal system. The economic and social life of many Japanese people gradually evolved into a whole, thus causing the development of intimate relationships among them. Intimacy in relationships, in turn, stimulated additional trust, respect, and willingness to cooperate in social and working environments. Moreover, the development of such a unique relationship enabled Japanese people to become more open and understanding toward each other. Some experts suggest that this form of relationship is fundamentally incompatible with Western industrial society, characterized by specialization of labor, frequent movement between employees, and an individualistic approach. The Japanese, however, have shown that a wholistic approach to industrial life is not only possible but may guide others in achieving success.[58]

As a result of his study, Ouchi concluded that despite many differences between Japanese (**Type J**) and American (**Type A**) companies, there are also certain similarities between them. He further identified a number of American companies that have characteristics similar to firms in Japan and referred to such companies as **Type Z organizations**. These organizations tend to have long-term employment, often for a lifetime, although the lifetime relationship is not formally stated. Type Z companies are among the fastest growing and most profitable of major American firms.[59] Hence, American managers are advised to examine their organizations (Type A) and seek ways of adopting some of the Japanese business management principles. A useful program developed by Ouchi outlines thirteen steps that should be undertaken by American managers keen to improve organizational performance. These steps are as follows:

1. Understand the Type Z organization and your role.
2. Audit your company's philosophy.

3. Define the desired management philosophy and involve the company leaders.
4. Implement the philosophy by creating both structures and incentives.
5. Develop interpersonal skills.
6. Test yourself and the system.
7. Involve the union.
8. Stabilize employment.
9. Decide on a system for slow evaluation and promotion.
10. Broaden career path development.
11. Prepare for implementation at the first level.
12. Seek out areas to implement participation.
13. Permit the development of wholistic relationships.[60]

The process of transforming an organization from Type A to Type Z is a lengthy one and requires substantial effort on the part of management and employees. Sometimes this process may take two years or even longer. However, Ouchi concludes that this process may help the organization improve its overall performance and secure its position in the marketplace. Additional details about Japanese management techniques, namely the Just-In-Time (JIT) methodology, are provided in Part 4 (Volume II).

1.21 Working Instructions and Forms

All information related to general management principles has been presented in Sections 1.01–1.20. It is essential to understand this information and to proceed with the compilation of forms provided at the end of Part 1. Working instructions for completing these forms follow immediately. These instructions require that management rates its knowledge of general management principles and evaluates company performance in the area of general management. Aggregate scores will help to identify possible problems and to assign priorities for implementing the most effective solutions. The sequence of activities pertinent to completion of working forms is presented in Exhibit 1–49.

Exhibit 1-49

Summary of Forms for Part 1

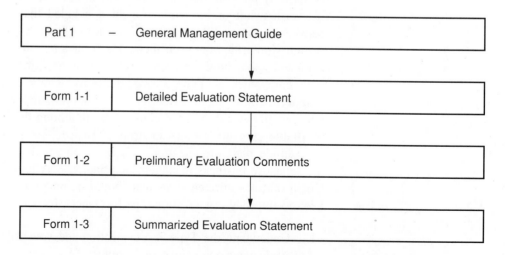

| Part 1 | – | General Management Guide |

| Form 1-1 | Detailed Evaluation Statement |

| Form 1-2 | Preliminary Evaluation Comments |

| Form 1-3 | Summarized Evaluation Statement |

Form 1-1   Detailed Evaluation Statement

1. Study the description of all checkpoints related to *general management principles* as outlined in Part 1.

2. Evaluate your personal knowledge in the area of general management and score your *personal knowledge level* of each checkpoint. Scores should be based on the scale shown below:

0–20(%)	Very poor level of knowledge
21–40(%)	Poor level of knowledge
41–60(%)	Fair level of knowledge
61–80(%)	Good level of knowledge
81–100(%)	Very good level of knowledge

3. Evaluate your company's performance in the area of general management and score your *company's performance level* on each checkpoint. Scores should be based on the scale shown below:

0–20(%)	Very poor level of performance (the checkpoint has never been implemented)
21–40(%)	Poor level of performance (the checkpoint is implemented sometimes)
41–60(%)	Fair level of performance (the checkpoint is implemented but not managed well)
61–80(%)	Good level of performance (the checkpoint is implemented and managed well)
81–100(%)	Very good level of performance (the checkpoint is constantly implemented and managed very well)

4. Determine the *average evaluation level* pertaining to your personal knowledge and the company's performance within each area of general management as follows:

$$\text{Average Evaluation Level } (\%) = \frac{\text{Total Score}}{\text{Number of Applicable Checkpoints}}$$

Form 1-2   Preliminary Evaluation Comments

5. State your personal opinion related to general management principles currently employed by your company and summarize *preliminary evaluation comments*.

Form 1-3   Summarized Evaluation Statement

6. Issue Form 1–1 and Form 1–2 to key executives within your company who are actively involved in the *general management activities* and ensure that both forms are completed in accordance with instructions.

7. Designate a *final evaluation level*[a] for each checkpoint as a result of a meeting between the company's executives.

See continuation of working instructions on page 192 (Part 2).

---

[a]The final evaluation level may not represent an average value of the individual results and should be determined by mutual consent.

GENERAL MANAGEMENT ANALYSIS
DETAILED EVALUATION STATEMENT

No.	DESCRIPTION	PERSONAL KNOWLEDGE LEVEL (%)	COMPANY'S PERFORMANCE LEVEL (%)				
			VERY POOR	POOR	FAIR	GOOD	VERY GOOD
		0 - 100	0 - 20	21 - 40	41 - 60	61 - 80	81 - 100
1.01	The Basic Management Process						
1.02	Evolution of Management Theory						
1.03	Business Engineering Method						
1.04	Environment and Organizational Culture						
1.05	Principles of Decision Making						
1.06	The Planning Process						
1.07	Strategic Planning						
1.08	Implementation of Strategic Plans						
1.09	Management by Objectives						
1.10	Operational Planning						
1.11	Plan of Management						
1.12	The Organizing Process						
1.13	Organizational Departmentation						
1.14	Management Structure						
1.15	Organizational Development						
1.16	The Leading Process						
1.17	Principles of Communication						
1.18	The Controlling Process						
1.19	Managerial Ethics						
1.20	Theory Z						
→	AVERAGE EVALUATION LEVEL						

NAME:	POSITION:	DATE:

GENERAL MANAGEMENT ANALYSIS
PRELIMINARY EVALUATION STATEMENT

No.	DESCRIPTION	PRELIMINARY EVALUATION COMMENTS
1.01	The Basic Management Process	
1.02	Evolution of Management Theory	
1.03	Business Engineering Method	
1.04	Environment and Organizational Culture	
1.05	Principles of Decision Making	
1.06	The Planning Process	
1.07	Strategic Planning	
1.08	Implementation of Strategic Plans	
1.09	Management by Objectives	
1.10	Operational Planning	
1.11	Plan of Management	
1.12	The Organizing Process	
1.13	Organizational Departmentation	
1.14	Management Structure	
1.15	Organizational Development	
1.16	The Leading Process	
1.17	Principles of Communication	
1.18	The Controlling Process	
1.19	Managerial Ethics	
1.20	Theory Z	

| NAME: | POSITION: | DATE: |

GENERAL MANAGEMENT ANALYSIS
SUMMARIZED EVALUATION STATEMENT

No.	DESCRIPTION	COMPANY'S PERFORMANCE LEVEL (%)				
		ASSESSED BY PRESIDENT	ASSESSED BY FINANCIAL EXECUTIVE	ASSESSED BY OPERATIONS EXECUTIVE	ASSESSED BY MARKETING EXECUTIVE	FINAL EVALUATION LEVEL
1.01	The Basic Management Process					
1.02	Evolution of Management Theory					
1.03	Business Engineering Method					
1.04	Environment and Organizational Culture					
1.05	Principles of Decision Making					
1.06	The Planning Process					
1.07	Strategic Planning					
1.08	Implementation of Strategic Plans					
1.09	Management by Objectives					
1.10	Operational Planning					
1.11	Plan of Management					
1.12	The Organizing Process					
1.13	Organizational Departmentation					
1.14	Management Structure					
1.15	Organizational Development					
1.16	The Leading Process					
1.17	Principles of Communication					
1.18	The Controlling Process					
1.19	Managerial Ethics					
1.20	Theory Z					
→	AVERAGE EVALUATION LEVEL					

NAME :	POSITION :	DATE :

1.22 References

1. Henry Mintzberg, *The Nature of Managerial Work* (New York: Harper & Row, 1973).
2. Stephen P. Robbins, *Management: Concepts and Applications*, 2nd ed. (Englewood Cliffs, NJ: Prentice-Hall, 1988), p. 13.
3. Frederick W. Taylor, *Principles of Scientific Management* (New York: Harper & Brothers, 1911).
4. Frank B. Gilbreth, *Motion Study* (New York: D. Van Nostrand, 1911).
5. Henry Fayol, *Industrial and General Administration*, translated by J. A. Coubrough (Geneva: International Management Institute, 1930). Reprinted in James A. F. Stoner, *Management*, 2e, ©1982, p. 40. Adapted by permission of Prentice Hall, Inc., Englewood Cliffs, New Jersey.
6. Stoner, pp. 41–42.
7. Patrick Montana and Bruce H. Charnov, *Management* (New York: Barron's Educational Series, 1987), pp. 20–21.
8. Ibid., pp. 24–25.
9. John Naisbitt, *Megatrends* (New York: Warner Books, 1984), p. 160.
10. Based on George G. Gordon and W. M. Cummins, *Managing Management Climate* (Lexington, Mass.: Lexington Books, 1979); and Chris A. Betts and Susan M. Halfhill, "Organization Culture: Theory, Definitions and Dimensions," presented at the National American Institute of Decision Sciences' Conference, Las Vegas, Nevada, Nov. 1985. Reprinted in Stephen P. Robbins, *Management*, 2e, ©1988, p. 66. Adapted by permission of Prentice Hall, Inc., Englewood Cliffs, New Jersey.
11. Robbins, p. 129.
12. Harold Koontz, Cyril O'Donnel, and Heinz Weinrich, *Essentials of Management*, 3rd ed. (New York: McGraw-Hill, 1982), pp. 75–79. Reprinted with permission.
13. Ibid., p. 81.
14. Ibid., p. 85.
15. Ibid., p. 86.
16. Michael H. Mescon, Michael Albert, and Franklin Khedouri, *Management*, 3rd ed. (New York: Harper & Row, 1988), p. 265.
17. Peter F. Drucker, *Management: Tasks, Responsibilities, Practices* (New York: Harper & Row, 1973), p. 61.
18. Mescon, Albert, and Khedouri, pp. 270–271.
19. Peter F. Drucker, *The Practice of Management*, (New York: Harper & Brothers, 1954), p. 63.
20. George A. Steiner and John B. Miner, *Management Policy and Strategy* (New York: Macmillan, 1977), p. 158.
21. Mescon, Albert, and Khedouri, *Management* pp. 288–289.
22. Steiner and Miner, p. 158.
23. Peter F. Drucker, *The Practice of Management*.
24. Anthony P. Raia, *Managing by Objectives* (Glenview Ill.: Scott, Foresman, 1974), p. 11.
25. Ibid.
26. Peter F. Drucker, *The Practice of Management* pp. 128–129.
27. Raia, p. 17.
28. Ibid., pp. 68–69.
29. Mescon, Albert, and Khedouri, p. 311.
30. Ibid.
31. Stoner, p. 262.
32. Ibid.
33. Ibid., p. 310.
34. Ibid., pp. 359–360.
35. Ross A. Webber, *Management* (Homewood, Ill.: Richard D. Irwin, 1979), pp. 389–391.

36. Joan Woodward, *Industrial Organization* (London: Oxford University Press, 1965) Reprinted in James A.F. Stoner, *Management*, 2e, ©1982, p. 365. Adapted by permission of Prentice Hall, Inc., Englewood Cliffs, New Jersey.

37. Larry E. Greiner, "Evolution and Revolution as Organizations Grow," *Harvard Business Review*, 50. 4, (July–August, 1972), pp. 37–46.

38. Koontz, O'Donnel, and Weinrich, p. 423.

39. Ibid., p. 424.

40. Stoner, p. 472–473.

41. Robert Tannenbaum and Warren H. Schmidt, "How to Choose a Leadership Pattern," *Harvard Business Review*, 51. 3 (May–June, 1973), pp. 162–164.

42. Fred E. Fiedler, "Engineer the Job to Fit the Manager," *Harvard Business Review*, 43. 5 (September–October, 1965), p. 116.

43. Robert J. House, "A Path-Goal Theory of Leader Effectiveness," *Administrative Science Quarterly*, 16 (1971), pp. 321–328; and Robert J. House and Terence R. Mitchell, "Path-Goal Theory of Leadership," *Journal of Contemporary Business*, 3.4 (Autumn, 1974), pp. 81–97.

44. Paul Hersey and Kenneth H. Blanchard, *Management of Organizational Behavior: Utilizing Human Resources*, 4th ed. (Englewood Cliffs, NJ.: Prentice-Hall 1982), p. 52. Copyrighted Material from Leadership Studies, Inc. All Rights Reserved. Used by Permission.

45. Robert J. Mockler, *The Management Control Process*, (Englewood Cliffs, NJ.: Prentice-Hall, 1972), p. 2.

46. Robbins, pp. 479–480.

47. William H. Newman, *Constructive Control: Design and Use of Control Systems*, (Englewood Cliffs, NJ.: Prentice-Hall, 1975), p. 33.

48. Keith Davis and William C. Frederick, *Business and Society: Management, Public Policy, Ethics*, 5th ed. (New York: McGraw Hill, 1984), pp. 28–41.

49. Robbins, pp. 627–636.

50. Reprinted by permission of *Harvard Business Review*. Raymond C. Baumhart, "How Ethical Are Businessmen?," *Harvard Business Review* 39.4 (July–August, 1961), p. 7. Copyright ©1986 by the President and Fellows of Harvard College; all rights reserved.

51. Reprinted by permission of *Harvard Business Review*. Saul W. Gellerman, "Why 'Good' Managers Make Bad Ethical Choices," *Harvard Business Review* 64.4 (July–August, 1986), p. 89. Copyright ©1961 by the President and Fellows of Harvard College; all rights reserved.

52. William Ouchi, *Theory Z*, ©1981, Addison-Wesley Publishing Co., Inc. Reading, Massachusetts. Reprinted with permission of the publisher.

53. Ibid., p. 7.

54. Ibid., pp. 15–59.

55. Ibid., p. 38.

56. Ibid., p. 39.

57. Ibid., p. 42.

58. Ibid., pp. 45–47.

59. Ibid., pp. 60–62.

60. Ibid., pp. 83–110.

Part 2

Personnel Management Guide

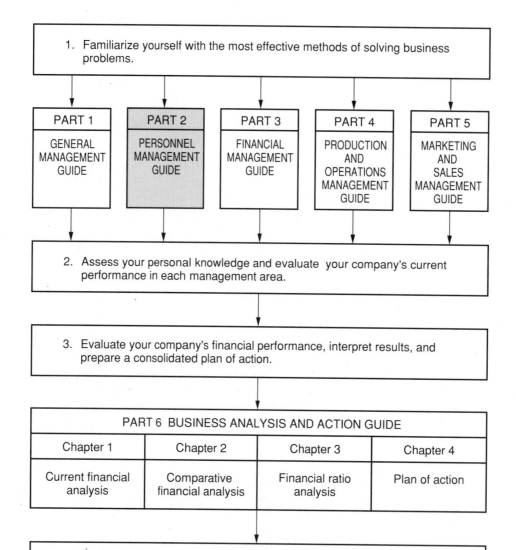

1. Familiarize yourself with the most effective methods of solving business problems.

PART 1	PART 2	PART 3	PART 4	PART 5
GENERAL MANAGEMENT GUIDE	PERSONNEL MANAGEMENT GUIDE	FINANCIAL MANAGEMENT GUIDE	PRODUCTION AND OPERATIONS MANAGEMENT GUIDE	MARKETING AND SALES MANAGEMENT GUIDE

2. Assess your personal knowledge and evaluate your company's current performance in each management area.

3. Evaluate your company's financial performance, interpret results, and prepare a consolidated plan of action.

PART 6 BUSINESS ANALYSIS AND ACTION GUIDE			
Chapter 1	Chapter 2	Chapter 3	Chapter 4
Current financial analysis	Comparative financial analysis	Financial ratio analysis	Plan of action

4. Implement most effective business solutions in accordance with guidelines contained in Parts 1 through 6.

5. Assess whether the action was implemented according to plan and adjust such action when necessary.

- *The 20 elements of practical personnel management*
- *Working instructions and forms for evaluating your company's personnel management*
- *Guidelines for implementing effective personnel management strategies and much more*

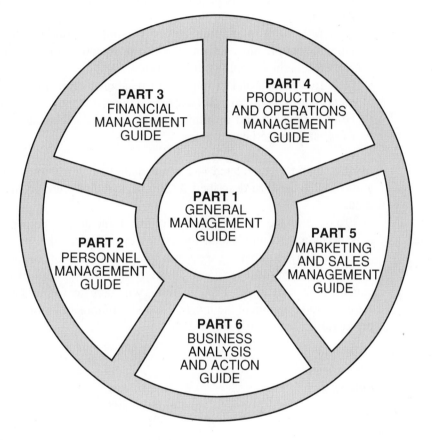

Contents

2.00 Introduction

The prime purpose of the **personnel management guide** is to identify business problems and implement the most effective solutions in the area of personnel management. This guide highlights a variety of issues, such as:

- How to analyze job requirements and prepare job descriptions and job specifications
- How to identify, plan, and forecast personnel requirements
- How to recruit, hire, screen, and test prospective employees
- How to conduct employment interviews
- How to establish and to implement personnel orientation, training, development, and motivation procedures
- How to develop and to implement basic job compensation, financial incentives, and fringe benefit plans

These and other related issues are addressed in the personnel management guide. All issues are described in **20 checkpoints** presented in **Sections 2.01–2.20**.

To develop the most suitable solutions in the area of personnel management, it is necessary to understand the issues discussed in this part. Thorough self-assessment by company executives and evaluation of company performance in the aforementioned area will indicate the effectiveness of current personnel management principles. This, in turn, will help to formulate a sound plan of action and to implement the most effective solutions in accordance with the **work program** presented in Exhibit 2–1.

Exhibit 2–1

Work Program for Part 2

Work Program

Planned Action	Objective
1. Study of personnel management principles	To attain an adequate level of knowledge in the area of personnel management
2. Self-evaluation of knowledge by members of the management team in area of personnel management	To identify individual strengths and weaknesses of members of the management team in the area of personnel management
3. Evaluation of company performance in the area of personnel management	To identify the level of company performance in the area of personnel management and to establish the average evaluation level
4. Formulation of a plan of action in the area of personnel management	To summarize the range of activities that must be undertaken in the area of personnel management
5. Implementation of the most effective business solutions in the area of personnel management	To develop a set of the most suitable solutions in accordance with guidelines presented in this part
6. Evaluation and control of actions in the area of personnel management	To assess whether the action was implemented according to plan and to adjust such action when necessary

Note: Please familiarize yourself with relevant working instructions prior to completing forms at the end of this part. Additional information on these forms is available from Business Management Club, Inc. upon request.

2.01 The Personnel Management Process

The main purpose of personnel management is to plan, organize, direct, and control effective utilization of human resources within an organization. These resources represent the employees who provide the company with their work, skills, talent, creativity, and motivation. Thus, among the most important leadership tasks of company executives is the development, implementation, and maintenance of the personnel management process.

Planning and control of the **personnel management process** entails a number of steps outlined in Exhibit 2–2. These steps generally fall under the following six operative functions:

1. **Staffing.** This is the process of obtaining suitable personnel to accomplish company objectives.
2. **Development.** This is the process of training to ensure high performance by personnel in the company.
3. **Compensation.** This is the process of establishing a fair and equitable level of personnel remuneration for their contribution toward the accomplishment of the organizational objectives.
4. **Integration.** This is the process of ensuring a positive level of personnel attitudes toward their work and harmony within the company.
5. **Maintenance.** This is the process of ensuring the continuation of adequate working conditions for personnel within the company.
6. **Separation.** This is the process of handling the return of personnel to society.

The personnel management process must be developed in accordance with various employment and compensation laws. Equal employment opportunity laws, for example, include Title VII of the 1964 Civil Rights Act, the Equal Pay Act of 1963, the Age Discrimination in Employment Act of 1967 and the Vocational Rehabilitation Act of 1973. Among the most important personnel compensation laws are the Social Security Act of 1935, the Fair Labor Standards Act of 1938, the Equal Pay Act of 1963, the Employee Retirement Income Security Act of 1974, and Workers' Compensation Laws. These and other laws are discussed later.

One of the first operational tasks in personnel management entails conducting a comprehensive job analysis and determining duties and skills for various positions within the organizations. All duties and skills need to be specified in accordance with the company's overall plans for the current fiscal period. Moreover, allocation of duties depends upon the specific nature of the company's existing organizational chart.

Comprehensive job analysis enables management to prepare detailed job descriptions and job specifications for various positions within the company. Job descriptions list all the relevant duties, responsibilities, authority and accountability of a specific job. Job specifications, on the other hand, outline the minimum level of personnel requirements necessary to ensure an acceptable standard of work.

Once various job descriptions and specifications are prepared, management needs to proceed with planning and forecasting of personnel requirements. The main purpose of this process is to secure the availability of specific types of employees with the skills, experience, and background necessary to meet company objectives. The personnel planning process entails consideration of several factors such as budget limitations, sales demands, production requirements, economic situation, and capabilities of existing employees.

Exhibit 2–2

Personnel Management Process

1. Be familiar with equal employment opportunity and compensation laws.
2. Determine duties and skill requirements for various positions within the company.
3. Prepare job descriptions and job specifications.
4. Identify short-, medium-, and long-term personnel requirements.
5. Initiate and maintain effective personnel recruitment and hiring procedures.
6. Establish and maintain sound procedures for screening, testing, and interviewing applicants.
7. Develop and implement an effective personnel orientation program.
8. Establish and maintain effective personnel training, development, and motivation programs.
9. Develop and implement effective personnel compensation plans.
10. Establish and maintain effective personnel evaluation procedures.
11. Develop suitable career management programs.
12. Establish sound labor-management relations and maintain effective collective bargaining and conflict-management procedures.
13. Develop and maintain effective personnel safety and health procedures.

Upon completion of the personnel planning and forecasting process, management must initiate the recruitment and hiring of employees. The main objective of personnel recruitment and hiring is to meet the company's specific requirements and employ people in accordance with existing organizational objectives. The personnel hiring process entails completion of a job application form by a prospective employee, screening, testing, interviewing, and selecting the most suitable applicants.

The main purpose of screening of applicants is to enable management to check the accuracy of information submitted by prospective employees. The hiring procedure sometimes entails preliminary testing of applicants. The prime objective of such testing is to evaluate the person's suitability for existing employment requirements and adaptability to future demands.

One of the central elements of the personnel hiring process is conducting of employment interviews. Such interviews enable management to "size-up" applicants and to evaluate their individual qualifications before completing the employee selection process. There are several types of employment interviews frequently used by managers: nondirective interviews, patterned interviews, structured interviews, and serialized interviews.

Once the selection of applicants is completed, each new employee must undergo orientation. The main purpose of personnel orientation is to ensure smooth integration of new employees into the existing organization. This process involves a formal introducing of employees to the company's rules and procedures, familiarizing with their jobs, and meeting fellow employees. Specific details of personnel orientation usually depend upon the status of a new employee within the organization.

Some new employees are not always entirely suited to their jobs and may require additional training. It is management's prime function, therefore, to identify the need for additional personnel training to ensure effective organizational performance. There are several types of personnel training methods used by management. Among these methods are on-the-job training, in-house training programs, apprenticeship training programs, and various educational courses.

In addition to the implementation of personnel training programs, it is necessary to initiate and to maintain a continuous management development process within the organization. The prime purpose of management development is to maximize the managers' abilities in performing their duties effectively and in providing sound guidance to their subordinates. Management development programs usually include managerial on-the-job training, professional coaching, and job rotation within the organization.

Another important managerial responsibility relates to motivating employees to perform their duties in the most efficient manner. This entails comprehension of basic human needs and development of suitable personnel motivation methods. These methods include an attractive compensation package, work security and satisfaction, the opportunity to advance, fair and competent management, and safe and comfortable working conditions.

One of the essential management functions is to provide basic job compensation to employees. This entails developing a suitable salary and wage structure in accordance with the company's existing financial condition and overall organizational objectives. To ensure consistency in salary and wage structure, management needs to establish a systematic relationship among basic compensation rates by evaluating various jobs within the company.

In addition to providing basic job compensation, managers need to develop and to implement suitable financial incentive plans for their employees. Such plans are usually classified as financial incentives for production personnel, for managers, for sales personnel, and for professional personnel. Financial incentives for production personnel, for example, include the piece work plan, the standard hour plan, and the group incentive plan. Financial incentives for managers, on the other hand, include several types of short- and long-term incentives.

Another element of personnel compensation entails the development and implementation of suitable fringe benefit plans. All fringe benefits are generally identified as nonworking time benefits, insurance benefits, retirement benefits, and service benefits. Nonworking time benefits, for example, include all additional compensation to employees for time not worked. Insurance benefits, on the other hand, include all additional compensation designed to cover various hazards commonly shared by employees.

Managers also need to ensure that the performance of all employees is appraised on a regular basis. The personnel performance appraisal enables management to provide employees with feedback on their performance and to identify their strengths and weaknesses in various areas of work. Moreover, regular appraisal of employees helps management to identify suitable candidates for promotion, to regulate the compensation level, and to develop suitable training programs.

Another important element of personnel management entails developing new career opportunities for employees within the organization. These opportunities should be identified and incorporated into an effective career development program. The main purposes of such a program are to ensure steady functional growth of employees, to maintain high morale and motivation, and to improve utilization of human resources within the organization.

Development of sound labor-management relations also represents an important managerial responsibility. Such relations should incorporate the principles of mutual acceptance and respect, a free enterprise system, and free collective bargaining. Labor-management relations are frequently influenced by labor unions and other similar organizations. Management, therefore, needs to be aware of labor union activities in their specific industry and be familiar with the standard unionization procedures.

When employees decide to join a labor union, managers should prepare themselves for the collective bargaining process. This process entails negotiating various elements of compensation, working conditions, and procedures between elected representatives of management and employees. Managers should also familiarize themselves with acceptable conflict management practices, employee grievance procedures, and disciplinary processes.

One of the most important managerial tasks requiring special attention relates to personnel safety and health. Effective safety and health procedures need to be developed and implemented to secure the welfare of employees, to meet appropriate legislation, to minimize injury compensation costs, medical expenses, and production losses. Managers, therefore, should familiarize themselves with the various safety and health procedures prescribed by the Occupational Safety and Health Administration (OSHA).

Management in every organization has to ensure adequate performance of the aforementioned functions to secure continued organizational success. Depending upon company size, these functions should be performed either by the chief executive or by the personnel manager.

2.02 Equal Employment Opportunity Laws

There are many laws that have a considerable impact on the development of personnel policies. These laws stipulate acceptable methods of employment and of compensation of manpower in various industries. It is essential, therefore, to adhere to these laws and to develop a comprehensive personnel management plan accordingly.

The underlying concepts of personnel management in the United States are developed in accordance with equal employment opportunity laws. One of the most important laws in this regard is Title VII of the 1964 Civil Rights Act. Title VII (as amended by the 1972 Equal Employment Opportunity Act) states that it is unlawful for an employer to

1. Fail or to refuse to hire or to discharge any individual or otherwise to discriminate against any individual with respect to compensation, terms, conditions, or privileges of employment because of such individual's race, color, religion, sex, or national origin; or

2. Limit, segregate, or classify employees or applicants for employment in any way that would deprive or tend to deprive any individual of employment opportunities or otherwise adversely affect his or her status as an employee because of such individual's race, color, religion, sex, or national origin.[1]

Title VII covers public and private employers, educational institutions, state and local governments with 15 or more employees, labor organizations with 15 or more members, public and private employment agencies, labor unions, and joint labor-management committees.

The enforcement of equal employment opportunity laws is carried out by an Equal Employment Opportunity Commission (EEOC). This commission consists of five members appointed by the president and confirmed by the Senate for a term of five years. The main function of the EEOC is to receive, to investigate, and to resolve employment discrimination complaints. When it finds that certain employment practices have been violated, the EEOC attempts to reach an agreement between the injured individual and the employer to eliminate all aspects of alleged discrimination. Under the Equal Employment Opportunity Act of 1972, the EEOC may also file discrimination charges on behalf of the employee, if such action is justified.

In addition to equal employment opportunity laws, several **presidential executive orders** have been issued in connection with the requirements imposed by Title VII. In 1965, for example, President Johnson issued Executive Order 11246. This law, as amended by Executive Order 11375, prohibits employment discrimination on the basis of race, color, religion, sex, or national origin by federal agencies, contractors, and subcontractors. Moreover, this executive order requires that contractors take **affirmative action** to ensure equal employment opportunity. The basic principles of the affirmative action are explained later.

The implementation of executive orders is the responsibility of the Office of Federal Contract Compliance Programs (OFCCP). This office is also responsible for ensuring the conciliation and contract compliance by federal contractors. **Contract compliance** means that in addition to quality, to timeliness, and to other requirements of federal contract work, contractors and subcontractors must also meet equal employment opportunity and affirmative action requirements. These cover all aspects of employment including recruitment, hiring, training, pay, seniority, promotion, and even benefits.[2]

To comply with equal employment opportunity regulations, management must be familiar with appropriate legislation. Some of the equal employment opportunity laws are summarized in Exhibit 2–3.

The EEOC has issued a number of guidelines designed to ensure compliance with these laws. These guidelines relate to issues such as equal pay, discrimination on the basis of national origin, religion, race, age, sex or pregnancy, affirmative action programs, and employee selection procedure.

The **affirmative action program** represents an advanced stage of the equal employment opportunity concept. This program requires that an employer make

Exhibit 2–3

Equal Employment Opportunity (EEO) and Affirmative Action (AA) Laws

Laws	Coverage	Basic Requirements	Agencies Involved
Title VII of Civil Rights Act, as amended by Equal Employment Opportunity Act	Employers with 15 or more employees, engaged in interstate commerce; federal service workers; and state and local government workers	Prohibits employment decisions based on race, color, religion, sex, or national origin; employers must develop affirmative action programs (AAPs) to recruit women and minorities	Equal Employment Opportunity Commission (EEOC)
Executive Order 11246 as amended by Executive Order 11375	Employers with federal contracts and subcontracts, with 50 or more employees, or with contracts over $50,000	Requires contractors to take affirmative action, including goals and timetables, to recruit, select, train, utilize, and promote minorities and women	Office of Federal Contract Compliance Programs (OFCCP), in the Labor Department
Age Discrimination in Employment Act	Employers with 20 or more employees	Prohibits employment discrimination against employees aged 40 to 70, including mandatory retirement before 70 (or 65 for tenured faculty and highly paid executives)	EEOC
Vocational Rehabilitation Act	Employers with federal contracts of $2,500 or more	Prohibits discrimination and requires contractor to develop AAPs to recruit and employ handicapped persons	OFCCP
Vietnam Era Veterans Readjustment Act	Employers with federal contracts	Requires contractors to develop AAPs to recruit and employ Vietnam-era veterans	OFCCP

SOURCE: L.C. Megginson, *Personnel Management,* 4th ed. (Homewood, Ill.: Richard D. Irwin, 1981), p. 87. Extracted from Bureau of National Affairs, *Fair Employment Practices* (Washington, D.C.: GPO,). Reprinted with permission.

a special effort to hire and to promote qualified persons who are part of the protected group. The affirmative action program includes several actions designed to eliminate existing effects of past discrimination in recruiting, hiring, compensating, and promoting employees. The EEOC guidelines regarding the affirmative action program suggest that an employer should take the eight steps outlined below. Ideally, the employer

1. Issues a written equal employment policy indicating that it is an equal employment opportunity employer, as well as a statement indicating the employer's commitment to affirmative action.
2. Appoints a top official with responsibility and with authority to direct and to implement the program.
3. Publicizes the equal employment policy and affirmative action commitment.
4. Surveys present minority and female employment by department and job classification to determine locations where affirmative action programs are especially desirable.
5. Develops goals and timetables to improve utilization of minorities, males, and females in each area where utilization has been identified.
6. Develops and implements specific programs to achieve these goals. According to the EEOC, this is the heart of the affirmative action program. Here the company should review its entire personnel management system (including recruitment, selection, promotion, compensation, and discipline)

to identify barriers to equal employment opportunity and to make needed changes.

7. Establishes an internal audit and reporting system to monitor and to evaluate progress in each aspect of the program.

8. Develops support for the affirmative action program, both inside the company (among supervisors, for instance) and outside the company in the community.[3]

Moreover, the EEOC suggests that management monitors the implementation of the affirmative action program within the organization and prepares a quarterly statistical report. This report is presented in Exhibit 2–4.

Exhibit 2–4

Affirmative Action Program—Quarterly Statistical Report

Form T	All Employees			Male				Female				Organizational Unit _____ Location _____ Time Period _____
Job Categories	Total	Male	Female	Negro	Oriental	American Indian	Spanish Surnamed American	Negro	Oriental	American Indian	Spanish Surnamed American	
Officials & Managers	(1)	(2)	(3)	(4)	(5)	(6)	(7)	(8)	(9)	(10)	(11)	
Professionals												
Technicians												
Sales Workers												
Office & Clerical												
TOTAL Lines 1-5												
Craftsmen (Skilled)												
Operatives (Semi-Skilled)												
Laborers (Unskilled)												
Service												
TOTAL Lines 7-10												
TOTAL All Lines												
In columns 1, 2, and 3, include all employees in the establishment including those in min. groups. (The data below shall be included in the figures for the appropriate occupation categories above.)												
On-the-job trainees Apprentices												
Production												
White Collar												
(Report only employees enrolled in formal on-the-job training programs.)												

Date of Survey _____   Person Preparing Reports _____
Name (Typed)   Signature

SOURCE: U.S. Equal Employment Opportunity Commission, *Affirmative Action and Equal Employment* (Washington D.C.: GPO, 1974)

2.03 Job Analysis

Sound personnel management practice prescribes creation of various jobs and positions designed in accordance with the specific organizational structure of a company. This task represents an important responsibility of the personnel manager and is usually accomplished by means of a job analysis. The prime purpose of **job analysis** is to determine duties and skill requirements for a particular job and the type of person who could be suitable for it.

The job analysis process is based on collection and study of information relevant to a specific position. Job analysis is frequently carried out by means of personal interviews, questionnaires, or observations and entails gathering of the following information:

- Identification of the job (title, department)
- Summary of the job
- Detailed list of responsibilities and duties performed
- Analysis of the accountability
- Analysis of performance standards
- Analysis of the available amount of supervision
- Summary of machine and tool requirements
- Summary of the physical demands of the job
- Summary of working conditions

Job analysis is particularly important in evaluating specific requirements for various managerial positions. This usually depends upon company size and nature of activities. Job analysis for managerial positions entails additional considerations in the following areas:

- Working with subordinates
- Organizing work of subordinates
- Work planning and scheduling
- Maintaining efficient quality and production
- Maintaining safe and clean work areas
- Maintaining equipment and machinery
- Compiling records and reports [4]

Job analysis is necessary for several reasons. First, it provides guidance throughout recruitment and selection of employees. In addition, this process helps management to understand the various requirements of a particular position and to develop an appropriate compensation package (e.g., salary, commission, bonus, fringe benefits). Finally, job analysis is useful in developing suitable training and development programs for employees.

The two prime products of job analysis are job descriptions and job specifications; both are discussed later. The interaction between these products and other elements of personnel management in the context of job analysis is summarized in Exhibit 2–5.

According to Gary Dessler, there are six steps in the job analysis process:

1. Identifying the use of the job analysis information. For example, it can be used in preparing a job description and job specification or in developing a compensation program.
2. Collecting and reviewing general information. This may include existing organizational charts, job descriptions, job specifications, or compensation reviews.

Exhibit 2–5

Job Analysis and Related Managerial Tasks

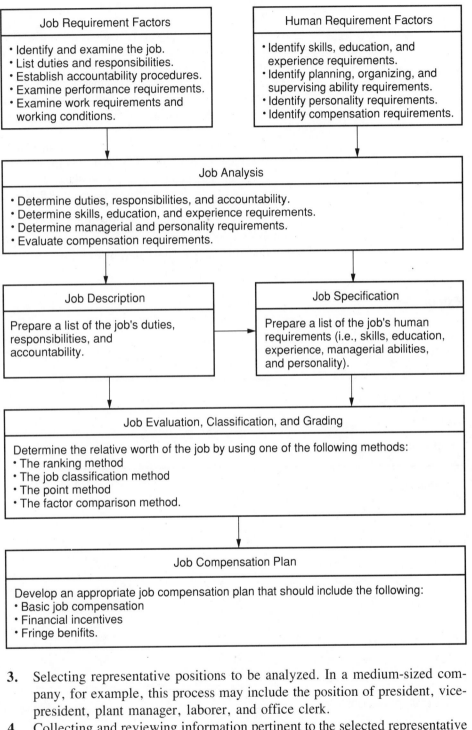

3. Selecting representative positions to be analyzed. In a medium-sized company, for example, this process may include the position of president, vice-president, plant manager, laborer, and office clerk.

4. Collecting and reviewing information pertinent to the selected representative positions. Relevant details have been outlined previously.

5. Reviewing the information with participants. This entails a general discussion with the particular employee who performs the job. The employee should understand and verify relevant details of job analysis information.

6. Developing a job description and job specification. These are the two prime results of the job analysis process. Job description lists the job's duties, responsibilities, and accountability while job specification summarizes human requirements for a particular position.

Some of the typical questions used during job analysis interviews have been summarized by Gary Dessler as follows:

- What is the job being performed?
- What are the major duties of your position?
- In what different physical locations do you work?
- What are the education, experience, skill, and (where applicable) certification and licensing requirements?
- In what activities do you participate?
- What are the responsibilities and duties of the job?
- What are the basic accountabilities or performance standards that typify your work?
- What do the activities you participate in involve?
- What are the physical, emotional, and mental demands of the job?
- What are the health and safety conditions?
- Are you exposed to any hazards or unusual working conditions?[5]

Managers in many small and medium-sized organizations often use a simple job analysis questionnaire to gather relevant information. A typical example of such a questionnaire is presented in Exhibit 2–6. Once all relevant questions are

Exhibit 2–6

Job Analysis Questionnaire

Job Analysis Questionnaire
Company name: _____ Department: _____
Job title   : _____
Reporting to   : _____
1. Summarize the job: _____
2. List duties and responsibilities: _____
3. Details of accountability: _____
4. Specify performance standards: _____

Exhibit 2–6

(concluded)

5. Specify required amount of supervision: _____

_____

6. Specify machine and tool requirements: _____

_____

7. Summarize the physical demands of the job: _____

_____

_____

8. Summarize working conditions: _____

_____

_____

_____

9. Suggested methods of accomplishing the work: _____

_____

_____

_____

_____

10. Details of relationships to other jobs: _____

_____

11. Participation in management meetings: _____

_____

12. Details of qualifications and experience requirements: _____

_____

_____

15. Additional information: _____

_____

Prepared by:	Approved by:	Date:

answered, it is necessary to summarize the appropriate results and to proceed with preparation of job descriptions and job specifications. These are used extensively in evaluating, classifying, and grading various jobs and in preparing appropriate compensation plans.

2.04 Job Descriptions and Job Specifications

The prime purpose of job analysis is to provide sufficient information to prepare comprehensive **job descriptions** that incorporate all the relevant duties, responsibilities, authority, and accountability of specific jobs as follows:

- *The job title, or job identification.* This specifies the title of the job (e.g., president, marketing manager, or typist).
- *The job summary.* This describes the nature of the job in a condensed form by listing the prime functions only.
- *Details of accountability.* These specify the reporting procedure, (i.e., to whom the person is accountable within the organization).
- *Details of responsibility and duties.* These include a detailed description of all responsibilities and duties of the job.
- *Details of authority.* These define the authority of the job holder within the organization and specify limits of authority in decision-making, direct supervision, expenditure, and other activities.
- *Participation in management teams.* This identifies the job holder's membership in specific management teams.

The core of any job description is the summary of all the duties prescribed for a specific job. This is achieved by means of detailed description of all activities and their corresponding goals. A well prepared job description represents one of the most effective tools that provides guidance and control of employees' performance in the company. A typical example of a job description is illustrated in Exhibit 2–7.

Another prime result of the job analysis process is development of **job specifications**. The main objective of a job specification is to outline the minimum level of personnel requirements necessary to ensure an acceptable standard of work. The initial stage of any job specification is usually based on a comprehensive assessment of the job description. The latter provides detailed information regarding any specified position within the company. The quality of the job specification depends primarily on the correct understanding of the relevant job's description (i.e., nature of work, specified duties and responsibilities, limits of authority and accountability). During the process of preparing a job specification a number of questions will have to be answered:

- What is the minimum standard of school, professional, or university education required?
- What is the minimum level of professional experience required?
- What knowledge, skills, and abilities does the job require?
- What is the period of experience required?
- Can specific knowledge, skills, and abilities be developed on the job and how long would it take?

Exhibit 2–7

Job Description

Job Description

Job title   : Chief Executive Officer or President
Job summary : To plan, organize, direct, and control the company's strategic and operational activities and to ensure a satisfying return on shareholders' investment.
Accountable to: Board of Directors

List of duties:

1. Establish the company's executive management team.
2. Develop and implement an effective decision-making process within the organization.
3. Formulate organizational objectives, strategies, policies, tactics, and rules in collaboration with other members of the executive management team.
4. Develop a sound and realistic plan of management for the forthcoming fiscal period.
5. Authorize and coordinate the implementation of all aspects of strategic and operational planning activities.
6. Develop an effective organizational structure and draw an organizational chart.
7. Allocate responsibilities, duties, and authority and determine the accountability of each member of the executive management team.
8. Ensure effective selection, appraisal, training, development, and compensation of management personnel and other employees.
9. Encourage and consider suggestions from subordinate executives regarding all company activities.
10. Lead the executive management team toward the achievement of organizational objectives.
11. Develop effective communication between all members of the executive management team.
12. Maintain continuous control over all major operational activities.
13. Deal on the company's behalf with various government, trade, and commercial organizations.
14. Ensure the existence of adequate arrangements to ensure the continuity of the company's operational activities.

Details of authority:

Not authorized to incur capital expenditure in excess of $. . . during one fiscal year without the specific approval of the Board of Directors

Immediate subordinates:

1. Vice President, Finance
2. Vice President, Production
3. Vice President, Marketing

Participation in management teams:

1. Chairman of the company's executive management team
2. Member of the company's operational management teams (i.e., financial, production, and marketing teams)

Job specifications can be prepared for a broad range of positions. A typical example of a job specification for a design engineer is illustrated in Exhibit 2–8.

The success of the employee-hiring process often depends upon the quality of the job specification developed in conjunction with a job description. Both

Exhibit 2–8

Job Specification

Job Specification
Job title: Design Engineer   Required by: June 1990
Accountable to: Vice President, Engineering
Background: Due to expansion of our manufacturing facility and to development of new products, it is essential to employ a suitable design engineer who will be able to handle the increased workload in the design department.
Job summary: To take full responsibility for new product and process design, testing, and collaboration with the manufacturing department in this regard.
Desired education: B.S. Mechanical Engineering
Desired experience: At least 2 years of product and process design experience in similar industry
Special requirements: The candidate needs to be familiar with plastic products manufacturing.
On-the-job training: The candidate should be prepared to receive additional on-the-job training during the initial period of employment.
Travel requirements: The candidate will be required to travel to customers and to deal with suppliers.
Salary range: $35, 000 - $40,000 per year
Fringe benefits: Medical and life insurance, pension plan, company vehicle, one month paid vacation
Additional information: The above position is suitable for a candidate who is eager to grow with the company.

the job descriptions and the job specifications, the prime products of the job analysis process, are commonly used in the following applications:

- Personnel planning and forecasting
- Personnel hiring procedures
- Personnel orientation programs
- Personnel training programs
- Personnel performance appraisal
- Personnel career development programs
- Personnel counseling procedures
- Examination of organizational structure and its effectiveness
- Specific job evaluation
- Examination of labor relations
- Modification of organizational structure
- Modification of specific jobs

Managers often underestimate the importance of job descriptions and job specifications. This may result in ineffective implementation of personnel management practices within the organization. It is necessary therefore, to ensure that a set of clear, short, and meaningful job descriptions and job specifications is prepared well in advance. This will equip managers with an important tool to handle a broad range of operational activities and provide effective guidance to subordinates.

2.05 Personnel Planning and Forecasting

Job descriptions and job specifications are widely used by management throughout the personnel planning and forecasting process. The main purpose of this process is to secure the availability of specific types of people with the skills, experience, and background necessary to meet the company's forthcoming objectives. The actual planning process consists of two stages:

1. Personnel demand forecasting.
2. Personnel supply forecasting.

Personnel planning deals with short- and long-term forecasting issues and is designed to provide sufficient information about employee requirements in the future. *Short-term personnel demand forecasting* is designed to assess the level of employee requirements to enable the company to meet its objectives during the forthcoming fiscal year. This type of forecasting has an immediate effect on the company's current situation. *Long-term personnel demand forecasting*, on the other hand, provides an optional indication of the company's future requirements based on one- to five-year periods.

It is appropriate to begin short-term personnel demand forecasting with a detailed analysis of current employee allocation. This involves completing the **personnel allocation status report** and summarizing relevant details about employees in various departments, sections, and shops. A typical personnel allocation status report is presented in Exhibit 2–9.

The information contained in the personnel allocation status report helps management to summarize data pertaining to current human resources within the organization. Moreover, this report indicates the possible need for replacing a particular employee based on the employee's past performance evaluation and personal work satisfaction. Various methods of personnel performance evaluation are discussed later.

The next stage in short-term personnel demand forecasting entails examination of the company's immediate operational objectives and assessment of relevant personnel requirements. The main factors which should be considered during this examination include the following:

- Current corporate budget
- Current production requirements
- Current sales demands
- Current economical situation
- Current capabilities of personnel

Upon completing the examination of all these factors, management should prepare a detailed **personnel requirements report** for the forthcoming fiscal

Exhibit 2–9

Personnel Allocation Status Report

Personnel Allocation Status Report					
Department, section, shop	Name of employee	Current position	Period of employment (years)	Annual income ($)	Need for replacement (Yes/?/No)
Administration dept.	A. Boss	President	6	60,000	No
Administration dept.	B. Richards	Secretary	1	30,000	No
Administration dept.	C. Peters	Receptionist	0.5	15,000	Yes
Financial dept.	D. Mayers	V.P. Finance	3	40,000	No
Financial dept.	C. Nicks	Bookkeeper	2	20,000	No
Financial dept.	A. Jones	Invoice Clerk	1	18,000	Yes
Operations dept.	A. Daniels	V.P. Operations	6	45,000	No
Press shop	B. Wilson	Foreman	5	30,000	No
Press shop	C. Cox	Operator	2	20,000	No
Press shop	D. Taylor	Operator	1	18,000	?
Press shop	S. Brown	Operator	0.5	16,000	Yes
Machine shop	C. White	Foreman	2	27,000	?
Marketing dept.	H. Black	V.P. Marketing	4	42,000	No
Marketing dept.	F. Green	Sales Manager	5	30,000	No
Marketing dept.	D. Chuck	Salesperson	2	25,000	?
Marketing dept.	J. Murdock	Salesperson	1	20,000	Yes
Name: A. Boss		Position: President		Date: August 1989	

period. This report contains detailed information summarizing the specific manpower requirements. A typical personnel requirements report is presented in Exhibit 2–10.

Once all personnel requirements for the forthcoming fiscal period are summarized, management should proceed with identifying appropriate sources of

Exhibit 2–10

Personnel Requirements Report

Personnel Requirements Report for 1990				
Department, section, shop	Position	Annual compensation ($)	Additional benefits	Period of requirement
Administration dept.	Receptionist	± 15,000	Med. insurance	Immediately
Financial dept.	Invoice clerk	± 18,000	≈	Immediately
Operations dept.			≈	
Press shop	Operator	± 18,000	≈	Immediately
Press shop	Operator	± 15,000	≈	May - June
Machine shop	Operator	± 15,000	≈	April - May
Marketing dept.	Salesperson	± 20,000	Company vehicle	Immediately
Marketing dept.	Salesperson	± 20,000	Company vehicle	April - May
Name: A. Boss		Position: President		Date: August 1989

personnel supply. This task represents an integral part of the process known as **personnel supply forecasting**.

The process of personnel supply forecasting requires management to identify the hidden talents of the people already employed by the company. This provides the employees with the opportunity for continuous challenge and development. In order to keep track of the employees' qualifications and development, it is necessary to introduce and to maintain an updated **manpower record system**. There are several types of manual systems applicable for this purpose:

- Personnel inventory and development record
- Management replacement chart

Personnel inventory and development record contains information that is compiled on each employee within the organization. This record includes information such as details of education, professional courses, career and development interests, additional training requirements, and details of skills and experience. A typical personnel inventory and development record is presented in Exhibit 2–11.

Another important element of the manual manpower record system is the **management replacement chart**. This chart includes names of several candidates for the most important positions within the organization and summarizes

Exhibit 2–11

Personnel Inventory and Development Record (appropriate for manual storage retrieval)

PERSONNEL INVENTORY AND DEVELOPMENT RECORD			Date: month, year

Department	Area or sub-department	Branch or section	Location

Company service date (month, day, year)	Birthdate (month, date, year)	Marital status	Job title

Education — Degree, year obtained, college, and major field of study

Grade school	High School
6 7 8	9 10 11 12 13

College
1   2   3   4   5

Courses (company sponsored)

Type of course	Subject or course	Year	Type of course	Subject or course	Year

Career and development interests

| Are you interested in an alternative type of work? | Yes ☐ No ☐ | Would you accept transfer to another division | Yes ☐ No ☐ | Would you accept lateral moves for further development | Yes ☐ No ☐ |

| If yes, specifically what type? | Comment on any qualifying circumstances |

Photo

What type of training do you believe you require to:

A) Improve your skills and performance in your present position

B) Improve your experience and abilities for advancement.

What other assignments do you believe you are qualified to perform now?

Last name

First name

Languages	Written	Spoken
	☐ English ☐ French ☐ Spanish ☐ Other	☐ English ☐ French ☐ Spanish ☐ Other

Middle name

SS Number

Societies and organizations — Memberships in community organizations, etc., within last five years, indicate name of association and office held, if any

Skills

Type of skill	Certification, if any	Type of skill	Certification, if any

Other significant work experience, and/or military service. (Omit repetitive experiences)

	Location	From yr.	To yr.	

Comments: Other significant experience, recreational activities, hobbies, interests, or personal data.

SOURCE: Gary Dessler, *Personnel Management*, 4e, ©1988, p. 114. Adapted by permission of Prentice-Hall, Englewood Cliffs, New Jersey.

present performance and promotion potential for each candidate. A typical management replacement chart is presented in Exhibit 2–12.

Sometimes, however, management will not find suitable candidates within the organization to fill certain positions. In this instance, management must ensure that additional candidates are available from external sources. The availability of suitable candidates depends upon several factors such as

- *General economic conditions.* These conditions depend upon overall economic conditions in the country, rate of unemployment, and anticipated economic trends.
- *Local labor conditions.* These conditions depend upon the economic situation in a specific city, county, or state.
- *Occupational market conditions.* These conditions depend upon availability and demand for professional people (e.g., engineers, accountants, computer programmers, and tradespeople).

The main advantage of the personnel planning process is that it enables management to make correct decisions regarding personnel who can meet the company's objectives and to deal more effectively with the following issues:

- Personnel hiring
- Personnel training
- Design of career management programs
- Design of productivity programs

Exhibit 2–12

Management Replacement Chart

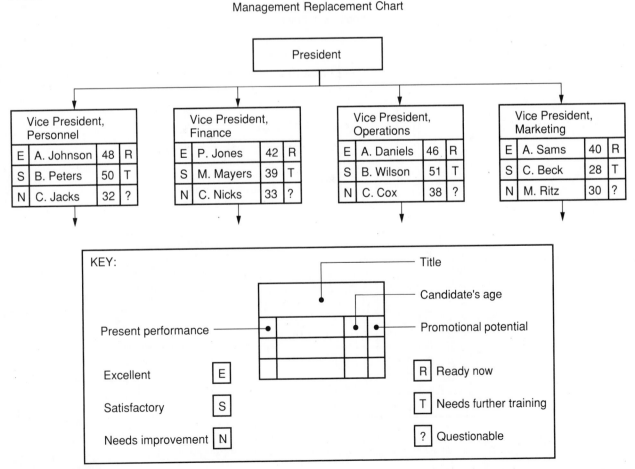

2.06 Personnel Recruitment and Hiring

Once the personnel planning and forecasting process has been accomplished, the search for and selection of new employees should begin. It is essential that this process conforms to equal employment opportunity guidelines prescribed by federal and state legislation. The search for and selection of new employees in small or medium-sized organizations involves a number of steps illustrated in Exhibit 2–13.

Exhibit 2–13

Search and Selection of New Employees

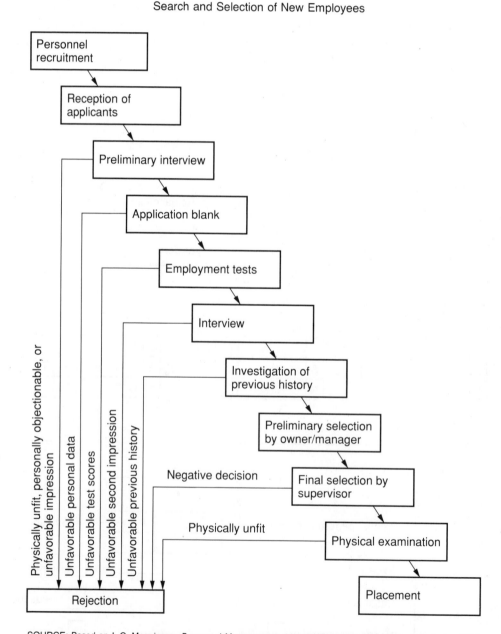

SOURCE: Based on L.C. Megginson, *Personnel Management*, 4th ed. (Homewood, Ill.: Richard D. Irwin, 1981), pp. 174 and 180. © 1981 by Richard D. Irwin, Inc. Reprinted with permission.

The first step in the process is the recruitment and hiring of new employees. The main objective of **personnel recruiting and hiring** is to fulfil the company's specific needs and to employ people who will satisfy most of the requirements set out by relevant job specifications and in accordance with existing organizational plans. As previously mentioned, the sources of employees can be specified into two categories—internal and external ones. Filling a job opening by means of internal personnel resources has the following important advantages:

- High level of stimulation for promotion
- Increased general level of morale
- Good knowledge of existing personnel
- Possibility for better overall results

Unfortunately, existing personnel resources cannot always provide enough candidates with the qualities required by the company to meet job specification needs. In this case, the management should use a recruiting method conducted by means of any of the following:

- Advertising
- Employment agencies
- Recommendations of current employees
- School or university graduates
- Labor unions
- Walk-ins and referrals

During the hiring process, certain information related to each specific applicant should be collected. This information must be compared subsequently with relevant details of the job specification and the general standard of personnel. The process of evaluating an applicant's abilities is considered to be one of the most important and difficult management tasks. There are no rules in this procedure that guarantee success; however, appropriate guidelines should be maintained.

The most effective method used during the personnel hiring process is the following:

- Completion of a job application form by a prospective employee
- Checking relevant references
- Testing and selection of prospective employees
- Employment interview
- Confirmation of employment acceptance
- Applicant's induction and orientation

The prime purpose of the **job application form** is to provide the company with a clear and condensed written report highlighting the applicant's details. This form must be designed in accordance with equal employment opportunity laws discussed earlier and may include information outlined in Exhibit 2–14.

The actual contents of a job application form depends upon the specific needs of the company and the nature of its activities. A typical job application form is presented in Exhibit 2–15.

Certain information may be requested by the company provided it claims that it is an *equal opportunity employer*, hiring without regard to race, religion,

Exhibit 2–14

Personnel History Items Useful in Developing Job Application Forms

Personal
Age*
Age at hiring
Marital status*
Number of years married
Dependents, number of
Age when first child born
Physical health
Recent illnesses, operations
Time lost from job for certain previous period
 (last 2 years, etc.)
Living conditions, general
Domicile, whether alone, rooming house, keep
 own house, etc.
Residence, location of
Size of home town
Number of times moved in recent period
Length of time at last address
Nationality*
Birth place*
Weight and height
Sex

General Background
Occupation of father
Occupation of mother
Occupation of brothers, sisters, other relatives
Military service and rank
Military discharge record
Early family responsibility
Parental family adjustment
Professionally successful parents
Stable or transient home life
Wife does not work outside home

Education
Education
Educational level of wife
Educational level of family relatives
Education finances—extent of dependence on
 parents
Type of course studied—grammar school
Major field of study—high school
Specific courses taken in high school or college
Subjects liked, disliked in high school
Years since leaving high school
Type of school attended, private/state

College grades
Scholarship level, grammar school and high school
Graduated at early age compared with classmates

Employment Experience
Educational—vocational consistency
Previous occupations (general type of work)
Held job in high school (type of job)
Number of previous jobs
Specific work experience (specific jobs)
Previous (selling) experience
Previous (life insurance sales) experience
Total length of work experience (total years, months)
Being in business for self
Previous employee of company now considering
 application
Seniority in present employment
Tenure on previous job
Minimum current living expenses
Salary requests, limits set for accepting job
Earnings expected (in future, 2 yrs., 5 yrs., etc.)

Social
Club memberships (social, community, campus, high
 school)
Frequency of attendance at group meetings
Offices held in clubs
Experience as a group leader
Church membership

Interests
Prefer outside to inside labor
Hobbies
Number of hobbies
Specific type of hobbies, leisure time activities
 preferred
Sports
Number of sports active in
Most important source of entertainment

**Personal Characteristics, Attitudes
Expressed**
Willingness to relocate or transfer
Confidence (as expressed by applicant)
Basic personality needs (5 types) as expressed by appli-
 cant in reply to question on application blank
Drive
Stated job preferences

---

 * Because of fair-employment guidelines, many of these must be used with caution.

SOURCE: George W. England, *Development and Use of Weighted Application Blanks*, rev. ed. (Minneapolis: Industrial Relations Center, University of Minnesota, 1971), pp. 16–19. Reprinted with permission.

Exhibit 2–15

Job Application Form

APPLICATION FOR EMPLOYMENT

Our organization is an equal opportunity employer. It is our policy to recruit, hire, compensate, and promote employees on the basis of merit, qualifications, and competence. This applies to all employees including managerial, professional, technical, and support personnel. All employment decisions are made on the basis of the applicant's qualifications as related to the requirements of the position being filled.

PLEASE PRINT ALL INFORMATION

1. PERSONAL DATA

Full name (first/middle/last):

Social Security No.: | U.S. Citizen ( ) Yes ( ) No

If no, do you possess a legal work permit in the U.S. ( ) Yes ( ) No

Address (apt. No., street, city, state, zip code):

Phone No.: (Home) (Work)

2. EMPLOYMENT PREFERENCES AND GENERAL DATA

Position desired: | Date available:

Work schedule desired: ( ) Full-time ( ) Part-time ( ) Other

Working shift desired: ( ) Mornings/Days ( ) Days/Evenings ( ) Evenings/Nights

Have you been employed by this company before? ( ) Yes ( ) No

Do you have any relatives employed by this company? ( ) Yes ( ) No

If yes, provide name(s):

3. DETAILS OF EDUCATION

School/College/University	Period	Location	Academic major	Degree

4. DETAILS OF AWARDS AND DISTINCTIONS

5. DETAILS OF MILITARY SERVICE

Branch of service: | Final rank:

Date entered: | Date discharged:

Exhibit 2–15

(continued)

6. DETAILS OF EMPLOYMENT

Please list all employment starting with present or most recent employer. Include U.S. military service, any part-time or temporary employment, and unemployment periods. Employment in this company is contingent on verification of employment history.

6.1 Employer's name:	Job title:
Supervisor's name and title:	Phone No.:
Employer's mailing address:	

Period of employment:	( ) Full-time	( ) Part-time
Starting salary/wage:	Ending salary/wage:	

Reason(s) for leaving:

Description of duties:

6.2 Employer's name:	Job title:
Supervisor's name and title:	Phone No.:
Employer's mailing address:	

Period of employment:	( ) Full-time	( ) Part-time
Starting salary/wage:	Ending salary/wage:	

Reason(s) for leaving:

Description of duties:

6.3 Employer's name:	Job title:
Supervisor's name and title:	Phone No.:
Employer's mailing address:	

Period of employment:	( ) Full-time	( ) Part-time
Starting salary/wage:	Ending salary/wage:	

Reason(s) for leaving:

Description of duties:

Exhibit 2–15

(continued)

6.4 Employer's name:	Job title:	
Supervisor's name and title:	Phone No.:	
Employer's mailing address:		
Period of employment:	( ) Full-time	( ) Part-time
Starting salary/wage:	Ending salary/wage:	
Reason(s) for leaving:		
Description of duties:		

6.5 Employer's name:	Job title:	
Supervisor's name and title:	Phone No.:	
Employer's mailing address:		
Period of employment:	( ) Full-time	( ) Part-time
Starting salary/wage:	Ending salary/wage:	
Reason(s) for leaving:		
Description of duties:		

6.6 Employer's name:	Job title:	
Supervisor's name and title:	Phone No.:	
Employer's mailing address:		
Period of employment:	( ) Full-time	( ) Part-time
Starting salary/wage:	Ending salary/wage:	
Reason(s) for leaving:		
Description of duties:		

7. PHYSICAL DATA

Do you have any physical or mental disabilities that would prevent you from performing the responsibilities of the position for which you are applying?
( ) Yes   ( ) No. If yes, explain:

Exhibit 2–15

(concluded)

8. CONVICTION RECORD
Have you ever been convicted of felony? ( ) Yes; ( ) No. If yes explain fully *:   *The existence of a criminal record does not necessarily bar you from employment

9. ADDITIONAL INFORMATION
Please provide any additional information (e.g., special interests, hobbies, etc.) in the space allocated below:

10. AUTHORIZATION AND CERTIFICATION

I hereby authorize _____(name of company) to verify all information contained in this application and any supplement thereto. I further authorize all former employers, companies, agencies, and persons contacted to release any and all information in their possession that has or may have bearing on my suitability for employment.

I certify that the above statements are true and complete to the best of my knowledge. I understand that any misrepresentation or material omission of information for this application and any supplement thereto may be cause for denial of employment or for dismissal if employed.

Once employed, I understand a copy of my birth certificate or other declaration of age will be required as proof of my eligibility for the retirement plan. Moreover, I understand that my employment is subject to a trial period imposed by my company.

Applicant's signature:	Date:

sex, color, national origin, or age. In this instance, the company should prepare a separate **equal employment opportunity disclaimer letter** and request the applicant to provide additional information on a strictly voluntary basis. A typical equal employment opportunity disclaimer letter is presented in Exhibit 2–16.

Exhibit 2–16

Equal Employment Opportunity Disclaimer Letter

EQUAL EMPLOYMENT OPPORTUNITY DISCLAIMER LETTER

In order to ensure compliance with the Civil Rights Act of 1964 (Title 42, U.S.C. Section 2000e et seq.) and related laws and regulations, the _____ (company's name) must monitor its equal employment opportunity position on a continuing basis. To aid this review process you are requested to identify your sex, group status (e.g., black, white, hispanic, asian), and age on this form. The information you furnish will be maintained only for the purpose of monitoring compliance with applicable laws and regulations concerning Equal Employment Opportunity and will not be used for any other purpose.[6]

EQUAL EMPLOYMENT OPPORTUNITY INFORMATION

Applicant's full name: _____

Social Security No.: _____

Date of birth: _____

Racial/ethnic data: ( ) Black   ( ) White   ( ) Hispanic   ( ) Asian
( ) Native American Indian or Alaskan   ( ) Asian/Pacific Islander.

Sex: ( ) Female   ( ) Male.

Do you have any disabling condition: ( ) Yes   ( ) No
If yes, please specify: _____

2.07 Screening and Testing of Applicants

Upon the completion of the job application form and the submission of all required documents and references, the information should be verified by means of screening and testing of applicants. The main purpose of these procedures is to assist the company further in evaluating the applicant and to confirm the accuracy of the submitted information.

Screening of applicants helps management to evaluate background, character, professional competence, experience, and other important factors. Willingness of the past or current employer to rehire the applicant may serve as an additional recommendation for employment. Such a recommendation, however, will be meaningful only if the person providing it.

1. Has had an adequate opportunity to observe the applicant in job-relevant situations.
2. Is competent to evaluate the applicant's job performance.
3. Can express such an evaluation in a way that is meaningful to the prospective employer.
4. Is completely candid.[7]

Unfortunately some written recommendations issued to employees by their past employers are not sufficiently accurate. It may be useful, therefore, to follow certain guidelines when searching for additional information from references about prospective employees:

- Request job-related information only; put it in written form to prove that your hire or no-hire decision was based on relevant information.
- Obtain from job candidates their written permission to check references prior to doing so.
- Stay away from subjective areas such as the candidate's personality.
- Evaluate the credibility of the source of the reference material. Under most circumstances, an evaluation by a past immediate supervisor will be more credible than an evaluation by a personnel officer.
- Wherever possible, use public records to evaluate on-the-job behavior or personal conduct (e.g., court, bankruptcy, workers' compensation records).
- Remember that the courts have ruled that a reference check of an applicant's prior employment record does not violate his or her civil rights as long as the information provided relates solely to work behavior and to reasons for leaving a previous job.[8]

One of the most effective methods of screening applicants is a telephone or personal interview with their former employers. Such an interview can be conducted by asking a broad range of questions or by using a **telephone or personal interview form**. This form helps the interviewer to ask relevant questions in an orderly manner without overlooking certain important issues. A typical telephone or personal interview form is presented in Exhibit 2–17.

Sometimes other organizations request that managers provide references on former employees. In this instance, managers need to be familiar with what they can or cannot say about former employees. Some of the laws which affect the employment reference procedures are as follows:

- The Freedom of Information Act of 1966
- The Fair Credit Reporting Act of 1970
- The Privacy Act of 1974
- The Family Education Rights and Privacy Act of 1974

Managers need to remember that the information which they provide to other organizations about former employees may eventually reach those employees. Hence, it is essential not to fall into a trap and provide any information that may be interpreted as defamatory. This will protect the organization from any legal action by such employees.

There are several guidelines which should be followed by managers while giving employment references to other organizations. Some of these guidelines are summarized in Exhibit 2–18.

In order to secure selection of suitable employees it may also be useful to conduct preliminary **testing of applicants**. The main objective of such testing is to

Exhibit 2–17

Telephone or Personal Interview Form

TELEPHONE OR PERSONAL INTERVIEW

☐ FORMER EMPLOYER
☐ CHARACTER REFERENCE

COMPANY ADDRESS PHONE

NAME OF PERSON CONTACTED POSITION OR TITLE

1. I WISH TO VERIFY SOME FACTS GIVEN BY (MISS, MRS.) MR. WHO IS APPLYING FOR EMPLOYMENT WITH OUR FIRM. WHAT WERE THE DATES OF HIS/HER EMPLOYMENT BY YOUR COMPANY? FROM 19 TO 19

2. WHAT WAS THE NATURE OF HIS/HER JOB? AT START

   AT LEAVING

3. HE/SHE STATES THAT HE/SHE WAS EARNING $ PER WHEN HE/SHE LEFT, IS THAT CORRECT? YES NO $

4. WHAT DID HIS/HER SUPERVISORS THINK OF HIM/HER?

   WHAT DID HIS/HER SUBORDINATES THINK OF HIM/HER?

5. DID HE/SHE HAVE SUPERVISORY RESPONSIBILITY? YES NO

   (IF YES) HOW DID HE/SHE CARRY IT OUT?

6. HOW HARD DID HE/SHE WORK?

7. HOW DID HE/SHE GET ALONG WITH OTHERS?

8. HOW WAS HIS/HER ATTENDANCE RECORD? PUNCTUALITY?

9. WHAT WERE HIS/HER REASONS FOR LEAVING?

10. WOULD YOU REHIRE HIM/HER? (IF NO) WHY? YES NO

11. DID HE/SHE HAVE ANY DOMESTIC, FINANCIAL, OR PERSONAL TROUBLE WHICH INTERFERED WITH HIS/HER WORK? YES NO

12. DID HE/SHE DRINK OR GAMBLE TO EXCESS? YES NO

13. WHAT ARE HIS/HER STRONG POINTS?

14. WHAT ARE HIS/HER WEAK POINTS?

REMARKS:

SOURCE: Reprinted by permission of publisher, from *Book of Employment Forms*

Exhibit 2–18

Guidelines for Defensible References

1. Don't volunteer information. Respond only to specific company or institutional inquiries and requests. Before responding, telephone the inquirer to check on the validity of the request.

2. Direct all communication only to persons who have a specific interest in that information.

3. State in the message that the information you are providing is confidential and should be treated as such. Use qualifying statements such as "providing information that was requested"; "relating this information only because it was requested"; or "providing information that is to be used for professional purposes only." Sentences such as these imply that information was not presented for the purpose of hurting or damaging a person's reputation.

4. Obtain written consent from the employee or student, if possible.

5. Provide only reference data that relates and pertains to the job and job performance in question.

6. Avoid vague statements such as: "He was an average student"; "She was careless at times"; "He displayed an inability to work with others."

7. Document all released information. Use specific statements such as: "Mr. ____ received a grade of C—an average grade"; "Ms. ____ made an average of two bookkeeping errors each week"; or "This spring, four members of the work team wrote letters asking not to be placed on the shift with Mr. ____."

8. Clearly label all subjective statements based on personal opinions and feelings. Say "I believe . . ." whenever making a statement that is not fact.

9. When providing a negative or potentially negative statement, add the reason or reasons why, or specify the incidents that led you to this opinion.

10. Do not answer trap questions such as "Would you rehire this person?"

11. Avoid answering questions that are asked "off the record."

SOURCE: Mary F. Cook, *Human Resources Director's Handbook* (Englewood Cliffs, N.J.: Prentice Hall, 1984), p. 93. Reprinted with permission.

measure a person's suitability to present employment conditions and adaptability to future demands. All tests must be conducted in accordance with various federal and state laws, including the 1964 Civil Rights Act and 1967 Age Discrimination in Employment Act which prohibit discrimination with respect to race, color, national origin, religion, sex, and age. The guidelines stipulated in the Equal Employment Opportunity Act of 1972 state that the employer must be able to prove that

- Testing of applicants relates to their potential success or failure on the job (validity of the test).
- Testing of applicants does not unfairly discriminate against the protected group.[9]

The American Psychological Association (APA) established certain standards for educational and psychological tests. In accordance with these standards, the testing of applicants is subject to privacy, confidentiality of test results, and the right to informed consent regarding the use of these results. Applicants also have the right to expect that only people qualified to interpret the scores will have access to them. Finally, applicants have the right to expect that the test is fair to all test takers in the sense of being equally familiar or equally unfamiliar so that the test results reflect the test takers' abilities.[10]

There are several types of tests used in industry. These tests should be conducted and validated in accordance with the Uniform Guidelines on Employee Selection Procedures approved by EEOC in 1978. Among these tests are the following:

- The intelligence test
- The aptitude test
- The achievement test
- The interest test
- The personality test

The intelligence test is an important instrument in assessing intelligence level, reasoning ability, verbal comprehension, word fluency, and memory. This type of testing is used in the process of identification and selection of management.

The aptitude test is used to establish and to evaluate the ability of a person to learn and to understand a given job. This test could assist in evaluating the capacity for future learning performance.

The achievement test is used alternatively to evaluate the level of understanding and degree of accomplishment as a result of professional training of a specific applicant or employee. This test relates to past learning performance and the degree of present achievement.

The interest test evaluates the similarity of interest levels between a specific applicant or employee and the actual job tasks. It is important to bear in mind that employees will do their jobs more effectively if there is a strong similarity of interest between them and their jobs.

The personality test evaluates the adaptability of a specific applicant or employee to other employees. It is essential to recognize the importance of this test for supervisory or management personnel, who are usually in a position of leading, motivating, and controlling subordinates.

2.08 Employment Interviews

Screening of applicants and evaluating their suitability for employment are essential elements of personnel selection. This process entails gathering of information about applicants, conducting reference checks, and finally interviewing suitable candidates. **Employment interviews** provide the employer with a distinct opportunity to "size-up" applicants and to assess their personal qualifications prior to making a final selection decision. These interviews, therefore, must be properly administered to obtain the most effective results.

There are several types of employment interviews frequently used by managers in small and medium-sized companies. Among these interviews are:

- Nondirective interview
- Patterned interview
- Structured interview
- Serialized interview

Nondirective interview does not follow a special format and is based on a general conversation between an interviewer and an applicant. The interviewer, however, may use a relevant job description and job specification as a guide to conduct the interview in a more meaningful manner.

Patterned interview, conversely, is conducted in accordance with a predetermined sequence of questions. These questions are provided in a set of patterned interview forms that are designed for various positions such as managerial, clerical, or technical. The prime purpose of the patterned interview is to obtain facts about the applicant's technical competence as well as to uncover personality patterns, attitudes, and motivation.[11] A typical **patterned interview form** used during such an interview is presented in Exhibit 2–19.

Structured interview is based on a series of job-related questions with predetermined answers that are consistently asked of all applicants for a particular job.[12] This type of interview is similar to a patterned interview in that both contain a set of predetermined questions. However, a structured interview involves many questions that are job-related and have been developed through analysis of a particular job. Furthermore, a selected team of supervisors prepares a set of suitable answers that is subsequently used to grade applicants' answers. Structured interviews usually provide more reliable results during the employee selection process since they are based on clearer consensus among interviewers regarding the applicants' performance during the interview. A typical **structured interview form** used during such an interview is presented in Exhibit 2–20.

Serialized interview is a method whereby an applicant is interviewed by two or more persons separately before the final selection decision is reached. Each interviewer may use any of the interview methods described above and rate the applicant on an individual basis. Subsequently, all applicant's ratings are compared before the hiring decision is made.

To secure the most effective employee selection result, it is essential that the interviewers understand the basic principles of conducting employment interviews and avoid common interviewing mistakes. Among these mistakes are:

- *First impression.*   Some interviewers often make up their mind about certain applicants even before the actual interview takes place. This may be attributed to the applicant's personal appearance or specific details in the application form.
- *Negative factors.*   Some interviewers are frequently more influenced by the negative facts about applicants than by their positive features.
- *Poor knowledge of the job.*   Some interviewers are not sufficiently familiar with particular job requirements or what kind of applicant would be most suitable for such a job, or both.
- *Urgency to hire.*   Some interviewers may be under pressure to hire an applicant for a particular position as a result of urgency in a specific employment situation.
- *Applicant order error.*   Some interviewers rate applicants on the basis of the preceding employment interviews. Thus, after several unsuitable candidates have been interviewed, an average candidate may be assessed in a more favorable manner.
- *Applicants communication skills.*   Some interviewers rate applicants on the basis of their communication abilities rather than on their professional skills. Thus, a more articulate person with lesser professional skills may often make a better impression than the less articulate person with higher professional qualifications.

Exhibit 2–19

Patterned Interview Form—Executive Position

PATTERNED INTERVIEW FORM — EXECUTIVE POSITION

Date _____ 19 _____

SUMMARY

Rating: | 1 | 2 | 3 | 4 |

Comments: _____
In making final rating, be sure to consider not only what the applicant can do but also his/her stability,

industry, perserverance, loyalty, ability to get along with others, self-reliance, leadership, maturity, motivation, and domestic situation and health.

_____

_____

_____

Interviewer: _____ Job Considered for: _____

Name _____ Date of birth _____ Phone No. _____

Present address _____ City _____ State _____ How long there? _____
Is this a desirable neighborhoood? Too High class? Too cheap?

Previous address _____ City _____ State _____ How long there? _____
Is this a desirable neighborhoood? Why did he/she move?

What kind of a car do you own? _____ Age _____ Condition of car _____
Will he be able to use his/her car if necessary?

Were you in the Armed Forces of the U.S.? Yes, branch _____

If not, why not? _____

Are you employed now? Yes ☐ No ☐ (If yes) How soon available? _____
What are his/her relationships with present employer?

Why are you applying for this position? _____
Is his/her underlying reason a desire for prestige, security, or earnings?

WORK EXPERIENCE. Cover all positions. This information is very important. Interviewer should record last position first. Every month since leaving school should be accounted for. Experience in Armed Forces should be covered as a job.

LAST OR PRESENT POSITION

Company _____ City _____ From _____ 19 ____ to _____ 19 ____
Do these dates check with his/her application?

How was job obtained _____ Whom did you know there? _____
Has he/she shown self-reliance in getting his/her jobs?

Nature of work at start _____ Starting salary _____
Will his/her previous experience be helpful on this job?

In what way did the job change? _____
Has he/she made good work progress?

Nature of work at leaving _____ Salary at leaving _____
How much responsibility has he/she had? Any indication of ambition?

Superior _____ Title _____ What is he/she like? _____
Did he/she get along with superior?

How closely does (or did) he/she supervise you? _____ What authority do (or did) you have? _____

Number of people you supervised _____ What did they do? _____
Is he/she a leader?

Responsibility for policy formulation _____
Has he/she had management responsibility?

To what extent could you use initiative and judgement? _____
Did he/she actively seek responsibility?

Exhibit 2–20

Structured Interview Form

Structured Interview Form (With answers)

Department: Marketing and Sales	Position: Salesperson

Instruction: Conduct questioning and complete the interview evaluation

1. Q: What does a successful salesperson need to know?
   A: His or her company's sales policy and objectives; products or services.

2. Q: What does a successful salesperson need to identify?
   A: New prospects; requirements of existing and potential customers; relevant developments and innovations in the marketplace.

3. Q: What does a successful salesperson need to do?
   A: Planning sales calls in advance; pursuing existing and potential customers through a direct or indirect selling approach; maintaining effective time management control; preparing and conducting effective sales presentations; preparing accurate and competitive cost estimates; conducting effective negotiations with customers; maintaining updated sales records; obtaining orders from customers.

4. Q: What does a successful salesperson need to accomplish?
   A: Meeting company's sales objectives; satisfying customer needs; securing sound relations between the company and its customers; contributing to the growth of the customer base.

5. Q: What are the basic stages in the personal selling process?
   A: Understanding the interaction between buyers and sellers; locating and qualifying prospects; developing a suitable approach to a customer; analysing the customer's specific requirements; preparing and conducting a formal presentation; overcoming customer objections and excuses; closing the sale to the customer; following-up the sale.

6. Q: What are the basic methods of closing a sale?
   A: Alternative choice; summary close; assumption close; special concession close; last chance close; confirmation close.

Interview Evaluation:					
Description	Very poor	Poor	Fair	Good	Very good
1. Understanding of the salesperson's functions and tasks					
2. Prior experience					
3. Potential selling ability					
Conclusion:					

Starting salary:		Starting date:	
Interviewer:	Approved:		Date:

To conduct an employment interview in the most effective manner, it is essential to adopt the following steps:

1. Plan the interview
2. Establish a friendly atmosphere
3. Ask the right questions
4. Close the interview
5. Review the interview
6. Select the most suitable candidate

Every interview should be planned in advance. The candidate's application form or a resume should be evaluated on a preliminary basis to identify strengths, weaknesses, and potential suitability for the job. Such an evaluation should be conducted in conjunction with a particular job description and specification requirements. Upon completion of the preliminary evaluation, it is useful to write down a number of questions in order to clarify matters of concern. Finally, it is important to allocate a private office for conducting the employment interview and to ensure that interruptions are kept to a minimum.

It is important to ensure that the applicant feels comfortable during the employment interview. It is useful, therefore, to spend the first few minutes of the interview in a general discussion concerning a particular topic of the day. This approach will reduce the tension and, hopefully, enable applicants to present themselves most effectively. Finally, by establishing a friendly atmosphere, the interviewer will have the opportunity to express human qualities toward the applicant, even if the job may ultimately be offered to another candidate.

The interviewer should select the most suitable type of employment interview and conduct it by asking relevant questions. It is advisable to ask questions to which the applicant will have the opportunity to provide detailed answers. The interviewer should avoid interrogating or patronizing the applicant during the interview. Instead, questions should be asked in an open-minded and constructive manner in order to encourage applicants to express themselves freely. A list of typical questions that could be asked by the interviewer are summarized in Exhibit 2–21.

Upon completing the questioning of an applicant, the interviewer should steer the interview toward its final stage. It is appropriate at this point to give to potentially suitable candidates more details about the company and to inform them that the final decision will be made shortly. It is advisable to close the interview in a friendly manner, whether the applicant may or may not be suitable for the position.

After the applicant has left, it is essential to summarize all issues discussed and notes taken during the interview. This should be done while all details are still fresh in the interviewer's mind. It is important to review the interview objectively and to avoid common mistakes described earlier.

Upon reviewing all information pertaining to each applicant and summarizing relevant details, it is essential to finalize the employee selection process as soon as possible. The selection decision should be made through a candid discussion with other members of the selection team, and each applicant should be informed accordingly.

Upon completing the screening and interviewing of applicants, management needs to proceed with the selection of the most suitable candidate. Once such candidate is selected, an appropriate job offer must be prepared. Various job offers for senior positions are usually accompanied by a **letter of appointment**,

Exhibit 2–21

Interview Questions from the Employer

Starters

- Can I see your résumé?
- How can I help you?
- Why do you want to join our company?
- What can you offer our company?
- Do you have suitable qualifications?
- What appeals to you about our company?

About education

- Outline your education in detail.
- What were your most favorite subjects?
- What was your major?
- Why did you choose your major?
- Where did you come in your class?
- What activities did you participate in?
- What merits did you earn?
- What was your average grade?
- Did you perform to your full potential? How come?
- What were your favorite courses at university? Why?

About experience

- Outline your experience in detail.
- Why do you think you should be hired?
- Why are you suited to this job?
- What role did you perform in the military?
- How could you improve our operations?
- What past responsibilities did you enjoy most/least? Why?
- What are your major strengths and weaknesses for this job?
- Who were your most/least favorite supervisors? Why?
- Who were you drawn to most/least as co-workers? Why?
- How many people did you supervise?
- Who were your most/least favorite subordinates? Why?
- With what machinery/equipment are you familiar?
- State your highest achievements.
- Why have you made so many job changes?
- Have you ever been terminated or asked to leave? Why?
- What is the biggest problem you ever encountered in your career?

About motivation

- Are you generally motivated and enthusiastic about your work?
- What has caused you to want to make the change?
- Why are you leaving military service now?
- Where would you like to be 1/3/5 years from now? Why?
- What job would you ideally like to do? Why?
- What type of work would you like to avoid doing? Why?
- With what were you occupied during the period excluded from your resume?
- What caused you to leave your past jobs?
- Do you have work samples to show me?
- How well do you perform as a subordinate/supervisor?
- How well do you handle pressure?
- What do you think are the key factors to perform your job well?
- Does your present employer know that you want to leave?

About expectations

- What salary/wages do you expect? What is the *minimum* you will accept?
- What are your expectations of working conditions?
- Do you prefer fixed or flexible hours?
- Do you want to work overtime and on the weekends if possible?
- Do you want to work second and third shifts when needed?
- Are you willing to relocate?
- What are your aspirations?
- What additional compensation and fringe benefits do you expect?
- Are you a team-player or do you prefer to work alone?
- When do you plan to retire?

SOURCE: Adapted from Richard Lathrop, *Who's Hiring Who* (Reston, Va: Reston Publishing, 1976), pp. 169–171. Reprinted in Gary Dessler, *Personnel Management*, 4th ed. (Englewood Cliffs, NJ.: Prentice Hall, 1988), pp. 217–218.

Exhibit 2–22

Specimen Letter of Appointment

Specimen Letter of Appointment of a Senior Manager

The text of a letter of appointment written by the Chief Executive on official company letterheads confirming the appointment of, say, a Marketing Executive may take the following format:

Dear (name):

<u>Marketing executive</u>

I am pleased to inform you that at a meeting of the Board of Directors held yesterday, my recommendation that you be appointed to the above position within the company was unanimously accepted.

Please accept this letter as confirmation of your appointment with effect from (date) together with Annexures I and II regarding matters of remuneration and conditions of service as discussed in our previous interviews. Your signature as indicated on the relevant copies returned at your early convenience will confirm your acceptance of this appointment.

I take this opportunity on behalf of myself and my colleagues to welcome you to our organization where, I am sure your background of achievement will prove of immense value in contributing to our program of development. I look forward to a long and mutually beneficial relationship.

Yours faithfully,

_____

(President)

Annexure I would contain the following details:

- Salary per annum and monthly
- Over-riding commission and/or bonus structure
- Incremental structure
- Expense account and limitations
- Motor vehicle type, usage, and running costs
- Method of payment of travelling and hotel expenses
- Vacation allowance
- Pension scheme contributions
- Family and/or educational benefits

Annexure II would outline the duties and responsibilities of the position of Marketing Executive together with the amount of delegated authority vested in this position.

---

which confirms such an offer in writing and briefly outlines the conditions of employment. A typical specimen letter of appointment is presented in Exhibit 2–22.

2.09 Personnel Orientation

Once the selection of applicants has been accomplished, it is essential to "convert" them into company employees. At this stage, the employment applications are accepted and the applicants should undergo a process of formal introduction to their jobs within the company as well as meeting with fellow employees. This process is known as **personnel orientation**.

The main purpose of personnel orientation is to facilitate a process of smooth integration of new employees into the existing organization. Furthermore, this process plays an important part in reducing the tension and anxiety of new employees during the initial working period. Apart from generating tension and anxiety, the job changing process may also be accompanied by a move to a new location, change of social environment, and possibly high expectations about the new job.[13] It is essential, therefore, that management understands the needs and expectations of employees and assists them in coping with new working conditions. Personnel orientation consists of three basic elements:

- *General company orientation.* This entails an overview of the organization, explanation of the company's policies, rules and regulations, details of compensation, benefits, safety information, unions, and physical facilities.
- *Specific departmental orientation.* This entails an overview of the departmental functions, policies, procedures, and job duties.
- *Socialization with other employees.* This entails a familiarization tour within the company and introduction to fellow employees.

Management in various companies develops orientation programs to meet specific organizational needs. Such programs range from brief introductions to lengthy and formal personnel orientation procedures. Some of the typical items pertinent to personnel orientation are summarized in Exhibit 2–23. These are generally categorized as follows:

Exhibit 2–23

Details of Personnel Orientation

General Company Orientation

The following items are among those typically included in this first phase:

1. Overview of the organization—brief history, what the organization does (products/services), where it does it (branches, etc), how it does it (nature of operations), structure (organization chart), etc.

2. Policies and procedures—work schedules, vacations, holidays, grievances, identification badges, uniforms, leaves of absence (sickness, educational, military, maternity/paternity, personal), promotion, transfers, training, etc.

3. Compensation—pay scale, overtime, holiday pay, shift differentials, when and how paid, time clock, etc.

4. Benefits—insurance, retirement, tax-sheltered annuities, credit union, employee discounts, suggestion system, recreational activities, etc.

5. Safety information—relevant policies and procedures, fire protection, first aid facilities, safety committee, etc.

6. Union—name, affiliation, officials, joining procedure, contract, etc.

7. Physical facilities—plant/office layout, employee entrance, parking, cafeteria, etc.

Specific Departmental Orientation

The following items are typically covered in this phase:

1. Department functions—explanation of the objectives, activities, and structure of the department along with a description of how the department's activities relate to those of other departments and of the overall company.

2. Job duties—a detailed explanation of the duties of the new employee's job (give him/her a copy of the job description) and how the job relates to the activities of the department.

3. Policies and procedures—those that are unique to the department such as breaks, rest periods, lunch hour, use of time sheets, safety, etc.

4. Department tour—a complete familiarization with the departmental facilities, including lockers, equipment, emergency exits, supply room, etc.

5. Introduction to departmental employees

SOURCE: "Let's Not Forget About New Employee Orientation" by R. W. Hollman. Reprinted with permission from *Personnel Journal*, Costa Mesa, California. Copyright May, 1976. All rights reserved.

- General company orientation items
- Specific departmental orientation items

Implementation of the orientation program depends upon the specific organizational structure of the company. The first phase of this process is usually handled by the personnel manager, who is familiar with all aspects of general

Exhibit 2–24

Orientation Program Checklist

ITEMS TO BE DISCUSSED BY DEPARTMENT HEAD OR SUPERVISOR WITH NEW EMPLOYEE:

First Day of Employment
☐ 1. Introduction to co-workers
☐ 2. Information on location of facilities

A. Coat room	D. Bulletin board
B. Cafeteria	E. Coffee service
C. Wash room	F. Provision for lunch

Rules and Policies
☐ 3. Hours: starting, lunch, dismissal time, hours per week
☐ 4. Pay: when, where, and how paid—overtime policy
      (Explain deductions when 1st check is received.)
☐ 5. Holidays and vacations in detail
☐ 6. Probationary period
☐ 7. Absences: Pay policies—before and after 5 months. When
         and whom to phone. Visit to medical dept. or
         doctor's note before return to work after absence
         of 3 or more days.
☐ 8. Organizational structure:
         Corporation—division—department—section
☐ 9. Rules on:
         Tardiness, telephone coverage, behavior, etc.

During First Two Weeks of Employment
☐ 10. Accident:
            Reporting accident or injury on job
☐ 11. Employee's discount on XYZ Company products
☐ 12. Salary checks—explanation of deductions
☐ 13. Salary reviews
☐ 14. Employee appraisal plan
☐ 15. Suggestion system
☐ 16. Reporting change in address, name, phone, etc.
☐ 17. Invite questions and help on problems

As indicated by check marks, all of the above items have been discussed with the employee.

The employee has been advised as to the time and extent of 1st vacation as shown by the Table on last page of this form.

Employee has been instructed to attend the second scheduled meeting and to bring this check list with him.

DEPARTMENT HEAD OR SUPERVISOR

DATE

Exhibit 2–24

(concluded)

NAME OF
EMPLOYEE _____   STARTING
                                          DATE _____

DEPARTMENT _____   LOCATION _____

ITEMS COVERED BY PERSONNEL RELATIONS DEPARTMENT OR
BRANCH OFFICE ON FIRST DAY OF ORIENTATION: (45 minutes)

PART 1—Organization and personnel policies & procedures

☐ 1. XYZ Company organization
☐ 2. Basic insurance benefits (*Paid in full by the company*)
  ☐ A. Hospitalization
  ☐ B. Short-term disability
  ☐ C. Basic life insurance
  ☐ D. Travel accident
☐ 3. Optional insurance benefits (*Paid for by you and the company*)
  ☐ A. Comprehensive medical
  ☐ B. Contributory life insurance
  ☐ C. Long-term disability
☐ 4. Vacations   ☐ 11. XYZ Company news
☐ 5. Holidays   ☐ 12. Tuition refund plan
☐ 6. Probationary period   ☐ 13. Building facilities
☐ 7. Compensation   ☐ 14. New building
☐ 8. Job evaluation   ☐ 15. XYZ Company and you
☐ 9. Medical absence   ☐ 16. Equal opportunity
☐10. Personal status change   employment
      notice

★★★★★★

APPOINTMENT FOR SECOND MEETING: (45 minutes)

DATE _____ *TIME* _____

        IMPORTANT: *BE SURE TO BRING THIS FORM BACK
                    WITH YOU, SIGNED BY YOUR MANAGER
                    WHEN YOU COME TO YOUR SCHEDULED
                    MEETING.*

PART II—Personnel policies and procedures

☐ 1. Review & questions on   ☐ 7. XYZ Company investment
      Part 1   plan
☐ 2. Retirement program   ☐ 8. U.S. savings bonds
☐ 3. College gift matching   ☐ 9. Employee activities
      plan   ☐10. Suggestion system
☐ 4. Time off the job   ☐11. Personnel inventory
☐ 5. Award for recruiting
☐ 6. Credit union

_____
PERSONNEL RELATIONS STAFF REPRESENTATIVE

_____
DATE

SOURCE: Joseph Famularo, *Modern Personnel Administration*, (New York: McGraw-Hill Inc, 1972). Reprinted with permission.

orientation. The second phase of the orientation program is normally handled by the departmental manager or the immediate supervisor of the new employee. A typical sequence of orientation procedures is illustrated in Exhibit 2–24.

2.10 Personnel Training

The first managerial task in individual development entails conversion of the applicant into a valuable employee. The successful applicant is not always entirely suited to the job and may require further training. Management's prime function is, therefore, to identify the need for **personnel training** to improve overall organizational performance. Additional results that management can expect from personnel training include the following:

- Increased productivity
- Reduced cost of materials and machine downtime
- Increased financial compensation to employees
- Higher morale and job satisfaction among employees
- Reduced turnover of employees
- Reduced level of supervision requirements
- Increased profitability of the organization

The training of personnel should be carried out in accordance with the equal employment opportunity laws described earlier. This process entails four basic steps:

1. Assessment of individual training requirements
2. Setting of specific training objectives
3. General and technical training of employees
4. Evaluation of training results

Assessment of individual training requirements can be accomplished through **job analysis, task analysis**, and **performance analysis**. Job analysis has been discussed earlier. This method results in the development of detailed job descriptions and job specifications, which are helpful in determining individual training requirements. The second method, task analysis, is particularly appropriate for new employees. This method is based on a detailed examination of a specific job and identification of appropriate skill requirements. Subsequently the employee's skills are assessed in accordance with basic skill requirements to establish the need for additional training. Some employers use a **task analysis record form** for determining training needs of new employees. This form summarizes information pertaining to a particular job and becomes the basic reference point for determining specific training requirements. A typical task analysis record form for a printing press operator is illustrated in Exhibit 2–25.

Another effective element of task analysis is a **job inventory form** for a specific position within the organization. Such a form helps to identify the importance of a particular task and to specify the amount of time that should be spent performing it. A typical example of a job inventory form for a salesperson is illustrated in Exhibit 2–26.

The third method entails the actual appraisal of the employee's performance on the job and identification of performance deficiencies. Significant perfor-

Exhibit 2–25

Task Analysis Record Form

Task Analysis Record Form					
Task list	When and how often performed	Quantity and quality of performance	Conditions under which performed	Skills or knowledge required	Where best learned
1. Operate paper cutter	4 times per day		Noisy pressroom: distractions		
1.1 Start motor					
1.2 Set cutting distance		± tolerance of 0.007 in.		Read gauge	On the job
1.3 Place paper on cutting table		Must be completely even to prevent uneven cut		Lift paper correctly	≈
1.4 Push paper up to cutter				Must be even	On the job but practice first with no distractions
1.5 Grasp safety release with left hand		100% of time, for safety		Essential for safety	
1.6 Grasp cutter release with right hand				Must keep both hands on releases	≈
1.7 Simultaneously pull safety release with left hand and cutter release with right hand				≈	≈
1.8 Wait for cutter to retract		≈		≈	≈
1.9 Retract paper				Wait till cutter retracts	≈
1.10 Shut off		≈			
2. Operate printing press					
2.1 Start motor					
Prepared:		Approved:		Date:	

SOURCE: Gary Dessler, *Personnel Management,* 4e, ©1988, p. 246. Adapted by permission of Prentice Hall, Inc., Englewood Cliffs, New Jersey.

mance deficiencies will define the need for further general or technical training. An ordinary performance analysis procedure consists of ten steps as follows:

1. Appraise your employee's current performance and determine whether this should be improved and to what extent.

Exhibit 2–26

Job Inventory Form

Job Inventory Form		
Department: Sales	Position: Salesperson	
Instruction	Task importance	Task frequency
Specify the importance and frequency of each task specified below	A - Very important B - Important C - Fairly important D - Slightly important E - Not important	A - Daily B - Weekly C - Monthly D - Semi-annually E - Annually
Task Description	A/B/C/D/E	A/B/C/D/E
1. Familiarize yourself with the company products	A	A
2. Familiarize yourself with the competitors' products	A	A
3. Familiarize yourself with personal selling techniques	A	A
4. Service existing company customers	A	A
5. Initiate contacts with potential customers	A	A
6. Update the sales literature and samples	A	C
7. Maintain detailed sales records	A	B
8. Prepare comprehensive sales reports	A	C
9. Maintain appropriate appearance on the job	A	A
10. Conform to the company's overall sales practices	A	A
11. Attend routine sales meetings	A	C
12. Attend seminars and training sessions	B	D
13. Prepare expense and entertainment reports	B	C
14. Adhere to the company's rules	A	A
Prepared by: B.Gray	Approved: A. Green	Date: 3.3.90

SOURCE: Kenneth Wexley and Gary Latham, *Developing and Training Human Resources*, (Glenview, Ill.: Scott, Foresman, 1981), p.44.

2. Conduct a cost/value analysis and determine whether additional expenses in training and for other efforts are justified in rectifying the existing problem. Ask, for example, "What is the cost of *not* solving the problem?"

3. Distinguish between *can't do* and *won't do* problems. The central question here is, "Could the employee do the job if he or she wanted to?" To distinguish between *can't do* and *won't do* problems ask such questions as: "Does the person know what to do and what you expect in terms of performance?" "Could the person do the job if he or she wanted to?" and "Does the person want to do the job, and what are the consequences of performing well?" If the problem is identified as *can't do*, proceed with step 4. If, on the other hand, the problem is identified as *won't do*, proceed with step 10.

4. Set appropriate performance standards and ensure that employees understand what is expected from them.

5. Identify and eliminate any obstacles in the system that cause a particular problem in employee performance.

6. Ensure that employees practice their skills continually.

7. Establish whether additional training may improve employee performance, and implement appropriate training methods.

8. Establish whether changing a particular job or task may improve the overall performance of an employee, and adjust job requirements accordingly.

9. Transfer or terminate those employees who fail to meet the required standards of performance despite all efforts undertaken by them and by management.

10. Develop suitable motivation techniques to improve the performance of those employees who are identified as *can do* but *won't do* the job. Motivation techniques may include special rewards or punishment, depending upon the specific circumstances within the organization.[14]

Evaluation of individual training requirements enables management to establish suitable training objectives for employees. The setting of these objectives should be carried out in accordance with job description requirements pertinent to specific jobs. Moreover, since training is essentially a learning process, managers should familiarize themselves with basic principles of learning. Some of these principles are as follows:

1. Start the training process by providing trainees with an overview of the learning material. This helps trainees to visualize the whole picture and provides better understanding of how each step fits into the learning process.

2. Use simple language, diagrams, and examples when presenting learning material to trainees. This helps trainees to understand each step of the learning process.

3. Subdivide learning material into smaller sections instead of presenting it all together. This enables trainees to absorb learning material in a more effective manner.

4. Maximize the similarity between training conditions and actual working conditions. This helps trainees to be better prepared for applying the learning material in a real working environment.

5. Label or identify important features of the task (e.g., "start the machine," "insert the work piece"). This helps trainees to memorize specific tasks and their sequence.

6. Provide trainees with the opportunity to apply learning material in a real life situation. This helps trainees to improve their skill in the actual working environment.

7. Provide trainees with feedback as soon and as often as possible. This helps trainees to understand whether or not they have absorbed material in an efficient manner.

8. Since learning abilities vary from one trainee to another, it is necessary to allow trainees to learn at their own pace. This enables trainees to absorb the learning material more effectively.

9. Motivate trainees during the learning process and explain the importance of additional training.[15]

There are several types of general and technical training methods frequently used by small and medium-sized companies. Some of these methods are

- On-the-job training
- In-house training program
- Apprenticeship training program
- Education courses

On-the-job training is probably one of the most popular personnel training methods. This method is used most effectively by managers in equipping employees with additional skills for improved performance. Training on the job occurs in the context of the actual working environment and has a distinct advantage due to its practical approach and effective motivation of employees. According to Gary Dessler, a useful step-by-step approach for providing a new employee with on-the-job training is summarized as follows:

Step 1: Preparation of the learner

1.1. Put the learner at ease—relieve the tension.

1.2. Explain why he or she is being taught.

1.3. Create interest, encourage questions, find out what the learner already knows about his or her job or other jobs.

1.4. Explain the reason for the whole job and relate it to some job the worker already knows.

1.5. Place the learner as close to the normal working position as possible.

1.6. Familiarize the worker with the equipment, materials, tools, and trade terms.

Step 2: Presentation of the operation

2.1. Explain quantity and quality requirements.

2.2. Go through the job at the normal work pace.

2.3. Go through the job at a slow pace several times, explaining each step. Between operations, explain the difficult parts or those in which errors are likely to be made.

2.4. Again go through the job at a slow pace several times, explaining the key points.

2.5. Have the learner explain the steps as you go through the job at a slow pace.

Step 3: Performance tryout

3.1. Have the learner go through the job several times slowly, explaining to you each step. Correct mistakes and, if necessary, do some of the complicated steps the first few times.

3.2. You, the trainer, run the job at the normal pace.

3.3. Have the learner do the job, gradually building up skill and speed.

3.4. As soon as the learner demonstrates ability to do the job, let the work begin, but don't abandon him or her.

Step 4: Follow-up

4.1. Designate to whom the learner should go for help if he or she needs it.

4.2. Gradually decrease supervision, checking work from time to time against quality and quantity standards.

4.3. Correct faulty work patterns that begin to creep into the work, and do so before they become habits. Show why the learned method is superior.

4.4. Compliment good work; encourage the worker until he or she is able to meet the quality and quantity standards.[16]

In-house training program is more effective where a substantial number of employees perform a similar function. On-the-job training, discussed earlier, might not be effective in this instance, since it requires unnecessary additional effort from the manager. The in-house training should be handled by a member of the management staff specially employed for this purpose.

Apprenticeship training program is one of the most professional educational methods and combines training on the job with the in-house training program. This program is widely used in industry to train various artisans, such as electricians, machine operators, turners, welders, grinders, and fitters. The apprenticeship training programs are usually developed by government labor departments in conjunction with certain professional educational institutions.

Education courses are designed to teach a substantial number of trainees by means of standard educational procedures such as sets of programmed courses, seminars, and audio-visual classes. This method is based on principles that provide specific objectives, a logical sequence of information, and active trainee participation. The program allows trainees to absorb information in accordance with their individual abilities and provides sufficient feedback on the effectiveness of a specific course.

The final stage of personnel training entails evaluation of training results. Managers often assume that the training of employees automatically leads to improved efficiency of performance. This, unfortunately, is not so. It is important, therefore, to determine the following:

- Did the employee find the training stimulating and useful?
- Did the employee learn new working methods or principles?
- Did the employee's individual performance change as a result of the training program?
- Did the personnel training improve overall performance results of the company?

In addition to development and implementation of effective personnel training programs, it is necessary to initiate and to maintain a continuous management development process. This process represents the cornerstone of successful organizational performance and is discussed next.

2.11 Management Development

Until fairly recently, the profession of manager had no clear descriptive definition unlike professions such as engineer, medical doctor, or accountant. This situation, however, has changed since the introduction of several professional management programs. Such programs include MBA courses offered by various universities and business schools and seminars offered by Business Management Club.

Management development is of prime importance to most organizations. It facilitates continuous growth, motivation, and promotion of employees to senior positions within the company. According to a recently conducted survey of 84 employers, 90% of supervisors, 73% of middle-level managers, and 51% of executives were promoted from within. Most of these managers, however, required additional training.[17]

Management development starts with a detailed assessment of managerial skills that may be required by the company in the future. This depends upon the company's short-, medium- and long-term plans and objectives. It is essential, therefore, to evaluate the promotion potential of managers currently employed by the company and to identify the need for further managerial development.

The promotion potential of managers can be evaluated by reviewing the individual personnel inventory and development record compiled on each employee. A typical illustration of such a record was presented earlier in Exhibit 2–11. This record highlights specific skills, education, experience, career preferences, and performance appraisal results of a particular manager.

Upon reviewing the individual personnel inventory and development record, it is useful to develop an updated management replacement chart. An example of such a chart has been presented earlier in Exhibit 2–12. This chart summarizes present performance, promotion potential, and required development details for each managerial candidate within the organization.

Management development needs depend upon the specific managerial level and are summarized in Exhibit 2–27. These needs are qualified as follows:

- Management needs for executive level
- Management needs for middle level
- Management needs for supervisory level

Management development is usually accomplished through suitable professional and educational training programs for supervisors and managers. These programs aim to ensure the development of sufficient skills, enabling the managers to perform their duties effectively and to provide adequate guidance to their subordinates.

There are several methods used in the process of management development. These methods include managerial on-the-job training, professional coaching, in-house workshops, job rotation, university and consulting programs, seminars, and self-study courses. The popularity of these methods varies among executive, middle, and supervisory management levels, as illustrated in Exhibit 2–28.

Managerial on-the-job training is considered one of the most popular management development methods used by small and medium-sized companies. This method is frequently supplemented by professional coaching, job rotation, and other in-house training programs. Managerial on-the-job training can provide the manager with invaluable practical experience. This experience will contribute to the improved level of job knowledge and development of general managerial skills.

Exhibit 2–27

Management Development Needs

Executive Level	Middle Level	Supervisory Level
1. Managing time	1. Evaluating and appraising employees	1. Motivating others
2. Team building	2. Motivating others	2. Evaluating and appraising others
3. Organizing and planning	3. Setting objectives and priorities	3. Leadership
4. Evaluating and appraising employees	4. Oral communication	4. Oral communication
5. Coping with stress	5. Organizing and planning	5. Understanding human behavior
6. Understanding human behavior	6. Understanding human behavior	6. Developing and training subordinates
7. Self-analysis	7. Written communication	7. Role of the manager
8. Motivating others	8. Managing time	8. Setting objectives and priorities
9. Financial management	9. Team building	9. Written communication
10. Budgeting	10. Leadership	10. Discipline
11. Setting objectives and priorities	11. Decision making	11. Organizing and planning
12. Holding effective meetings	12. Holding effective meetings	12. Managing time
13. Oral communication	13. Delegation	13. Counseling and coaching
14. Labor/management relations	14. Developing and training subordinates	14. Selecting employees
15. Decision making	15. Selecting employees	15. Decision making
16. Developing strategies and policies		

Professional coaching in conjunction with on the job experience is considered to be another highly effective management training method used by small and medium-sized companies. The manager-in-training is given an opportunity not only to encounter actual day-to-day management problems and to provide feasible solutions but also to obtain simultaneous and professional feedback from a coaching supervisor. The task of effective management coaching requires a delicate balance of direction, professionalism, and freedom of choice. The manager-in-training should also occasionally be given an opportunity to fail and to learn by personal experience how to get back up. A certain amount of freedom of choice will allow the managers-in-training to develop their own managerial styles, thus ensuring further personal growth.

Job rotation method is based on a principle whereby the manager-in-training will spend a limited period of time with various departments and will subse-

Exhibit 2–28

Popularity of Various Types of Management Development Methods

Type of Development	Percent Receiving		
	Executive	Middle	Supervisory
External conference/seminars	27.7%	26.1%	17.3%
In-house workshops	22.9	21.6	34.7
Coaching plus on-the-job experience	13.3	29.5	33.4
Participation in university programs	10.8	10.2	4.0
Association/professional conferences and workshops	16.8	4.5	0
Consultant programs	7.2	5.7	5.3
Self-study courses	1.2	2.3	5.3

quently receive overall management experience. This method is particularly useful for recent college graduates. It helps them to identify new areas of interest and to discover which jobs they prefer. Job rotation of managers also improves cooperation between departments and enhances organizational flexibility. One of the disadvantages of this method is the periodic disruption caused by the actual process of job rotation. Some managers could become discouraged from settling down within the company and subsequently not be able to perform in the most efficient manner.

Seminars, professional conerences, workshops and **self-study courses** have also gained popularity in recent years. These are provided by several organizations such as Business Management Club, the American Management Associations (AMA), the Small Business Administration (SBA), American Society for Training and Development, and many others. A typical list of such organizations is presented in Exhibit 2–29.

Exhibit 2–29

A List of Some Organizations Offering Management Development Programs

Organization	Services
American Management Association	Trains leaders and provides program materials for numerous in-house courses in supervisory and management development.
Business Management Club	Offers "be-your-own-management-consultant" programs to business owners, conducts seminars and develops specialized business methods.
Addison-Wesly Publishing Company	Publishes books, audio-cassette programs, film strips, programmed texts, video programs, and reference materials.
AMR International, Inc.	Conducts management seminars and in-company programs on a variety of subjects including: management by objectives, successful negotiating, project financing, merging and selling companies, and others.
American Society for Training and Development	Sponsors workshops and seminars in supervisory and management development and publishes directories, workbooks, and handbooks on management development.
Battelle Memorial Institute	Offers a subscription program (Technical inputs to planning) designed to bridge the management-technology gap.
Conference Board	Offers management/executive conferences, seminars, publications, custom research, chief executive lunches.
Mantread, Inc.	Is a clearing house for management-training programs and services. Offers evaluation of training programs offered by others.
Sterling Institute	Conducts both standard and custom-tailored management courses either in-house or in outside facilities. Develops training modules for general use.
Strategic PLanning Institute	Is a data bank based on information from 150 companies—analyzes data for corporate members.
Westinghouse Learning	Offers numerous courses, workbooks, filmstrips, etc. for individual and group instruction.
Xerox Educational Systems	Develops custom-tailored programs and offers specialized packaged programs in a variety of managerial areas.

Note: This list contains only a sampling of organizations offering educational services or materials. A comprehensive list is published periodically by the American Society for Training and Development, Inc., P.O. Box 5307, Madison, Wisc. 53705.

SOURCE: From Donald P. Crane, *Personnel: The Management of Human Resources,* 4th ed. (Boston: Kent Publishing Company, 1986), p. 328. © by Wadsworth, Inc. Reprinted by permission of PWS-KENT Publishing Company, a division of Wadsworth, Inc.

2.12 Personnel Motivation

Personnel motivation describes management's ability to stimulate the employees to work willingly and enthusiastically. In order to accomplish this important managerial task, it is essential to examine various types of employees and to understand their needs and wants. Abraham Maslow, a famous psychologist, suggested that all basic human needs form a hierarchy, as illustrated in Exhibit 2–30, and may be categorized as follows:

- *Physiological needs*. The first level in Maslow's hierarchy covers physiological needs such as food, water, shelter, and rest.
- *Safety needs*. When the physiological needs are reasonably satisfied, the safety needs become important. These needs include a desire for safety, protection against danger, and security.
- *Social needs*. Once the physiological and safety needs are satisfied, they no longer influence behavior. At this stage the social needs become activated. These needs include a desire for friends, social interaction, and giving and receiving affection.
- *Ego needs*. The next level in the hierarchy contains the ego needs, which have been interpreted by Douglas McGregor as follows:
  1. Those needs that relate to one's self-esteem—needs for self-confidence, for independence, for achievement, for knowledge, and
  2. Those needs that relate to one's reputation—needs for status, for recognition, for appreciation, for the deserved respect of one's fellows.
- *Self actualization needs*. Finally, when the aforementioned needs are reasonably satisfied, the self-actualization needs start to motivate human behavior. These needs relate to a person's desire for fulfilment or personal accomplishment in certain areas of activity such as education or business.[18]

There are various methods that can be successfully implemented by management to motivate personnel. These methods include the following:

Exhibit 2–30

Maslow's Hierarchy of Human Needs

Self-actualization
needs

(becoming the
person you
know you are
capable of
becoming)

Ego needs

(recognition, etc.)

Social needs

(friends, etc.)

Safety needs

(a secure job, etc.)

Physiological
needs

(food, etc.)

SOURCE: Gary Dessler, *Personnel Management*, 4e, ©1988, p. 315. Adapted by permission of Prentice Hall, Inc., Englewood Cliffs, New Jersey.

- Attractive remuneration
- Fringe benefits
- Work security
- Interpersonal functional relations
- The opportunity to advance
- Work satisfaction
- Safe and comfortable working conditions
- Fair and competent management
- Correct guidance and reasonable orders
- Credit for good performance
- Sound social organizational structure

Attractive remuneration represents one of the most important wants of the employee that will satisfy physiological needs and will provide a sense of psychological security. Very often attractive remuneration alone cannot motivate the employee, so there is a need to satisfy other requirements.

Fringe benefits represent another important method of satisfying the employee's wants and of compensating ego needs.

Work security represents one of the high priority issues. The fulfilment of this desire will satisfy the employee's need for stability and security.

Interpersonal functional relations represent a human desire to be accepted by others and to become an important functional link within a specific working group. Management can assist in this task by means of effective advanced planning of the working process.

The opportunity to advance provides an essential solution to employees with a high level of motivation. It must be clarified that not all employees are willing to advance; therefore, it remains management's duty to identify appropriate candidates.

Work satisfaction provides an invaluable source of personal motivation for most employees. Management can help fulfil this need by means of a methodical approach to various operational tasks, ensuring their accomplishment to the mutual satisfaction of both the company and the employee. Most employees have a definite need to perform a meaningful function and to satisfy their desire for recognition.

Safe and comfortable working conditions represent the human desire to ensure the fulfilment of physiological needs for security and comfort. Management can assist in satisfying these needs by adhering to the principles of general safety and by creating suitable environmental conditions.

Fair and competent management has the essential responsibility to provide personnel with a feeling of security related to the stable future of the company and, subsequently, to the employee.

Correct guidance and reasonable orders should be used by management in the process of channeling information required by employees to fulfil their duties within the company. Incorrect guidance or unreasonable orders may cause unnecessary aggravation and frustration among personnel and serious damage to the company's interests.

Credit for good performance represents one of the ego needs of a human being. Management should be able to express its appreciation related to the working achievements of the employee. This can be done by means of verbal praise or specific monetary reward.

Sound social organizational structure represents the human need for higher social expectations as it is fulfilled during the working period within a company. This need is based on a human desire for self-esteem and necessitates management to maintain an acceptable level of organizational activities.[19]

Just as employees attempt to satisfy wants and needs, the company has to satisfy its own organizational objectives. To ensure a smooth alignment between these objectives and the wants of employees, management should provide sufficient motivation in the right direction. The underlying success of motivating personnel depends heavily on management's ability to identify basic human needs and to ensure their smooth integration in the process of achieving the organizational objectives.

According to William A. Cohen, there are 15 things that managers can do to motivate their employees:

1. Care about the people who work for you. The people who work for you don't have to become friends, but they are people and you should recognize them as such. You should be concerned with their problems and their opportunities both on the job and off.

2. Take responsibility for your actions. This means that, when you make a mistake, you should acknowledge it freely; don't try to blame it on an employee.

3. Be tactful with your employees. They are not pieces of machinery. They have feelings, thoughts, and ambitions. Therefore, they deserve respect and to be treated with tact.

4. Give praise when a job is well done. If your employee does something good, show that you appreciate it by your public recognition.

5. So far as possible, foster independence in your employees. Let them have as much authority and responsibility as they can handle.

6. Be willing to learn from your employees. You are not an expert on everything. Acknowledge expertise of those who work for you.

7. Always exhibit enthusiasm and confidence. Enthusiasm and confidence are infectious; if you are enthusiastic and confident, your employees will be also.

8. Keep open lines of communication to your employees so they can express their opinions, even if they disagree with you.

9. If your employee has a problem doing his or her job, don't just give orders. Give as much help as you can in order to allow your employee to do the job as best as he or she can.

10. Set standards for yourself and your company. Communicate these standards to your employees.

11. Always let your employees know where they stand—when you are happy with them and when you are unhappy. Never let them be in doubt.

12. Keep your employees informed about what's going on in the way of future plans in your company. If your employees can understand "the big picture," they can help you better by orienting their jobs to your overall objectives.

13. Encourage initiative, innovation, and ingenuity in your employees. Don't turn off ideas submitted by someone who works for you simply because he or she is not supposed to come up with ideas. Good ideas are hard to come by, and you want all you can get.

14. Be aware of your own prejudices and biases toward certain people. Do not allow these prejudices or biases to interfere with the way you treat them or your evaluation of their performance.

15. Always be flexible. The fact that you have done something one way since you started your business does not mean that it has been done right. Always be ready to change for something better.[20]

Adherence to the these principles enables managers to maintain a high level of personnel motivation, thereby ensuring successful organizational performance.

2.13 Basic Job Compensation

One of the prime operative functions of personnel management is developing and implementing an effective **personnel compensation plan**. This plan entails determination of fair and equitable remuneration, incentives, and nonfinancial benefits to employees. The main objectives of a personnel compensation plan are as follows:

- To attract suitable employees to the company
- To motivate personnel toward superior performance
- To retain personnel services during a specific period of time

Development of a suitable personnel compensation plan requires familiarization with equal employment opportunity and compensation laws. Some of these laws have been discussed earlier and summarized in Exhibit 2–3. Compensation laws established by the federal and state governments relate to the minimal level of wages, overtime rates, and benefits payable to employees. Some of the major compensation laws are summarized in Exhibit 2–31.

There are many other laws and regulations that have a considerable impact on establishing appropriate pay rates for employees. It is essential to adhere to these laws and to develop a comprehensive personnel compensation plan accordingly. Such a plan should include three major elements as follows:

- Basic job compensation
- Financial incentives
- Fringe benefits

Basic job compensation to employees is expressed in terms of monthly salaries and weekly wages and constitutes one of the highest costs incurred by the organization during its operating activities. Moreover, this type of compensation is of notable importance to company personnel. It represents a single source of the employees' financial support and is one of the most influential factors in determining their status in society.

The most significant factors affecting the determination of a basic job compensation, apart from personnel compensation laws, are as follows:

- The principle of supply and demand
- Labor unions
- The company's financial condition
- Cost-of-living factor

Employers and employees will always be in a situation of continuous and reciprocal need. Organizations require professional personnel and skilled labor to meet their corporate objectives. People need jobs to keep them occupied and to earn a living. The process of satisfying mutual needs and wants is based on a service for money exchange and is regulated by the *principle of supply and demand*.

The main objective of *labor unions* is to provide general support for employees and to establish an important mechanism regulating the process of supply and demand of skills on an open labor market. This factor is designed to determine a minimum level of salaries and wages payable to employees in the company. The actual hourly remuneration rates are usually developed on the basis of employees' abilities and work experience, thus ensuring a fair level of compensation and a "square deal" for both the company and the employee.

Exhibit 2–31

Summary of Major Compensation Laws

Laws	Coverage	Basic Requirements	Agencies Involved
Public Construction Act (Davis-Bacon Act)	Employers with federal construction contracts, or sub-contracts, of $2,000 or more	Employers must pay not less than the wages prevailing in the area as determined by the Secretary of Labor; overtime is to be paid at 1 1/2 times the basic wage for all work over 8 hours per day or 40 hours per week	Wage and Hour Division of the Labor Department
Public Contracts Act (Walsh-Healy Act)	Employers with federal contracts of $10,000 or more	Same as above	Same as above
Fair Labor Standards Act (wage and hour law)	Private employers engaged in interstate commerce, and retailers having annual sales of $325,000; many groups are exempted from overtime requirements	Employers must pay a minimum of $3.35* per hour; and at the rate of 1 1/2 times the basic rate for work over 40 hours per week; and are limited (by jobs and school status) in employing persons under 18	Same as above
Equal Pay Act	All employers	Men and women must receive equal pay for jobs requiring substantially the same skill, effort, responsibility, and working conditions	EEOC
Service Contracts Act	Employers with contracts to provide services worth $2,500 or more per year to the federal government	Same as Davis-Bacon	Same as Davis-Bacon

The minimum wage will increase to $3.80 by April 1990 and $4.25 by April 1991.

SOURCE: L.C. Megginson, *Personnel Management*, 4th ed. (Homewood, Ill.: Richard D. Irwin, 1981), p. 101. Reprinted with permission. Extracted from The Bureau of National Affairs, *BNA Policy and Practice Series: Wages and Hours* (Washington, D.C. GPO).

The *company's financial condition* normally determines its ability to employ suitable personnel to meet organizational objectives. The question is whether or not the company can afford to retain the services of a certain employee. Obviously, if the company is going through a difficult period, management will be forced to reduce the number of employees to a functional minimum. However, if the company is prospering, management will be in a position to offer an above average package, thus attracting the most suitable people to the organization.

The *cost-of-living factor* depends mainly upon the overall economic situation, rate of inflation, and specific geographic location. Sometimes this factor is regulated by the *cost-of-living adjustment (COLA)* provision, which was first adopted by the United Auto Workers in 1950. At present approximately one half of all major labor union contracts contain a COLA provision. The cost-of-living factor provides a realistic measure related to the salaries and wages adjustment process and, subsequently, enables management to review the company's remuneration policy from time to time.

The process of establishing a basic job compensation generally necessitates that management carry out the following tasks:

1. Conduct a compensation survey.
2. Evaluate a range of jobs.
3. Group similar jobs into pay grades.
4. Allocate pay rates to each pay grade.
5. Fine tune pay rates.[21]

Salary and wage surveys play a major part in the process of determining the basic job compensation for employees. Such surveys may be useful in establishing a preliminary compensation range for jobs that are comparable with other jobs in similar organizations. Furthermore, the compensation surveys may assist the management in classifying various jobs in the order of their relative worth to the company. Finally, these surveys provide important data about additional benefits such as medical insurance or leave pay offered in the open market.

Compensation surveys are conducted and published by several reliable sources. Among the prime sources of information are:

- *Bureau of Labor Statistics.* This organization conducts three types of surveys every year:
  1. Area wage surveys for clerical and manual jobs in manufacturing and nonmanufacturing industries.
  2. Industry wage surveys for different industries.
  3. Professional, administrative, technical, and clerical (PATC) surveys in fields such as legal and accounting services, engineering, and chemical industries.
- *The American Management Association (AMA).* This organization conducts surveys and provides executive, managerial, and professional compensation data as one of its services. The AMA also publishes extensive reports on middle management compensation covering a wide range of jobs and industries on a regional and national basis.[22]

Other organizations that provide useful information about personnel compensation are Administrative Management Society (AMS), American Society for Personnel Administrators, and Financial Executives Institute. Many small and medium-sized companies develop their basic job compensation policies solely on information provided by these organizations. If, however, management wants to ensure consistency in salary and wage structure and to establish a systematic relationship among basic compensation rates, it should evaluate various jobs within the company. There are a number of **job evaluation** methods available for this purpose:

- The ranking method
- The job classification method
- The point method
- The factor comparison method[23]

The **ranking method** is considered to be one of the most useful and inexpensive methods of job evaluation. This method necessitates that management prepares brief job descriptions for all major jobs within the company and ranks them in order of importance. During the actual ranking process the most important job will be selected as the top of the range and the least significant job will represent the bottom of such a range. All jobs in between will be compared with one another and will be placed according to their considered worth.

The **job classification method** is a simple and widely used method, whereby jobs are grouped into grades, or classes. This method necessitates that management selects a range of compensable factors and then develops a scale of grades or classes for different groups of jobs. The federal classification system, for example, includes the following factors:

1. Difficulty and variety of work
2. Supervision received and exercised
3. Judgment exercised
4. Originality required
5. Nature and purpose of interpersonal work relationships
6. Responsibility
7. Experience
8. Knowledge required

Each job is measured as a whole, compared with other jobs, and finally classified on the basis of the established scale of compensable factors.

The **point method** is considered to be one of the most popular methods of the job evaluation process. A standard procedure describing this process is as follows:

- Selection of job factors (such as education, skill, responsibility, effort, etc.)
- Construction of the job factor scales based on points (e.g., 1–10)
- Evaluation of the job according to the job factor scales
- Completion of salaries and wages survey
- Development of salaries and wages structure
- Adjustment of salaries and wages structure

The **factor comparison method** is based on a job-to-job comparison method reduced to the detailed evaluation of relevant job factors. A typical procedure describing this process follows:

- Selection of job factors
- Identification of key jobs
- Determination of correct rates for relevant key jobs
- Ranking of key jobs by selected job factors
- Allocation of correct rates for identified key jobs
- Evaluation of other jobs using these factors
- Development of salaries and wages structure
- Adjustment of salaries and wages structure

The process of job evaluation provides management with the ability to create a systematic remuneration structure based on the *principle of equity and compensation* so as to ensure satisfaction and a high level of motivation among company employees. Once the evaluation of jobs has been completed and their relative worth has been established, it is necessary to group similar jobs into specific pay grades.

A **pay grade** is generally comprised of jobs of similar complexity or importance as determined by the job evaluation process. The pay grade may be comprised of all jobs that fall into two or three ranks, if a ranking method was used, or a range of classes, if job classification method was used. Irrespective of the job evaluation method used, all jobs should be included in a range of pay grades. A medium-sized company, for example, may have five pay grades for the following jobs:

- Pay grade 1. This is for the president and executive vice-president.
- Pay grade 2. This is for vice presidents—finance, production and marketing.
- Pay grade 3. This is for managers, supervisors, and foremen.
- Pay grade 4. This is for senior production, office, and sales personnel.
- Pay grade 5. This is for junior production, office, and sales personnel.

The next step is to allocate pay rates to each pay grade in accordance with the prevailing level of compensation in the market place. A range of pay rates for a medium-sized company, for example, may be illustrated as follows:

- Pay grade 1. $50,000 - $70,000
- Pay grade 2. $40,000 - $50,000
- Pay grade 3. $30,000 - $40,000
- Pay grade 4. $20,000 - $30,000
- Pay grade 5. $10,000 - $20,000

Finally, it is necessary to adjust the salaries and wages structure for all jobs in every pay grade. This adjustment, or "fine tuning," of compensation to specific employees should be carried out in accordance with the job evaluation results.

2.14 Financial Incentives

Financial incentives represent an additional method of attracting personnel to a company. This method equips management with a distinct means of remunerating employees in accordance with their individual or group performance. Financial incentives expressed in monetary terms provide employees with an additional motivational force. The magnitude of this force relates directly to two factors:

- The degree of importance of additional remuneration to the employee
- The strength of expectancy of additional remuneration by the employee

To determine the effect of the motivational force on the employee, it is important to have some knowledge of the existing level of human needs. Despite various attitudes toward the motivational ability of monetary compensation, there is much evidence that money is an attractive and important motivational factor.

The level of expectancy of additional remuneration depends substantially upon the employee's perception of the following:

- Confidence in his or her own ability to perform in accordance with the established norm
- Confidence in the ability of management to provide additional remuneration

Management can assist its employees in building up their confidence by means of additional training and steady encouragement during the working process. Management can also increase the level of general confidence of personnel by creating a healthy atmosphere within the company.

There are several types of financial incentive plans used in various industries at present. Among these plans are

- Financial incentives for production personnel
- Financial incentives for managers
- Financial incentives for sales personnel
- Financial incentives for professional personnel[24]

Financial incentives for production personnel include a piece-rate plan, standard-hour plan, and group incentives plans. The *piece-rate*, or *piecework plan*, is probably the oldest and the most popular method of providing financial incentives to operators. In accordance with this plan, each operator's wages are calculated on the basis of his or her production output, or a piece rate. Thus if a welder gets $1 for welding a frame, then he or she will earn $30 for welding 30 frames a day or $50 for welding 50 frames. The piece-rate plan necessitates development of production standards, or *norms*, for various operations. These norms are usually expressed in terms of standard time per unit (e.g., minutes per operations, hours per part) or number of units per standard time (e.g., number of operations per minute, number of parts per hour).

Since the introduction of the Fair Labor Standards Act most companies are obliged to guarantee their workers a minimum hourly wage. This implies that the worker will be paid $3.80 per hour (minimum wage in 1990), regardless of the production output. It is useful, therefore, to introduce a piece-rate incentive plan in conjunction with the minimum hourly wage in order to stimulate the motivation of production employees and to increase overall productivity within the company.

The *standard-hour plan* is similar to the piece-rate plan, with one basic difference. In a piece-rate plan the operator is paid a specific rate per unit produced. In the standard-hour plan, the operator is guaranteed a minimum hourly wage and further rewarded with a bonus based on performance above a predetermined norm. If, for example, an operator completes a certain job in eight hours that normally takes ten hours, it means that two hours, or 20% of time, were effectively saved. Such an operator can be, therefore, awarded a time bonus based on time saved. Thus, if the normal wage rate is $5 per hour, the operator should be paid an additional 20%, or $6 per hour, for an appropriate working period.

The *group incentive plan* is designed to offer a financial incentive to a team of production employees. One of the approaches of this plan is to set a production standard for the whole team and to provide equal compensation to each member in accordance with the team's performance. Such a plan may prove to be effective when a particular task requires a team effort and cooperation among employees. Group incentive plan also stimulates a more effective on-the-job training since each member of the team is motivated to train new members in order to increase overall production output. The final compensation for a group effort can be based on a group piece-rate plan or a group standard-hour plan. Each of the aforementioned financial incentive methods has certain advantages and disadvantages. These methods, generally, are simple to calculate and easy to understand. The first two methods, however, are more advantageous if workers prefer individual financial incentives. The group incentive plan does not reward each worker on his or her personal effort.

Financial incentives for managers relate to the additional compensation system designed specifically for the company's managerial personnel. Such incentives are highly important since managers play a critical role in maintaining the company's performance on a desired level. All financial incentives for managers may be categorized as follows:

- *Short-term incentives* such as individual performance bonus, or corporate performance bonus.
- *Long-term incentives* such as stock options, book value plan, stock appreciation rights, performance achievement plan, restricted stock plans, and phantom stock plans.

Short-term financial incentives are generally offered to management in the form of an *annual cash bonus*. The value of such bonus may vary from 10% to 50% or more of a particular manager's monthly salary. There are several methods of determining the actual value of the cash bonus. Perhaps, the most effective method is to divide the bonus into two parts. One part is based on the individual performance, and the other part is based on the company's performance. Regardless of the method being used, it is important to remember the following:

> truly outstanding performers should never be paid less than their normal reward, regardless of organizational performance, and should get substantially larger awards than do other managers. They are people the company cannot afford to lose, and their performance should always be adequately rewarded by the organization's incentive system . . . marginal or below average performers should never receive awards that are normal or average, and poor performers should be awarded nothing. The money saved on these people should be given to above average performers.[25]

Long-term financial incentives, on the other hand, are designed to motivate and compensate senior managerial personnel for the long-term growth and success of the company. Such incentives are particularly useful in encouraging executives to stay and to grow with the organization for their mutual benefit. Long-term incentives are based on providing executive managers with an opportunity to accumulate capital or stock over an extended period. Among these incentives are:

- *Stock options.* This plan provides the right to purchase a certain number of shares of a company's stock at a prearranged price during a specific period of time. Such an option may be attractive to an executive who may assume that the price of the company's stock will increase.
- *Book value plan.* This plan serves as an alternative to a stock option and permits purchase of the company's stock at its current book value. Executives who participate in such a plan can earn dividends on stock in their possession and benefit from future increases in stock value.
- *Stock appreciation rights.* This plan provides the right to enjoy full benefit of stock holding without an obligation to purchase actual stock. Thus, it is the executive manager's choice whether to acquire the stock or simply to receive compensation for its appreciated value.
- *Performance achievement plan.* According to this plan executive managers should be awarded shares of the company's stock if they accomplish a predetermined range of financial objectives. Such objectives may include specific improvement of the company's annual net income or an increase of return on shareholders' equity.
- *Restricted stock plan.* This plan generally provides the right to obtain shares of the company's stock free of charge but with certain restrictions. These restrictions are specified in the Internal Revenue Code and impose a minimum period of service by the executive manager in order to avoid forfeiture of the stock.

- *Phantom stock plan.* This plan provides executive managers with special "units" that are equivalent to shares of the company's stock. Subsequently, managers are entitled to receive a monetary compensation equal to the appreciation of the "phantom" stock in their possession.

Financial incentives for sales personnel generally include sales commissions and, sometimes, special awards and bonuses. The sales commission percentages vary from one industry to another and usually depend upon the basic salary offered to a salesperson. In fact, monetary compensation offered to salespeople may be solely in the form of a straight salary, or basic salary and sales commission, or sales commission only. Each method has its advantages and disadvantages and is discussed in detail in Part 5 (Volume II).

Straight salary plan, for example, may provide the salesperson with a guaranteed income at the end of the month. The employer, on the other hand, may also prefer to have a fixed and predictable level of sales expenditure. One of the main disadvantages of this plan, however, is that it does not motivate sales personnel to substantially increase their level of sales.

Straight commission plan, conversely, is developed with the sole purpose of motivating salespeople in generating additional sales and producing results. Thus, a commission plan offers attractive compensation to high-performing salespeople. The company's interests are also served in a better way since its sales costs are proportional to the level of sales. One of the drawbacks of this plan is that it demotivates salespeople to serve small and not so profitable accounts. In addition, this plan does not provide stable income to salespeople and may fluctuate depending upon external economic conditions.

A *combination plan* is probably the most popular method of compensating sales personnel. This method offers the sales person a stable minimal level of income at the end of each month as well as an opportunity to earn additional commissions. The combination plan often consists of 80 percent base salary and 20 percent commission. Sometimes, however, the proportion may change to a 70%/30% split or a 60%/40% split.[26] One of the major disadvantages of the combination plan is the complexity of its administration and the monitoring of results.

Financial incentives for professional personnel should be combined with mentally stimulating work programs. The development of these incentives often requires a special approach. Professionals such as engineers, accountants, or scientists are often motivated by the quality of work rather than solely by monetary reward. It is essential, therefore, to ensure that professional employees are given the opportunity to utilize their skills effectively and be provided with equitable financial incentives. These incentives may be expressed in the form of a special bonus for innovation, financial support for further educational purposes, profit-sharing plans, or employee stock ownership plans.

The *profit-sharing plan* is a method whereby a company offers organization-wide incentives to virtually all its employees. There are several methods of providing financial incentives to employees under the profit-sharing plan. However, the most popular method probably is the *cash plan,* according to which a certain percentage of profits (between 15 percent to 20 percent) is distributed as a profit share.

Sometimes profit is distributed on a deferred basis. This type of incentive is known as *deferred profit-sharing plan.* Under this plan a certain percentage of profits is deposited in a special trust for the benefit of employees. Furthermore, this plan provides a distinctive tax advantage since employees receive the additional income only upon retirement and are taxed at a lower rate.

The *employee stock ownership plan (ESOP)* is another method whereby the company offers an organization-wide incentive to all employees. Under this plan, a company contributes shares of its own stock, or cash equivalent, to a special trust that is established with the purpose of purchasing same stock for the company's employees.[27] These contributions are usually made once a year in proportion to total employee remuneration but not exceeding 15 percent of its value. The cash and stock are held in such a trust for the benefit of employees and distributed to them upon retirement or separation (provided the employee is eligible for stock ownership).

The employee stock ownership plan has certain advantages. All contributions made by the company in accordance with this plan are fully tax deductible. The deduction is determined in accordance with the fair market value of shares transferred to the trust. Employees, on the other hand, are taxed only upon receiving their shares, usually at retirement when the tax rate is minimal. In addition, the Employee Retirement Income Security Act (ERISA) permits the company to borrow funds, using employee stock held in trust as security, and later to repay the loan with pre-tax rather than after-tax dollars. This represents an important tax incentive to the company.[28] Finally, this plan encourages employees to develop a sense of ownership and real participation in their company's affairs.

The *production sharing scheme*, also known as *gain-sharing plan*, is the final example of providing financial incentives to employees on an organization-wide basis. One form of this plan is the *Scanlon plan*, developed in 1937 by Joseph Scanlon.[29] It takes into account the required level of compensation related to the normal labor cost per unit of product manufactured. If, for instance, it becomes possible to reduce this cost as a result of improved cooperation among employees within a particular production team, it will create additional savings. This plan points to a distribution of such savings fully or partially among all the members of the team in the form of a bonus. Sometimes it is acceptable to allocate 75 percent of the savings to the production team and the balance of 25 percent to management. This scheme has a twofold function. First, it provides an attractive incentive for cooperation among various employees within a specific production team. Second, it fosters an essential liaison between employees and general management within the organization.

2.15 Fringe Benefits

Fringe benefits represent another method of additional compensation designed to attract personnel to the company. The main objective of this method is to ensure the process of long-term retention of employees. All fringe benefits can be classified into the following four categories:

- Nonworking time benefits
- Insurance benefits
- Retirement benefits
- Service benefits[30]

The first category, **nonworking time benefits**, includes all additional compensation to employees for time not worked. This includes vacation and holiday pay, sick leave pay, severance pay, and unemployment insurance.

Vacation and holiday pay is probably one of the most costly fringe benefits offered by a company. The extent of this benefit depends upon the company's policy with regard to length of vacation period allowed to employees and the number of paid public holidays.

Paid vacations generally vary from one week per year to four weeks or more, depending upon the employee's seniority and period of service with the company. It is essential to formulate the company's policy with regard to the vacation period and to develop a suitable plan. Some plans, for example, prescribe a gradual accumulation of vacation time such as one hour of vacation for each week of service.

The number of paid public holidays may vary from five to thirteen and generally includes the following: New Year's Day, Memorial Day, Independence Day, Labor Day, Veterans Day, Thanksgiving Day, Friday after Thanksgiving Day, Christmas Day.

Sick leave pay provides the employee with compensation during absence from service as a result of illness. Employers generally allow up to 12 days of absence per year on account of sick leave (i.e., an average of one day for each month of service). Sometimes employers compensate employees for being healthy and not using paid sick leave. This policy, however, may not produce the desired results since it can motivate certain employees to come to work sick.

Severance pay may be offered to employees upon termination of their employment. This is a one-time payment that may vary from a few days' wages to as much as six or more months of salary. Severance pay also depends upon the notice period given to the employee. Thus, it may be feasible to offer an extended notice period to a particular employee in conjunction with reasonable severance pay. Such a gesture may further allow the employee to find a new job and to terminate his present employment with minimal difficulties.

Unemployment insurance is designed to provide eligible employees with weekly unemployment benefits. The premium for this insurance is levied on each employer in accordance with the Federal Unemployment Tax Act (FUTA). This act is a part of the U.S. social security program, and it prescribes payments not exceeding 6.2 percent of the first $7,000 earned by each employee. Furthermore, the employer is allowed a credit against this federal tax for unemployment taxes paid to the state. The maximum credit is 5.4 percent of the first $7,000 of each employee's earnings. Most states, generally, set their rate at this maximum. Therefore, the FUTA paid is 0.8 percent (6.2–5.4 percent) of the taxable wages.[31]

The second category, **insurance benefits**, includes all additional compensation designed to cover various hazards commonly shared by employees. These include workers' compensation, hospitalization, medical and disability insurance, and life insurance.

Workers' compensation laws are designed to provide employees with a secure, prompt income and medical benefits in case of an accident in the workplace. These benefits are paid to accident victims or their dependents regardless of fault.[32] In order to be eligible for workers' compensation, all that is necessary is to prove that an accident took place while the employee was on the job. In this event the benefits will be paid to the employee in the form of cash or medical coverage, or both, for a period not exceeding 800 weeks. The amount of monetary compensation depends upon the degree of the employee's disablement and, usually, varies between 50 percent to 75 percent of the worker's average wage.

Workers' compensation insurance is generally handled by state administrative commissions. It is, however, the employer's responsibility to arrange appropriate coverage through suitable insurance companies. Moreover, employers are required to make regular payments into special workers' compensation funds to provide coverage for their employees.

Hospitalization, medical, and disability insurance is one of the most important benefits offered to employees. This insurance provides protection in the event of the employee's hospitalization, incurring of medical costs or of a disability arising from off-the-job causes. Employers have the option of selecting and purchasing a suitable insurance policy from various organizations (e.g., life or casualty insurance companies such as Blue Shield or Blue Cross). Most health insurance policies cover, at least, basic medical, surgical, and hospitalization expenses for all eligible members of the particular group. All employees aged 65 and over are in any event covered by the federally funded Medicare health insurance plan.

The Health Maintenance Organization (HMO) Act of 1973 was designed to promote an alternative health care plan to employees. The HMO is a medical organization that offers membership to employers and provides a comprehensive medical service to its employees for a nominal fee. The HMO also charges a fixed annual membership fee per employee from employer.[33]

Life insurance is offered by many organizations to their personnel. Companies usually purchase life insurance policies for a group of employees in order to obtain lower rates and more flexible conditions. As a result, employees may have the opportunity of joining a particular life insurance plan regardless of their personal state of health or physical condition.

The employer usually pays the full base premium, thus providing the employee with a life insurance coverage equal to approximately two years income. An employee may also contribute to the payment of the insurance premium, if higher coverage is desired. In other instances, the employer and employee split the payment for the base premium in a prearranged proportion (e.g., 50 percent/50 percent or 70 percent/30 percent).

The third category, **retirement benefits**, includes all additional compensation designed to provide steady income to employees upon their retirement. This includes social security and various pension plans.

The *social security program* was developed and introduced by the federal government in the 1930s. The central part of this program is the Social Security Act of 1935. The prime purpose of this act and its amendments is to protect American workers from total economic poverty if termination of employment occurs outside of their control. In accordance with this act, employers and employees must contribute equal payments to a special fund on a monthly basis. In addition, this act provides for unemployment compensation to jobless workers for a period of 26 weeks.

The social security program also offers retirement and disability benefits to all employees who retire at age 62 or thereafter. Furthermore, this program offers survivor's benefits or death benefits to the employee's dependents, regardless of age at death. Finally, this program provides disability payment to employees and their dependents in case of an employee's temporary or permanent disability. One of the major additions to this program is the provision of hospitalization and medical insurance for persons over 65 years old.

The social security program is financed by taxes on employers, employees, and self-employed individuals. The magnitude of these taxes is determined in accordance with the Federal Insurance Contributions Act (FICA). The 1990 schedule prescribes a deduction of 7.65 percent from the employee's taxable income up to $50,400 and an equal contribution by the employer.

Pension plans include three basic types.[34] First, there is a *group pension plan*, whereby the employer and the employee make regular contributions to a pension fund. Second, under a *deferred profit-sharing plan*, a certain portion of the company's profits is transferred to each employee's account. Finally, there is a *savings plan*, whereby employees transfer a fixed portion of their income into a special retirement fund. The employer, normally, contributes an equivalent amount, or more, to the same fund.

Pension plans are governed by several federal laws and their planning often represents a complex task. One of the major restrictions on pension plans is imposed by the Employee Retirement Income Security Act of 1974 (ERISA). This act stipulates conditions related to pension contracts between employers and employees. It provides for the establishment of government-controlled employer-financed corporations that will secure employees' interest in special pension plans. Furthermore, this act regulates *vesting rights* of employees (i.e., access to the equity that employees accumulate in their pension plan should their employment be terminated prior to retirement). The employee's *portability rights* (i.e., the transfer of vesting rights from one company to another) are also covered by this act.

The final category, **service benefits**, includes all additional compensation offered to employees in the form of services and executive perquisites. Service benefits may include personal services such as social or legal counseling and job-related benefits such as subsidized employee transportation or education subsidies. Executive perquisites, or "perks," are generally offered to senior managers and may include a company car, gas allowance, interest free loans, and many other benefits.

2.16 Personnel Performance Appraisal

Once employees are selected, trained, and motivated, management must conduct regular **personnel performance appraisals**. The main purposes of this process are:

- To review the employees' performance during a specific period of employment
- To provide employees with feedback regarding their performance and to identify their strengths and weaknesses in various areas of work
- To provide employees with an opportunity to express their opinions concerning their work
- To identify suitable candidates for short- or long-term promotions and salary or wage increases
- To identify employees whose performance is not in accordance with company standards
- To develop training programs in order to improve the employees' performance deficiencies
- To identify candidates for replacement

Personnel performance appraisal is considered one of the most important managerial functions. Unfortunately, this process if often carried out spontaneously and without any preliminary planning. There are, however, numerous methods of providing a systematic approach to the personnel performance appraisal. Probably, the simplest and the most widely used method of appraisal is a **descriptive graphic rating scale**. This method is based on a personnel performance rating applied to numerous performance factors such as:

- *Quality of work.* This includes evaluation of working skills, experience, accuracy, and thoroughness of the employee.

- *Quantity of work.* This reflects work output by the employee under normal conditions and under pressure.
- *Required supervision.* This reflects need for advice, direction, or coordination by the employee.
- *Attendance.* This reflects regularity, dependability, and promptness of performance by the employee.
- *Conservation.* This reflects the employee's effort in preventing waste, spoilage, and protection of equipment.
- *General attitude.* This reflects the employee's attitudes toward the company and fellow employees.

Performance appraisal of an employee entails a separate rating of each of the aforementioned factors in terms such as:

- Unsatisfactory performance
- Fair performance
- Good performance
- Superior performance
- Exceptional performance.

Once the employee's performance appraisal is completed, all individual ratings should be condensed into a **performance appraisal form**. A typical illustration of such a form is presented in Exhibit 2–32.

Management's performance appraisal in small and medium-sized companies may be conducted in a similar manner. Such an appraisal, however, should be applied to different performance factors such as:

- *Planning skills.* These include the manager's ability to assess the existing situation, to establish priorities in the area of his or her responsibility, to formulate attainable plans, and to foresee possible problems.
- *Organizing skills.* These include the manager's ability to group activities for the most effective use of human and material resources, to clearly define responsibilities and authority limits of subordinates, and to maximize the efficiency in work operations.
- *Leading skills.* These include the manager's ability to guide, conduct, direct, and motivate subordinates to meet specific organizational objectives.
- *Controlling skills.* These include the manager's ability to monitor the subordinates' work progress and identify deviations from planned objectives, to adjust deviations in work, and to ensure that established goals are met.
- *General attitude.* This includes the manager's attitude toward the company and fellow employees.
- *Special duties.* This includes the manager's ability to perform special duties within the organization.

Upon completing the manager's performance appraisal, all individual ratings should be summarized in a **management appraisal form**. A typical illustration of such a form is presented in Exhibit 2–33.

Performance appraisal of all employees must be carried out in accordance with fair employment practice principles. The actual appraisal process should be conducted by each employee's supervisor, who is usually in the best position to assess the subordinate's performance. The supervisor is expected to demonstrate an unbiased and reasonable attitude toward the employee during the appraisal

Exhibit 2–32

Performance Appraisal Form

PERFORMANCE APPRAISAL FORM					
Employee : _____ Job Title : _____ Date: _____					
Department: _____ Job Number: _____ Rate: _____					

FACTOR	SCORE - RATING				
	UNSATIS-FACTORY So definitely inadequate that it justifies release	FAIR Minimal; barely adequate to justify retention	GOOD Meets basic requirement for retention	SUPERIOR Definitely above norm and basic requirements	EXCEPTIONAL Distinctly and consistently outstanding
QUALITY OF WORK Accuracy, thoroughness, appearance, and acceptance of output					
QUANTITY OF WORK Volume of output and contribution					
REQUIRED SUPERVISION Need for advice, direction, or correction					
ATTENDANCE Regularity, dependability, and promptness					
CONSERVATION Prevention of waste, spoilage; protection of equipment					
GENERAL ATTITUDE Attitude toward the company and fellow employees					

Reviewed by: _____ (Reviewer comments on reverse)

Employee comment: _____

Date: _____ Signature or initial: _____

SOURCE: Dale Yoder, *Personnel Management*, 6e, ©1970, p. 240. Reprinted by permission of Prentice Hall, Inc., Englewood Cliffs, New Jersey.

Exhibit 2–33

Management Appraisal Form

MANAGEMENT APPRAISAL FORM					
Employee : _____ Job Title : _____ Date: _____					
Department: _____ Job Number: _____ Rate: _____					
FACTOR	SCORE - RATING				
	UNSATIS-FACTORY So definitely inadequate that it justifies release	FAIR Minimal; barely adequate to justify retention	GOOD Meets basic requirement for retention	SUPERIOR Definitely above norm and basic requirements	EXCEPTIONAL Distinctly and consistently outstanding
PLANNING SKILLS Ability to analyze results, establish priorities, and formulate plans					
ORGANIZATION SKILLS Ability to group activities for most effective use of material and labor resources					
LEADING SKILLS Ability to guide, conduct, direct, and motivate subordinates					
CONTROLLING SKILLS Ability to monitor progress of work, and to identify and adjust deviations in work					
GENERAL ATTITUDE Attitude toward the company and fellow employees					
SPECIAL DUTIES Ability to perform special duties					
Reviewed by: _____ (Reviewer comments on reverse) Employee comment: _____ Date: _____ Signature or initial: _____					

process. In addition, it may be useful to issue a **confidential questionnaire** to selected employees in order to obtain their opinions on relevant work-related issues. This action may further enhance the clarity of performance appraisal results. A typical confidential questionnaire is presented in Exhibit 2–34.

The outcome of the performance appraisal indicates whether the employee's performance is satisfactory or not. These results determine the nature and objectives of subsequent **appraisal interviews**.[35] Should performance be *satisfactory*, the manager must assess whether the employee is promotable or not. If the manager concludes that the subordinate is promotable, it is necessary to conduct an interview wherein the employee's future development is discussed. If it is felt, however, that the employee has reached his or her ceiling and is thus not promotable, then the objective of the interview should be how to maintain the current performance level.

Should performance be *unsatisfactory*, the manager must assess whether this is correctable or not. If the employee's performance is correctable, the manager must conduct an interview with the objective of developing a suitable correction plan. However, if the performance is not correctable, then the manager must simply decide whether to tolerate the situation or dismiss the employee.

In preparation for the appraisal interview, it is necessary to assemble all relevant information including the current appraisal form and the questionnaire completed by the employee. The person's job description should be carefully studied and used as a standard for performance appraisal. Furthermore, it is necessary to review the file containing previous appraisal results and to identify if there has been improvement over a certain period of time.

An employee should be notified about the pending performance appraisal interview at least one week in advance and informed that it is a routine procedure. For the interview to be successful, both the manager and the subordinate must have an opportunity to express their views as openly as possible. All problem areas need to be identified during the interview and a suitable plan of action must be developed. Such a plan should include a description of specific goals and time limits in which these should be attained. All details pertaining to the plan of action should be summarized in a **plan of action schedule**, as illustrated in the Exhibit 2–35.

The performance appraisal interview incorporates principles of management by objectives (MBO) discussed earlier in Part 1. The main purpose of the MBO approach is to provide employees with clear guidelines and specific objectives directly related to their duties and responsibilities within the company. This approach is particularly useful in developing a set of meaningful and measurable goals for managers:

- Objectives for vice president, finance: a 10 percent reduction of overdraft by September 1990 and a 20 percent reduction of accounts receivable by October 1990.
- Objectives for vice president, manufacturing: a 10 percent increase of production output by September 1990 and a 20 percent reduction of production reject by October 1990.

The MBO approach has certain limitations in being too individualistic rather than organizationally oriented. Furthermore, this approach is sometimes ineffective for certain nonmanagerial positions. However, management should view the aforementioned methods as an integral aspect of managerial responsibility in ensuring a high standard of personnel performance.

Exhibit 2–34

Confidential Questionnaire

Confidential Questionnaire		
Employee's name:		Department:
Main function:		
Describe most satisfactory duties		Describe least satisfactory duties
Who gives you instructions?		
Are working conditions correct for your job?		
Do you actually like the work you do?		
How satisfied are you with your own performance?		
What other functions would you like to perform?		
How can the company assist you to achieve better work satisfaction?		
Do you have any problems with other members of the staff?		
Summarize you suggestions that could benefit both you and the company:		
Signature:		Date:

Exhibit 2–35

Plan of Action Schedule

Plan of Action Schedule	
To: Shirley Sunn - Credit Controller	
Problem	Objective
1. The age and value of accounts receivable is too high. 2. Recent rise in bad debts.	1. To reduce the age and value of accounts receivable. 2. To introduce stricter credit control methods.

Plan of action		
Action step	Date required	Expected result
1. Collect all accounts aged 60 days and over.	September 30, 1990	1. Outstanding period of accounts receivable should not exceed 60 days.
2. Review all credit application forms.	September 30, 1990	2. Bad debts should be minimized.
Prepared by: A. Jones, Vice President, Finance		Date: August 4, 1990

2.17 Personnel Career Management

Career development can be described as the process of separate but related working activities undertaken to satisfy a person's ambitions. The **career development process** is designed to provide an effective method of ensuring a steady functional growth of employees within a company. This process also contributes to satisfying the ever increasing organizational needs for new personnel. The advantages of the career development process are as follows:

• Increased level of morale and motivation of personnel
• Avoidance of personnel "retirement on the job"
• Reduction of personnel turnover
• More effective personnel planning process
• Improved utilization of internal personnel resources

The work life of employees does not stand in isolation from their family life. The company's management should, therefore, consider the employees' private lives as an important factor in the career development process. Every person undergoes the five distinct stages during the life cycle that are outlined below:

1. **Growth stage.** This period lasts from birth to approximately age 14, when the person passes through the childhood stage. During this period, the person develops a self-image by identifying and interacting with family, friends, and teachers. Toward the end of this period, the adolescent develops some preliminary ideas about his or her particular interests and preferences.

2. **Exploration stage.**   This period lasts approximately from ages 15 to 24, when the person passes through the young, unmarried adulthood stage. During this period the person explores various educational and occupational options and tries to select a suitable direction based on his or her personal interest and preferences. Toward the end of this period the person develops strong interests and preferences which guide him or her throughout the active working life.

3. **Establishment stage.**   This period lasts approximately from ages 25 to 44, during which the person is likely to marry and start a family. The establishment stage generally comprises three substages. First, there is a *trial substage* which lasts from about 25 to 30. During this period the person ascertains whether or not the selected area of work is suitable. If not, then a change of direction may take place. Second, there is a *stabilization substage*, which lasts from about 30 to 40. This is, generally, the most critical stage in the person's life, when his or her dreams and aspirations are to be fulfilled. Finally, the person may enter into a *mid-career crisis substage* sometime between the mid-30s and mid-40s. During this period, the person is expected to adjust his or her ambitions to the real world and to reorient accordingly.

4. **Maintenance stage.**   This period lasts approximately from ages 45 to 65, when the person passes through a married adulthood stage and raises children. During this period the person consolidates occupational activities and maintains strong use of skills and experience. Toward the end of this period, the person gradually slides into a less active working environment and prepares for eventual retirement.

5. **Decline stage.**   This period starts at age 65, when the person's family is grown up and children lead separate lives. Decline stage also entails a possible loss of spouse. During this period the person operates on a reduced level of responsibility and shares experiences with a younger generation of employees. Toward the end of this period, the person retires from active service and enters into a postretirement stage.[36]

There are numerous factors affecting the employee's career development process within the company. These factors are directly related to the employee's background and personal qualities as well as to the company's relevant policies.

Employees generally tend to perform better at jobs in which they have special interests and skills. It is essential, therefore, to start the career development process with the identification of such interests and skills in order to establish the **personal orientation** of each employee.

There are six basic types of personal orientation, as illustrated in Exhibit 2–36:

1. Realistic orientation
2. Investigative orientation
3. Social orientation
4. Conventional orientation
5. Enterprising orientation
6. Artistic orientation[37]

In the context of the business environment, the personal orientation types can be interpreted as follows:

• A *realistic orientation* is characteristic of production engineers, technicians, mechanics, tool and die makers, drivers, carpenters, and tradespeople in general.

- An *investigative orientation* is characteristic of design engineers, managers, and management consultants.
- A *social orientation* is characteristic of managers in general and particularly of personnel managers.
- A *conventional orientation* is characteristic of accountants, bookkeepers, credit managers, storekeepers, and office workers.
- An *enterprising orientation* is characteristic of executive managers, buyers, and sales personnel.
- An *artistic orientation* is characteristic of design engineers, architects, advertising managers, artists, and interior decorators.

Most people usually fall into two or more orientation types. Engineers, for example, may have realistic and investigative orientations, while many managers have investigative and enterprising orientations. Career counseling expert J. Holland suggests that, the more compatible orientation types are, the more decisive the person will be in making an individual career choice. This may be further illustrated by the placement of personal orientation types in one of the

Exhibit 2–36

Personal Orientation Types

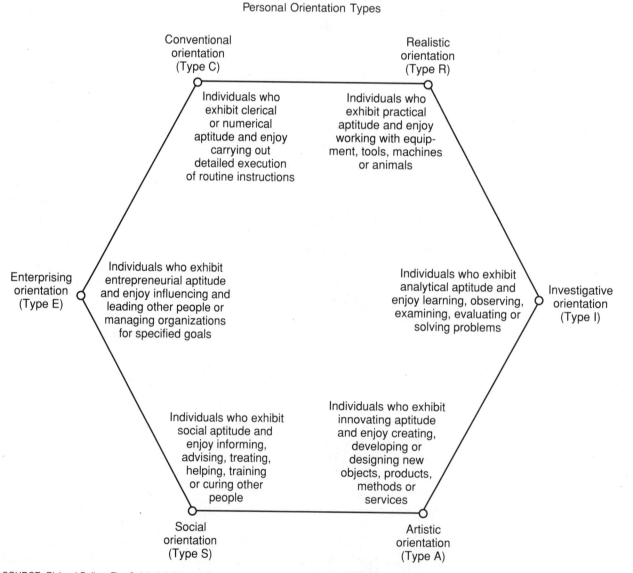

SOURCE: Richard Bolles, *The Quick Job Hunting Map* (Berkeley, CA: Ten Speed Press, 1979), p.5.

corners of a hexagon as in Exhibit 2–36. Thus, the closer two orientations are in the hexagon, the more compatible they are.

By examining employees, managers can identify their **occupational orientation level** (i.e., to what degree their personal orientation types are compatible). This may lead to the following classification of employees:

- *Employees with high occupational orientation.* These include people whose personal orientation is placed in adjacent corners of the hexagon (e.g., enterprising-conventional, or realistic-investigative).
- *Employees with low occupational orientation.* These include people whose personal orientation is placed in opposite corners of the hexagon (e.g., artistic-conventional, or realistic-social).

The career development process depends upon personal skills, talents, needs, values, and ambitions of employees. This is further enhanced by employee's gradual inclination toward individual **career anchors** or preferences. Edgar Schein has identified five career anchors as follows:

- Technical/functional competence
- Managerial competence
- Creativity
- Independence
- Security

Technical/functional competence is usually selected by people with distinctive functional abilities and an overriding interest in their specific jobs. These people generally avoid activities that would drive them toward general management; instead they tend to specialize in their selected professional areas such as engineering, accounting, medicine, or science.

Managerial competence is a goal usually selected by people with distinctive leadership qualities and an overriding interest in management activities. These people are inclined to wield considerable managerial responsibility; to have an ability to work with, influence, and control employees; and to have the skills to identify, evaluate, and solve problems.

Creativity is a direction usually selected by people with a distinctive desire to discover new solutions. This direction enables people to utilize their creative abilities and, consequently, to fulfil personal and professional ambitions. This inclination necessitates that people have a substantial sense of personal responsibility, high self-motivation, and fair expectation of material gain.

Independence is a direction usually selected by people with a distinctive drive for personal autonomy. This direction enables people to express their life aspirations, personal creative abilities, and desire for freedom of choice. This inclination necessitates that people have a substantial sense of personal responsibility and high self-motivation and are prepared to temporarily sacrifice material benefits.

Security is a direction usually selected by people with a distinctive need for personal peace of mind. This direction does not require people to express their ambitions or to demonstrate their managerial talent. It does, however, require a certain ability to wield personal responsibility and to have sufficient skills and experience in selected areas of work.[38]

The identification of all these factors plays an important role in the process of planning for personnel career development. A properly designed **career development program** usually has three main objectives, which are as follows:

- To assist employees in evaluating their own internal career needs
- To develop new career opportunities in the company
- To match career opportunities in the company with the employee's needs and abilities

Career development is a highly individual and very important aspect in the human life cycle. Management, therefore, should provide employees with an opportunity for making their own decisions in this regard and assist them in the decision-making process. Employees should be asked to consider the relative importance of factors such as managerial or technical competence, security, creativity, independence, and family life; this consideration will help to improve the quality of their own career planning.

The process of developing new career opportunities necessitates that management design specific **career routes** corresponding to various functions. Certain positions within the company, termed *low ceiling jobs*, will prove to have limited opportunities for significant careers. Such jobs should be identified and made known to employees, particularly those who have a distinctive need for security. Relevant information in regard to the duties of such jobs should be provided, as well as details of the necessary training or development requirements.

Upon completing the process of identifying and evaluating employees' internal career needs and the company's career opportunities, management will be able to plan the alignment of the above by means of a career development program. Such a program should incorporate all the major elements of individual and organizational development processes, namely: operative, management and organizational training, performance appraisal, and management by objectives. The ultimate result of a well-planned and efficiently executed career development program will be the process of employees' smooth transfer and promotion within the company. This process will enable management to utilize internal personnel resources in accordance with the company's specific needs in order to meet its organizational objectives.

Sometimes, however, the company does not meet its planned objectives as a result of reduced sales or profits. This may necessitate temporary or permanent **discharge** or **layoff** of a certain number of employees. Most layoff procedures are generally based on seniority of employees, or length of their employment period. On other occasions, employees are requested to take **voluntary time off** or a **shorter working week** in order to reduce the company's payroll expenses.

If the performance of a particular employee does not meet on a continuous basis the company's standards, such an employee is a subject to **dismissal**. Among additional reasons for dismissal may be the employee's misconduct or lack of suitable qualifications for the job. Dismissal of employees, in general, must be conducted in accordance with fair employment laws and practices discussed earlier. It is essential to establish an effective dismissal procedure, which may include the following:

- *Warning discussions.* These should be conducted between a supervisor and an employee in order to inform the latter about his or her poor performance. These discussions must be supported by appropriate documentation which will be kept by the supervisor.
- *Final warning.* This should be given to an employee if his or her performance continues to be unsatisfactory in spite of previous warnings. In this instance, the employee must be informed that the next step is dismissal from the company's employment. Final warning must be accompanied by an appro-

priate written confirmation to protect the interest of both the company and the employee.

- *Pay in lieu of notice* should be exercised if the presence of a particular employee may adversely affect the morale of fellow workers.[39] Severance pay is calculated on the basis of one week of compensation for each year of service up to a prescribed maximum.[40]

Managers must remember that employees cannot be dismissed "at will," or without sound reason. This is further enforced by the Civil Rights Act and by appropriate federal and state employment laws. Violation of these laws may force employees to seek out a legal recourse against the employer. This will result in an unnecessary expenditure of time, money, and effort on the part of the company.

Thus, if an employee has to be dismissed, it is essential to conduct a **termination interview**. Guidelines for such an interview, according to consultants at May Associates, are as follows:

1. Plan the interview carefully.
   - Schedule the meeting on a day early in the week.
   - Make sure the employee keeps the appointment time.
   - Never inform an employee over the phone.
   - Ten minutes should be sufficient for notification.
   - Avoid Fridays, pre-holidays, and vacation times.
   - Use a neutral site; never use your own office.
   - Have employee agreements, personnel file, and release announcement (internal and external) prepared in advance.
   - Be available at a time after notification.
   - Have phone numbers ready for medical and/or, security emergencies.

2. Inform the employee about the dismissal decision in a straightforward manner.
3. Spend no more than 5 to 15 minutes in explaining reasons for the dismissal decision and emphasize that the decision is final and irrevocable.
4. Allow the employee to express his or her opinion on the dismissal decision.
5. Discuss all elements of the severance package.
6. Provide the employee with an appropriate employment reference.[41]

Finally, if management needs to prepare some of its employees for retirement, it is essential to arrange for pre-retirement counseling. This procedure is expected to smooth the retirement process and to ensure dignified treatment of employees.

2.18 Labor-Management Relations

One of the most important managerial tasks is to ensure sound labor-management relations within a company. Such relations represent an essential ingredient of every organizational structure and should be based on the following principles:

- Mutual acceptance and respect
- A free enterprise system

- Free collective bargaining
- A problem-solving attitude

Labor-management relations are influenced by labor unions or other similar organizations. A **labor union** or a **trade union** is an organization of employees established to protect, to promote, and to improve the economic, social, and political interests of its members. The main objective of the labor union is to secure the economic well-being of workers in various industrial sectors. It is important, therefore, to evaluate the objectives of labor unions and to assess how they compare with the usual interests of the company's management.

At present over 20 million American workers, or about 25 percent of the total work force, belong to labor unions. The American Federation of Labor (AFL), formed in 1886, merged with the Congress of Industrial Organizations (CIO) in 1955 to become the biggest labor organization in U.S. history. The AFL-CIO is a voluntary federation of 109 national and international labor unions with about 15 million members.

In addition, there are about 5 million workers who belong to labor unions other than the AFL-CIO. About 75 percent of these workers belong to two major independent unions—the Teamsters (about 2 million members) and the United Auto Workers (about 1.5 million members).[42]

Labor unions play an important role in the working lives of millions of people nationwide. Sometimes workers join the labor union because it is easier to obtain employment through the union than on the open labor market. In other instances workers expect the labor union to protect their rights during the process of conflict management between the company and employees. In addition, labor unions are instrumental in the process of wage-rates adjustment procedures. They also mediate during the process of collective bargaining between the company and employees.

Federal legislation and the modern business environment facilitated the development of the following types of labor–management relations:

- **Closed shop.** In this instance, only union members can be hired by a company. This provision was outlawed in 1947. However, it still remains in effect in certain industries in some states.
- **Union shop.** In this instance, non-union employees can be hired by a company. However, they have to join the union within a prescribed period of time and to pay dues in order not to be fired from the job.
- **Agency shop.** In this instance, all company employees, including non-union members, must pay union dues. It is assumed here that the union's efforts benefit all employees.
- **Open shop.** In this instance, union membership decision rests with employees. Those employees who do not join the union are not liable for union dues.
- **Maintenance of membership arrangement.** In this instance, employees are not obliged to belong to a union. Those employees who are union members, however, must maintain their membership in the union during the employment period.[43]

As a result of labor union activities, certain federal laws have been passed and implemented since about 1930. Among the important laws are the following:

- The Norris-La Guardia Act of 1932. This was the first law that encouraged the activities of labor unions and guaranteed each employee the right to collective bargaining, "free from interference, restraint, or coercion." This law also restricted the courts' powers against activities such as picketing and payment of strike benefits.

- The Wagner Act of 1935. This law banned certain types of unfair labor practices, provided for secret ballot elections for unionization of employees, and created the National Labor Relations Board (NLRB) for enforcing the aforementioned provisions.

The Wagner Act stipulates that the following five employer practices are considered **unfair labor practices:**

1. It is unfair for management to "interfere with, restrain, or coerce employees" in exercising their legally sanctioned right of self-organization.
2. It is an unfair practice for company representatives to dominate or to interfere with either the formation or the administration of labor unions. Among other management actions found to be unfair under stipulation 1 and 2 are: bribery of employees, company spy systems, moving a business to avoid unionization, and blacklisting union sympathizers.
3. Companies are prohibited from discriminating in any way against employees for their legal union activities.
4. Employers are forbidden from discharging or discriminating against employees simply because the latter had filed "unfair practice" charges against the company.
5. Finally, this act defines as an unfair labor practice employers' refusal to bargain collectively with their employees' duly chosen representatives.[44]

Subsequent labor laws passed in the late 1940s and 1950s reflected a less enthusiastic approach toward unions. Among the most important laws adopted during the period include:

- The Taft-Hartley Act of 1947. This law prohibited unfair labor practices by unions, specified the rights of employees as union members, stipulated the rights of employers, and permitted the President of the United States to temporarily prohibit national emergency strikes.
- The Landrum-Griffin Act of 1959. This law, also known as the Labor–Management Reporting and Disclosure Act, was designed to protect union members from possible misconduct on the part of their unions.

The Taft-Hartley Act provides employers with explicit collective bargaining rights as well as with freedom of expressing their opinion about labor organizations. A manager, for example, may tell employees that, in his opinion, unions are "worthless, damaging to the economy, and serve no purpose." Furthermore, the manager may suggest that unionization and subsequent additional wage demands might cause a permanent shutdown of the company. The Landrum-Griffin Act, on the other hand, stipulates additional restrictions imposed on employers in the event of unionization. Companies, for example, are prohibited from paying their employees in an effort to discourage them from joining the union. Employers and unions are also required to submit extensive reports prior to employment of labor-relation consultants.

It is important that managers be familiar with the standard unionization procedure. Such a procedure generally includes the following basic steps:[45]

1. **Initial contact.** The first contact may be initiated by a representative of a union that seeks to expand its activities or by a dissatisfied employee

who would like to see the company unionized. The representative visits the company to establish whether a sufficient number of employees are interested in joining the union. Those employees who may become part of an organizing committee are also identified. The main purpose here is to "educate the committee about the benefits of forming a union, the law and procedures involved in forming a local union, and the issues management is likely to raise during a campaign."[46] Federal legislation does permit union organizers to solicit employees for membership provided solicitation does not interfere with work or pose a safety hazard in the workplace.

2. **Authorization cards.** The union needs to justify to the National Labor Relations Board that a substantial number of employees might be interested in the company's unionization. For this purpose, union organizers have to obtain signed authorization cards from employees. At least 30% of the employees must sign these cards before an election can be petitioned. During the petition process, both the union's representatives and management may propagate for or against the unionization process. The union may claim that it will improve working conditions and increase compensation for employees. Management, conversely, may accuse the union of an unconstructive role or attack it on moral or ethical grounds. Employees, however, must be left alone to make their final decision whether to join the union or not.

3. **The hearing.** If management does not oppose union recognition, no hearing is required and the election of the union can be held immediately. Management, however, may contest the election by claiming, for example, that a substantial number of its employees do not wish to join the union. In this instance, the union's representative approaches the National Labor Relations Board (NLRB) and requests a hearing. Subsequently, the hearing is conducted by a NLRB's hearing officer, who listens to both the union representative's and management's arguments. The two purposes of such a hearing are to establish whether at least 30% of employees signed the authorization cards and to identify a bargaining unit. The *bargaining unit* is a group of employees who authorize the union to represent them in any negotiations with management. Finally, if the results of the hearing favor unionization, the NLRB will issue a notice about pending elections.

4. **The campaign.** Prior to the election day, both the union's representatives and management have an opportunity to appeal to employees in an effort to win their votes. The union's representatives usually base their campaign on promises of overall improvement of working conditions, higher salaries, wages, and other benefits, and of additional rights and privileges for employees. Management, on the other hand, may explain that improvements promised by the union do not depend upon unionization or that financial costs of union dues outweigh the anticipated gains. Management may also stress that a union is an outsider and its activities can lead to a strike and possible loss of jobs. Neither side, however, is allowed to bribe, threaten, or coerce employees.

5. **The election.** The final election may take place when the union succeeds in obtaining the following: 30% of signed authorization cards, agreement concerning the bargaining unit, and approval by the NLRB. Employees and management are notified about the election, which is subsequently held within 30 to 60 days. The actual election process is facilitated, conducted, and certified by representatives of the NLRB. The union, in order to win the election, needs to get a majority of employees' votes. If, however, this is not achieved, management will succeed in maintaining the existing conditions and win the election.

Exhibit 5–42

List of Fringe Benefits Offered by Different Companies

Benefits	Percentage of Firms Offering
Hospital	99
Life insurance	92
Accident insurance	85
Moving expenses	65
Salary continuation plan	62
Educational assistance	60
Pension plan	56
Personal use of company car	52
Club or association membership	38
Profit sharing	36
Dental insurance	25
Stock purchase	18

SOURCE: Adapted from data in John Steinbrink's, "How to Pay Your Sales Force," *Harvard Business Review*, Vol. 56 (July–August, 1978), p. 121.

daily food allowance, or $60 hotel allowance. The prime purpose of this plan is to motivate the salesperson to control selling expenses.

Fringe benefits are another form of compensation and are frequently used to attract suitable salespeople. There are several types of benefits which can be offered to salespeople depending upon the seniority of their position and their overall importance to the organization. Some of these benefits are summarized in Exhibit 5–42.

Once all parameters of the sales force compensation package are established, the sales manager should evaluate the plan in terms of overall organizational objectives and its acceptance by salespeople. Finally, upon its approval, the compensation plan must be implemented and monitored consistently.

5.18 Sales Force Management and Motivation

The effective management and motivation of a sales force represents another major responsibility of a sales manager. This process entails evaluating, selecting, and designing sales territories; assigning salespeople and allocating sales quotas; implementing a territorial coverage plan; motivating salespeople; and conducting regular sales meetings. A typical **sales force management and motivation process** is illustrated in Exhibit 5–43.

The word "sales territory" is misleading because it does not relate to a specific geographic area alone. A **sales territory** represents a quantifiable and identifiable group of existing and potential buyers. A territory thus focuses upon sales potential from the company's point of view, and would be a slice of the total pie that the company hopes to obtain in sales.[40] There are several reasons for establishing sales territories:

- Ensuring thorough coverage of the existing and potential market
- Increasing motivation and efficiency of sales personnel
- Optimizing the level of selling costs
- Providing better control and evaluation of the sales force
- Facilitating improved customer relations

Prior to selecting and designing suitable sales territories, the sales manager must evaluate several **territorial planning factors** which include the following:[41]

Exhibit 2–37

A List of Mandatory Bargaining Items

Mandatory Bargaining Items

Wages	Procedures for income tax withholding
Hours	Severance pay
Discharge	Nondiscriminatory hiring hall
Arbitration	Plant rules
Holidays—paid	Safety
Vacations—paid	Prohibition against supervisors' doing unit work
Duration of agreement	Superseniority for union stewards
Grievance procedure	Checkoff
Layoff plan	Partial plant closing
Reinstatement of economic strikers	Hunting on employer forest reserve where previously granted
Change of payment from hourly base to salary base	Plant closedown and relocation
Union security and checkoff	Change in operations resulting in reclassifying workers from incentive to straight-time, or cut work force, or installation of cost-saving machine
Work rules	
Merit wage increase	
Work schedule	Plant closing
Lunch periods	Job-posting procedures
Rest periods	Plant reopening
Pension plan	Employee physical examination
Retirement age	Union security
Bonus payments	Bargaining over "Bar List"
Price of meals provided by company	Truck rentals—minimum rental to be paid by carriers to employee-owned vehicles
Group insurance—health, accident, life	
Promotions	Musician price list
Seniority	Arrangement for negotiation
Layoffs	Change in insurance carrier and benefits
Transfers	Profit-sharing plan
Work assignments and transfers	Motorcarrier-union agreement providing that carriers use own equipment before leasing outside equipment
No-strike clause	
Piece rates	
Stock-purchase plan	Overtime pay
Work loads	Agency shop
Change of employee status to independent contractors	Sick leave
Management-rights clause	Employer's insistence on clause giving arbitrator right to enforce law
Cancellation of seniority upon relocation of plant	Company houses
Discounts on company products	Subcontracting
Shift differentials	Discriminatory racial policies
Contract clause providing for supervisors' keeping seniority in unit	Production ceiling imposed by union
	Most-favored nation clause

SOURCE: Reed Richardson, *Collective Bargaining by Objectives* ©1977, pp. 113-115. Reprinted by permission of Prentice Hall, Inc., Englewood Cliffs, New Jersey.

Management and employees normally start the collective bargaining process by presenting their demands to each other. These demands are examined, negotiated, and subsequently reduced to bring about a possible agreement that will satisfy both parties. Finally, when all the differences are settled, a formal agreement is signed.

Collective bargaining expert Reed Richardson has a number of important suggestions for negotiators:

1. Be sure you have set clear objectives on every bargaining item and make sure you understand on what grounds the objectives were established.
2. Do not hurry.
3. When in doubt, caucus with your associates.
4. Be well prepared with firm data supporting your position.
5. Always strive to keep some flexibility in your position. Do not get yourself out on a limb.
6. Do not just concern yourself with what the other party says and does; find out why. Remember that economic motivation is not the only explanation for the other party's conduct and action.
7. Respect the importance of face saving for the other party.
8. Constantly be alert to the real intentions of the other party with respect not only to goals, but also priorities.
9. Be a good listener.
10. Build a reputation for being fair but firm.
11. Learn to control your emotions; do not panic. Use emotions as a tool, not as an obstacle.
12. Be sure as you make each bargaining move that you know its relationship to all other moves.
13. Measure each move against your objectives.
14. Pay close attention to the wording of every clause negotiated; words and phrases are often a source of grievances.
15. Remember that collective bargaining negotiations are, by their nature, part of a compromise process. There is no such thing as having all the pie.
16. Learn to understand people and their personalities.
17. Consider the impact of present negotiations on those in future years.[48]

Sometimes management and employees are not able to reach a compromise during the collective bargaining process. In this case, it is advisable to seek assistance through a third party, which may perform one of the following functions:

• Embarkation upon a fact-finding mission
• Mediation of a conflict
• Final arbitration of a conflict

The objective of **mediation** is to stimulate management and employees by means of listening, suggesting, communicating, explaining, and convincing both parties to reach an amicable agreement. **Arbitration**, on the other hand, aims to collect all the pertinent facts related to a dispute between the company's management and employees and to provide a decision that will be final and binding on both parties.

Management should also be aware that if an agreement with employees is not reached, a strike may ensue. A **strike** is a process of organized, temporary refusal to provide services to the company by employees. It is essential, therefore, to prepare for the possibility of a strike and to have a proper plan of action in the case of work stoppage. It must also be realized that each strike is a costly exercise and should thus be avoided.

When management and employees finally reach an agreement, a contract must be signed by both parties. Such a contract should cover all relevant details agreed upon during the negotiating process and may include the following major subjects:

1. Management rights
2. Union security and dues checkoff
3. Grievance procedures
4. Arbitration of grievances
5. Disciplinary procedures
6. Compensation rates
7. Hours of work and overtime
8. Benefits: vacations, holidays, insurance, pensions
9. Health and safety provisions
10. Employee security–seniority provisions
11. Contract expiration date[49]

One of the important outcomes of the labor contract is the development and implementation of **grievance procedures**. These procedures are designed to handle employees' complaints, to prevent or manage conflicts between employees and management, and to ensure a healthy environment in the organization. If such grievances do occur, the management is advised to handle them in the following manner:

- To receive the complaint or grievance
- To establish the nature of dissatisfaction
- To obtain all the relevant facts
- To analyze the current situation
- To make an appropriate decision
- To act in accordance with the above decision
- To ensure the implementation and follow-up of the above action

If a particular grievance is not resolved, the employee may be expected to approach the union for further assistance in the matter. A union representative will then negotiate with the management on the employee's behalf with the purpose of reaching an amicable solution.

It is important that employees' grievances are handled equally effectively in both unionized and non-unionized companies. Management is advised, therefore, to act promptly and objectively when the employees' complaints are received in order to stimulate high morale and productivity within the organization.

Management is sometimes required to take specific actions in relation to certain employees to ensure the complete implementation of the grievance handling procedure. These actions relate to the **disciplinary process**, which has the distinctive objective of ensuring a specific level of employees' conduct within the company. The first task of this process is to establish managerial responsibility for the administration and implementation of relevant **disciplinary actions**. The second task of such a process is to develop and to clarify the employees' expected code of behavior within the company. This code normally consists of various written rules and regulations prescribing a recommended style of employee conduct and defining all the forbidden activities.

When management is required to exert specific control over a particular employee, it is suggested to enforce the **disciplinary action penalties** in the following sequence:

1. Verbal warning
2. Written warning

3. Temporary loss of benefits
4. Disciplinary layoff
5. Demotion
6. Discharge

The main objective of any disciplinary action is to prevent further contravention of the company's code of conduct. If the application of penalties is still required, management is advised to use some of the following recommendations:

- The disciplinary action should be conducted in private.
- The imposed penalty should be constructive.
- The disciplinary action should be applied by the immediate supervisor.
- The disciplinary action should be taken without delay.
- The disciplinary action should be applied on a consistent basis.
- The disciplinary action should never be applied to supervisors in the presence of their immediate subordinates.
- Management should assume a normal attitude toward the employee after applying a disciplinary action.

Finally, if the application of disciplinary actions does not produce the desired result, management should consider discharging a particular employee. In this instance, an **employee separation report** indicating the reasons for the employee's separation should be prepared. A typical employee separation report is presented in Exhibit 2–38.

Exhibit 2–38

Employee Separation Report

Employee Separation Report		
Name: _____ Soc.Sec.No.: _____		
Date Employed: _____ Separation Date: _____		
Details of circumstances leading to separation:		
Supervisor:	Approved:	Date:

2.20 Personnel Safety and Health

One of the most important managerial tasks is the provision of adequate working conditions to ensure personnel safety and health. The U.S. Public Health Service reports that during one year there were almost $8\frac{1}{2}$ million injuries as a result of accidents at work. The National Safety Council reports over 14,000 deaths over the same period.[50] Many safety experts believe that the actual figures are, in fact, much higher. Furthermore, these figures neither reflect the pain and suffering of employees and their families nor include the tremendous costs of medical treatment, lost working hours, and litigation expenses.

Safety expert Willie Hammer suggests that management should develop and implement effective **safety and health procedures** for

- *Moral reasons* to secure the welfare of employees and their families.
- *Legal reasons* to meet appropriate legislation.
- *Economic reasons* to reduce injury compensation costs, medical expenses, and production losses.

The development of these procedures necessitates that management plans certain actions in advance. Some of these actions are as follows:

- To select a person among the managerial personnel who will be responsible for the safety and health of employees
- To ensure safety within the organization and particularly operational safety within the production department
- To provide sufficient education in safe operational performance to employees
- To keep sufficient records related to safety maintenance procedures
- To analyze accidents in order to prevent their repetition
- To formulate and to enforce all instructions related to personnel safety and health

The safety and health procedures should be developed in accordance with standards set by the Occupational Safety and Health Administration (OSHA). The basic OSHA standard states that every employer "shall furnish to each of his employees employment and a place of employment which are free from recognized hazards that are causing or are likely to cause death or serious physical harm."[51]

Under the provisions of the Occupational Safety and Health Act of 1970, OSHA's standards are enforced nationwide through the offices of the Department of Labor. These standards are very comprehensive and apply to all employers except self-employed persons, self-employed farmers and members of their families, and other work places that are regulated by similar standards. OSHA's standards for general industry, for example, are set for the following:

- Walking–working surfaces
- Means of egress
- Powered platforms, lifts, and vehicle-mounted work platforms
- Occupational health and environmental control (ventilation, etc.)
- Hazardous materials
- Personnel protective equipment
- General environmental controls (sanitation, etc.)
- Medical and first aid

- Compressed gas and compressed air equipment
- Materials handling and storage
- Machinery and machine guarding
- Hand and portable powered tools and other hand-held equipment
- Welding, cutting, and braising
- Special industries (textiles, etc.)
- Electrical
- Toxic and hazardous substances
- Fire protection [52]

Safety programs in small and medium-sized companies are usually developed by managerial personnel who are directly involved in the production and operational activities of the firm. As safety expert Willie Hammer suggests:

> A prime requisite for any successful accident prevention program is to leave no doubt in the mind of any employee that his managers are concerned about accident prevention. The most effective means by which this can be done is for the manager at the highest level possible to issue a directive indicating his accident prevention policies and then to insure that his lower level manager, supervisors, and other employees carry them out. . . . For the workers the foreman represents management. He has to see that the intention and orders of management are carried out by exerting his personal authority and influence. If the foreman does not take safety seriously, those under him will not either . . . . [53]

It is essential, therefore, to examine the company's specific safety requirements and ensure, whenever necessary, that

- The factory is well lit, properly ventilated, and kept in generally clean condition.
- Mechanical equipment is adequately safeguarded.
- Electrical installations are sufficiently insulated and grounded.
- Production and operational processes involving various mechanical movements, such as press brake or guillotine, have a dual activation system.
- Tanks containing poisonous liquids or chemical solutions are isolated and surrounded by safety guards, false floor installations, and fume protection systems.
- Tanks and boilers operating under high temperature and pressure have sufficient thermal insulation and proper structural reinforcement.
- Dust-producing plants incorporate efficient air pollution control systems.
- Operators are issued special safety overalls, goggles, boots, gloves, and other protective items.

Management should also ensure that employees do not attempt to modify safety precautions that usually present some form of a mechanical delay or an additional operation. Furthermore, it is essential to enforce that employees wear all personal protective equipment during working hours.

Education and training of employees represents another important avenue of ensuring conditions for safe performance within the company. This education should start during the process of employees' orientation to their jobs and should continue throughout the job performance by means of the following:

- Safety instructions during the orientation and training sessions
- Safety precautions during on-the-job training program
- Safety procedures established by management

- Operational safety meetings
- Explanatory posters and charts describing the safety procedures

Safety experts believe that there are two distinctive factors related to the accident causes in the industry:

- Technical factors
- Human factors

The **technical factor** represents a cause related to plant, equipment, tools, materials, and overall working environment deficiencies. This may include the following:

- Improperly guarded equipment
- Defective equipment
- Hazardous arrangement of procedure in, on, or around, machines or equipment
- Unsafe storage—congestion, overloading
- Improper illumination—glare, insufficient light
- Improper ventilation—insufficient air change, impure air source [54]

The **human factor** represents a cause related to unsafe behavior of employees in the workplace. This may be illustrated by the following:

- Failing to secure equipment
- Failing to use safe attire or personal protective equipment
- Throwing materials
- Operating or working at unsafe speeds, either too fast or too slow
- Making safety devices inoperative by removing, adjusting, disconnecting them
- Using unsafe equipment or using equipment unsafely
- Using unsafe procedures in loading, placing, mixing, combining
- Taking unsafe positions under suspended loads
- Lifting improperly
- Distracting, teasing, abusing, startling, quarreling, horseplay.[55]

Approximately 80% of all accidents in the industry are caused by the human factor. Management should realize, therefore, that a well designed safety program combined with steady education and occupational training of employees may substantially contribute to the company's accident-free performance.

According to OSHA requirements, every employer with 11 or more employees must maintain a set of occupational injury and illness records. Small businesses with fewer than 11 employees are generally exempt from the record-keeping procedure. Basic details of this procedure are summarized in the Exhibit 2–39.

Management should ensure a complete and updated recordkeeping system related to the company's accidents and should conduct a proper accident analysis, which should reflect among others the following points:

- Details of an employee's injury
- Reasons for the accident
- Costs of replacing the injured employee
- Cost of the personnel investigating the accident
- Cost of damage to the production facility, equipment, and materials caused by the accident

Exhibit 2–39

Reporting of Work Related Accidents under Occupational Safety and Health Act (OSHA)

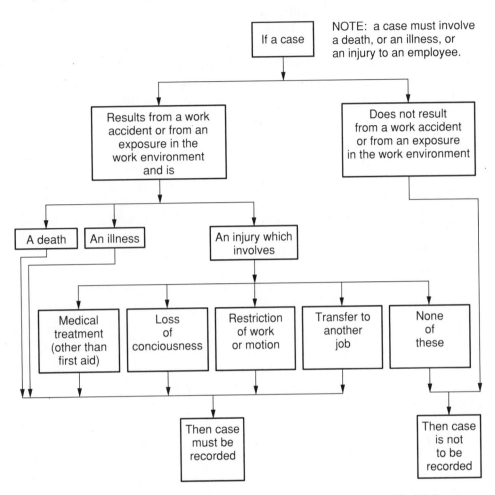

SOURCE: *What Every Employer Needs to Know about OSHA Recordkeeping*, (Washington, D.C.: U.S. Department of Labor, 1978), p. 3.

- Cost of compensation paid out to the injured employee and his or her family as a result of the accident
- Miscellaneous costs related to the accident

Health of the company's personnel represents another important factor in the process of maintaining an accident-free working environment. Management, therefore, should provide working conditions that will prevent any adverse effect on the physical and mental state of the employees. In order to achieve this objective, management should

- Analyze all aspects of the company's operational activities and identify the stage that represents potential health hazards.
- Prepare a standard procedure related to the actual accident-handling process.
- Formulate a health and medical insurance policy.
- Sponsor medical examinations for all employees exposed to health hazards.
- Provide systematic attention to industrial hygiene and sanitation.
- Encourage regular medical examinations for all employees.

Management of medium-sized companies is advised to call on the services of an industrial hygienist to establish an adequate level of health and a hazard-free working environment within the organization. The industrial hygienist is trained to identify operational health hazards, to assess the probability of possible accidents, and to design health programs that will ensure desirable working conditions.

Managers should be prepared to deal with health problems such as drug addiction, alcoholism, or emotional illness. These problems may sometimes occur as a result of **occupational stress**, or **job stress**. Occupational stress places an undesirable burden on the mental and physical state of the employee and may be detrimental to his or her health. In order to prevent such a condition, it is essential to identify and assess the following:

• *Environmental factors.* These include the degree of safety and comfort in the workplace and workload, the nature of duties, the number and types of customers, and the sense of job security.
• *Personal factors.* These include the employee's personality, ability to handle stress, attitude toward work and fellow employees, stress in personal life, and state of physical and mental health.

Regardless of its source, occupational stress affects the well-being of employees and has adverse effects on job performance. These adverse effects, in turn, cause increased frustration, absenteeism and turnover rate of employees, and subsequent deterioration of the company's performance.

2.21 Working Instructions and Forms

All information related to personnel management principles has been presented in Sections 2.01–2.20. It is essential to understand this information and to proceed with the compilation of forms provided at the end of Part 2. Working instructions for completing these forms follow immediately. These instructions require that management rates its knowledge of personnel management principles and evaluates company performance in the area of personnel management. Aggregate scores will help to identify possible problems and to assign priorities for implementing the most effective solutions. The sequence of activities pertinent to completion of working forms is presented in Exhibit 2–40.

Exhibit 2–40

Summary of Forms for Part 2

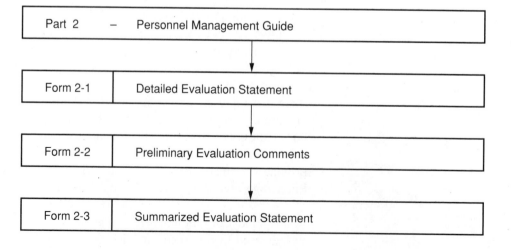

Form 2-1   Detailed Evaluation Statement

8. Study the description of all checkpoints related to *personnel management principles* as outlined in Part 2.

9. Evaluate your personal knowledge in the area of personnel management and score your *personal knowledge level* of each checkpoint. Scores should be based on the scale shown below:

0–20(%)	Very poor level of knowledge
21–40(%)	Poor level of knowledge
41–60(%)	Fair level of knowledge
61–80(%)	Good level of knowledge
81–100(%)	Very good level of knowledge

10. Evaluate your company's performance in the area of personnel management and score your *company's performance level* on each checkpoint. Scores should be based on the scale shown below:

0–20(%)	Very poor level of performance (the checkpoint has never been implemented)
21–40(%)	Poor level of performance (the checkpoint is implemented sometimes)
41–60(%)	Fair level of performance (the checkpoint is implemented but not managed well)
61–80(%)	Good level of performance (the checkpoint is implemented and managed well)
81–100(%)	Very good level of performance (the checkpoint is constantly implemented and managed very well)

11. Determine the *average evaluation level* pertaining to your personal knowledge and the company's performance within each area of personnel management as follows:

$$\text{Average Evaluation Level}(\%) = \frac{\text{Total Score}}{\text{Number of Applicable Checkpoints}}$$

Form 2-2   Preliminary Evaluation Comments

12. State your personal opinion related to personnel management principles currently employed by your company and summarize *preliminary evaluation comments*.

Form 2-3   Summarized Evaluation Statement

13. Issue Form 2–1 and Form 2–2 to key executives within your company who are actively involved in the *personnel management activities* and ensure that both forms are completed in accordance with instructions.

14. Designate a *final evaluation level*[a] for each checkpoint as a result of a meeting between the company executives.

See continuation of working instructions on page 309 (Part 3).

---

[a]The final evaluation level may not represent an average value of the individual results and should be determined by mutual consent.

PERSONNEL MANAGEMENT ANALYSIS
DETAILED EVALUATION STATEMENT

No.	DESCRIPTION	PERSONAL KNOWLEDGE LEVEL (%)	COMPANY'S PERFORMANCE LEVEL (%)				
			VERY POOR	POOR	FAIR	GOOD	VERY GOOD
		0 - 100	0 - 20	21 - 40	41 - 60	61 - 80	81 - 100
2.01	The Personnel Management Process						
2.02	Equal Employment Opportunity Laws						
2.03	Job Analysis						
2.04	Job Descriptions and Job Specifications						
2.05	Personnel Planning and Forecasting						
2.06	Personnel Recruitment and Hiring						
2.07	Screening and Testing of Applicants						
2.08	Employment Interviews						
2.09	Personnel Orientation						
2.10	Personnel Training						
2.11	Management Development						
2.12	Personnel Motivation						
2.13	Basic Job Compensation						
2.14	Financial Incentives						
2.15	Fringe Benefits						
2.16	Personnel Performance Appraisal						
2.17	Personnel Career Management						
2.18	Labor-Management Relations						
2.19	Collective Bargaining and Conflict Management						
2.20	Personnel Safety and Health						
→	AVERAGE EVALUATION LEVEL						

| NAME: | POSITION: | DATE: |

PERSONNEL MANAGEMENT ANALYSIS
PRELIMINARY EVALUATION COMMENTS

No.	DESCRIPTION	PRELIMINARY EVALUATION COMMENTS
2.01	The Personnel Management Process	
2.02	Equal Employment Opportunity Laws	
2.03	Job Analysis	
2.04	Job Descriptions and Job Specifications	
2.05	Personnel Planning and Forecasting	
2.06	Personnel Recruitment and Hiring	
2.07	Screening and Testing of Applicants	
2.08	Employment Interviews	
2.09	Personnel Orientation	
2.10	Personnel Training	
2.11	Management Development	
2.12	Personnel Motivation	
2.13	Basic Job Compensation	
2.14	Financial Incentives	
2.15	Fringe Benefits	
2.16	Personnel Performance Appraisal	
2.17	Personnel Career Management	
2.18	Labor-Management Relations	
2.19	Collective Bargaining and Conflict Management	
2.20	Personnel Safety and Health	

| NAME: | POSITION: | DATE: |

NAME OF COMPANY:

PERSONNEL MANAGEMENT ANALYSIS
SUMMARIZED EVALUATION STATEMENT

No.	DESCRIPTION	COMPANY'S PERFORMANCE LEVEL (%)				
		ASSESSED BY PRESIDENT	ASSESSED BY FINANCIAL EXECUTIVE	ASSESSED BY OPERATIONS EXECUTIVE	ASSESSED BY MARKETING EXECUTIVE	FINAL EVALUATION LEVEL
2.01	The Personnel Management Process					
2.02	Equal Employment Opportunity Laws					
2.03	Job Analysis					
2.04	Job Descriptions and Job Specifications					
2.05	Personnel Planning and Forecasting					
2.06	Personnel Recruitment and Hiring					
2.07	Screening and Testing of Applicants					
2.08	Employment Interviews					
2.09	Personnel Orientation					
2.10	Personnel Training					
2.11	Management Development					
2.12	Personnel Motivation					
2.13	Basic Job Compensation					
2.14	Financial Incentives					
2.15	Fringe Benefits					
2.16	Personnel Performance Appraisal					
2.17	Personnel Career Management					
2.18	Labor-Management Relations					
2.19	Collective Bargaining and Conflict Management					
2.20	Personnel Safety and Health					
→	AVERAGE EVALUATION LEVEL					

NAME:　　　　　　　　　POSITION:　　　　　　　　　DATE:

2.22 References

1. U.S. Congress. Senate. Committee on Labor and Public Welfare. Subcommittee on Labor. *The Equal Employment Opportunity Act of 1972.*

2. U.S. Department of Labor. Employment Standards Administration. Office of Federal Contract Compliance Programs. *Making EEO and Affirmative Action Work.* (Washington, D.C.: 6PO, 1979)

3. U.S. Equal Employment Opportunity Commission. *Affirmative Action and Equal Employment* (Washington, D.C. (GPO, 1974); Reprinted by permission of *Harvard Business Review*, Antonia Handler Chayes, "Make Your Equal Opportunity Program Court Proof," *Harvard Business Review* (Sept. 1974), pp. 81–89, Copyright ©1974 by the President and Fellows of Harvard College; all rights reserved; Gary Dessler, *Personnel Management*, 4e, ©1988, p. 55. Adapted by permission of Prentice Hall, Inc., Englewood Cliffs, New Jersey.

4. B. E. Dowell and K. N. Wexley, "Development of a Work Behavior Taxonomy for First-line Supervisors," *Journal of Applied Psychology,* 63 (1978), pp. 563–572.

5. Adapted from Dessler, pp. 75–79.

6. Adapted from Merrill Lynch Pierce Fenner & Smith, Inc., Equal Employment Opportunity Disclaimer Letter for Applicants.

7. E. J. McCormick and D. R. Ilgen, *Industrial Psychology,* 7th ed. (Englewood Cliffs, NJ.: Prentice Hall, 1980).

8. J. D. Rice, "Privacy Legislation: Its Effect on Pre-employment Reference Checking," *Personnel Administrator,* 23 (1978), pp. 46–51; C. Sewell, "Pre-employment Investigations: The Key to Security in Hiring," *Personnel Journal* 60 (1981), pp. 376–379.

9. James Ledvinka and Lyle Schoenfeldt, "Legal Developments in Employment Testing: Albemarle," *Personnel Psychology,* 31.1 (Spring 1978), p. 9.

10. Dessler, p. 176.

11. Arthur Pell, *Recruiting and Selecting Personnel* (New York: Regents Publishing Co., 1969), pp. 120–121.

12. Elliott Purcell, Michael Campion, and Sara Gaylord, "Structured Interviewing: Avoiding Selection Problems," *Personnel Journal,* 59 (Nov. 1980), pp. 907–912.

13. Kenneth Wexley and Gary Latham, *Developing and Training Managers,* (Glenview, IL.: Scott, Foresman, 1981), p. 104.

14. Adapted from Donald F. Michalack and Edwin G. Yager, *Making the Training Process Work* (New York: Harper & Row, 1979).

15. Kenneth Wexley and Gary Yukl, *Organizational Behavior and Personnel Psychology* (Homewood, IL.: Richard D. Irwin, 1977), pp. 289–295. Reprinted with permission.

16. Dessler, pp. 254–255.

17. Ibid., p.271.

18. Douglas McGregor, "The Human Side of Enterprise," *The Management Review* (November 1957), pp. 22–28, 88–92. Reprinted in Dessler, pp. 314–315.

19. Edwin B. Flippo, *Personnel Management,* 6th ed. (New York: McGraw-Hill, 1984), pp. 390–391.

20. William A. Cohen, *The Entrepreneur & Small Business Problem Solver,* (New York: John Wiley & Sons, 1983), p. 264. Reprinted with permission.

21. Dessler, p. 337.

22. Ibid., pp. 338–342.

23. Ibid., pp. 345–350.

24. Ibid., pp. 385–405.

25. F. Dean Hildedrand, Jr., "Individual Performance Incentives," *Compensation Review,* 10. 3 (1978), p. 32.

26. John Steinbrink, "How to Pay Your Sales Force." *Harvard Business Review* (July-August 1978), p. 115.

27. Randy Swad, "Stock Ownership Plans: A New Employee Benefit," *Personnel Journal* (June 1981), pp. 453-455.

28. Donald Sullivan, "ESOPs," *California Management Review,* 20. 1 (Fall 1977), pp. 55–56.

29. Brian Moore and Timothy Ross, *The Scalon Way to Improved Productivity: A Practical Guide* (New York: John Wiley & Sons, 1978), p. 2.

30. Dessler, pp. 416–450.

31. B. Needless, H. Anderson, and J. Caldwell, *Financial and Managerial Accounting,* (Boston, Mass.: Hougton Mifflin, 1988), p. 347.

32. Richard Henderson, *Compensation Management* (Reston, Va. : Reston Publishing, 1979), p. 250.

33. Thomas Snodeker and Michael Kuhns, "HMO's Regulations, Problems, and Outlook," *Personnel Journal* (Aug. 1981), pp. 629–631.

34. Everett Allen, Jr., Joseph Melone, and Jerry Rosenbloom, *Pension Planning* (Homewood, IL.: Richard D. Irwin, 1981).

35. Robert Johnson, *The Appraisal Interview Guide* (New York: Amacom, 1979), pp. 45–50.

36. Donald Super et al., *Vocational Development: A Framework for Research* (New York: Teachers College Press, 1957); Edgar Schein, *Career Dynamics: Matching Individual and Organizational Needs* (Reading, MA: Addison-Wesley, 1978).

37. John Holland, *Making Vocation Choices: A Theory of Careers* (Englewood Cliffs, N.J.: Prentice Hall, 1973).

38. Schein, pp. 128–129.

39. Joseph Famularo, *Handbook of Modern Personnel Administration.*

40. U. S. Bureau of National Affairs, "Severance Pay Perusal," *Fair Employment Practices* 13 Jan. 1983, p. 7.

41. William J. Morin and Lyle York, *Outplacement Techniques* (New York: Amacom, 1982), pp. 101–131; Reprinted in Dessler, pp. 515–516.

42. "Boardroom Reports," *The Conference Board,* 15 Dec. 1976, p. 6.

43. Richard Hodgetts, *Introduction to Business* (Reading, MA.: Addison-Wesley, 1977), pp. 213–214.

44. Dessler, p. 582.

45. William F. Glueck, "Labor Relations and the Supervisor," in M. Jean Newport, *Supervisory Management: Tools and Techniques* (St. Paul, MN.: West Publishing, 1976), pp. 207–234.

46. William Fulmer, "Step by Step Through a Union Election," *Harvard Business Review* (July-August 1981), pp. 94–102.

47. Matthew Goodfellow, University Research Center. Reprinted in Dessler, p. 600.

48. Reed Richardson, *Collective Bargaining by Objectives,* p. 150. Reprinted in Dessler, pp. 617–618.

49. Dessler, p. 621; based on a contract clause finder published by The Bureau of National Affairs, Washington D.C.

50. Willie Hammer, *Occupational Safety Management and Engineering* (Englewood Cliffs, N.J.: Prentice Hall, 1976), p. 6.

51. U.S. Department of Labor. Occupational Safety and Health Administration. *All about OSHA.* (Washington, D.C.: 1980).

52. U.S. Department of Labor. OSHA, *General Industries Standards.* (Washington, D.C.: 1978).

53. Hammer, *Occupational Safety Management and Engineering.*

54. *A Safety Committee Man's Guide,* Aetna Life and Casualty Insurance Company, Catalog 872684.

55. Ibid.

Part 3

Financial Management Guide

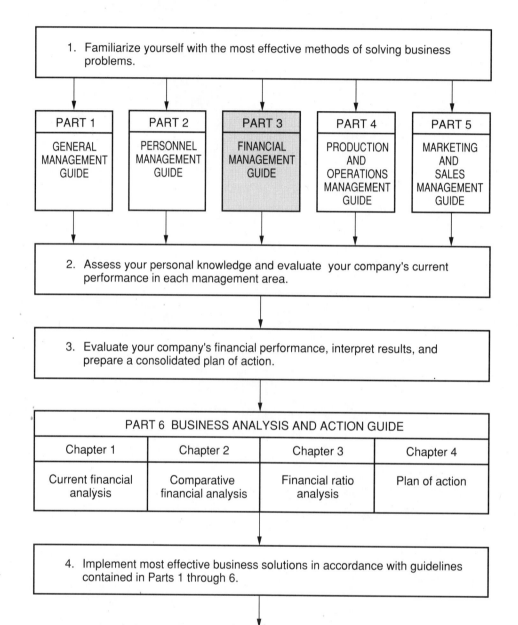

1. Familiarize yourself with the most effective methods of solving business problems.

PART 1	PART 2	PART 3	PART 4	PART 5
GENERAL MANAGEMENT GUIDE	PERSONNEL MANAGEMENT GUIDE	FINANCIAL MANAGEMENT GUIDE	PRODUCTION AND OPERATIONS MANAGEMENT GUIDE	MARKETING AND SALES MANAGEMENT GUIDE

2. Assess your personal knowledge and evaluate your company's current performance in each management area.

3. Evaluate your company's financial performance, interpret results, and prepare a consolidated plan of action.

PART 6 BUSINESS ANALYSIS AND ACTION GUIDE			
Chapter 1	Chapter 2	Chapter 3	Chapter 4
Current financial analysis	Comparative financial analysis	Financial ratio analysis	Plan of action

4. Implement most effective business solutions in accordance with guidelines contained in Parts 1 through 6.

5. Assess whether the action was implemented according to plan and adjust such action when necessary.

- *The 20 elements of practical financial management*
- *Working instructions and forms for evaluating your company's financial management*
- *Guidelines for implementing effective financial management strategies and much more*

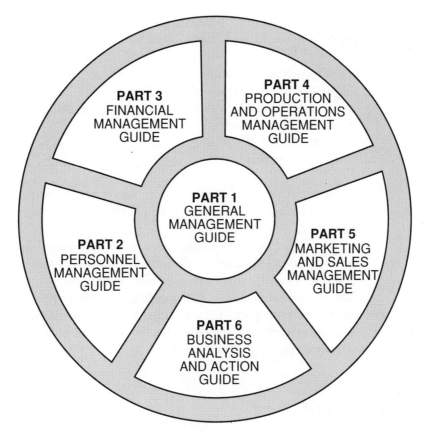

Contents

3.00 Introduction

The prime purpose of the **financial management guide** is to identify business problems and implement the most effective solutions in the area of financial management. This guide highlights a variety of issues, such as:

- How to develop and to maintain a simple bookkeeping system
- How to evaluate the company's performance and to interpret financial statements
- How to prepare operating, capital expenditure, and cash budgets
- How to formulate effective tax strategies
- How to control the company's cash, purchases, disbursements, credit, inventory, and capital assets
- How to control the company's cost structure and to evaluate management accounting reports

These and other related issues are addressed in the financial management guide. All issues are described in **20 checkpoints** presented in **Sections 3.01–3.20**.

To develop the most suitable solutions in the area of financial management, it is necessary to understand the issues discussed in this part. Thorough self-assessment by company executives and evaluation of company performance in the aforementioned area will indicate the effectiveness of current financial management principles. This, in turn, will help to formulate a sound plan of action and to implement the most effective solutions in accordance with the **work program** presented in Exhibit 3-1.

Exhibit 3–1

Work Program for Part 3

Work Program	
Planned Action	**Objective**
1. Study of financial management principles	To attain an adequate level of knowledge in the area of financial management
2. Self-evaluation of knowledge by members of the management team in the area of financial management	To identify individual strengths and weaknesses of members of the management team in the area of financial management
3. Evaluation of company performance in the area of financial management	To identify the level of company performance in the area of financial management and to establish the average evaluation level
4. Formulation of a plan of action in the area of financial management	To summarize the range of activities that must be undertaken in the area of financial management
5. Implementation of the most effective business solutions in the area of financial management	To develop a set of the most suitable solutions in accordance with guidelines presented in this part
6. Evaluation and control of actions in the area of financial management	To assess whether the action was implemented according to plan and to adjust such action when necessary

Note: Please familiarize yourself with relevant working instructions prior to completing forms at the end of this part. Additional information on these forms is available from Business Management Club, Inc., upon request.

3.01 The Financial Management Process

Financial management represents one of the most critical functions within any organization. It is essential, therefore, that top managers pay serious attention to this function and develop, implement, and maintain the financial management process. In simple terms, financial management entails development, implementation, and control of systems aimed at securing the most efficient use of an organization's material and financial resources.

Many business practitioners confuse financial management with accounting, bookkeeping, budgeting, tax preparation, cost accounting, pricing, and management accounting. Although all these functions are interrelated, it is necessary to understand how each function fits into the total responsibility of the financial executive.

The most important task of the financial executive is to initiate a **financial management process** and to develop a financial department within the organization. Planning and control of the financial management process entails a number of steps outlined in Exhibit 3–2.

The financial management process begins with the design and installation of a suitable bookkeeping system. The prime purpose of this system is to enable the company's bookkeeper to record all financial transactions continuously. The ordinary bookkeeping system consists of two sets of books, namely journals and ledgers. All transactions are first recorded in the journals and thereafter posted to appropriate ledger accounts. Subsequently, all balances from the ledger accounts are transferred to a work sheet, and a trial balance is prepared.

An orderly recording of all business transactions pertinent to the company's operations facilitates timely compilation of financial statements. These statements are prepared from the trial balance at least once a year and include a balance sheet, an income statement, and a statement of cash flows. Each statement contains important information about the company's financial condition, past performance, and flow of funds.

Financial statements are used extensively by top managers for evaluating financial performance and for submitting information to existing and potential shareholders, the Internal Revenue Service (IRS), and existing and potential creditors. Evaluation of financial performance thus represents an important managerial responsibility. This evaluation includes current financial analysis covering the most recent fiscal period, comparative financial analysis covering the three preceding fiscal periods, and financial ratio analysis.

Once the financial manager completes the evaluation of the company's present condition and results, performance trends, and financial ratios, it is necessary to initiate the financial planning or budgeting process. This process represents an integral part of the overall planning effort undertaken by top managers within the organization. The prime purpose of the financial planning process is the development of budgets aimed at guiding the company's performance in the future.

Financial planning represents one of the most important responsibilities of the financial manager. The central element of this process is a master budget, which is usually prepared for one fiscal year. The master budget comprises three basic financial plans: operating budget, capital expenditure budget, and cash budget. Each budget is of particular significance to the organization and is discussed in detail later in this part.

Another aspect of financial planning entails formulation of the most effective tax strategies. Since every business is expected to produce profits, it is logical to assume that the organization will be liable to pay a certain portion of that profit

Exhibit 3–2

The Financial Management Process

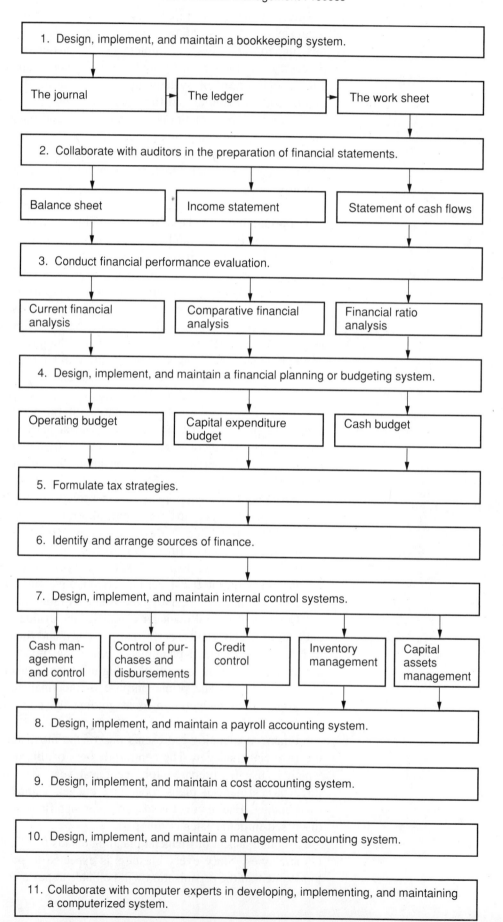

1. Design, implement, and maintain a bookkeeping system.

| The journal | The ledger | The work sheet |

2. Collaborate with auditors in the preparation of financial statements.

| Balance sheet | Income statement | Statement of cash flows |

3. Conduct financial performance evaluation.

| Current financial analysis | Comparative financial analysis | Financial ratio analysis |

4. Design, implement, and maintain a financial planning or budgeting system.

| Operating budget | Capital expenditure budget | Cash budget |

5. Formulate tax strategies.

6. Identify and arrange sources of finance.

7. Design, implement, and maintain internal control systems.

| Cash management and control | Control of purchases and disbursements | Credit control | Inventory management | Capital assets management |

8. Design, implement, and maintain a payroll accounting system.

9. Design, implement, and maintain a cost accounting system.

10. Design, implement, and maintain a management accounting system.

11. Collaborate with computer experts in developing, implementing, and maintaining a computerized system.

in the form of taxes to the federal, state, and local tax authorities. Hence, one of the prime responsibilities of the financial manager is to plan the company's activities in such a manner that the tax liability will be minimized.

Once the development of financial plans is accomplished, it is necessary to implement such plans by integrating financial objectives with the overall operating activities within the organization. This process, however, cannot be accomplished without identifying and developing appropriate sources of finance. Hence, it is necessary to determine how much capital is required to fund the company's operations, over what period, and how it will be used. In addition, it is necessary to establish when and how borrowed funds will be repaid.

The next stage of the financial management process entails the design, implementation, and maintenance of effective internal control systems. These systems comprise cash management and control, control of purchases and disbursements, credit control, and inventory and capital assets management. Each type of control is discussed in detail later in this part.

The financial management process also entails development and installation of a comprehensive payroll accounting system. This system is concerned with determining, recording, and controlling salaries, wages, employees' withholdings, and company contributions. Moreover, an effective payroll accounting system enables the company to meet its obligations toward employees and to comply with relevant regulations imposed by tax authorities.

Design, implementation, and maintenance of a suitable cost accounting system represents another important responsibility of the financial manager. The prime purpose of this system is to ensure that the company recovers all its costs and makes profits while manufacturing and supplying products or rendering services to customers. An effective cost accounting system also facilitates the development of sound pricing methods which are subsequently used throughout the cost estimating and pricing procedures.

In order to ensure effective control within the financial department and to monitor the company's operational performance, it is necessary to design, implement, and maintain a comprehensive management accounting system. The prime purpose of this system is to facilitate the collation of financial data pertinent to the company's actual performance and to compare such data with corresponding budget projections. The comparison between actual and projected results enables the financial manager to determine variances and to identify whether the company meets its planned objectives.

Another aspect which should not be overlooked by the financial manager is the need for computerization of certain functions within the financial department. Such a need may arise, depending upon the requirements of the organization. It is necessary, therefore, to identify the company's particular needs and to seek professional advice from computer experts.

Once all elements of the financial management process are identified, it is necessary to develop the financial department. The person in charge of the financial department in a small or medium-sized company holds the title of **vice president, finance**. This person is responsible for the development, implementation, and maintenance of the financial management system described earlier. The execution of prime functions within the financial department in larger organizations may be allocated to two managers: the controller and the treasurer.[1]

The **controller** is in charge of accounting services and is usually responsible for the following:

- Design, implementation, and maintenance of accounting systems, including a computerized system
- Collaboration with auditors in preparing financial statements for external users
- Evaluation of the company's financial performance
- Design, implementation, and maintenance of a financial planning or budgeting system
- Design, implementation, and maintenance of internal control systems
- Development, implementation, and maintenance of procedures for complying with federal, state, and local tax authorities
- Design, implementation, and maintenance of a cost accounting system (sometimes this function is carried out by a cost accountant)
- Design, implementation, and maintenance of a management accounting system
- Provision of special information requested by management

The **treasurer** is another staff position within the financial department and is usually responsible for the following:

- Development of plans for obtaining short-, medium-, and long-term financing
- Formulation of cash management policies and implementation of cash management and control procedures
- Formulation of credit control policies and implementation of credit control procedures
- Development of plans for investing the company's funds
- Liaison with insurance companies to provide adequate insurance coverage

The company may require additional employees within the financial department, depending upon its particular needs. These employees may include a **bookkeeper** responsible for maintaining the bookkeeping system, a **credit control clerk** responsible for maintaining a credit control system, and others. The final decision pertaining to the allocation of responsibilities within the financial department rests with the company's financial executive.

3.02 Accounting Information

The prime purpose of the financial management process is to develop, implement, and maintain an effective accounting system within the organization. The **accounting system** is designed "to provide quantitative information, primarily financial in nature, about economic entities that is intended to be useful in making economic decisions."[2] An *economic entity* is an independent business enterprise that may be organized as a sole proprietorship, a partnership, or a corporation. Different forms of business organization are discussed later in this part.

Managers are constantly faced with the necessity of making decisions pertaining to various activities of their organization. One manager, for example, may want to know about the company's profitability during a certain operating period, while the other may seek to determine an adequate selling price for a new product or service. In other instances, managers are requested to provide financial information to institutions when applying for additional funds or when preparing special reports for governmental organizations. It is apparent that such information, known as **accounting information**, plays an integral part in the business process.

Accounting information "is a tool and, like most tools, cannot be of much direct help to those who are unable or unwilling to use it or who misuse it. Its use can be learned, however, and (accounting) should provide information that can be used by all—nonprofessionals as well as professionals—who are willing to use it properly."[3] This information is instrumental in coordinating important management decisions and in undertaking appropriate action in accordance with the overall objectives of the organization. An effective financial management system usually provides two different types of accounting information:

- **External reports** to present and potential shareholders, creditors, and tax authorities
- **Internal reports** to management

The emphasis of each type of accounting report differs substantially. External reports, also known as **financial accounting reports**, include three basic financial statements: the balance sheet, the income statement, and the statement of cash flows. These reports are usually submitted to company shareholders, present and potential creditors (e.g., banks and investors, and tax authorities). Financial accounting reports provide important information pertaining to three basic elements of the company's well-being:

- The **balance sheet** illustrates how solvent the company is (i.e., by how much its assets exceed its liabilities, or net worth).
- The **income statement** illustrates how profitable the company is (i.e., by how much its revenues exceed its expenditures, or net income).
- The **statement of cash flows** illustrates how liquid the company is (i.e., whether more cash is flowing into the company than out).

Internal reports, on the other hand, are designed for use in strategic planning, operational planning, and routine controlling activities. These reports, also known as **management accounting reports**, include a broad range of statements developed by the company's financial executive in accordance with the specific needs of the organization. Some of the most popular management accounting reports are as follows:

- **Monthly revenue and expenditure statement.** This statement summarizes monthly and year-to-date revenues and expenses, compares same with corresponding budget projections, and determines variances.
- **Monthly income statement.** This statement summarizes monthly and year-to-date income (or loss), compares same with corresponding budget projections, and determines variances.
- **Monthly debtors (or creditors) age analysis.** This statement summarizes in alphabetical order the amounts owed by the company's customers (or owed by the company to its suppliers) on a 1–30, 31–60, and 61–90 day basis.

The basic differences between financial and management accounting reports are summarized in Exhibit 3–3.

Exhibit 3–3

Differences Between Financial and Management Accounting Reports

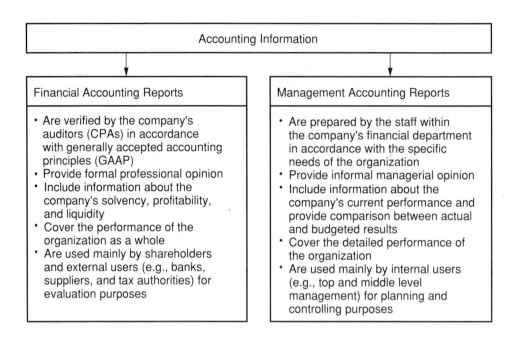

Financial accounting information is recorded in accordance with a particular set of rules known as *generally accepted accounting principles (GAAP)*. The American Institute of Certified Public Accountants (AICPA) has defined these principles as follows:

> Generally accepted accounting principles encompass the conventions, rules, and procedures necessary to define accepted accounting practice at a particular time.[4]

The generally accepted accounting principles have been developed by accountants over a period of years and are subject to change in accordance with prevailing conditions and governmental requirements. Among the organizations that constantly influence these principles are the AICPA, the Financial Accounting Standards Board (FASB), the Securities and Exchange Commission (SEC), the Government Accounting Standards Board (GASB), the American Accounting Association (AAA), and the Internal Revenue Service (IRS).

Financial accounting reports, or financial statements, are verified by the company's auditors, who are *certified public accountants (CPA)*. Independent CPAs are licensed by each state in a manner similar to the legal or medical professions. These CPAs are independent in the sense that they operate their own accounting practices and are not directly employed by the company whose statements they examine. As a part of their service, CPAs perform an unbiased audit of their clients' books. This entails careful examination of the company's accounting and internal control systems, verification of accounting records and inventory existence, identification of amounts owed by the company to its suppliers, and analysis of amounts owed to the company by its customers. As a result of the company's audit, the CPA will be able to express an opinion about the conformance of the company's financial statements to generally accepted accounting principles. The CPA does not express an opinion as to the "fairness" of what the statements represent.

3.03 Bookkeeping System

The first important task of the financial manager is to design, implement, and maintain a suitable **bookkeeping system**. This system, also known as a **double-entry bookkeeping system**, consists of sets of records or books and formal instructions for placing information on these books.

The fundamental rule of double-entry bookkeeping states *that every transaction affects at least two accounts*. Each **account** represents one item that appears on the financial statements (i.e., an asset, liability or owner's equity). In its simplest form, an account consists of three parts:

- A **title** that describes the account
- A left side, or the **debit** side
- A right side, or the **credit** side

This form of the account is termed a **T-account** because of its similarity to the letter *T*. An ordinary T-account is illustrated in Exhibit 3–4.

In accordance with accounting terminology, the term *debit* means "left," from the Latin word *debere* (abbreviated Dr.). The term *credit* means "right," from the Latin word *credere* (abbreviated Cr.). Thus, every entry made on the left side of the T-account is a debit, or a **debit entry**; every entry made on the right side of the T-account is a credit, or a **credit entry**. The terms debit and credit are also used by accountants as verbs. The act of recording a debit in a specific account is called *debiting* the account, while recording a credit is called *crediting* the account.

In an ordinary accounting system, all accounts are classified under suitable headings and coded numerically for easier reference. A list of such coded accounts is known as a **chart of accounts** and comprises five basic categories as follows:

- Assets
- Liabilities
- Shareholders' equity
- Revenue
- Expenses

Assets represent total resources controlled by the organization and utilized for the purpose of obtaining future benefits. Assets are provided to the organization by two prime sources: owners, or shareholders, and outside investors, or creditors. As a result of their investment, shareholders and creditors acquire

Exhibit 3–4
A T-Account

Title of Account

Left or debit side	Right or credit side

a special interest in the organization, which is respectively termed **shareholders' equity** and **creditors' claims**. Thus, according to the basic accounting equation:

Assets = Creditors' Claims + Shareholders' Equity

Liabilities represent the total creditors' claims against assets utilized by the organization. In other words, liabilities represent the total debt of the organization. Such a debt may include money owed by the organization to its employees, suppliers, banks, tax authorities, and various creditors. Thus, according to the basic accounting equation:

Liabilities = Creditors' Claims = Assets – Shareholders' Equity

Shareholders' equity represents the owners' interest in the organization and is equal to the **net worth** of the company. The value of shareholders' equity represents the excess of total company assets over total liabilities. Thus, according to the basic accounting equation:

Shareholders' Equity = Net Worth = Assets – Liabilities

Revenues represent the total value earned by an organization during a specified accounting period. Service organizations, for example, earn revenue by rendering service to customers. The revenue earned may be in either the form of cash or as a receivable. Merchandising and manufacturing organizations, on the other hand, earn revenues as a result of delivering goods to customers. Thus:

Revenue = Total Fees Earned (not necessarily collected) by an Organization

Expenses represent the total cost incurred for services rendered or goods sold by an organization during a specified accounting period. Thus:

Expenses = Total Cost of Sales Incurred (not necessarily paid) by an Organization

The aforementioned accounts are further subdivided into various groups as follows:

- Assets are classified as current assets, capital assets, long-term investments, and intangible assets.
- Liabilities are classified as current liabilities and long-term liabilities.
- Revenues may be classified as revenues from services, gross sales, and net sales (depending upon the nature of company activities).
- Expenses may be classified as cost of goods manufactured, cost of goods available for sale, cost of goods sold, and operating expenses (depending upon the nature of company activities).

A detailed breakdown and explanation of each account is provided in the first chapter of Part 6 (Volume II) and is presented in Forms 6–1 to 6–5.

The basic requirement of a double-entry bookkeeping system is *the equality of debits and credits*. Thus, according to this requirement, equal amounts of debit and credit entries must be recorded for every business transaction. A method of recording these transactions for different types of accounts is presented in Exhibit 3–5.

The fundamental rules for recording transactions in a double-entry bookkeeping system are as follows:

Exhibit 3–5

Rules for Recording Transactions in a Double Entry Bookkeeping System

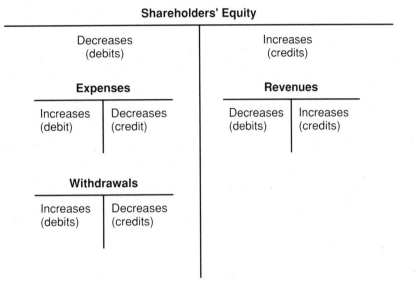

SOURCE: B. E. Needles, Jr., H. R. Anderson, and J. C. Caldwell, *Financial & Managerial Accounting*, (Boston, MA: Houghton Mifflin, 1988), pp. 55–56. Reprinted with permission.

- Increases in assets are debited to asset accounts. Decreases in assets are credited to asset accounts.
- Increases in liabilities are credited to liability accounts. Decreases in liabilities are debited to liability accounts.
- Increases in shareholders' equity are credited to the shareholders' equity account. Decreases in shareholders' equity are debited to the shareholders' equity account.
- Increases in expenses and withdrawals by debits decrease the shareholders' equity account. Decreases in expenses and withdrawals by credits increase the shareholders' equity account.
- Increases in revenues by credits increase the shareholders' equity account. Decreases in revenues by debits decrease the shareholders' equity account.

A typical application of these rules is illustrated in Exhibit 3–6.

An ordinary bookkeeping system consists of two different types of **books of account**:

- **A journal.** This book facilitates the initial entry in a chronological sequence of all transactions from source documents. The process of entering transactions into the journal is called *journalizing*.
- **A ledger.** This book facilitates the transfer of all journal entries in a chronological sequence to individual accounts. The process of recording journal entries into the ledger is called *posting*.

Exhibit 3–6

Application of Rules in a Double-Entry Accounting System

May 1: The owner invested $30,000 in his business

Cash

May 1 30,000	

Owner's Equity

	May 1 30,000

Transaction: Investment in business

Analysis: Assets (i.e., Cash, increased and Owner's Equity increased)

Rules: Increases in assets are debited to assets accounts. Increases in owner's equity are credited to the owner's equity account.

Entry: The Cash account is debited by $30,000 .
The Owner's Equity account is credited by $30,000.

May 2: The owner rented an office and paid rent in advance $1,500.

Cash

May 1 30,000	May 2 1,500

Prepaid Rent

May 2 1,500	

Transaction: Expense paid in advance

Analysis: Asset (i.e., Prepaid Rent, increased) Asset (i.e., Cash, decreased)

Rules: Increase in assets are debited to assets accounts. Decreases in assets are credited to assets accounts.

Entry: The Prepaid Rent account is debited by $1,500. The Cash account is credited by $1,500.

May 3: The owner ordered office supplies ($300).
Analysis: No transaction has occurred; therefore, no entry is made. There is no liability until office supplies are delivered, and there is an obligation to pay for them.

May 4: The owner purchased equipment for $3,000 paying $2,000 and agreeing to pay the balance next month.

Cash

May 1 30,000	May 2 1,500
	May 4 2,000

Equipment

May 4 3,000	

Accounts Payable

	May 4 1,000

Transaction: Purchase of equipment, partial payment.

Analysis: Asset (i.e., Equipment, increased) Asset (i.e., Cash, decreased) Liability (i.e., Accounts Payable, increased)

Rules: Increases in assets are debited to assets accounts. Decreases in assets are credited to assets accounts. Increases in liability are credited to liability accounts.

Entry: The Cash account is credited by $2,000. The Equipment account is debited by $3,000. The Accounts Payable account is credited by $1,000.

SOURCE: Adapted from B.E. Needles, Jr., H.R. Anderson, and J.C. Caldwell, *Financial & Managerial Accounting*, (Boston, MA.: Houghton Mifflin, 1988), pp. 56–61. Reprinted with permission.

A standard procedure for recording transactions in a double-entry bookkeeping system represents an integral part of the **accounting cycle**. This procedure consists of nine steps and is presented in Exhibit 3–7.

Every business transaction must be analyzed and entered into the appropriate journal. At the outset of a company's development, the number of transactions

Exhibit 3–7

Standard Bookkeeping Procedures in an Accounting Cycle

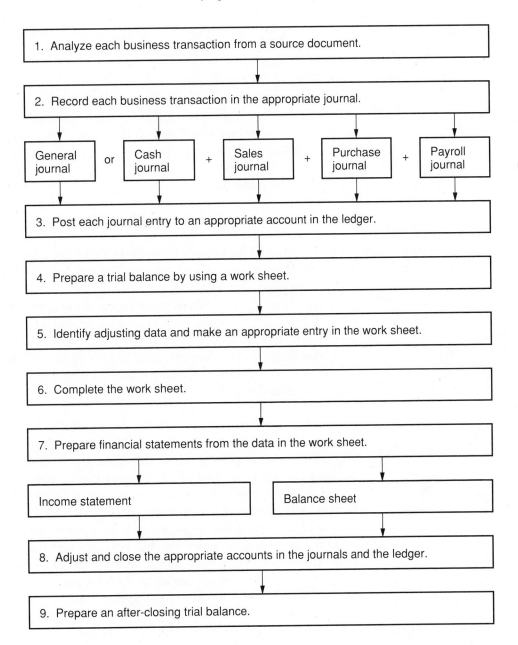

is usually very small. For this reason, all transactions can be entered into one journal known as the **general journal**. When the company grows, however, more and more transactions take place. This growth necessitates the introduction of several journals and the recording of transactions on the following basis:

- All cash receipts and payments are recorded in a **cash journal** or **cash receipts journal**, and **cash payments journal**.
- All credit sales are recorded in a **sales journal**.
- All credit purchases are recorded in a **purchase journal**.

- All salaries, wages, and appropriate deductions are recorded in a **payroll journal** or **payroll register**.

A typical application of various journals is illustrated in Exhibit 3–8. The information contained in a general journal is as follows:

- Date of the transaction
- Description of an account that should be debited
- Description of an account that should be credited
- Posting reference (post. ref.) (i.e., the account's number or code) in a chart of accounts in the ledger
- The debit amount
- The credit amount

Transactions recorded in the general journal reflect the following events:

- On May 1, Jack Jones invested $10,000 in cash into his company. Hence, the Cash account is debited with $10,000 and "Jack Jones, Capital" account is credited with $10,000.
- On May 2, the company purchased equipment and paid $5,000 in cash. Hence, the "Equipment" account is debited with $5,000 and the "Cash" account is credited with $5,000.
- On May 3, the company paid $1,000 to one of its suppliers. Hence, the "Accounts Payable" account is debited with $1,000 and the "Cash" account is credited with $1,000.

Additional transactions which are recorded in other journals are also illustrated in Exhibit 3–8.

The next step in a standard bookkeeping procedure entails posting each journal entry to an appropriate account in the **ledger**. In a manually operated accounting system, a ledger consists of a set of individual pages, or **ledger cards,** that are placed together in a special book or file. Each ledger card contains a record of every transaction pertinent to a particular account. All accounts, in turn, are classified under suitable headings and coded numerically for easier reference. A ledger card summarizes all increases and decreases to a single account in chronological sequence. There is one ledger card for "Cash," one for "Inventory," one for "Accounts Payable," and so on. A typical illustration of posting of data to the ledger is presented in Exhibit 3–9. In this example, $10,000 is debited to the "Cash" account No. 101 and the same amount is credited to the "Jack Jones, Capital" account No. 300 in the general ledger.

Journalizing and posting all business transactions represents a routine bookkeeping task that should be carried out on a daily basis. Periodically, however, it is essential to check that all transactions have been properly recorded and relevant books of account can be balanced. This bookkeeping procedure can be accomplished by preparing a **trial balance** at the end of a selected accounting period. In order to prepare a trial balance, bookkeepers use a special form known as the **work sheet**. In a manually operated bookkeeping system, a work sheet represents the balance of all accounts recorded in the ledger at the end of a selected accounting period. A work sheet contains a number of columns, as illustrated in Exhibit 3–10.

First, the individual balances of each ledger account at a specified date must be entered into the "trial balance" column in the work sheet. All debits (Dr.)

Exhibit 3–8

A Typical Illustration of Journal Entries

General Journal					Page 1
Date	Description		Post. Ref.	Debit	Credit
	Account Debited	Account Credited			
May 1	Cash	Jack Jones, capital		10,000	10,000
2	Equipment	Cash		5,000	5,000
3	Accounts payable	Cash		1,000	1,000

Cash Receipts Journal								Page 1
Date	Account Debited/Credited	Post. Ref.	Debits			Credits		
			Cash	Sales Discount	Other Discount	Sales	Accounts Receivable	Other Accounts
May 4	Jack Jones, capital		10,000					10,000
5	Cash sales		10,000			10,000		
6	Payment by customer		475	25			500	

Cash Payments Journal									Page 1
Date	Check No.	Payee	Account Credited/ Debited	Post. Ref.	Credits			Debits	
					Cash	Purchase Discount	Other Accounts	Accounts Payable	Other Accounts
May 3	100	Jack Jones	Salary		1,000				1,000
9	101	ABC properties	Rent		500				500
10	102	Supplier A	Purchases		1,440	60		1,500	

Sales Journal						Page 1
Date	Account Debited	Invoice No.	Post. Ref.	Debit	Credit	
				Accounts Receivable	Sales Taxes Payable	Sales
May 11	Customer A	100		318	18	300
May 12	Customer B	101		530	30	500
May 13	Customer C	102		848	48	800

Purchase Journal								Page 1
Date	Account Credited	Date of Invoice	Terms	Post. Ref.	Credit	Debit		
					Accounts Payable	Purchases	Services	Other Accounts
May 15	Supplier A	5/15	2/15		1,000	1,000		
May 16	Supplier B	5/16	n/30		500		500	
May 17	Supplier C	5/17	n/30		800			800

Payroll Journal												Week No: 10
Employee	Total Hours	Earnings—Gross			Deductions						Payment	
		Normal Time	Over Time	Total	FICA Tax	Fed. Income Tax	Union Dues	Insurance		Other	Net	Check No.
								Medical	Life			
Jack A.	50	350.00	100.00	450.00	50.00	40.00	3.00	30.00	20.00	—	307.00	201
Peter B.	40	300.00	—	300.00	30.00	25.00	3.00	20.00	—	—	222.00	202
Joan C.	35	200.00	—	200.00	20.00	15.00	3.00	—	—	—	162.00	203

Exhibit 3–9

A Typical Illustration of a Posting Procedure

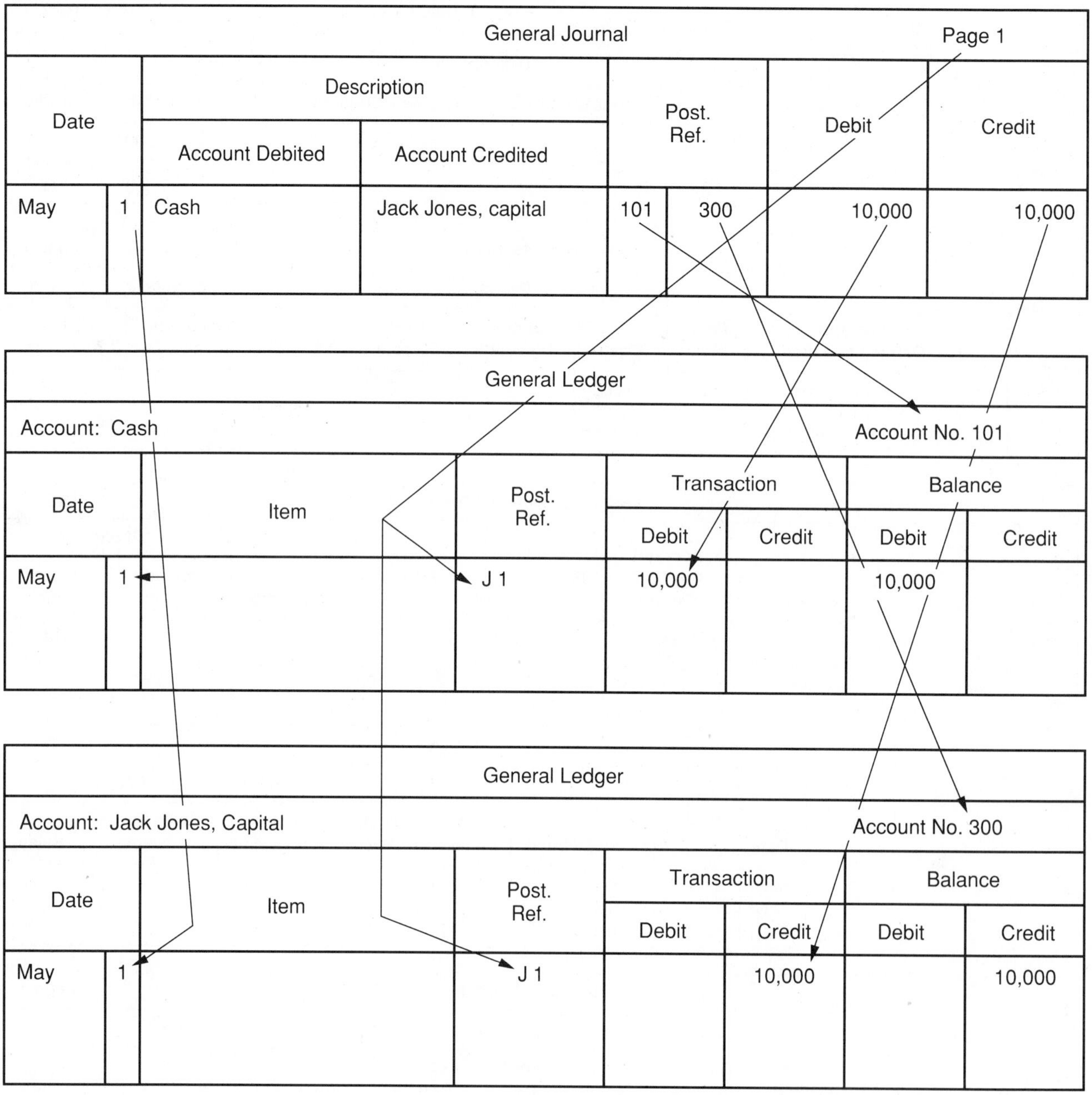

General Journal					Page 1
	Description		Post. Ref.	Debit	Credit
Date	Account Debited	Account Credited			
May 1	Cash	Jack Jones, capital	101 | 300	10,000	10,000

General Ledger

Account: Cash — Account No. 101

Date	Item	Post. Ref.	Transaction		Balance	
			Debit	Credit	Debit	Credit
May 1		J 1	10,000		10,000	

General Ledger

Account: Jack Jones, Capital — Account No. 300

Date	Item	Post. Ref.	Transaction		Balance	
			Debit	Credit	Debit	Credit
May 1		J 1		10,000		10,000

and credits (Cr.) must be summarized and a trial balance obtained. Sometimes, however, bookkeepers experience difficulty in balancing books of account as a result of erroneous journalizing or posting of a particular business transaction. For this reason, it is necessary to double-check all entries and to identify the recording error in a specific account. Once the error is identified, an adjustment must be entered into the "Adjustments" column. This adjustment necessitates addition of all corresponding balances recorded in the first two columns and enables the bookkeeper to balance all debits and credits in an "Adjusted trial balance" column.

The next stage of the bookkeeping procedure entails preparation of preliminary financial statements—namely, the income statement and the balance sheet.

Exhibit 3–10

A Typical Illustration of Entries in a Work Sheet

ABC Corporation
Work Sheet
For the Month Ended May 31, 1989

Description	Trial Balance Dr.	Trial Balance Cr.	Adjustments Dr.	Adjustments Cr.	Adjusted Trial Balance Dr.	Adjusted Trial Balance Cr.	Income Statement Dr.	Income Statement Cr.	Balance Sheet Dr.	Balance Sheet Cr.
Cash	2,900				2,900				2,900	
Accounts Receivable	1,500				1,500				1,500	
Office Supplies	1,400			(b) 300	1,100				1,100	
Prepaid Rent	600			(a) 200	400				400	
Equipment	6,000				6,000				6,000	
Accumulated Depreciation, Equipment				(c) 100		100				100
Accounts Payable		1,200				1,200				1,200
Jack Jones, Capital		10,000				10,000				10,000
Jack Jones, Withdrawals	1,200				1,200				1,200	
Service Fees Earned		4,000		(d) 500		4,500		4,500		
Wage Expense	1,400		(e) 400		1,800		1,800			
Utility Expense	150				150		150			
Telephone Expense	50				50		50			
	15,200	15,200								
Rent Expense			(a) 200		200		200			
Office Supply Expense			(b) 300		300		300			
Depreciation Expense, Equipment			(c) 100		100		100			
Accrued Fees Receivable			(d) 500		500				500	
Accrued Wages Payable				(e) 400		400				400
			1,500	1,500	16,200	16,200	2,600	4,500	13,600	11,700
Net Income							1,900			1,900
							4,500	4,500	13,600	13,600

In order to accomplish this task, it is necessary to extend the adjusted balances of all revenue and expense accounts to the "Income statement" column and all assets, liabilities and shareholders' (owners') equity accounts to the "Balance sheet" column. Doing so will enable the bookkeeper to prepare preliminary financial statements, which will remain subject to verification by the company's auditors.

The last stage of the bookkeeping procedure entails adjusting and closing the appropriate accounts in the journals and the ledger. Once this procedure is accomplished, the bookkeeper may prepare an after-closing trial balance, thereby providing the company's auditors with tangible proof of accurate recording of all business transactions.

3.04 Financial Statements

Accurate and comprehensive maintenance of the bookkeeping system facilitates timely preparation of financial statements. These statements consist of three important documents:

- Balance sheet
- Income statement
- Statement of cash flows

The **balance sheet** is a statement of the company's financial position at a specific moment in time. It is referred to as a "snapshot" of the organization's resources and obligations and is intended to describe the financial condition of the company on the date of closing the books of account. The resources, or assets, available to management are classified as:

- **Current assets** such as cash, accounts receivable, inventory (merchandise, direct materials, work-in-process, and finished goods), notes receivable, prepaid expenses, refundable deposits, and short-term investments
- **Capital assets**, also known as **fixed assets** or **long-term assets**, such as land, buildings, equipment, furniture, and vehicles purchased for use
- **Long-term investments** such as land, buildings, or equipment purchased for speculative reasons
- **Intangible assets** such as patents, copyrights, trademarks, and goodwill

The obligations, or claims, against these assets are made by creditors and shareholders and are classified as follows:

- **Current liabilities** such as accounts payable, bank overdraft, current portion of a long-term debt, deferred revenues, dividends payable, notes payable, payroll liability, taxes payable, product warranty liability, and other accrued liabilities
- **Long-term liabilities** such as bonds payable, capital leases, mortgages payable, and pension liability
- **Shareholders' equity** for issued stock and retained earnings

The balance sheet is usually drawn up on a regular basis covering a particular period of the company's operating activities. This period is termed the **accounting period** and represents an important milestone in the company's life. The length of the accounting period is commonly accepted as one full year, known as the **fiscal year** or **financial year**. Management has the option of selecting the beginning of the company's fiscal year in accordance with the particular operating conditions and other relevant factors. Sometimes the balance sheet may be drawn up on a half-yearly, quarterly, or monthly basis, depending upon the specific requirements of the shareholders. In any event, the balance sheet does not indicate whether the company makes profits or incurs losses. It merely summarizes the financial position and provides details of all assets and liabilities of the organization at a given date.

The balance sheet can be presented in several forms and may contain, among other details, the information illustrated in Exhibit 3–11. Additional information about all financial statements is provided in Part 6 (Volume II).

The main purpose of the **income statement** is to communicate financial information related to the company's operating activities and to summarize

Exhibit 3–11

Balance Sheet

ABC Service Company
Balance Sheet
Date: December 31, 1989

Assets			Liabilities		
Current Assets:			**Current Liabilities:**		
			(+) Accounts payable		$18,000
			Long-Term Liabilities:		
(+) Cash		$20,000			
(+) Accounts receivable		35,000			
(+) Notes receivable		5,000	(+) Capital lease		7,000
(+) (=) Total current assets		60,000	(=) Total liabilities		25,000
Capital Assets:			**Owner's Equity:**		
(+) Building		30,000	(+) Jack Jones, capital		85,000
(+) Office equipment		3,000			
(+) Vehicles		17,000			
(+) (=) Total capital assets		50,000			
(=) Total assets		$110,000	(=) Total liabilities and owner's equity		$110,000

the amounts of **revenues** earned and **expenses** incurred during a specific accounting period. The prime result of the income statement is the determination of **gross margin from sales** (for merchandising and manufacturing companies) and **net income**.

The final presentation form of revenues, expenses, and net income depends upon the nature of the company's operating activities. This is reflected in three different forms of income statements:

- Income statement for a *service* company
- Income statement for a *merchandising* company
- Income statement for a *manufacturing* company (including statement of cost of goods manufactured)

An illustration of a typical income statement for a service company is presented in Exhibit 3–12. Revenues include all amounts earned by the company as a result of rendering services or selling goods to customers during the accounting period, while expenses include all costs incurred by the company during the same period. These costs are classified either as **operating expenses** (for all companies) or as **manufacturing costs** (for manufacturing companies only).

Furthermore, the income statement contains detailed information pertaining to the value of inventory carried by the organization during a particular accounting period. The classification of inventory also depends upon the nature of the company's activities:

- A service company usually does not carry inventory except for certain consumable items (e.g., supplies, or spare parts).
- A merchandising company carries inventory for resale known as **merchandise inventory.**
- A manufacturing company carries three types of inventory—**direct materials inventory, work-in-process inventory,** and **finished goods inventory.**

Exhibit 3–12

Income Statement for a Service Company

ABC Service Company
Income Statement
For a Period: January 1, 1989 - December 31, 1989

Revenues

(+)	Service fees earned			$250,000
	Operating Expenses			
	(+) Advertising expenses		$ 20,000	
	(+) Audit and secretarial fees		3,000	
	(+) Communication expenses		12,000	
	(+) Depreciation, capital assets		8,000	
	(+) Insurance expenses		6,000	
	(+) Office supples and expenses		17,000	
	(+) Rent		20,000	
	(+) Salaries and wages		100,000	
	(+) Traveling and entertainment		8,000	
	(+) Utilities		6,000	
(−) (=)	Total operating expenses			200,000
(=)	Income from operations			50,000
(−)	Interest expense			10,000
(=)	Income before taxes			40,000
(−)	Income taxes expense			12,000
(=)	Net income			$ 28,000

Additional information pertinent only to manufacturing companies is included in the **statement of cost of goods manufactured**. The main purpose of this statement is to summarize all manufacturing costs incurred during a specific accounting period and to establish the cost of goods manufactured. This information is essential to the process of determining the income for a manufacturing company.

An income statement, or **profit and loss account (P and L account)**, is usually computed on a monthly basis to ensure sufficient control over the company's operating activities. The statement summarizing twelve months of the company's performance is termed the **annual income statement** and represents the second important financial statement.

Each financial statement provides essential information pertinent to company activities during a specified accounting period. The balance sheet, for example, illustrates at a point in time the assets and liabilities of the company. The income statement, on the other hand, summarizes the results of the company's operating performance during the accounting period.

There are, however, certain important issues that are not addressed by these financial statements. These issues relate to the actual flow of cash into and from the organization during the accounting period. It may be necessary, for example, to identify whether the company generated a positive cash flow or a negative cash flow as a result of its operating activities and whether investing and financing activities yield or consume cash.

Positive cash flow signifies that the company received, but not necessarily earned, more cash than it has issued during a particular accounting period. *Negative cash flow*, conversely, means that the company issued, but not necessarily spent, more cash than it has received during the same period.

Furthermore, the company may be involved in various activities apart from providing services, purchasing merchandise for resale, or manufacturing goods for sale to customers. The company may also purchase capital assets, such as machinery and equipment for operational use, or a piece of land for investment purposes, or it may repay a debt to one of its creditors. All such activities should be classified either as operating, investing, or financing activities as follows:

- **Operating activities.** These include transactions that relate to the determination of net income (i.e., revenues received from customers, interest received from investments, manufacturing costs, operating expenses, interest, and tax expenses).
- **Investing activities.** These include only transactions that relate to the purchase or sale of capital assets and of marketable securities and advance or collection of loans to and from borrowers.
- **Financing activities.** These include only transactions that relate to obtaining and returning funds from and to shareholders and creditors.

All information related to the inflow and outflow of cash as a result of these activities is summarized in the **statement of cash flows**. This is the third important financial statement. It summarizes all cash receipts and cash payments during a particular accounting period. An illustration of a typical statement of cash flows is presented in Exhibit 3–13.

Exhibit 3–13

Statement of Cash Flows

ABC Service Company
Statement of Cash Flows
For a Period: January 1, 1989 - December 31, 1989

Cash Flows from Operating Activities:

(+)		Receipts from revenue from services	$200,000	
(+)		Receipts from miscellaneous revenue	10,000	
(−)		Payments for operating expenses	(180,000)	
(−)		Payment for interest expenses	(10,000)	
(−)		Payments for tax expenses	(5,000)	
(+)	(=)	Net cash flow from operating activities		$15,000

Cash Flows From Investing Activities:

(+)		Proceeds from sales of capital assets	2,000	
(+)		Proceeds from sales of marketable securities	4,000	
(−)		Payments to purchase capital assets	(10,000)	
(−)		Payments to purchase marketable securities	(8,000)	
(+)	(=)	Net cash flow from investing activities		(12,000)

Cash Flows from Financing Activities:

(+)		Proceeds from short- and long-term borrowing	20,000	
(−)		Repayments of short- and long-term borrowing	(10,000)	
(−)		Payments of dividends	(6,000)	
(+)	(=)	Net cash flow from financing activities		4,000
(=)		Net increase (decrease) in cash		7,000
(+)		Cash balance at the start of the period		50,000
(=)		Cash balance at the end of the period		$ 57,000

3.05 Financial Performance Evaluation

The timely preparation and the availability of financial statements assists top management in the process of examining the condition and performance of a company. This process, known as **financial performance evaluation**, serves to identify the company's strengths and weaknesses in terms of dollars and percentages. Financial performance evaluation, for example, indicates whether the company

- Has enough cash to meet all its obligations.
- Generates sufficient volume of sales to justify recent investment.
- Collects outstanding accounts from customers without creating a burden on its cash flow.
- Makes timely payments to suppliers to take advantage of discounts.
- Utilizes the inventory in an efficient manner.
- Has sufficient working capital.
- Generates an adequate profit margin.
- Produces sufficient return on investment.

All these and other conditions must be met to ensure effective organizational performance and an acceptable level of return on the shareholders' investment. To determine whether such conditions are met, management must evaluate company performance on a regular basis (say once every three, six, or twelve months) and analyze results in terms of:

- Predetermined standards.
- Past performance.
- Acceptable norms within an industry.

Evaluation of the company's performance in terms of predetermined standards provides the most significant management information and helps in the decision-making process. Such an evaluation entails comparison of current or most recent results achieved by the organization with corresponding financial plans. Hence, it is necessary to have a set of well-defined plans to ensure sound evaluation of the company's financial performance.

Comparison of the company's current or most recent results with the corresponding results of previous years is particularly useful in identifying trends. Examination of trends helps management to develop an "early warning system" and provides tangible signs of potential problems in various areas of company activities.

An effective evaluation of the company's performance also entails comparison of financial results attained by the organization with corresponding results acceptable in a particular industry. Such a comparison is usually accomplished by means of special ratios, known as **financial ratios**. These ratios are frequently used not only by managers, but also by investors, creditors, and various financial institutions.

Financial performance evaluation thus represents an important managerial responsibility and comprises three elements, as illustrated in Exhibit 3–14:

- Current financial analysis
- Comparative financial analysis
- Financial ratio analysis

Exhibit 3–14

Financial Performance Evaluation

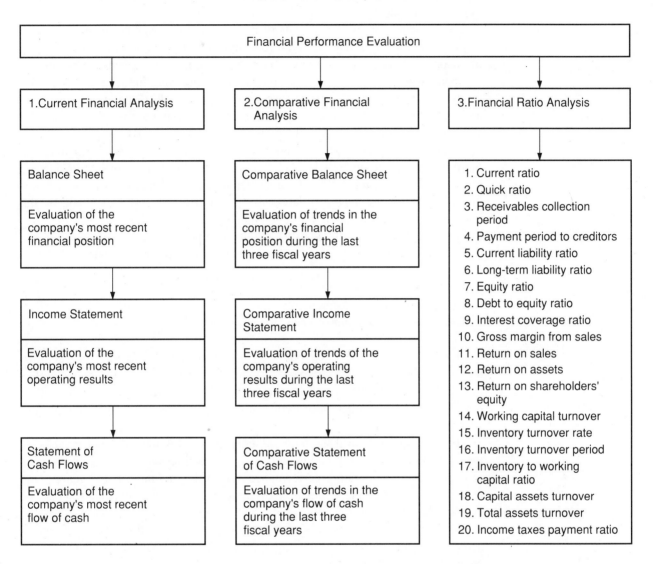

The prime purpose of **current financial analysis** is to evaluate the most recent financial condition and operating results achieved by the company. The central question that is addressed at this stage of the financial performance evaluation is: "Where is the company now in terms of dollars and percentages?"

Current financial analysis entails a comprehensive examination of the company's latest available financial statements as follows:

- Balance sheet
- Income statement
- Statement of cash flows

Examination of the latest balance sheet enables management to achieve the first objective of the current financial analysis—to measure the company's most recent financial condition. This results in detailed evaluation of assets, liabilities, working capital (the difference between current assets and current liabilities), and shareholders' equity.

Examination of the latest income statement helps management to achieve the second objective of the current financial analysis—to measure the company's most recent operating performance. This leads to the comprehensive evaluation of revenues and expenses and the determination of cost of goods sold, gross margin from sales, and net income.

Examination of the latest statement of cash flows enables management to achieve the third objective of the current financial analysis—to measure the flow of incoming and outgoing funds. Such an examination indicates whether the company is generating a positive cash flow (i.e., incoming funds exceed outgoing funds) or, conversely, a negative cash flow as a result of its operating, investing, and financing activities. A detailed explanation pertaining to the current financial analysis is provided in the first chapter of Part 6 (Volume II).

The prime purpose of the **comparative financial analysis** is to evaluate the trends in the company's financial condition and operating results during the last three fiscal years. The central question that is addressed at this stage of the financial performance evaluation is: "What are the trends developed by the company in terms of dollars and percentages?"

Comparative financial analysis entails comprehensive examination of the company's financial statements covering three preceding fiscal years:

- Comparative balance sheet
- Comparative income statement
- Comparative statement of cash flows

Examination of the three balance sheets enables management to achieve the first objective of the comparative financial analysis—to interpret changes in the company's financial condition during the last three fiscal years. This results in detailed evaluation of trends of assets, liabilities, working capital, and shareholders' equity.

Examination of the three income statements helps management to achieve the second objective of the comparative financial analysis—to interpret changes in the company's operating performance during the last three fiscal years. This leads to comprehensive evaluation of trends of revenues, expenses, costs of goods sold, gross margins from sales, and net income.

Examination of the three statements of cash flow enables management to achieve the third objective of comparative financial analysis—to interpret the changes in cash flows that have occurred in the company during the last three fiscal years. This results in detailed evaluation of trends of cash flows as a result of the company's operating, investing, and financing activities. A detailed explanation pertaining to the comparative financial analysis is provided in the second chapter of Part 6 (Volume II).

Financial ratio analysis enables management to evaluate the company's financial condition and operating results. The central question that is addressed at this stage of the financial performance evaluation is: "How does the company's financial condition and operating performance compare with the industry norms?"

Financial ratio analysis illustrates the relationship between two specific values extracted from an appropriate balance sheet or income statement. The main purpose of financial ratio analysis is to provide management and other parties with important information related to the company's:

- Liquidity
- Solvency
- Profitability
- Ability to manage assets

The **liquidity** of the company is its ability to meet current obligations upon their maturity by means of converting available assets into cash and to pay current liabilities. Evaluation of the company's liquidity entails computation and interpretation of the following financial ratios:

- **Current ratio.**   This ratio measures the number of times that current liabilities could be paid out of current assets.
- **Quick ratio.**   This ratio measures the number of times that current liabilities could be paid out of current assets (excluding inventory).
- **Receivables collection period.**   This is the average period of time required to collect cash after a sale on credit.
- **Payment period to creditors.**   This is the average period of time required to pay cash after a purchase on credit.

The **solvency** of the company is its ability to meet all obligations and pay debts as they come due, whether such liabilities are current or long-term ones. Evaluation of the company's solvency entails computation and interpretation of the following financial ratios:

- **Current liability ratio.**   This ratio measures the number of times current liabilities could be paid out of total assets.
- **Long-term liability ratio.**   This ratio measures the number of times long-term liabilities could be paid out of total assets.
- **Equity ratio.**   This ratio measures the extent of shareholders' contribution in the process of acquiring company assets.
- **Debt to equity ratio.**   This ratio measures the proportion of financing provided to the company by outside creditors against the funds introduced by its shareholders.
- **Interest coverage ratio.**   This ratio measures the amount earned from operating activities that is available to pay the interest burden.

The **profitability** of the company reflects its ability to generate revenues, to produce a sizeable net income, and to produce an acceptable return on investment. Evaluation of the company's profitability entails computation and interpretation of the following financial ratios:

- **Gross margin from sales.**   This ratio measures the cost of goods sold in relation to net sales generated by the company.
- **Return on sales.**   This ratio compares net income against net sales generated by the company.
- **Return on assets.**   This ratio compares net income against the average value of total assets employed by the company.
- **Return on shareholders' equity.**   This ratio compares net income against the average value of shareholders' equity.

The company's **ability to manage assets** reflects the degree of utilization of working capital, inventory, capital, and other assets in the process of generating funds during a specific accounting period. Evaluation of the company's ability to manage assets entails computation and interpretation of the following financial ratios:

- **Working capital turnover.**   This ratio compares net sales generated by the company against the average value of working capital employed.

- **Inventory turnover rate.** This ratio compares the cost of goods sold against the average value of inventory kept by the company.
- **Inventory turnover period.** This is the average period of time during which the company undergoes a complete cycle of replacing inventory.
- **Inventory to working capital ratio.** This ratio compares the average value of inventory kept by the company against the average value of working capital employed.
- **Capital assets turnover.** This ratio compares net sales generated by the company against the average value of capital assets employed.
- **Total assets turnover.** This ratio compares net sales generated by the company against the average value of total assets employed.
- **Income taxes payment ratio.** This ratio compares income tax expense against the income before tax generated by the company.

As a result of financial ratio analysis, management can compare the company's financial condition and operating performance against an appropriate set of norms in a particular industry. Such norms, or **industry averages,** can be obtained from Dun & Bradstreet, Business Management Club, Robert Morris Associates, and various trade organizations. A detailed explanation pertaining to the financial ratio analysis is provided in the third chapter of Part 6 (Volume II).

3.06 Operating Budget

The evaluation of financial statements provides management with essential information and assists throughout the financial planning process. The main objective of this process is to prepare a set of plans, or budgets, for the forthcoming fiscal period. In accounting terms, a **budget** is defined as a comprehensive quantitative plan for utilizing the resources of the organization within a specified period of time.

The process of preparing a budget, or a **budgeting process**, is an integral part of the company's operational planning activities. This process has several important advantages

- Management ideas can be converted into tangible objectives and formal plans.
- Objectives and plans can be communicated throughout the organization.
- Strategic and operational plans can be implemented efficiently to achieve organizational objectives.
- Coordination of operational activities within the organization can be improved.
- Standards for evaluating management performance in various departments are provided.
- Effective management control is facilitated.

Hence, the budgeting process is one of the most important managerial responsibilities. This process starts with a corporate appraisal by top management in conjunction with establishing preliminary parameters for the company's financial performance. In conducting a corporate appraisal, managers should ask themselves the following questions:

- What business are we really in?
- Do we have unique or valuable skills?
- Who are our customers and how do they view us?

- What is our position in the marketplace?
- Who are our competitors and how do they view us?
- What is our position in the industry?
- What are our major strengths and weaknesses?
- What should be done to improve our performance?
- Where do we want to be in one to five years from now?
- Do we have to incur additional capital expenditure?
- How can we finance our future development?
- What steps do we have to take to achieve our objectives?

Once these questions are answered in a suitable manner, managers should establish appropriate financial objectives concerning company performance and proceed with the budgeting process. Budgets are usually compiled for one fiscal year and then subdivided into monthly periods, providing the necessary level of management control. Preparation of budgets entails decisions related to

- Objectives to be fulfilled.
- Activities required for fulfilling those objectives.
- Facilities to be utilized in carrying out those activities.
- Cost of those facilities.

The final outcome of the budgeting process is a **master budget**, which consists of two major components:

1. **Operating budget.** This is a financial plan that provides a description of a company's future operating results. It includes sales budget, production (cost of sales) budget, operating expenses budget, and budgeted income statement.
2. **Financial budget.** This is a financial plan that provides a description of a company's future financial condition. It includes capital expenditure budget, cash budget (cash flow projection), and budgeted balance sheet.

All individual budgets are strongly interrelated and must be prepared in a particular sequence. The formal relationship between these budgets and the sequence of their preparation is illustrated in Exhibit 3–15.

The operating budgeting process starts with the preparation of a **sales budget.** This budget must be prepared by the sales manager in accordance with realistic estimates of sales volume likely to be achieved during the forthcoming fiscal period. The main factors that usually influence the sales budgeting process are as follows:

- Nature of the company's products and services
- History of previous sales
- Seasonal variations in product demand
- The company's current position in the marketplace
- Influence by competitors
- The company's plans for new product or service development
- Expected product or service demand in the marketplace
- Economic stability in the marketplace
- Rate of inflation

As a result of detailed evaluation of these factors, the sales manager is expected to prepare accurate sales forecasts pertaining to all products or services offered by the company. These forecasts provide quantitative estimates of the

Exhibit 3–15

Sequence of Preparation of Individual Components of the Master Budget

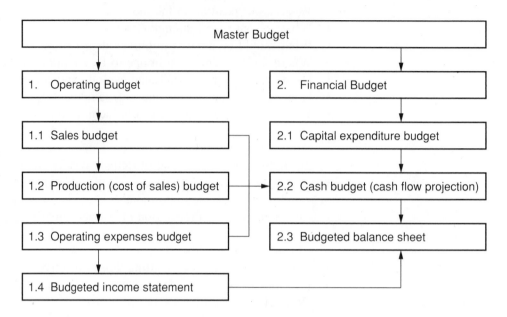

level of sales, expressed in monetary terms, or units of product to be sold, or units of service to be rendered during the budgeted period. Sales forecasts are usually prepared for one fiscal year, thereby providing the first important parameter for the overall budgeting process. Additional details pertaining to the sales budgeting process are provided in Part 5 (Volume II). A typical sales budget is presented in Exhibit 3–16.

The second stage in the operating budgeting process entails preparation of supporting budgets. These budgets may differ depending upon the type of the company's operations:

- Service operations
- Merchandising operations
- Manufacturing operations

A *service company* provides a range of specific services to customers and incurs certain operating expenses as a result of its activities. Hence, in addition to the sales budget, it is necessary to prepare an **operating expenses budget,** which should include all sales and administrative costs estimates. Once the operating expenses budget is completed, it should be integrated with the sales budget into a **budgeted income statement**. A typical budgeted income statement for a service company is presented in Exhibit 3–17.

Exhibit 3–16

Sales Budget

ABC Company Sales Budget For a Period: January 1, 1990 - December 31, 1990	
Description	**Estimated Value**
Product (service) range A	$ 300,000
Product (service) range B	500,000
Product (service) range C	400,000
Total	$1,200,000

Exhibit 3–17

Budgeted Income Statement for a Service Company

		ABC Service Company Budgeted Income Statement For a Period: January 1, 1990 - December 31, 1990			
		Account Description	**Budget Value ($)**		**Percentage of Net Sales**
			Annual	**Monthly**	
+		Service fees earned	300,000	25,000	100.0
	+	Advertising expenses	21,600	1,800	7.2
	+	Audit and secretarial fees	2,400	200	0.8
	+	Communication expenses	13,200	1,100	4.4
	+	Depreciation, capital assets	8,400	700	2.8
	+	Insurance expenses	7,200	600	2.4
	+	Office supplies and expenses	19,200	1,600	6.4
	+	Rent	21,600	1,800	7.2
	+	Salaries and wages	115,200	9,600	38.4
	+	Traveling and entertainment	9,600	800	3.2
	+	Utilities	3,600	300	1.2
−	=	Total operating expenses	222,000	18,500	74.0
=		Income from operations	78,000	6,500	26.0
−		Interest expense	6,000	500	2.0
=		Income before taxes	72,000	6,000	24.0
−		Income taxes expense	24,000	2,000	8.0
=		Net income	48,000	4,000	16.0

A *merchandising company* is engaged in the buying and selling of products to customers at a profit. This type of operation requires that the company carries a sufficient quantity of merchandise inventory in its stores. In addition, the merchandising company incurs sales and administrative expenses as a result of its activities. Thus, the operating budgeting process for a merchandising company entails preparation of two additional budgets:

- **Cost of goods sold budget.** This budget includes the estimated net cost of merchandise purchases and the difference between the estimated inventory values at the start and at the end of the budgeted period.
- **Operating expenses budget.** This budget includes all sales and administrative cost estimates.

Upon estimating all costs and relevant inventory values, both budgets must be integrated with the sales budget to prepare a budgeted income statement. A typical budgeted income statement for a merchandising company is presented in Exhibit 3–18.

A *manufacturing company* is engaged in converting raw materials into finished goods by means of utilizing labor and equipment. This type of operation requires that the company carries three different kinds of inventory: raw materials, work-in-process, and finished goods. Furthermore, the manufacturing company incurs manufacturing, sales, and administrative expenses as a result of its activities. Thus, the operating budgeting process for a manufacturing company entails preparation of three additional budgets:

- **Cost of goods manufactured budget.** This budget, also known as the **production budget,** includes the estimated net cost of all direct (raw) materials

Exhibit 3–18

Budgeted Income Statement for a Merchandising Company

ABC Merchandising Company Budgeted Income Statement For a Period: January 1, 1990 - December 31, 1990					
		Account Description	**Budget Value ($)**		**Percentage of Net Sales**
			Annual	**Monthly**	
	+	Gross sales	1,236,000	103,000	103.0
	−	Sales returns and allowances	24,000	2,000	2.0
	−	Sales discounts	12,000	1,000	1.0
+	=	Net sales	1,200,000	100,000	100.0
	+	Merchandising inventory (beginning)	150,000	150,000	12.5*
	+	Net purchases	720,000	60,000	60.0
	=	Cost of goods available for sale	870,000	210,000	72.5*
	−	Merchandising inventory (ending)	162,000	151,000	13.5*
−	=	Cost of goods sold	708,000	59,000	59.0
=		Gross margin from sales	492,000	41,000	41.0
	+	Advertising expenses	4,800	400	0.4
	+	Audit and secretarial fees	3,600	300	0.3
	+	Communication expenses	7,200	600	0.6
	+	Depreciation, capital assets	6,000	500	0.5
	+	Freight out expenses	7,200	600	0.6
	+	Insurance expenses	6,000	500	0.5
	+	Office supplies and expenses	4,800	400	0.4
	+	Property taxes	2,400	200	0.2
	+	Rent	28,800	2,400	2.4
	+	Salaries and wages	79,200	6,600	6.6
	+	Traveling and entertainment	4,800	400	0.4
	+	Utilities	6,000	500	0.5
−	=	Total operating expenses	160,800	13,400	13.4
=		Income from operations	331,200	27,600	27.6
−		Interest expense	12,000	1,000	1.0
+		Net miscellaneous revenue	4,800	400	0.4
=		Income before taxes	324,000	27,000	27.0
−		Income taxes expense	110,400	9,200	9.2
=		Net income	213,600	17,800	17.8
* Percentage of Annual Net Sales of $1,200,000					

purchases, direct labor and subcontracting service costs, total plant* overhead costs, and the difference between estimated inventory (raw materials and work-in-process) values at the start and at the end of the budgeted period.

- **Cost of goods sold budget.** This budget includes the estimated cost of goods manufactured, as described above, and the difference between estimated inventory (finished goods) values at the start and at the end of the budgeted period.
- **Operating expenses budget.** This budget includes all sales and administrative cost estimates.

The production budget is prepared by the company's production manager, who is expected to be familiar with all information pertinent to his department.

---

* Plant is defined by Webster as "the tools, machinery, fixtures, buildings, grounds, etc. of a factory or business."

Exhibit 3–19

Production Budget for a Manufacturing Company

		ABC Manufacturing Company Production Budget For a Period: January 1, 1990 - December 31, 1990			
		Account Description	*Budget Value ($)*		**Percentage of Net Sales**
			Annual	**Monthly**	
	+	Direct materials inventory (beginning)	60,000	60,000	5.0*
	+	Direct materials purchases (net)	348,000	29,000	29.0
	=	Cost of direct materials available for use	408,000	89,000	34.0*
	−	Direct materials inventory (ending)	78,000	61,500	6.5*
+	=	Cost of direct materials used	330,000	27,500	27.5
+		Direct labor costs	156,000	13,000	13.0
+		Direct subcontracting service costs	4,800	400	0.4
	+	Depreciation, production equipment	14,400	1,200	1.2
	+	Indirect labor and supervision costs	64,800	5,400	5.4
	+	Indirect materials purchases (net)	3,600	300	0.3
	+	Insurance, production equipment	3,600	300	0.3
	+	Maintenance, production equipment	4,800	400	0.4
	+	Property taxes	1,200	100	0.1
	+	Rent	28,800	2,400	2.4
	+	Rental expense, production equipment	1,200	100	0.1
	+	Utilities	8,400	700	0.7
+	=	Total plant overhead costs	130,800	10,900	10.9
=		Total manufacturing costs	621,600	51,800	51.8
+		Work-in-process inventory (beginning)	70,000	70,000	5.8*
=		Total cost of work-in-process	691,600	121,800	57.6*
−		Work-in-process inventory (ending)	88,000	71,500	7.3*
=		Cost of goods manufactured**	603,600	50,300	50.3

* Percentage of Annual Net Sales of $1,200,000

** Transfer this cost to the budgeted income statement (refer to Exhibit 3–20)

This budget is prepared in accordance with sales forecasts for the projected period and entails estimating the use of raw materials, labor, subcontracting services, and plant overhead costs. Subsequently, all manufacturing costs must be accurately estimated and summarized in the production budget. A typical production budget for a manufacturing company is presented in Exhibit 3–19.

The next step in the operating budgeting process for a manufacturing company entails estimation of the cost of goods sold and operating expenses. Upon estimating costs and relevant inventory values at the start and end of the budgeted period, all budgets must be integrated with the sales budget to prepare a budgeted income statement. A typical budgeted income statement for a manufacturing company is presented in Exhibit 3–20.

Exhibit 3–20

Budgeted Income Statement for a Manufacturing Company

| | | | Budget Value ($) | | Percentage |
		ABC Manufacturing Company Budgeted Income Statement For a Period: January 1, 1990 - December 31, 1990			
		Account Description	**Annual**	**Monthly**	**Percentage of Net Sales**
	+	Gross sales	1,236,000	103,000	103.0
	−	Sales returns and allowances	24,000	2,000	2.0
	−	Sales discounts	12,000	1,000	1.0
+	=	Net sales	1,200,000	100,000	100.0
	+	Finished goods inventory (beginning)	80,000	80,000	6.7*
	+	Cost of goods manufactured (from production budget)	603,600	50,300	50.3
	=	Cost of goods available for sale	683,600	130,300	57.0*
	−	Finished goods inventory (ending)	68,000	79,000	5.7*
−	=	Cost of goods sold	615,600	51,300	51.3
=		Gross margin from sales	584,400	48,700	48.7
	+	Advertising expenses	2,400	200	0.2
	+	Audit and secretarial fees	3,600	300	0.3
	+	Communication expenses	7,200	600	0.6
	+	Depreciation, office equipment and vehicles	2,400	200	0.2
	+	Freight out expenses	7,200	600	0.6
	+	Insurance, vehicles	4,800	400	0.4
	+	Office supplies and expenses	4,800	400	0.4
	+	Salaries and wages, administration and sales	30,000	2,500	2.5
	+	Salaries, officers	60,000	5,000	5.0
	+	Traveling and entertainment	4,800	400	0.4
−	=	Total operating expenses	127,200	10,600	10.6
=		Income from operations	457,200	38,100	38.1
−		Interest expense	18,000	1,500	1.5
+		Net miscellaneous revenue	4,800	400	0.4
=		Income before taxes	444,000	37,000	37.0
−		Income taxes expense	144,000	12,000	12.0
=		Net income	300,000	25,000	25.0

* Percentage of Annual Net Sales of $1,200,000

Once the operating budgeting process is completed, all estimated values specified in the budgeted income statement must be entered into the management accounting reporting system. Each estimated value of revenues, expenses, and income should be compared with the corresponding actual values on a monthly and a year-to-date basis. Doing so will enable management to determine *variances* between budgeted and actual values, thereby identifying possible deviations from the original plan. Additional details pertaining to the use of the operating budgets as an important controlling device are provided later in this part.

3.07 Capital Expenditure Budget

An important task that executive managers frequently encounter is choosing appropriate capital investments. A **capital investment** may be defined as the outlay of company cash for specific objectives with the expectation that the outlay will produce future profit and generate a positive cash flow. Capital investment decisions represent an integral part of the overall financial planning process. They involve utilization of substantial company funds for a long period, a commitment that may be impossible or very difficult to reverse. Capital investment decisions are usually made for the following purposes:

- Purchase of new capital assets (e.g., property, equipment, vehicles)
- Replacement of existing capital assets
- Expansion of the current product and service range
- Research and development of new products and services
- Acquisition of an additional company

The capital investment decision-making process entails preparation of estimates pertaining to additional costs and potential benefits related to a specific long-term project. The ultimate aim of this process is the preparation of a comprehensive capital expenditure budget.

The **capital expenditure budget** is an important financial document that summarizes estimated benefits and costs pertaining to the acquisition of capital assets or the participation in long-term projects. The capital expenditure decision-making process, or **capital expenditure decision cycle**,[5] entails a number of steps that are summarized in Exhibit 3–21.

The capital expenditure decision cycle starts with the identification of capital investment opportunities. New ideas pertaining to capital investment opportunities may be originated by managers in various departments. A production manager, for example, can prepare a list of additional capital equipment that may substantially improve overall performance efficiency in the production department. A marketing manager, on the other hand, can submit suggestions about new product lines to improve the company's position in the marketplace. These and similar proposals need to be examined in terms of short-, medium- and long-term company objectives in order to summarize possible capital expenditure requirements. A typical **schedule of capital expenditure requirements** is illustrated in Exhibit 3–22.

Once a detailed schedule of possible capital expenditure requirements is summarized, a formal request for capital expenditure needs to be prepared. Such a request is prepared by an appropriate manager who is directly involved with a specific proposal. The proposed request should provide a detailed description of capital equipment under review or specify relevant details pertaining to a particular long-term project (e.g., new product development, or acquisition of a new property). Additional details that should be included in this request are as follows:

- Calculation of the capital cost of the project and determination of its operational life period (e.g., equipment replacement study)

Exhibit 3–21

Capital Expenditure Decision Cycle

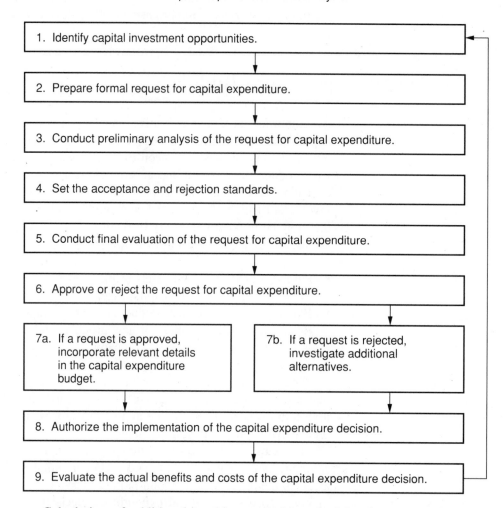

1. Identify capital investment opportunities.

2. Prepare formal request for capital expenditure.

3. Conduct preliminary analysis of the request for capital expenditure.

4. Set the acceptance and rejection standards.

5. Conduct final evaluation of the request for capital expenditure.

6. Approve or reject the request for capital expenditure.

7a. If a request is approved, incorporate relevant details in the capital expenditure budget.

7b. If a request is rejected, investigate additional alternatives.

8. Authorize the implementation of the capital expenditure decision.

9. Evaluate the actual benefits and costs of the capital expenditure decision.

- Calculation of additional working capital required by the new project and determination of possible operating savings
- A forecast of additional cash flow (i.e., cash receipts and cash payments, not revenues and expenses, arising from the new project)
- A forecast of tax liability arising from additional earnings and possible tax savings accruing from the above investment

The bulk of capital expenditure requests in small and medium-sized companies are concerned with purchase of new equipment and replacement of the old.

Exhibit 3–22

A Schedule of Possible Capital Expenditure Requirements

Schedule of Capital Expenditure Requirements			
Required by	**Description of Capital Expenditure**	**Quantity**	**Price Estimate**
Early 1990	Lathe (new)	1	$ 4,000
Middle 1990	Milling machine (used)	1	2,000
End 1990	Press brake (used)	2	1,000
Early 1990	Development of a new product line	–	4,000
Middle 1990	Painting plant (new)	1	10,000
End 1990	Power saw (new)	2	20,000
Early 1991	Surface grinder (used)	1	3,000

Such requests are usually prepared by the production manager in accordance with a comprehensive **equipment replacement program**. Development of equipment replacement programs is discussed in detail in Part 4 (Volume II).

Once all information pertaining to a specific request for capital expenditure is summarized, it should be analyzed by the financial manager. Preliminary analysis of capital expenditure requests entails reviewing relevant details and ascertaining their compatibility with the short-, medium-, and long-term financial objectives and plans. Without incurring excessive investigation costs, the financial manager provides a major contribution to this activity by identifying suitable and unsuitable proposals.

The next step in the capital expenditure decision cycle entails setting appropriate standards for accepting and rejecting various proposals. Setting of such standards is particularly important for small and medium-sized companies with limited financial resources. Among the most commonly used acceptance-rejection standards are:

- **Minimum desired rate of return.** This is the lowest rate of return on capital expenditure acceptable to company shareholders.
- **Minimum cash flow payback period.** This is the shortest period of time during which the company can generate additional cash flow equal to capital expenditure.

The following step in the capital expenditure decision cycle entails final evaluation of proposals. This involves verifying decision variables (e.g., operating costs—materials, labor, and overheads), estimated operating life period, and salvage value of the investment. Each variable in a particular proposal needs to be checked for accuracy.

Final evaluation of capital expenditure proposals is essential to meaningful investment appraisal and provides a guarantee for sound management decisions. Thus it is important to allocate sufficient time and effort to ensure a high quality of information, thereby avoiding unnecessary and costly mistakes. There are several methods of measuring the profitability of capital projects. Some of these methods are as follows:

- Accounting rate-of-return method
- Payback period method
- Discounted cash flow method

Accounting rate-of-return method is a crude, but simple, approach for estimating the performance of a capital investment. Because of its simplicity, this method is often used to obtain a preliminary indication of the viability of a proposed capital expenditure. This method provides a measure for expected capital expenditure performance by using two variables:

1. Estimated annual after-tax net income from the project
2. Average investment cost[6]

The basic equation for determining the accounting rate of return by applying these variables is as follows:

$$\text{Accounting rate of return} = \frac{\text{Project's average annual after-tax net income}}{\text{Average investment cost}}$$

Key:

$$\frac{\text{Projects average annual}}{\text{after-tax net income}} = \frac{(\text{Annual revenue - Annual operating cost}) \times}{(1.0 - \text{Company's income tax rate})}$$

and

$$\text{Average investment cost} = \frac{(\text{Total investment cost–Salvage value})}{2}$$
$$+ \text{Salvage value}$$

Assume, for example, that ABC Corporation is considering purchasing new equipment at a total investment cost of $30,000. In accordance with estimates, equipment is expected to generate annual cash revenue of $13,500 at an operating cost of $6,000 per year (including depreciation). The estimated salvage value of new equipment (i.e., the value at the end of equipment's service life period) is $5,000. If the company's income tax rate is 30 percent, the accounting rate of return can be determined as follows:

$$\text{Accounting rate of return} = \frac{(\$13,500 - \$6,000)(1.0 - 0.3)}{\left(\frac{\$30,000 - \$5,000}{2}\right) + \$5,000}$$
$$= \frac{\$5,250}{\$17,500} = 30.0\%$$

Management should desire a rate of return on capital expenditure at least 10 percent above the annual rate of inflation. Thus, for example, if the current annual rate of inflation is about 5 percent, the desired rate of return on capital expenditure should be at least 15 percent. Since the accounting rate of return in the example exceeds the minimum desired rate, it provides a positive indication of the economic viability of the proposed plan.

Despite its simplicity, the accounting rate-of-return method has several drawbacks. First, the use of average values tends to equalize relevant data, thereby leading to possible inaccuracy in the calculation. Second, this method does not provide reliable results when estimated annual net income fluctuates from one year to the next. Finally, the future devaluation of the dollar is not accounted for in this method (i.e., present and future dollar amounts are treated as having equal value or purchasing power).

Payback period method is the second method for measuring the economic viability of a specific capital expenditure proposal. This method is concerned with measuring the period of time it will take to recuperate the capital investment from future cash inflows. This payback period can be determined as follows:

$$\text{Payback period (in years)} = \frac{\text{Total investment cost}}{\text{Average annual net cash inflow}}$$

Key:

$$\begin{array}{l}\text{Average annual} \\ \text{net cash inflow} \\ \text{(in dollars)}\end{array} = \begin{array}{l}\text{Project's average annual} \\ \text{after-tax net income}\end{array} + \frac{\text{Total investment cost} - \text{Salvage value}}{\text{Service life period (in years)}}$$

The application of the payback period method can be illustrated by using data from the previous example. Assuming that the proposed equipment's estimated service life period is 10 years, the payback period can be determined as follows:

Payback period (in years)

$$= \frac{\$30,000}{(\$13,500 - \$6,000) \times (1.0 - 0.3) + \left(\frac{\$30,000 - \$5,000}{10 \text{ years}}\right)}$$
$$= \frac{\$30,000}{\$7,750} = 3.87 \text{ years}$$

If the desired payback period on capital expenditure is four to five years, this proposal could be acceptable to the company's management.

Although the payback period method is simple in its application and is widely used by managers, it also has several drawbacks. These drawbacks are similar to the ones discussed earlier in the context of the accounting rate-of-return method.

Discounted cash flow method is the most accurate method for measuring the economic viability of a specific capital expenditure proposal. Instead of measuring the accounting rate of return or payback period on a particular investment, this method measures present cash flow values generated from such an investment. This approach to capital investment analysis is termed the **present-value method**.

The discounted cash flow method entails the use of *present-value tables* (Tables A–1, A–2, A–3, and A–4 in Appendix A), which are provided at the end of this part. Each table contains a series of *multipliers* that help to determine the present value of the future cash flow. This process is called **cash flow discounting** and it has two basic variables:

- Annual interest rate or minimum desired rate of return
- A period of time during which the cash flow is discounted

Typical examples of cash flow discounting can be illustrated as follows:

1. Determine the future value of $1,000 deposited now that will earn 10 percent interest compounded annually for five years. From Table A–1, the necessary multiplier for five years at 10 percent is 1.611. Hence, the answer is:

$$\$1,000 \times 1.611 = \$1,611$$

2. Determine the future value at the end of five years if $1,000 is deposited annually on January 1, assuming 10 percent interest compounded annually. From Table A–2, the necessary multiplier is 6.105. Hence the answer is:

$$\$1,000 \times 6.105 = \$6,105$$

3. Determine the present value of $1,000 to be received five years from now, assuming a 10 percent annual interest rate. From Table A–3, the necessary multiplier is 0.621. Hence, the answer is:

$$\$1,000 \times 0.621 = \$621$$

4. Determine the present value of a $1,000 total investment, payable in five equal, annual installments, assuming a 10 percent annual interest rate. From Table A–4, the necessary multiplier is determined as follows:

   If the first installment is paid now, the multiplier is determined for a period N–1 (i.e., four years at the same interest rate). The answer is:

$$\frac{\$1,000}{5} + \frac{\$1,000}{5} \times 3.170 = \$834$$

   If the first installment is paid one year from now, the multiplier is determined for a full period N (i.e., five years at the same interest rate). The answer is:

$$\frac{\$1,000}{5} \times 3.791 = \$758.2$$

These examples clearly illustrate fluctuation of present and future values depending upon the annual interest rate and the period of time during which the cash flow is discounted. An additional example will help to illuminate the application of the discounted cash flow method for evaluating capital expenditure proposals. Suppose ABC Company needs to make an investment decision pertaining to two machines on the basis of the following information:

	Machine X	Machine Y
Purchase price on 1–1–90	$17,000	$17,000
Salvage value	0	0
Expected service life period	5 years	5 years
Desired rate of return	20%	20%
Estimated net cash inflows:		
1990	$6,000	$4,000
1991	$6,000	$5,000
1992	$6,000	$6,000
1993	$6,000	$7,000
1994	$6,000	$8,000

Machine X is expected to generate equal annual net cash inflows of $6,000 per year over 5 years. The present value of cash inflows can be determined from Table A–4 by using the 20 percent annual interest rate:

(+)	Present value of cash inflows	$6,000 \times 2.991 = $17,946
(−)	Purchase price of the machine	($17,000)
(=)	Net present value	$946

Machine Y is expected to generate unequal, annual net cash inflows ranging from $4,000 to $8,000 per year over 5 years. The present value of cash inflows in this case can be determined from Table A–3 by using 20 percent annual interest rate:

Present value of cash inflows

1990	$4,000 \times 0.833	= $3,332
1991	$5,000 \times 0.694	= $3,470
1992	$6,000 \times 0.579	= $3,474
1993	$7,000 \times 0.482	= $3,374
1994	$8,000 \times 0.402	= $3,216

(+)	Total cash inflows	$16,866
(−)	Purchase price of the machine	($17,000)
(=)	Net present value	($ 134)

It is apparent from this example that Machine X with a positive net present value of $946 is economically more viable in comparison with Machine Y, which has a negative net present value of $134.

Another important factor that should be considered during the capital expenditure decision cycle is the effect of income taxes on the company's cash flow and profitability. Additional details related to selection of suitable tax strategies are discussed later in this part.

The last step in the capital expenditure decision cycle entails the final approval or rejection of a specific request. Upon its approval, each capital expenditure request must be implemented and subsequently evaluated in terms of the actual benefits received.

3.08 Cash Budget

One of the major responsibilities of the financial manager is to ensure that funds are available when needed by the company. This necessitates detailed examination of cash requirements and identification of sources of cash for a specific fiscal period. As a result of such an investigation, the financial manager is expected to develop a comprehensive **cash flow projection** or **cash budget**.

The cash budget represents an important stage in the financial planning process and is an integral part of the master budget. The cash budget provides a period-by-period projection of the following:

1. Cash on hand at the start of the budgeted period, or the *opening bank balance*
2. Expected *cash receipts* during the budgeted period
3. Expected *cash disbursements* during the budgeted period
4. Cash on hand at the end of the budgeted period, or the *closing bank balance*

An accurate cash budget is of paramount importance to the effective functioning of the company. Some of the major benefits provided by the cash budget are as follows:

- It summarizes all cash receipts and disbursements pertinent to company activities.
- It helps to identify periods when the company may experience a cash shortage so that additional loans may be negotiated in advance and obtained at the most favorable rates.
- It helps to identify periods when the company may experience a cash surplus so that additional funds may be invested in a planned manner at the most favorable rates.
- It describes the company's liquidity to banks and other financial institutions.
- It helps to determine whether the company can commit itself to new capital expenditure without raising additional funds.

Preparation of a cash budget, or a **cash budgeting process**, entails selection of the purpose and the period for which finance is required, computation of the amount of funds required, and the selection of appropriate sources of funds. There are three major types of company activities that should be considered when computing the amount of funds required during a particular fiscal period. These activities have been classified earlier in the statement of cash flows as follows:

- Operating activities
- Investing activities
- Financing activities

As a result of these activities certain amounts of cash will flow into and out of the company. The **cash inflow,** for example, may be classified as follows:

- *Operating activities.* The receipts from sales of goods or rendering of services to customers and receipts of interest or dividends on loans and investment
- *Investing activities.* The proceeds from the sale of property, equipment, and other capital assets, proceeds from the sale of marketable securities, and collection of loans from borrowers

- *Financing activities*. The proceeds from the sale of stock to shareholders and the receipt of loans from creditors

The **cash outflow**, on the other hand, may be categorized on the following basis:

- *Operating activities*. The payments for salaries and wages to employees, for purchasing goods and services from suppliers, for general operating expenses, for interest on debt, and for taxes
- *Investing activities*. The payments for purchasing property, equipment, and other capital assets and for purchasing marketable securities and advance of loans to borrowers
- *Financing activities*. The payments for reacquiring stock from shareholders, for repayment of debt to creditors, and for dividends to shareholders

Cash budgets are prepared in advance for monthly, quarterly, semi-annual, and annual periods. The cash budgeting process starts with the examination of the budgeted income statement for the corresponding period. This statement summarizes revenue and expenditure projections pertinent to the company's planned operating activities. The information contained in the budgeted income statement is obtained from the following sources:

- Sales budget. This budget provides revenue projections from cash and credit sales.
- Production (cost of sales) budget. This budget provides direct material, direct labor, subcontracting service, and plant overhead costs projections.
- Operating expenses budget. This budget provides selling, administrative, and general expenses projections.

Additional information that needs to be examined relates to company policy and to subsequent actions pertinent to collection of revenues arising from credit sales and payment of disbursements arising from credit purchases. All outstanding amounts owed to the company by its customers (termed **accounts receivable**) are classified in monthly debtors-age-analysis reports on the basis of 1–30, 31–60, 61–90 days, and over 91 days. All outstanding amounts owed by the company to its suppliers (termed **accounts payable**) are classified in monthly creditors-age-analysis reports in a similar manner. The information contained in both types of reports needs to be summarized for a full fiscal period to determine annual average percentages pertinent to collection of revenues and payment of disbursements. This information is illustrated in Exhibit 3–23.

Exhibit 3–23
Illustration of Annual Collection of Revenues and Payment of Disbursements

Collection of Revenues (Annual Average Percentages)		Payment of Disbursements (Annual Average Percentages)	
Cash	10%	Cash	20%
1–30 days	30%	1–30 days	40%
31–60 days	30%	31–60 days	10%
61–90 days	20%	61–90 days	25%
Over 91 days	10%	Over 91 days	5%
	100%		100%

Exhibit 3–24

Example of a Cash Budget for a Three-Month Period

ABC Company
Cash Budget
For Period: January 1, 1990 - March 31, 1990

		Description	January	February	March	Total
Cash receipts:						
	(+)	Cash sales	2,000	2,500	2,800	7,300
	(+)	Credit sales	20,000	25,000	28,000	73,000
(+)	(=)	Total receipts	22,000	27,500	30,800	80,300
Cash disbursements:						
	(+)	Direct materials	5,500	6,000	8,500	20,000
	(+)	Direct labor and benefits	6,600	7,100	7,900	21,600
	(+)	Subcontracting services	500	1,000	2,000	3,500
	(+)	Plant overheads (excluding depreciation)	2,500	2,600	2,800	7,900
	(+)	Selling expenses	1,500	1,600	2,400	5,500
	(+)	General and administrative expenses	500	500	1,000	2,000
	(+)	Capital expenditures	800	1,000	2,000	3,800
	(+)	Income taxes	—	—	4,000	4,000
	(+)	Loan repayment	—	3,000	3,000	6,000
(−)	(=)	Total disbursements	17,900	22,800	33,600	74,300
(=)		Cash increase (decrease)	4,100	4,700	(2,800)	6,000
(+)		Beginning cash balance	10,000	14,100	18,800	16,000
(=)		Ending cash balance	14,100	18,800	16,000	22,000

The next stage in the cash budgeting process entails examination of the capital expenditure budget and identification of time and values of individual disbursements. Each capital expenditure disbursement must be entered into the cash budget in accordance with the respective payment date. Furthermore, it is necessary to identify periods for all lump-sum payments such as taxes, interest, loan repayment, or vacation pay and to enter relevant amounts into the cash budget.

A simplified example of the cash budget is presented in Exhibit 3–24. This budget is prepared for a three-month period and incorporates information presented in Exhibit 3–23.

3.09 Tax Strategies

Income taxes are an important factor in the overall financial planning process, and they often influence business decisions. Selection of the most effective **tax strategies** represents, therefore, an integral part of the budgeting process and necessitates continuous cooperation between business people and accountants.

Tax strategies depend firstly upon the form of the business organization. The three basic forms of business organization, as illustrated in Exhibit 3–25, are:

- Sole proprietorship
- Partnership
- Corporation

A **sole proprietorship** is an unincorporated business formed and owned by one individual. This form of business provides its owner with exclusive

Exhibit 3–25

Comparative Features of the Various Forms of Business Organization

		Sole Proprietorship	Partnership	Corporation
1.	Legal status	Not a separate legal entity	Not a separate legal entity	Separate legal entity
2.	Risk of ownership	Owner's personal resources at stake	Partners' resources at stake	Limited to investment in corporation
3.	Duration or life	Limited by desire or death of owner	Limited by desire or death of each partner	Indefinite, possibly unlimited
4.	Transferability of ownership	Sale by owner establishes new company	Changes in any partner's percentage of interest requires new partnership	Transferable by sale of stock
5.	Accounting treatment	Separate economic unit	Separate economic unit	Separate economic unit

SOURCE: B. E. Needles, Jr., H. R. Anderson, and J. C. Caldwell, *Financial & Managerial Accounting*, (Boston, MA: Houghton Mifflin, 1988), p. 15. Reprinted with permission.

control of operating activities and can be initiated in a relatively simple manner. Legally, sole proprietorship represents the same economic entity as its owner. Consequently, the owner is entitled to receive all profits from operations; however, he or she is also liable for all losses and other obligations of the business. In addition, the owner must pay all taxes on net income earned by the business. These taxes are based on individual income tax rates, which range from 15 to 33 percent for 1990. Furthermore, most states impose additional income taxes on the individual proprietor. The life of a sole proprietorship may last for as long as the owner may desire or until the owner's death or incapacitation.

A **partnership** is an unincorporated business formed and owned by two or more individuals. This form of business enables its owners to share control of operating activities in accordance with prearranged and mutually acceptable conditions. These conditions also stipulate the basis upon which all partners share profits and losses of the business. All partnerships are further classified as *general partnerships* and *limited partnerships*. Both types of businesses are not liable for federal income tax, although they are required to file an informational income tax return. All partnership's income taxes are payable by its partners on an individual basis and in accordance with their share of net income from operations. Furthermore, many states impose state income taxes on each partner's share. The life of a partnership may last as long as the partners wish it to, until the ownership changes, or until one of the partners leaves or dies. If the business continues, a new partnership must be formed.

A **corporation** is a business entity that is legally separated from its owners. The ownership of corporation is effected through owning shares of stock by *shareholders*. Every corporation has certain distinguishing characteristics such as:

- *Continuous life.* A corporation does not have to be dissolved upon retirement, bankruptcy, or death of any of its shareholders.
- *Limited liability.* A shareholder does not carry personal liability for the debts incurred by or claims against the corporation.
- *Free transfer of shares.* Shareholders generally have the right to sell without restriction their shares of stock to any person.
- *Independent management.* Shareholders elect a board of directors who manage the corporation for the benefits of shareholders.

Exhibit 3–26

1989 Corporate Income Tax Rates

Taxable Income Range	Tax Liability and Percentage of the Amount Over
0 - $ 50,000	15% of the taxable income
$ 50,001 - 75,000	$ 7,500 + 25% of the amount over $ 50,000
75,001 - 100,000	13,750 + 34% of the amount over 75,000
100,001 - 335,000	22,250 + 39% of the amount over 100,000
335,001 - Over	113,900 + 34$ of the amount over 335,000

A regular corporation is liable to pay federal income tax on net income earned during a particular accounting period. The 1989 corporate income tax rates are summarized in Exhibit 3–26.

For example, a corporation with a taxable net income of $120,000 will have a federal income tax liability as follows (refer to range $100,001 − $335,000):

$$\$22,250 + 0.39 \times (\$120,000 - \$100,00) = \$22,250 + \$7,800$$
$$= \$30,500$$

Special consideration should be given to the **S corporation**. Management may elect to have an otherwise ordinary corporation taxed as a subchapter *S* corporation. In essence, the *S* corporation status stipulates that net income earned by the corporation is to be taxed at the individual shareholder's level. Hence, shareholders report corporate income or loss in their personal income taxes return and still enjoy all the benefits offered by an ordinary corporation. No corporate tax is paid to the federal government. The *S* corporation status has been specifically designed to accommodate the needs of small and medium-sized organizations with no more than 35 shareholders.

It is advisable that small and medium-sized companies keep their accounting and tax records on the same basis to ensure that income tax expense accrued from operations equals income tax liability payable to IRS. In addition to federal income tax, regular corporations are also liable for the state income tax in 44 different states.

The process of minimizing taxes through planning also involves issues of operational and capital budgeting nature. Some of these issues are:

- Selection of a tax year for ordinary corporations. The *Tax Reform Act of 1986* prescribes that sole proprietorships, partnerships, and *S* corporations adopt the tax year of their principal partners or shareholders.
- Selection of a suitable accounting method. There are two basic accounting methods for recordkeeping and income tax calculation: the cash method and the accrual method.
- Selection of the amortization method for such items as start-up and organizational expenses, research and development costs, and other preliminary expenses.
- Selection of a suitable inventory-count method (e.g., FIFO or first-in, first-out, LIFO or last-in, first-out, and others).
- Selection of a suitable method of acquiring capital assets (e.g., operating lease, or capital lease, or cash).
- Selection of a suitable method of depreciating capital assets (e.g., straight-line depreciation or reducing balance depreciation).

- Selection of suitable owners, or shareholders, and employees compensation methods. This includes salaries, stock options, fringe benefits, and other allowances.
- Selection of a suitable method of financing. This entails examination of the debt financing method versus equity financing method.

Since most tax laws change every year, it is virtually impossible to keep track of all such changes. It is essential, therefore, to obtain regular updates from the company's tax advisors, who are expected to have expertise in the field of taxation. Once the latest tax information is obtained, management will be in a better position to develop the most effective tax reduction strategies, thereby improving overall company results.

3.10 Sources of Capital

One of the major elements of financial planning is the search for the additional capital that may be required by a company during a particular accounting period. Identification of appropriate sources of capital represents, therefore, an important function of the financial manager.

The company may need additional capital for several reasons, depending upon the nature of its activities, stage of development, profitability, and the aspirations of its shareholders. Some of the typical examples of capital requirements are as follows:

- A new company needs start-up and working capital.
- An existing company needs additional capital for research and development of new products or services, acquisition of capital assets, or financing of an increased volume of sales.
- A company needs additional capital to compensate for an anticipated cash shortage during a specific accounting period.

Irrespective of the reason for additional capital requirements, the financial manager needs to provide satisfactory answers to the following questions:

- Who requires the capital?
- How much capital is required?
- When is the capital required?
- For how long is the capital required?
- How will the capital be used?
- When will the capital be paid back?
- What guarantees can be provided?

Once acceptable answers to these questions have been provided, the search for suitable sources of capital should begin. The first step in this process entails identification of the most viable method of financing. Two commonly used methods of financing are:

- Debt financing
- Equity financing[7]

Debt financing essentially means borrowing money from outside sources or creditors at prearranged repayment conditions. Such conditions stipulate the length of the loan period, rate of interest, repayment procedures, and penalties on late payments. The debt financing method has several advantages, which can be summarized as follows:

- The cost of interest can be estimated in advance in accordance with the prevailing prime bank rate.
- Creditors do not have any claim on the future earnings of the company.
- Debt may be used to produce an additional return on shareholders' equity (this is known as "leverage" and is discussed later).
- The cost of interest is an operating expense, which is tax deductible.
- Debt does not affect the status of shareholders within the company.

Despite its advantages, the debt financing method also has several disadvantages. Some of them are as follows:

- The cost of interest creates a constant burden on the company's cash flow and decreases its profitability.
- Debt is not permanent capital and must be repaid accurately to avoid penalties and deteriorated credit rating.
- Additional loans must be arranged to pay existing creditors if current debts cannot be paid at maturity.
- Debt requires a pledge of the company's shareholders' assets to creditors, thereby restricting shareholders' control over the company.

Equity financing, on the other hand, means acquisition of the company's stock by its shareholders. By investing their personal capital into the company, shareholders acquire additional interest, or *equity*, in the business. The major difference between equity and debt financing is that equity financing is provided by shareholders without prearranged repayment conditions. The equity financing method has several advantages, which are outlined below:

- Equity financing does not incur a fixed cost since interest payment procedure on the invested capital is regulated by shareholders.
- Equity financing in the form of stock provides permanent capital, which usually does not have to be paid back.
- A higher level of equity enables shareholders to raise additional capital through debt financing.

The equity financing method also have several disadvantages, which can be summarized as follows:

- Equity financing by additional investors reduces the nominal value of stock held by an individual shareholder.
- Since equity is not tax deductible when repaid in the form of dividends to shareholders, it has a higher cost in comparison with debt financing.
- Equity financing provides investors with additional control over the business.

Once the advantages and disadvantages of both methods of financing are clarified, the most appropriate sources of capital need to be selected. There are three important factors that should be considered during the finance selection process. These factors are as follows:

- *Cost.* How much will capital ultimately cost shareholders?
- *Cash flow.* How will additional capital help to solve existing and potential cash flow problems?
- *Risk.* What is the risk of losing control over the business?

Another important aspect of financing that needs to be understood relates to leveraging of creditors funds. In simple terms, **leverage** is the ability of company shareholders to increase the return on their equity by using creditors' capital. Consider, for example, two identical organizations: Company X and Company Y. Both companies have the same equity capital of $100,000—provided by shareholders—and debt capital of $20,000—borrowed from creditors. Both companies earn the same rate of return on total capital before interest and taxes (15 percent), pay the same tax deductible fixed interest on debt (10 percent) and are in the same tax bracket (30 percent). Later, Company Y borrows an additional $80,000 from creditors, thereby increasing its total capital to $200,000. This, in turn, causes an increase of net earnings from $11,200 to $14,000 and subsequent increase of the rate of return on shareholders' equity from 11.2 to 14.0 percent. Such an increase is the direct result of more effective leveraging of creditors' capital. This is illustrated in Exhibit 3–27.

It is apparent from this example that leveraging of creditors' capital provides shareholders with several advantages. Some of these advantages are as follows:

- By borrowing and properly utilizing additional capital supplied by creditors, shareholders may increase the overall return on their equity.
- An increased level of capital may enhance the company's growth and help to find additional opportunities in the marketplace.
- By borrowing additional capital from outside sources, shareholders do not relinquish direct control over their company.

Borrowing capital from outside sources also has certain disadvantages, described earlier in the context of debt financing. Moreover, financial leveraging may have negative effects if management is not capable of utilizing the borrowed

Exhibit 3–27

Example of Financial Leverage

	Description	Company X	Company Y
(+)	Long-term debt	$ 20,000	$ 100,000
(+)	Shareholders' equity	100,000	100,000
(=)	Total capital	120,000	200,000
(+)	Earnings before interest and taxes (at 15%)	18,000	30,000
(−)	Interest expense (at 10% of long-term debt)	2,000	10,000
(=)	Earnings before taxes	16,000	20,000
(−)	Taxes (at 30%)	4,800	6,000
(=)	Net earnings	11,200	14,000

Rate of return on shareholders' equity
is calculated as follows:

$$\frac{\text{Net earnings}}{\text{Shareholders' equity}} \qquad \frac{\$\ 11,200}{\$100,000} = 11.2\% \qquad \frac{\$\ 14,000}{\$100,000} = 14.0\%$$

capital in an efficient manner. This may result in paying interest on the debt in excess of the company's rate of earnings, thereby decreasing the rate of return on shareholders' equity.

Upon selecting the debt financing method, it is necessary to identify appropriate sources of financing well in advance instead of waiting until the last moment. This is particularly important in securing the most favorable conditions of loan repayment. Prior to approaching potential lenders, such as banks and other financial institutions, a detailed financial plan needs to be prepared.

This plan must specify the size, period, and purpose of the loan requirement, how it will be repaid, and what securities can be offered to the lender. The company's request for additional capital must be supported by the most recent financial statements and comprehensive budget projections for the forthcoming fiscal period. Once all information is available, the potential lender will be in a better position to make an appropriate decision.

Additional sources of finance that are frequently utilized by various companies include the following:

- *Revolving line of credit.* Such credit is usually provided by a bank that carries the company's current account. In terms of this arrangement, the bank makes certain funds available to the company on a continuous basis and imposes a total credit limit. The company, in return, is required to provide the bank with adequate securities such as pledge of accounts receivable and personal guarantees of shareholders.
- *Factoring,* or *accounts receivable financing.* In terms of this arrangement, the company concedes the right to collect accounts receivable to a financial institution. In return, the company receives cash upon shipping finished products to customers without waiting for their payment. This type of financing is usually expensive and, therefore, is left as the last resort for raising capital.
- *Inventory financing.* The company usually purchases the bulk of materials or merchandise inventory on credit and pays its suppliers within 1 to 90 days or later, depending upon the specific arrangement. The inventory, in turn, can be used by the company in a manufacturing process or sold directly to customers, thereby generating additional revenue.
- *Capital leasing.* This is a long-term financial arrangement that enables the company to obtain the right of using expensive capital equipment without paying its full price to the supplier. In accordance with this arrangement, the purchaser may derive immediate benefits from leased equipment and generate additional revenues as a result of its usage. The ownership of leased equipment remains with the suppliers until the full amount is paid by the purchaser. However, the purchaser may depreciate the leased equipment, thereby obtaining additional benefit in the form of a reduced tax liability.
- *SBA loans.* The company may arrange a special loan from Small Business Administration (SBA), provided the company qualifies. SBA loans are usually offered to smaller companies for development purposes. Hence, it may be useful to investigate this option and to approach the local SBA office.

Regardless of the financing method used, management needs to ascertain whether or not such a method helps to improve overall company performance and profitability. This can only be accomplished if the company pays reasonable rates of interest on borrowed capital and manages to utilize additional finance in the most efficient manner.

3.11 Internal Control and Cash Management

One of the prime responsibilities of the financial manager is to design, install, and maintain stringent internal control within the financial department. **Internal control** is defined by AICPA as "the plan of organization and all of the coordinate methods and measures adopted within a business to safeguard its assets, check the accuracy and reliability of its accounting data, promote operational efficiency, and encourage adherence to prescribed managerial policies."[8] This broad definition relates specifically to two types of internal control:

- Internal accounting control
- Internal administrative control

The main purpose of **internal accounting control** is to ensure the completeness, accuracy, validity and maintenance of accounting records and physical security of assets. Some of the basic requirements of internal accounting control are outlined below:

- Transactions are executed in accordance with management's general or specific authorization.
- Transactions are recorded as necessary to permit preparation of financial statements in conformity with generally accepted accounting principles and to maintain accountability for assets.
- Access to assets is permitted only in accordance with management's authorization.
- The recorded accountability for assets is compared with existing assets at reasonable intervals, and appropriate action is taken with respect to any differences."[9]

Effectively implemented internal accounting control helps to achieve important objectives within the financial department and provides the following benefits:

- It prevents losses of cash and inventory from theft or fraud.
- It facilitates preparation of accurate records related to company transactions with customers, suppliers, and creditors.

The main purpose of **internal administrative control,** on the other hand, is to ensure high operational efficiency within the financial department and adherence to managerial policies related to accounting function. This type of control entails developing special training programs and teaching employees such administrative tasks as:

- How to deal with the company's customers, suppliers, and creditors
- How to authorize business transactions pertaining to purchase and sale of goods or services
- How to maintain a proper bookkeeping system
- How to maintain steady control over company assets such as cash, inventory, and capital assets
- How to maintain an updated payroll accounting system
- How to maintain an effective credit control system
- How to gather cost accounting information
- How to prepare management accounting reports
- How to maintain a computerized accounting system

Internal accounting and administrative controls are strongly interrelated. Both types of control, therefore, need to be developed at the same time and implemented in accordance with the company's specific requirements.

In order to maintain effective internal control within the financial department and in the organization as a whole, management is advised to adhere to the following:

- *Separation of duties.* It is important to ensure that all critical areas of accounting control are handled by more than one person to minimize mistakes and chances of possible embezzlement of cash and other assets.
- *Development of a sound accounting system.* It is essential to develop, implement, and maintain simple but effective procedures for bookkeeping and control over assets, liabilities, revenues and expenses. Such a system should also prescribe regular balancing of books of account and allow spontaneous audit.
- *Implementation of effective personnel policies.* This entails selection of qualified and reliable employees, continuous supervision and possible rotation of employees in key positions, and regular personnel performance appraisal and training.
- *Review of internal control policies.* It is necessary to conduct regular reviews of the company's internal control policies and to identify possible inefficiencies in the financial department.

One of the major elements of internal control relates to **cash management and control.** Cash, the most liquid form of assets, must be administered with particular care. The control of cash represents a difficult task since it is utilized throughout the company's business activities, which follow a typical operational cycle:

Cash $\rightarrow\rightarrow\rightarrow$ Purchases $\rightarrow\rightarrow\rightarrow$ Operations$\rightarrow\rightarrow\rightarrow$ Sales$\rightarrow\rightarrow\rightarrow$ Cash

Cash is usually defined as the sole medium of monetary exchange that is totally negotiable and free of restrictions. One of the weakest points related to the use of cash is its vulnerability to misappropriation. It is essential, therefore, to install and maintain a sound cash management and control system to ensure that

- The function of handling cash is separated from the bookkeeping function.
- The number of employees who have access to cash is limited.
- Employees who handle cash are specifically designated and their background is checked thoroughly.
- Cash received by mail is handled by at least two employees.
- Cash received over the counter is controlled through the use of cash registers and sometimes through the use of prenumbered sales tickets.
- Cash receipts are recorded daily.
- Cash received is deposited daily.
- Cash is stored in a safe place.
- The amount of cash is verified against relevant documentation or bank statements.
- All payments are made by check, except some small payments made out of a petty cash fund.
- Petty cash is controlled on a daily basis.
- Cash journal is reconciled periodically with appropriate bank statements.

Because of its vulnerability, cash should not be kept on the company premises and, instead, should be deposited in an appropriate **bank account**. Banking facilities play an important role in safeguarding cash and other valuable business documents such as stocks and bonds. Moreover, the use of checks for cash disbursements helps to minimize the amount of cash on hand and provides a permanent record of all payments. Hence, it is apparent that control of a company's bank accounts is an integral part of cash management and control. The financial manager needs to develop, implement, and maintain effective and safe banking procedures, which include the following:

- Daily deposit of cash from cash sales and other cash receipts
- Weekly withdrawal of cash for wages and petty cash
- Monthly reconciliation of bank statement with the cash journal

Daily deposits of cash must be accompanied by a **deposit ticket** prepared in duplicate by the person responsible for handling cash. All deposit tickets must be kept in a special file and, if necessary, be used for reconciliation of bank statements.

Weekly withdrawal of cash for wages is necessary if such wages are paid in cash to the company's hourly paid employees. Salaried employees, on the other hand, are normally paid by check on a biweekly or monthly basis. In addition, withdrawal of small amounts of cash may be required to maintain a steady level in the *petty cash fund*. The withdrawal of cash must be effected by a **cash withdrawal slip** prepared in duplicate by the person responsible for handling cash.

Once a month the company must receive a **bank statement**. This statement summarizes all transactions on the company's bank account (i.e., deposits of cash and checks, withdrawal of cash, issued checks, accrual of interest, service, and interest charges). All previously issued checks that have gone through the bank account are also returned to the company together with the bank statement.

The cash balances on the bank statement and in the cash journal rarely coincide with one another. This happens for several reasons:

- *Outstanding checks.* These checks have been issued by the company, recorded in the cash journal, but not yet presented to the bank for payment.
- *Deposits in transit.* These deposits have been placed in the bank, recorded in the cash journal, but not processed in time to be reflected on the monthly bank statement.
- *Service charges.* These charges are reflected only on the bank statement for usual services provided by the bank to a particular company.
- *Interest earned fee.* This fee is commonly paid by commercial banks on balance in a savings account maintained by the company.
- *Interest charged fee.* This fee is commonly charged by commercial banks on the credit line balance utilized by the company.
- *Non-sufficient funds (NSF) checks.* These checks are collected by the company from its customers and deposited in the bank account. However, these checks are not covered by sufficient funds in the customer's bank account and are subsequently returned to the company.
- *Miscellaneous charges and credits.* These relate to special services provided by the bank to the company (e.g., printing of checks, collection and payment of promissory notes, and stopping payment on checks).

Exhibit 3–28

Bank Reconciliation Statement

ABC Company
Bank Reconciliation Statement
Date: July 31, 1989

(1)	Balance per bank, July 31		$1,234.56
(2)	Add deposit in transit on July 31		200.00
			$1,434.56
(3)	Less outstanding checks		
	No. 200	$ 100.00	
	No. 203	20.10	
	No. 205	314.46	434.56
(4)	Adjusted cash balance per bank		$1,000.00
(5)	Balance per books, July 31		$2,345.67
(6)	Add credit memoranda:		
	Notes receivable collected by bank	$ 200.00	
	Interest earned	20.50	220.50
			$2,566.17
(7)	Deduct debit memoranda:		
	Service charges	$ 15.00	
	Interest charges	70.00	
	Collection fees	10.00	
	NSF check from XYZ Company	1,471.17	1,566.17
(8)	Adjusted cash balance per books		$1,000.00

SOURCE: Adapted from B.E. Needles, Jr., H.R. Anderson, and J.C. Caldwell, *Financial & Managerial Accounting,* (Boston, MA: Houghton Mifflin, 1988), pp. 229–234. Reprinted with permission.

An important element of cash management and control entails regular reconciliation of the bank statement with the cash journal. This process, termed **bank reconciliation**, must be carried out on a monthly basis. The specific steps in preparing a bank reconciliation are illustrated in Exhibit 3–28. These steps are as follows:

1. Enter the cash balance as reflected on the latest bank statement.
2. Compare deposits reflected on the bank statement with deposits recorded in the company's books. Any deposits in transit should be added to the bank balance. Moreover, any deposits in transit from the previous month that are not yet listed on the bank statement should be investigated immediately.
3. Trace returned checks to the bank statement, making sure that each check issued by the company is correctly charged to the company's account and signed by an authorized person. Arrange all paid checks returned with the bank statement in numerical order and compare them with the record of checks issued. List all issued checks that are not reflected on the bank statement as outstanding checks and deduct these checks from the bank balance. Any outstanding checks from the previous month should be included.
4. Determine the adjusted cash balance as per bank statement.
5. Enter the cash balance as reflected in the company's books.
6. Add to the cash balance any credit memoranda issued by the bank not yet recorded in the company's books (e.g., notes receivable collected by the bank, interest earned).
7. Deduct from the cash balance any debit memoranda issued by the bank not yet recorded in the company's books (e.g., service charges, interest charges, collection fees, and NSF checks).

8. Determine the adjusted cash balance as per the company's books and compare this with the adjusted cash balance as per bank statement. In the event of a discrepancy, repeat the process until both cash balances are reconciled.

9. Make journal entries for each item on the bank statement not yet recorded in the company's books.

3.12 Control of Purchases and Disbursements

The vulnerability of cash to fraud and embezzlement represents a serious problem for small and medium-sized companies in which the separation of duties is less distinctive than in larger organizations. It is essential, therefore, to ensure continuous **control of purchases and disbursements** in order to minimize theft.

The process of purchasing materials and services is illustrated in Exhibit 3–29. This process must begin with an appropriate **purchase requisition** specifying the description and quantity of required items. The purchase requisition, illustrated in Exhibit 3–30, must be authorized by the head of department for which the materials or services are required. Upon approval, this requisition should be forwarded to the company's buyer, who is responsible for placing a **purchase**

Exhibit 3–29
Internal Control for Purchasing and Payment for Goods and Services

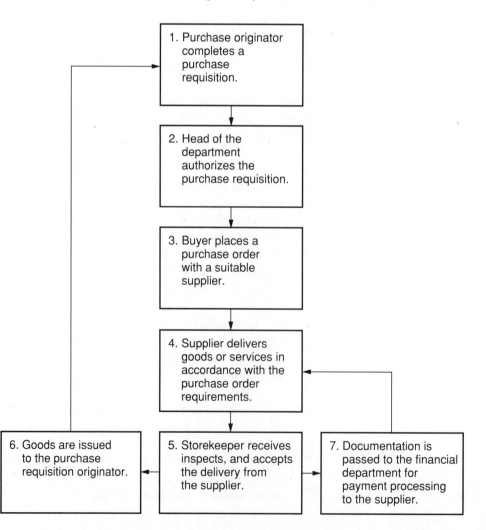

Exhibit 3–30

Purchase Requisition

ABC Company Address: Purchase Requisition		No. :
From:	Department:	
To:	Date of request:	
Please purchase the following items:		
Description		Quantity
Reason for request:		
Approved by:		
To be completed by the buyer:		
Order No.	Date of order:	

order with the most suitable supplier. The purchase order, illustrated in Exhibit 3–31, contains detailed information pertinent to the supply of goods or services:

- Description of goods or services
- Quantity required
- Unit cost and total price
- Terms of payment and possible discounts

Exhibit 3–31

Purchase Order

ABC Company Address: Purchase Order			No. :	
To: Supplier's name and address		Date of order:		
		Date required:		
		Terms:		
Delivery address:				
Please deliver the following items:				
Description	Quantity	Price ($)		
			Unit	Total
Ordered by:		Total amount:		

Exhibit 3–32

Delivery Note

XYZ Supply Company Address: Delivery Note			No. :	
To: The purchaser's name and address		Your purchase order No.		
		Delivery address:		
Description	Quantity		Comments upon delivery	
	Ordered	Supplied		
Confirmation of goods received (signature):			Date:	

- Delivery date required
- Other shipping instructions

Upon receiving the purchase order, the supplier is expected to deliver the goods or to render services strictly in accordance with details specified therein. Such a delivery should be accompanied by the supplier's **delivery note** or **bill of lading** (in duplicate) or **invoice,** or both. The delivery note, illustrated in Exhibit 3–32, contains a detailed description and an indication of the quantity of goods. The invoice, in addition, specifies the price and terms of payment, as illustrated in Exhibit 3–33. When the ordered goods arrive in the company's stores, they must be immediately inspected and counted, if possible, by the

Exhibit 3–33

Invoice

XYZ Supply Company Address: Invoice			No. :	
To: The purchaser's name and address		Your purchase order No.		
		Delivery address:		
Description	Quantity		Price	
	Ordered	Supplied	Unit	Total
Terms of payment:		Total price:		

Exhibit 3–34

Materials Received Report

ABC Company			
Materials Received Report			Page:
Stores:		Location:	
Date	Description	Quantity received	Name of supplier

storekeeper. The storekeeper should subsequently sign both delivery notes and return one to the supplier as *proof of delivery*. In addition, the storekeeper must enter the relevant details pertaining to the delivered goods into the **materials received report**, as illustrated in Exhibit 3–34, and thereafter into the inventory control system. At a later stage, the storekeeper must forward the second delivery note to the financial department for further processing of the transaction.

In the financial department, the supplier's delivery note, or a copy of the material received report, and invoice are compared with the company's purchase order and, if all is correct, a **check authorization** is completed. Finally, the check authorization, illustrated in Exhibit 3–35, together with the three supporting documents must be forwarded to the company's treasurer, who should again examine the evidence and issue a **check** for the net amount of the invoice (i.e., gross amount less discount allowed). Sometimes it is useful to send a check with an attached **remittance advice**, which indicates for what purpose the check is issued. This is illustrated in Exhibit 3–36.

Exhibit 3–35

Check Authorization

ABC Company Check Authorization	
Description of document	Reference
Purchase requisiton Purchase order Delivery note and invoice Material received report	No.: No.: No.: Page:
Total price:	
Less discount:	
Net amount:	
Approved for payment Signature:	Check No.:

Exhibit 3–36

Check with Attached Remittance Advice

ABC Company Address:			Check No. Date:	
Pay to the order of _____ $ _____				
_____ dollars				
Name of bank:				
For: _____		Signed by: _____		

- -

ABC Company

Remittance Advice

Date	P.O. No.	Description	Amount

All procedures that relate to the purchase of goods or services and to the disbursement of cash should be continuously maintained in the financial department. These procedures are summarized in Exhibit 3–37.

Although it is essential to issue checks for all payments, the company may need to pay cash for small items or services. For this reason it is convenient to establish and to maintain a **petty cash fund**. Cash for this fund is provided by

Exhibit 3–37

Internal Control Procedures for Purchase of Goods or Services and Disbursement of Cash

	Business Document	Prepared by	Sent to	Verification and Related Procedures
1.	Purchase requisition	Requesting department	Purchasing department	Purchasing verifies authorization.
2.	Purchase order	Purchasing department	Supplier	Supplier sends goods or services in accordance with purchase order.
3.	Delivery note	Supplier	Receiving department	Receiving department returns a signed copy of delivery note to supplier as a proof of delivery.
4.	Invoice	Supplier	Accounting department	Accounting receives invoice from supplier.
5.	Receiving report	Receiving department	Accounting department	Accounting compares invoice, purchase order, and receiving report. Accounting verifies prices.
6.	Check authorization (or voucher)	Accounting department	Treasurer	Accounting staples check authorization to top of invoice, purchase order, and receiving report.
7.	Check	Treasurer	Supplier	Treasurer verifies all documents before preparing check.
8.	Deposit ticket	Supplier	Supplier's bank	Supplier compares check with invoice. Bank deducts check from buyer's account.
9.	Bank statement	Buyer's bank	Accounting department	Accounting compares amount and payee's name on returned check with check authorization.

SOURCE: Adapted from B. E. Needles, Jr. , H. R. Anderson, and J. C. Caldwell, *Financial & Managerial Accounting*, (Boston, MA: Houghton Mifflin, 1988), p. 226. Reprinted with permission.

Exhibit 3–38

Monthly Creditors Age Analysis Report

ABC Company Monthly Creditors Age Analysis Report						
Date: August 31, 1989	Outstanding Period (Days)				Total	
Creditor	1–30	31–60	61–90	91–over	Amount	Comments
Supplier A	$1,000	—	$200	—	$1,200	
Supplier B	500	$1,000	400	—	1,900	
Supplier C	200	—	500	$800	1,500	
Total	$1,700	$1,000	$1,100	$800	$4,600	

drawing a check for a limited amount known as the **petty cash float**. The source of this float is provided in its entirety by the company's normal trading receipts, thus creating a single exception to the aforementioned rule. Records of all petty cash transactions are entered into the **petty cash journal** and controlled by means of the petty cash control account in the ledger.

Control of cash disbursements and purchases also entails continuous monitoring of **accounts payable** to suppliers, or **trade creditors**, in order to ensure that the company does not overcommit itself financially. It is necessary, therefore, to establish and maintain thorough control of accounts payable and to summarize information that reflects the extent of the company's liabilities at any stage of trading.

It is essential to identify all accounts payable by the company to its trade creditors and to summarize them in monthly **creditors age analysis reports** in accordance with the outstanding periods of time. These reports enable the financial manager to evaluate and to control the level of accounts payable in accordance with the specific requirements of the company. A illustration of a typical monthly creditors age analysis report is presented in Exhibit 3–38.

3.13 Credit Control

One of the important tasks of the financial manager is to develop, implement, and maintain special procedures related to business transactions with the company's customers. These transactions often take place on a credit basis and necessitate the development of stringent **credit control**. Most firms follow a set policy of credit control governing the amounts of credit that may be granted to customers, or **trade debtors**, as well as the period allowed for the repayment of such amounts, known as **accounts receivable**.

Generally, **credit** represents the authority to obtain finance, materials, and services on the basis of a promise to pay for them at a certain date in the future. All credit transactions have three important elements:

- The element of future payment
- The element of confidence
- The element of risk

Unfortunately, there is always a certain amount of risk involved in doing business on a credit basis. It may happen that a particular customer will not pay on the due date or not pay at all, leading to a **bad debt**. The main function of the **credit controller** is, therefore, to minimize risk and to ensure that the element of confidence is supported by a practical policy of evaluating the ability of the company's customers to meet their payment commitments. A sound credit control policy usually has the following objectives:

- To minimize the amount of credit losses
- To minimize the proportion of slow paying accounts
- To maximize the contribution toward the profitability of the organization
- To ensure effective evaluation of customers' credit rating
- To define the conditions of credit covering maximum value, credit period, and cash discounts
- To ensure efficient collection of outstanding accounts with some flexibility particularly in respect to valued customers

One of the main tasks of credit control is to establish a correct rating for all customers through obtaining suitable information from various sources. Some of the major sources of credit information are:

- Information provided by the prospective customer
- Credit ratings published by Dun & Bradstreet and other reputable agencies
- Bankers' references, usually obtained through the company's bank
- Trade references provided by the prospective customer
- References from trade associations
- Financial statements provided by the prospective customers

The first step in obtaining information about the prospective customer entails completion of the **credit application form**. This form, illustrated in Exhibit 3–39, must be prepared by an executive officer of the company that requires credit for purchasing goods or services. All information supplied by the prospective customer must be treated with the utmost confidentiality.

Once the credit application form is submitted to the company, all information contained therein needs to be thoroughly checked by the credit controller. This entails approaching each trade reference and verifying information provided by the prospective customer. The trade reference inquiry is based on evaluating answers on such questions as:

- How long has the subject of inquiry (i.e., the prospective customer) been known to you?
- If a recently opened account, were satisfactory references given?
- What amount of credit do you allow to the subject of inquiry?
- What are your credit terms?
- Are payments made regularly and in accordance with your terms?
- Is there any additional information pertaining to the subject of inquiry?

Upon obtaining trade references and verifying information provided by the prospective customer, the credit controller needs to decide whether the credit should be approved. If the credit is approved, the maximum amount of credit, terms of repayment, and securities required from the prospective customer must be specified. Once appropriate securities are obtained and credit terms

Exhibit 3–39a

Credit Application Form

ABC Company
Application for Credit

1. Name of company/individual (in full): _____

   _____

2. Full names of directors/partners: _____

   _____

3. Street address (where business is carried out): _____

   _____

4. Postal address: _____

5. Business telephone No: _____ After hours: _____

6. Registered office address (if a company): _____

7. Name of bankers _____ Branch: _____ Phone No.: _____

8. Two trade references:

   (a) Name: _____ Phone No.: _____

   (b) Name: _____ Phone No.: _____

9. Period of business activity: _____

10. If a company, are the officers prepared to bind themselves as sureties and co-principal debtors?   ( ) Yes   ( ) No

11. Monthly credit requirements: _____

12. Sales tax exemption number: _____

   (Please attach a copy of the certificate)

I, the undersigned _____
                   (Please print name in full)

being the owner/partner/director of the applicant referred to in paragraph 1 above, do hereby:

(a) warrant that I am entitled to bind the above company,
(b) warrant that if credit is granted to the applicant I fully understand that all accounts are payable strictly 30 (thirty) days from date of statement, unless otherwise agreed to by both parties in writing,

---

are accepted by the prospective customer, both companies may begin a normal trading relationship. Credit terms and conditions imposed by the company do not have to be the same for every customer. It is advisable, in fact, to maintain sufficiently flexible credit terms to ensure a continuous flow of business. Such terms should be specifically applied to the most valuable customers (i.e., those who place significant purchase orders on a continuous basis).

Sometimes, however, the company may require immediate payment upon the delivery of goods supplied to customers. In this case, the transaction takes

Exhibit 3–39b

(continued)

Application for credit (continued)

(c) warrant that in the event of your having to institute action against the applicant
for any amounts due, whether in excess of the _____ Court limit or not, although
in your discretion to sue in the Court, I hereby consent to the jurisdiction of the
_____ Court in terms of Section _____ of the _____ Court Act No. _____
of 19__ as amended.

The applicant further warrants that all information given in this application form is true
and correct and any credit granted to the applicant has been based on the truth and
accuracy of the information furnished herein:

Signed at _____ this _____ day of _____ 19 _____

_____
The applicant (who warrants that he/she is duly authorized to sign hereto)

Witnesses by:

1. _____ 2. _____

On behalf of the management and staff of _____ I thank you for
your assistance and cooperation in supplying the above information.

****

For office use only

1. Bank reference: _____

2. Credit reference: _____

3. Credit reference: _____

Credit reference checked by: _____ Date: _____

Credit granted in the sum of _____ per month

_____ Total

Authorized by: _____

Subject to the conditions referred to above

Credit forms sent by _____ Date: _____

---

place on a **cash on delivery (COD)** basis. Many companies also offer **cash discounts** to their customers to stimulate payments of accounts receivable within a specified period of time. For example, a cash discount structure may look as follows:

- Cash discount of 5 percent if payment is received on a COD basis, or 5 percent COD
- Cash discount of 2.5 percent if payment is received within 30 days from delivery, or 2.5 percent/30 days
- No cash discount if the payment is received within 60 days from delivery, or net/60 days

Irrespective of the particular credit terms offered to customers, all outstanding accounts should be continuously monitored and the following measures should apply:

- Customers' credit ratings must be evaluated prior to the granting of credit.
- All transactions between the company and its customers must be recorded in the appropriate books of account.
- Monthly statements of account must be forwarded to all customers.
- Contact with customers should be on a continuous basis to ensure agreement on the outstanding balances.
- Outstanding amounts must be collected promptly.

Accounts receivable represent an important part of the company's current and liquid capital, and it is essential to ensure their timely collection. The first step in ensuring timely collection of accounts receivable entails preparing **monthly statements** of customers' accounts. Each statement summarizes the dates, invoices, and amounts that reflect customers' purchases during a particular month. In addition, all outstanding amounts are summarized in accordance with the outstanding period of time, ranging from 1 to 90 days or more. An illustration of a typical monthly statement of account is presented in Exhibit 3–40.

Once all monthly statements are prepared, each statement must be immediately sent to the appropriate customer. Moreover, all details related to outstanding amounts owed by the customers must be entered into the monthly **debtors age analysis report**. Each report summarizes all customer accounts in accordance with the outstanding period of time, ranging from 1 to 90 days or more. An illustration of a typical monthly debtors age analysis report is presented in Exhibit 3–41.

Additional measures that sometimes need to be undertaken by the credit controller entail sending special letters to those customers who do not pay on time. Such letters usually consist of three different types as follows:

- **Overdue account letter.** This is the first measure to be applied to customers who may be late with their payment. The overdue account letter must specify the dates, invoice numbers, and amounts which are in arrears. Moreover, the letter should contain a request for payment within seven days.

Exhibit 3–40

Monthly Statement of Account

ABC Company Monthly Statement of Account				
To: Customer A Address:		Your account with us: No. 546 Date of statement: August 31, 1989		
Date	Invoice No.	Your Order No.	Amount	Terms
8.01.89 8.05.89 8.20.89	123 139 160	385 390 420	$ 200.00 400.00 600.00	COD. 5% / COD. net60
Outstanding Period (days)				Payment Instructions
1–30	31–60	61–90	91–over	Total Amount
$1200.00	$600.00	$300.00	$100.00	$2,200.00

Payment Instructions
Please remit a payment of $400.00 which is overdue.

Exhibit 3–41

Monthly Debtors Age Analysis Report

Date: August 31, 1989	Outstanding Period (Days)				Total Amount	Comments
Debtor	1–30	31–60	61–90	91–over		
ABC Company — Monthly Debtors Age Analysis Report						
Customer A	$1,200	$600	$300	$100	$2,200	
Customer B	1,000	200	—	—	1,200	
Customer C	—	1,000	400	600	2,000	
Total	$2,200	$1,800	$700	$700	$5,400	

- **Final reminder letter.**   This letter should be sent if no response has been received to the previous one. The final reminder letter must emphasize that the customer's failure to comply with credit conditions offered by the company may jeopardize future supplies. Moreover, the letter should contain a request for immediate payment.
- **Final demand.**   This letter should be sent by certified mail if no response has been received on the previous one. The final demand letter must clarify that the customer's failure to comply with immediate payment will result in legal action. Such action should be undertaken within seven days without further notice to the customer. Moreover, all deliveries and credit facilities should be suspended until the matter is rectified.

   Another function of the credit controller is to review existing credit terms granted by the company to its customers. Such a review should be carried out on a regular basis (possibly once every six months) and should include the following details:

- *Name of the customer.*   Who is the customer?
- *Size of the customer.*   Is it a small, medium-sized, or large company?
- *Business period.*   How many years has the customer purchased goods or services from the company?
- *Credit risk.*   Does the customer present a good, fair, or questionable credit risk?
- *Current credit.*   What is the current credit amount allowed by the company and actual amount owed to it?
- *Annual business volume.*   What are the current and potential values of purchases generated by the customer?
- *Payment period.*   What is the average payment period secured by the customer during this year?

   Once each aspect of the history of business relations between the company and a particular customer is thoroughly examined, final conclusions may be reached. By reaching such conclusions, the credit controller will be in a better position to decide whether to increase or to reduce credit terms offered to the customer.

3.14 Inventory Management

One of the major responsibilities of the financial manager is to develop, implement, and maintain an effective **inventory management system** within a company. Development of such a system is particularly important since the company often commits a substantial part of its capital to inventory.

Many companies frequently experience serious problems related to inventory management. Some typical inventory problems are as follows:

- The value of inventories is increasing at a faster rate than the level of sales.
- There is a disparity between the actual value of inventories in the stores and in relevant accounting records.
- There is a substantial quantity of slow moving and obsolete inventories in the stores.
- There is a frequent shortage of fast moving items, which results in a loss of sales.
- Shortage of certain inventories creates an unnecessary burden on production planning efforts and causes an increase in machine setup times.
- Inventory turnover rate is below the norm acceptable in a particular industry.

Different types of inventory may be used by the company depending upon the nature of its activities. In an earlier discussion about the financial statements, all inventories have been classified as follows:

- **Merchandise inventory.** This represents all spare parts used by a service company and all goods purchased for resale by a merchandising company.
- **Direct materials inventory.** This represents all raw materials purchased by a manufacturing company. These materials, used in a manufacturing process, are converted into **work-in-process inventory** and, subsequently, into **finished goods inventory.**

Inventory is usually converted into cash during an accounting period not exceeding one year, and for this reason it is considered a current asset. Inventory consists of all goods that are owned by the company at any point in time and their value must be measured on a regular basis. The AICPA states that "a major objective of accounting for inventories is the proper determination of income through the process of matching appropriate costs against revenues".[10] Hence, inventory management plays an important role in determining the final results of the company's activities during a specific accounting period.

Inventory owned by the company at the start of an accounting period is termed **beginning inventory**, while inventory that remains at the end of the accounting period is termed **ending inventory**. The determination of inventory costs is essential in calculating such values as cost of goods manufactured, cost of goods available for sale, cost of goods sold, gross margin from sales, and net income.

It is important, therefore, to ensure that the values of inventory at the start and at the end of the fiscal period are stated correctly. An understatement or an overstatement of inventory values leads to inaccurate results on financial statements. A typical effect of an error on the computation of results specified in the income statement in ending inventory is illustrated in Exhibit 3–42.

An error in the ending inventory for one fiscal period will be transferred as an error in the beginning inventory for the succeeding fiscal period. This, in turn,

Exhibit 3–42

Effect of an Error on Results Specified in the Income Statement in Ending Inventory

ABC Company
Income Statement
For a Period: January 1, 1989 - December 31, 1989

Description of Account		Correct Statement of Ending Inventory	Incorrect Statement of Ending Inventory
(+)	Revenue from sales	$200,000	$200,000
	Cost of goods sold		
	Merchandise inventory,		
(+)	January 1, 1989	$ 25,000	$ 25,000
(+)	Net purchases	100,000	100,000
(=)	Cost of goods available for sale	125,000	125,000
	Merchandise inventory		
(−)	December 31, 1989	15,000	20,000
(−) (=)	Cost of goods sold	110,000	105,000
(=)	Gross margin from sales	90,000	95,000
(−)	Total operating expenses	60,000	60,000
(=)	Income from operations	30,000	35,000

will cause incorrect computation of results similar to those described above.

The cost assigned to inventory depends on two basic measurements: *quantity* and *unit cost*. Quantity is determined by a systematic physical count of inventory, or simply **taking inventory**, at the end of the fiscal year. When taking inventory, all materials should be arranged in a suitable order to ensure that items are neither counted twice nor omitted altogether. Furthermore, it is essential to establish correct ownership of materials at the inventory-taking date or a predetermined **cut-off point**. Only inventory that is the property of the company should be included in the count. All other materials that may have been sold but not yet dispatched to customers or materials received on consignment from suppliers (not yet purchased) must be excluded form the inventory count.

The AICPA states that "the primary basis of accounting for inventory is cost, which has been defined generally as the price paid or consideration given to acquire an asset. As applied to inventories, cost means in principle the sum of applicable expenditures and charges directly or indirectly incurred in bringing an article to its existing condition and location."[11] Thus, inventory should be recorded at its cost, which includes not only the net purchase price but also all additional expenses in acquiring the material such as freight or transportation costs, transit insurance, custom and excise duties or tariffs, and handling charges.

Since the company's investment in inventory often constitutes a significant part of the total assets, it is very important to ensure accurate valuation of inventory. There are several generally accepted methods of costing inventory, each based on a different assumption:

- **Specific identification method.** This method is based on the assumption that the cost of each inventory item can be identified.
- **Average cost method.** This method is based on the assumption that the cost of ending inventory is the average cost of beginning inventory plus the net cost of all purchases during the period.

- **First-in, first-out (FIFO) method.** This method is based on the assumption that the first merchandise purchased is the first merchandise sold. As a result, the ending inventory consists of the most recently purchased merchandise.
- **Last-in, first-out (LIFO) method.** This method is based on the assumption that the most recently purchased merchandise is the first merchandise sold. As a result, the ending inventory consists of the merchandise purchased during the earlier period.

Each of these inventory costing methods can be adopted by the company regardless of whether or not the actual flow of merchandise corresponds with the relevant assumption. But once a particular method is selected, it must be used consistently from one year to the next to meet the requirements of the IRS. Hence, the final selection of the most suitable method rests with the financial manager. Selection of a specific inventory costing method often entails comparison of results pertaining to the application of each method. Such a comparison is illustrated in Exhibit 3–43.

It is apparent from the comparison of inventory costing methods that there is a significant variation in the value of ending inventory, cost of goods sold, and subsequently in the gross margin from sales. Hence, such variation may affect the costing of finished goods as well as the tax liability of the company. All four methods are regarded as acceptable accounting practice and used in determining taxable income. The popularity of each method, however, differs, as presented in Exhibit 3–44.

The LIFO method appears to be the most popular for several reasons. First, this method most accurately represents the measurement of net income based on the current costs. Second, this method helps to produce lower taxable income, thereby reducing the tax liability.

The FIFO method is used less frequently because many accountants believe that, as a result of applying this method, the company's taxable profit is overstated. This leads to increased tax liability and, subsequently, lower net income.

The average cost method is becoming less popular since it has an effect similar to the FIFO method. An additional disadvantage of the average cost method is that is it conceals changes in current replacement costs of inventory since these costs are averaged with the older ones. As a result of cost averaging, the reported taxable income may not reflect true market conditions.

Exhibit 3–43

Comparison of Four Methods of Inventory Costing

Description of Account		Specific Identification Method	Average Cost Method	First-In, First-Out Method	Last-In, First-Out Method
(+)	Revenue from sales	$1,000	$1,000	$1,000	$1,000
	Cost of goods sold:				
	(+) Beginning inventory	100	100	100	100
	(+) Net purchases	500	500	500	500
	(=) Cost of goods available for sale	600	600	600	600
	(−) Ending inventory	250	230	300	200
(−)	(=) Cost of goods sold	350	370	300	400
(=)	Gross margin from sales	650	630	700	600

Exhibit 3–44

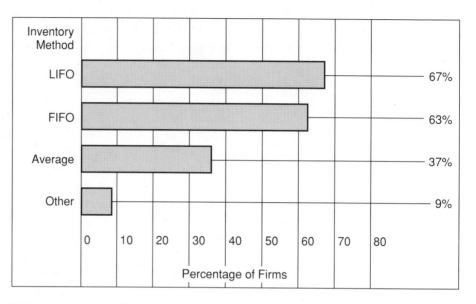

Inventory Cost Methods Used by 600 Large Companies

Total percentage exceeds 100 because some companies used different methods for different types of inventory.

SOURCE: American Institute of Certified Public Accountants, *Accounting Trends and Techniques* (New York: AICPA, 1985). Reprinted with permission.

The specific identification method is used least frequently despite its apparent reasonableness. This method might be used in pricing expensive inventory items such as automobiles, jewelry, or heavy machinery. In other instances, this method proves to be impractical since it is very difficult to keep track of the purchase and sale of low- and medium-cost inventory items. Moreover, if the company buys and sells identical items at different costs, the use of the specific identification method may lead to faulty pricing decisions and miscalculation of net income.

There are two basic systems of **inventory control** that can be used by the company. These systems are as follows:

• Periodic inventory system
• Perpetual inventory system

Periodic inventory system is based on counting and costing inventory on a periodic basis, possibly once every six months or once a year. Under this system, no detailed record of inventory movement need be kept during the year, thus resulting in low cost recordkeeping and shelf-monitoring procedures. Periodic inventory system, however, also has several disadvantages such as:

• Lack of detailed records of what items of inventory are available at any point in time
• Inability to respond efficiently to manufacturing inquiries concerning availability of raw materials and work-in-process inventories
• Inability to prepare accurate income statements on a monthly basis

But, the low cost of recordkeeping and shelf monitoring often seems to outweigh the disadvantages.

Perpetual inventory system, on the other hand, is based on the recording on a continuous basis of every transaction pertaining to the movement of inventory.

Exhibit 3–45

Perpetual Inventory Record Card

Perpetual Inventory Record Card								
Description: _____ Part No. 12345 _____						Inventory No.: __ 100 __		
Reorder Level: __ 100 __			Minimum Level: __ 50 __			Location: __ Store A __		
Date	Received			Sold			Balance		
	Units	Cost		Units	Cost		Units	Cost	
		Unit	Total		Unit	Total		Unit	Total
5.1.89							50	5.00	250.00
5.6.89	100	5.00	500.00				150	5.00	750.00
10.6.89				90	5.00	450.00	60	5.00	300.00
16.6.89	100	6.00	600.00				60	5.00	
							100	6.00	900.00

Under this system every purchase, entry, withdrawal, and sale of inventory is recorded in a **perpetual inventory record card**. In order to maintain detailed perpetual inventory records, an individual inventory card must be prepared for every item of inventory kept by the company. A typical inventory card is presented in Exhibit 3–45.

Although the perpetual inventory system provides accurate information about the quantity and cost of inventory on hand at any given point in time, it does not eliminate the need for physical inventory counting at the end of the fiscal period. The perpetual inventory records indicate what should be in the stores, not necessarily what is in the stores. Hence, there may be a discrepancy between actual and recorded values of inventories due to possible theft or spoilage of goods. Any noted loss in inventory should be recorded by debiting inventory loss (not cost of goods sold) and by crediting the inventory account.

The process of inventory valuation is usually based on the inventory's actual cost. Sometimes, however, the market value of inventory may decline below the original cost paid by the company. In this instance, inventory should be valued at the lower cost or market value by applying the **lower-of-cost-or-market (LCM) rule**. There are three basic methods of valuing inventory according to this rule:

- **Item-by-item method.** This method entails comparison of original cost and market value for each item in the inventory and subsequent valuation of inventory at lower values.
- **Major category method.** This method entails comparison of total costs and total market values for each major category of items in the inventory and subsequent valuation of inventory at lower values.
- **Total inventory method.** This method entails comparison of total costs and total market values for all items in the inventory and subsequent selection of the lower total value.

It is often necessary to value the ending inventory on a monthly basis. This is required for accurate preparation of financial statements and computation of

Exhibit 3–46

The Retail Method of Inventory Valuation

	Description	Cost	Retail
(+)	Beginning inventory	$ 20,000	$ 33,000
(+)	Net purchases for the period (including freight in)	100,000	167,000
(=)	Merchandise available for sale	120,000	200,000

$$\text{Cost-to-retail price ratio} = \frac{\$120,000}{\$200,000} = 60\%$$

		Cost	Retail
(−)	Net sales during the period		150,000
(=)	Estimated ending inventory at retail		$ 50,000
(×)	Cost-to-retail price ratio	60%	
(=)	Estimated cost of ending inventory	$ 30,000	

net income. Since the physical counting of ending inventory is a time-consuming and expensive task, the **retail method** may be used to estimate the value of inventory.

The retail method is generally used in retail merchandising organizations. The use of this method is based on the availability of inventory values at the beginning of the period *at cost* and *at retail* (i.e., the original cost and marked selling price). Additional records which are required include the value of new purchases and net sales during the period. The retail method entails calculation of a **ratio of cost-to-retail price** and subsequent application of this ratio to the estimated ending inventory value. An illustration of a typical retail method of inventory valuation is presented in Exhibit 3–46.

Ending inventory can also be estimated by a **gross profit method**. This method is based on the assumption that the **gross profit margin** remains relatively steady from one year to the next. However, since gross profit margin may change from year to year, this method cannot be used for financial statement preparation. It may be used, on the other hand, for insurance claims when inventory is destroyed. This method is simple in application and does not require details of retail prices of inventory and net purchases. An illustration of a typical gross profit margin method of inventory valuation is presented in Exhibit 3–47. In this example an estimated gross profit margin of 40 percent is assumed.

Exhibit 3–47

The Gross Profit Method of Inventory Valuation

(+)	Beginning inventory at cost		$ 20,000
(+)	Net purchases at cost for the period		100,000
(=)	Cost of goods available for sale		$120,000
	(+) Net sales during the period	$150,000	
	(−) Estimated gross profit margin of 40%	60,000	
(−)	(=) Cost of goods sold		90,000
(=)	Estimated cost of ending inventory		$ 30,000

A sound inventory management policy prescribes economical utilization of materials within the company. This is outlined by the **Just-In-Time (JIT)** operating philosophy. The basic objective of this philosophy is the elimination of waste of materials, equipment, working time, and space. Effective implementation of the JIT philosophy may result in a reduction of overall manufacturing expenses and in more efficient utilization of inventory. Additional details about the inventory control and JIT philosophy are discussed in Part 4 (Volume II).

3.15 Capital Assets Management

Apart from utilizing inventory throughout the process of generating funds, the company has a need to acquire and to use additional assets in order to accomplish its commercial objectives. These assets have a useful life of more than one year and are known as **capital assets**, **fixed assets**, or **long-term assets**. Accounting procedures related to capital assets management are mainly concerned with the determination and recording of the cost of assets, methods of depreciation, disposal, and disclosure of assets in financial statements. There are two basic types of capital assets:

- **Tangible capital assets.** These include land, buildings, production and office equipment, furniture, and vehicles.
- **Intangible capital assets.** This include patents, copyrights, trademarks, leaseholds, leasehold improvements, franchises, licenses, formulas, processes, and goodwill.

Capital assets management ensures thorough control over the purchase, utilization, storage, and disposal of company assets. The price of these assets normally includes all costs incurred during their acquisition, transportation, and installation on the company's premises. Full details of purchased assets should be entered into the **capital asset register** at cost. This register includes individual **capital asset records** for equipment, vehicles, and other long-lived assets. A typical capital asset record is presented in Exhibit 3–48.

The useful life of all tangible capital assets, except land, is limited to a certain number of years. For this reason, the total cost of such assets must be distributed over the expected period of useful service and applied as an operating expense. This procedure is known as the **depreciation** of capital assets, and it should be recorded in the capital asset register in accordance with a particular depreciation method selected by management. The life span of capital assets depends primarily upon the nature of their utilization and can be classified as follows:

- Technical life span
- Economical life span

The **technical lifespan** is determined by various factors of an operational nature and terminates when the asset cannot provide further service for which it was purchased originally. The **economic lifespan** depends upon various external factors, such as technological improvements or changing requirements, and

Exhibit 3–48

Capital Asset Record

Capital Asset Record				
Description: _____Vehicle_____			Allocation: Sales department	
Purchase Date: _1.01.89_	Serial No.: ___12345___		Original Cost: ___$20,000___	
Estimated Service Life: __5 (years)__	Estimated Salvage Value: __$5,000__		Method of Depreciation: _Straight line_	
Disposal Date: _1.01.93_	Method of Disposal: ☐ Sold ☐ Trade-in ☐ Scrap			
Year	Beginning Book Value	Annual Depreciation Expense	Accumulated Depreciation	Ending Book Value
1989	$20,000	$3,000	$3,000	$17,000
1990	17,000	3,000	6,000	14,000
1991	14,000	3,000	9,000	11,000
1992	11,000	3,000	12,000	8,000
1993	8,000	3,000	15,000	5,000
Continue record on the back of this card if necessary				

terminates when the asset's performance becomes uneconomical. As soon as it has been selected, purchased, and installed on the company's premises, the asset starts to lose its original value due to depreciation and obsolescence. According to AICPA:

> The cost of a productive facility is one of the costs of the services it renders during its useful economic life. Generally accepted accounting principles require that this cost be spread over the expected useful life of the facility in such a way as to allocate it as equitably as possible to the periods during which services are obtained from the use of the facility. This procedure is known as depreciation accounting, a system of accounting which aims to distribute the cost or other basic value of tangible capital assets, less salvage (if any), over the estimated useful life of the unit . . .in a systematic and rational manner. It is a process of allocation, not of valuation.[12]

There are several factors that affect the computation of depreciation for a specific accounting period. These factors are as follows:

- **Cost.** This is the net purchase price paid to acquire a capital asset. Cost of an asset also includes all relevant transportation and installation expenses.
- **Salvage value.** This is the estimated net price that is expected to be obtained once the capital asset is disposed (i.e., sold, traded-in, or scrapped). The salvage value is also termed **disposal value**, or **residual value**.
- **Depreciable cost.** The depreciable cost of a capital asset is the difference between its cost and salvage value. For example, a vehicle that costs $20,000 and has a salvage value of $5,000 would have a depreciable cost of $15,000.
- **Estimated service life.** This is the total number of service units expected from a capital asset. Service units are usually measured in terms of the number of years the asset is expected to be in use (e.g., building or equipment). Sometimes, however, the estimated service life is measured in different terms (e.g., expected mileage from a vehicle or a truck, or a number of units expected to be produced by a particular machine).

Several methods of depreciation are used by accountants to allocate the cost of a capital asset to a specific accounting period. Some of the most commonly used methods of depreciation are as follows:

- The straight-line method
- The production method
- The double-declining-balance method

The **straight-line method** prescribes an equal distribution of depreciation over the estimated service life of a capital asset, taking into account its salvage value. Thus, according to the straight-line method, the depreciation expense can be determined as follows:

$$\text{Annual depreciation} = \frac{\text{Cost} - \text{Salvage value}}{\text{Estimated service life}}$$

Consider, for example, that an asset costs \$20,000, its estimated service life period is five years, and its salvage value is \$5,000. In this case, **annual depreciation** is determined as follows:

$$\text{Annual depreciation} = \frac{\$20,000 - \$5,000}{5\,\text{years}} = \$3,000$$

The depreciation schedule for the asset, based on the straight-line method, is presented in Exhibit 3–49.

The straight-line method is characterized by the same depreciation expense during each year and a gradual increase in **accumulated depreciation**. At the end of the estimated service life of the capital asset, its **book value**, or **carrying value** (i.e., the difference between the cost of the asset and accumulated depreciation) equals the estimated salvage value.

The **production method** is based on allocating an equal depreciation expense in accordance with the actual use of a capital asset. This method completely ignores the passage of time during which the asset is used and aims at determining the **depreciation per unit of service**. Thus, according to the production method, the depreciation expense can be determined as follows:

$$\text{Depreciation per unit of service} = \frac{\text{Cost} - \text{Salvage value}}{\text{Estimated units of service life}}$$

Consider, for example, a company vehicle that has an estimated service life of 100,000 miles. If the net cost of the vehicle is \$20,000 and its salvage value is \$5,000, *the depreciation per mile* can be determined as follows:

$$\frac{\text{Depreciation}}{\text{per mile}} = \frac{\$20,000 - \$5,000}{100,000\ \text{miles}} = \$0.15\ \text{per mile}$$

Exhibit 3–49

Depreciation Schedule Based on the Straight-Line Method

Date	Cost	Annual Depreciation	Accumulated Depreciation	Ending Book Value
Date of purchase	$20,000	— —	— —	$20,000
End of 1st year	20,000	$3,000	$ 3,000	17,000
End of 2nd year	20,000	3,000	6,000	14,000
End of 3rd year	20,000	3,000	9,000	11,000
End of 4th year	20,000	3,000	12,000	8,000
End of 5th year	20,000	3,000	15,000	5,000

Exhibit 3–50

Depreciation Schedule Based on the Production Method

Date	Cost	Miles	Annual Depreciation	Accumulated Depreciation	Ending Book Value
Date of purchase	$20,000	— —	— —	— —	$20,000
End of 1st year	20,000	15,000	$2,250	$ 2,250	17,750
End of 2nd year	20,000	25,000	3,750	6,000	14,000
End of 3rd year	20,000	30,000	4,500	10,500	9,500
End of 4th year	20,000	20,000	3,000	13,500	6,500
End of 5th year	20,000	10,000	1,500	15,000	5,000

Hence, the depreciation schedule for the company's vehicle will depend upon estimated annual mileage, as illustrated in Exhibit 3–50. Since vehicles and trucks are usually kept for a period not exceeding five years, this schedule covers the same period.

The production method is characterized by unequal depreciation during each year of use. The depreciation expense is determined in direct relation to actual output obtained for the capital asset (e.g., the mileage of the company vehicle). At the end of the asset's estimated service life (i.e., passage of 100,000 miles), its ending book value equals the estimated salvage value (provided, of course, that there were no accidents).

The **double-declining-balance** method is an *accelerated method of depreciation* that prescribes application of a fixed percentage against the ending book value of the capital asset. The fixed percentage used in this method equals twice the straight-line percentage. Thus, if the estimated service life of the asset is 5 years, the annual percentage for depreciation, in this case, is as follows:

$$\text{Annual depreciation rate} = 2 \times \frac{100\%}{5 \text{ years}} = 40\%$$

The use of data from the straight-line method and application of a fixed 40 percent annual depreciation rate to the ending book value provides the results illustrated in Exhibit 3–51.

The double-declining-balance method is characterized by very substantial depreciation during the first year of the asset's use and declining depreciation during each year thereafter. Final depreciation is limited to the amount necessary to reduce the ending book value to the estimated salvage value of the asset. For this reason, depreciation in the example below is applied in full only during the first two years. Partial depreciation of $2,200 is applied during the third year to bring the ending book value of the asset to $5,000 (i.e., the estimated salvage value).

Exhibit 3–51

Depreciation Schedule Based on the Double-Declining-Balance Method

Date	Cost	Annual Depreciation	Accumulated Depreciation	Ending Book Value
Date of purchase	$20,000	— —	— —	$20,000
End of 1st year	20,000	40% × 20,000 = $8,000	$ 8,000	12,000
End of 2nd year	20,000	40% × 12,000 = $4,800	12,800	7,200
End of 3rd year	20,000	— —	2,200*	5,000
End of 4th year	20,000	— —	— —	5,000
End of 5th year	20,000	— —	— —	5,000

* Depreciation is limited to an amount necessary to reduce the ending book value to salvage value.

A recent survey of 600 companies suggests that the straight-line method is the most acceptable method of depreciation. A comparison of results is presented in Exhibit 3–52.

Capital assets are not usually purchased at the beginning or end of the accounting period. In most cases such assets are purchased when they are needed and disposed of when they are no longer useful. Consequently, it is often necessary to determine depreciation for partial accounting periods. If an asset has been purchased at some point during a particular accounting period, the depreciation calculation should be rounded off to the nearest month as follows:

- If the purchase date is between the 1st and the 15th of the month, the calculation of depreciation should start from the first day of that month.
- If the purchase date is between the 16th and the 31st of the month, the calculation of depreciation should start from the first day of the next month.

Assume, for example, that the company's fiscal year starts on January 1 and ends on December 31. If a capital asset was purchased on August 15, the depreciation must be recorded for five full months. The five months depreciation based on the data from the straight-line method example is calculated as follows:

$$\frac{(\text{Cost} - \text{Salvage value})}{\text{Estimated service life}} \times \frac{\text{Depreciation period}}{12 \text{ months}}$$

$$= \frac{(\$20,000 - \$5,000)}{5 \text{ years}} \times \frac{5}{12} = \$1,250$$

In 1981, Congress approved a new method of depreciation, the **Modified, Accelerated Cost Recovery System (MACRS)**. In accordance with this method, the concepts of service life and salvage value of a capital asset could be discard-

Exhibit 3–52

Depreciation Methods Used by 600 Large Companies

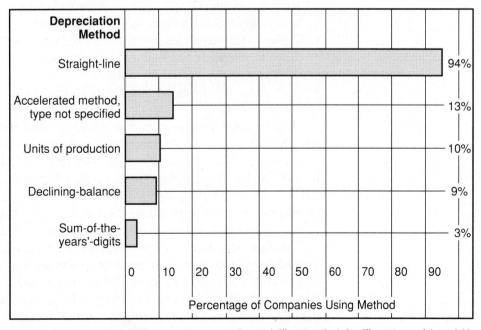

Total percentage exceeds 100 because some companies used different methods for different types of depreciable assets.

SOURCE: American Institute of Certified Public Accountants, *Accounting Trends and Techniques* (New York, AICPA, 1985). Reprinted with permission.

ed, and, instead, a cost recovery allowance would have to be computed on the following basis:

1. On the unadjusted cost of capital assets being recovered
2. Over a period of years prescribed by the law for all capital assets of a similar type
3. By applying the straight-line method or by prescribed percentages not exceeding 150 percent the declining balance method with a half-year convention[13]

The capital asset to be recovered under MACRS was generally defined as tangible property subject to depreciation and placed in service after December 31, 1980 and before January 1, 1987.

In 1986, Congress passed the Tax Reform Act of 1986, outlining new federal tax laws. In accordance with these laws, the basic MACRS concepts were retained despite the following changes:

1. The accelerated method prescribed by the new law for most capital assets, excluding real estate, is based on a 200 percent declining balance with a half-year convention.
2. The new law applies to all capital assets placed in service after December 31, 1986.
3. The MACRS applies to all capital assets placed in service before January 1, 1987. However, for capital assets placed in service after July 31, 1986 and before January 1, 1987, the new law may apply, based on an asset-by-asset evaluation.

Under new federal tax laws, the cost of some capital assets can be recovered in the following periods:

- 3 years—Special tools and devices
- 5 years—Computers, typewriters, copiers and other office equipment, computer-based telephones, central office switching equipment, cars, light and heavy duty trucks, trailers and cargo containers
- 7 years—Production equipment and machinery, office furniture and fixtures
- 10 years—Vessels and liquid transportation equipment
- 27.5 years—Residential buildings
- 31.5 years—Commercial and industrial buildings

Capital asset management also entails control over **capital expenditures**, which relate to additions and betterments of existing assets. **Additions** are enlargements of the physical capacity of an asset (e.g., an additional floor is added to the existing building). **Betterments**, on the other hand, are improvements to capital assets that do not change its physical size (e.g., an air-conditioning system installed in the existing building). In both cases, the expense must be capitalized over a number of years and depreciated as an ordinary capital asset.

Another important element of capital asset management relates to **revenue expenditure**. This type of expenditure includes cost of repairs, maintenance, consumables, and other items needed to operate and to maintain a capital asset. All revenue expenditures must be charged to the operating expense account since they provide a benefit only during the current accounting period. It is necessary, however, to distinguish between ordinary and extraordinary repairs.

Ordinary repairs relate specifically to maintaining a capital asset in good working condition and are treated as an operating expense. **Extraordinary repairs**

are more significant in nature (e.g., overhaul of a boiler) and result in extension of the estimated service life of a capital asset. The total cost of extraordinary repairs must be debited to the accumulated depreciation of the asset, thereby increasing its book value. Subsequently, the asset must be depreciated again by applying the usual depreciation method.

Once a capital asset is no longer required or cannot be used by the company, it should be disposed of. Some of the **methods of assets disposal** are as follows:

- **Sale.** In this case, the asset is sold to another party for cash.
- **Trade-in.** In this case, the asset is used as a down-payment to purchase or is exchanged for another asset.
- **Scrap.** In this case, the asset does not have meaningful value and is sold as scrap or simply given away.

Regardless of the method of disposal, it is necessary to determine a gain or loss disposal of the capital asset. The gain or loss on disposal is determined as follows:

Exhibit 3–53

Accounting for Intangible Capital Assets

Type	Description	Special Accounting Problems
Patent	An exclusive right granted by the federal government for a period of 17 years to make a particular product or use a specific process.	The cost of successfully defending a patent in a patent infringement suit is added to the acquisition cost of the patent. Amortize over the useful life, which may be less than the legal life of 17 years.
Copyright	An exclusive right granted by the federal government to the possessor to publish and sell literary, musical, and other artistic materials for a period of the author's life plus 50 years. Includes computer programs.	Record at acquisition cost, and amortize over the useful life, which is often much shorter than the legal life. For example, the cost of paperback rights to a popular novel would typically be amortized over a useful life of two to four years.
Leasehold	A right to occupy land or buildings under a long-term rental contract. For example, Company A, which owns but does not want to use a prime retail location, sells Company B the right to use it for ten years in return for one or more rental payments. Company B has purchased a leasehold.	Debit leasehold for the amount of the payment, and amortize it over the remaining life of the lease. Payments to the lessor during the life of the lease should be debited to lease expense.
Leasehold improvements	Improvements to leased property that become the property of the lessor (the person who owns the property) at the end of the lease.	Debit leasehold improvements for the cost of improvements, and amortize the cost of the improvements over the remaining life of the lease.
Trademark, brand name	A registered symbol or name giving the holder the right to use it to identify a product or service.	Debit the trademark or brand name for the acquisition cost, and amortize it over a reasonable life not to exceed 40 years.
Franchise, license, formula, process	A right to an exclusive territory or to exclusive use of a formula, technique, or design.	Debit the franchise, license, formula, or process for the acquisition cost, and amortize it over a reasonable life not to exceed 40 years.
Goodwill	The excess of the cost of a group of assets (usually a business) over the market value of the assets individually.	Debit goodwill for the acquisition cost, and amortize it over a reasonable life not to exceed 40 years.

SOURCE: B. E. Needles, Jr., H. R. Anderson, and J. C. Caldwell, *Financial & Managerial Accounting*, (Boston, MA: Houghton Mifflin, 1988), p. 390. Reprinted with permission.

- If the cash received through disposal of the asset exceeds its ending book value, the difference is termed the **gain on disposal**.
- If the cash received through disposal of the asset is less than its ending book value, the difference is termed the **loss on disposal**.

Capital assets management also entails control over purchase, recording, and disposal of intangible assets (e.g., patents, copyrights, trademarks, goodwill, and others as described earlier). Accounting problems that relate to intangible assets are the same as those related to tangible ones. According to the Accounting Principles Board, these problems include the following:

1. Determination of an initial carrying amount (i.e., initial cost)
2. Reduction of the initial cost, after acquisition, under normal business conditions through periodic write-off, or **amortization**, in a manner similar to depreciation
3. Accounting for the initial cost if the asset's value declines substantially and permanently [14]

In addition to these problems, intangible assets have no physical qualities, and their value and service life may be quite difficult to estimate. In accordance with the decision of the Accounting Principles Board, all intangible assets purchased from others must be recorded as assets and written off through periodic amortization. If, however, intangible assets are developed by the company, all development costs must be treated as operating expenses. Additional information related to intangible assets is summarized in Exhibit 3–53.

3.16 Payroll Accounting System

One of the major operating expenses incurred by most companies relates to salaries, wages, and commissions paid and benefits provided to employees. In fact, in many labor-intensive manufacturing and service industries, the payroll cost represents the largest operating expense. Hence, one of the important tasks of financial management is development, implementation, and maintenance of an effective **payroll accounting system.**

An ordinary payroll accounting system is associated with three general types of liabilities:

1. Liabilities for employee compensation
2. Liabilities for employee payroll withholdings
3. Liabilities for employer payroll taxes [15]

The payroll accounting system concerns solely those individuals who are directly employed, supervised, controlled, and paid by the company. Such individuals or employees receive wages, salaries, or commissions and are paid on an hourly, daily, weekly, biweekly, or monthly basis (depending upon the employment agreement between the company and the individual). The payroll accounting system does not apply to outside contractors, who may provide the company with a wide range of services (e.g., accounting, legal, consulting, or plumbing).

Liabilities for employee compensation include wages, salaries, and commissions paid by the company. **Wages** are paid to employees for their work in the company at an hourly rate or on a piecework basis. The Fair Labor Standards Act of 1938*, as amended in 1983, specifies a minimum hourly wage rate of

$3.35, maximum working time of 40 hours per week, overtime pay equal to 1.5 times normal wage rate, child labor provisions, and recordkeeping requirements. In addition, this law prescribes special overtime pay arrangements for work on Saturdays, Sundays, and public holidays.

Consider, for example, that employee John Peters is employed on the following basis:

- Regular wage: $5.00 per hour.
- Overtime wage: $1.5 \times \$5.00 = \$7.50$ per hour.
- Saturdays, Sundays, and public holidays: $2.0 \times \$5.00 = \$10.00$ per hour.
- Regular time: 8 hours per day $\times$ 5 days a week = 40 hours per week.

The total weekly wage earned by John Peters depends upon the number of hours worked during a specific week as reflected in the **payroll timecard**. A typical payroll timecard is presented in Exhibit 3–54.

Salaries refer to fixed amounts of compensation paid to managerial, administrative, and sales employees on a biweekly or monthly basis. Salaried employees are expected to work at least 40 hours per week or longer, depending on the workload within the company. When salaried employees work overtime, they usually do not get additional pay. Diligence and commitment of employees, however, should be compensated when their salaries and wages are reviewed by management.

Exhibit 3–54

Weekly Payroll Timecard

Payroll Timecard							
Name: ____John Peters____				Employee No.: _____12_____			
Department: ____Production____				Pay period ended: ____8.15.1989____			
Day	Morning		Afternoon		Overtime		Hours	
	In	Out	In	Out	In	Out	Regular	Overtime
Mon.	8:00	12:00	1:00	5:00	5:00	7:00	8	2
Tue.	7:58	12:02	1:01	5:01			8	—
Wed.	8:02	12:01	12:58	5:01	5:01	6:59	8	2
Thu.	8:01	12:00	12:59	5:02	5:02	6:03	8	1
Fri.	7:57	12:04	1:00	5:00			8	—
Sat.	8:03	12:01					—	4
Sun.	8:01	10:02					—	2
Description		Hours		Rate		Amount	
Regular		40		$ 5.00		$200.00	
Overtime (1.5)		5		$ 7.50		37.50	
Overtime (2.0)		6		$10.00		60.00	
Total hours		51		Total pay		297.50	

* The minimum wage will increase to $3.80 by April 1990 and $4.25 by April 1991.

Commission is another form of compensation that can be paid to the company's employees for their work. Commissions are usually paid to salespeople in accordance with their sales performance. In this instance, commissions are often coupled with basic monthly salaries. Moreover, commissions may be paid to supervisors in the form of a bonus for efficient performance of their section or department.

Consider, for example, that Linda Peters is employed as a saleswoman and receives a basic biweekly salary of $300.00 and a 1 percent sales commission on all net sales generated. The total payment due to Linda Peters is summarized in a **commissions record** on a biweekly basis. A typical commissions record is presented in Exhibit 3–55.

Liabilities for employee payroll withholdings represent a second major element of an ordinary payroll accounting system. These liabilities include all **deductions** that must be withheld by law from employees' earnings and sent directly to the appropriate government agencies. This group of liabilities include the following:

- FICA tax
- Federal income tax
- State income tax

Additional withholdings made from the employees' earnings relate to various benefit programs designed for employees. These withholdings may include the following:

- Pension payments
- Medical insurance premiums
- Life insurance premiums
- Union dues
- Charitable contributions

FICA tax must be withheld from every employee's earnings in accordance with the Federal Insurance Contributions Act (FICA). The prime purpose of FICA tax is to provide the federal government with additional funds in support of the U. S. Social Security program. This program offers retirement and disability benefits, medical and hospitalization benefits, and survivor's benefits. In addition to funds withheld from employees, this program is also financed by

Exhibit 3–55

Commissions Record

Commissions Record		
Employee name: Linda Peters	Employee No. 45	
Regular biweekly salary: $300.00	Commission: 1%	
Department: Sales	Pay period ended: 8.15.1989	
Sales on account .... $5,000.00 Cash and credit card sales 7,500.00		**Amount**
Total sales .... 12,500.00 Less: sales discounts .... $300.00 sales returns and allowances 200.00 500.00		Regular biweekly salary plus commission on net sales
Net sales $12,000.00 Commission on net sales (1%) 120.00		$300.00 120.00
Total pay		**$420.00**

funds paid by employers and self-employed individuals. The FICA tax schedule for 1990 for both the employer and employee is as follows:

FICA tax rate: 7.65%
Maximum wage taxed under present laws: $50,400
Present maximum tax: $50,400 × 0.0765 = $3,855.60

The FICA tax currently applies to the amount paid to employees not exceeding $50,400. Thus, according to the present law, the maximum tax that could be withheld from an employee is $3,855.60 per year. The employer must deduct the FICA tax from each employee's wages, add an equal amount contributed by the company, and deposit the total amount with the government.

Federal income tax is the largest deduction from most employees' earnings. This tax must be withheld from each employee's earnings by the employer on the basis of "pay as you earn" and sent to the IRS. The amount of federal income tax withheld depends upon the employee's gross earnings and the number of exemptions. Employees are required by law to indicate their exemptions by completing **Employee's Withholding Exemption Certificate (Form W-4).** In accordance with the Tax Reform Act of 1986, each employee is entitled to one exemption for himself or herself and one for each dependent (e.g., spouse and children).

The IRS provides employers with a **Wage Bracket Table** to calculate the correct amount of federal income tax withheld. An example of such a table is presented in Exhibit 3–56.

Thus, if John Peters' total weekly wage is $297.50 and he has three exemptions (himself, his wife, and one child), the federal income tax withholding is $24.00.

State income tax is an additional deduction from employees' earnings and is regulated by the existing tax laws in a specific state. Most states require that employers withhold certain amounts from their employees' earnings and send these taxes to the local IRS. Procedures for calculating state taxes are similar to the ones described above.

Other withholdings from employees' earnings have been described earlier. These withholdings include pension payments, medical insurance premiums, life

Exhibit 3–56

Wage Bracket Table

And the wages are:		Weekly Payroll Period—Employee Married										
		And the number of withholding allowances claims is:										
At least	But less than	0	1	2	3	4	5	6	7	8	9	10 or more
		The amount of income tax to be withheld shall be:										
$200	$210	$20	$17	$14	$11	$ 8	$ 6	$ 3	$ 1	$ 0	$0	$0
210	220	21	18	15	12	9	7	4	2	0	0	0
220	230	22	19	17	14	11	8	6	3	1	0	0
230	240	24	21	18	15	12	9	7	4	2	0	0
240	250	26	22	19	16	14	11	8	6	3	1	0
250	260	27	24	21	18	15	12	9	7	4	2	0
260	270	29	25	22	19	16	13	11	8	5	3	1
270	280	30	27	24	21	18	15	12	9	7	4	2
280	290	32	29	25	22	19	16	13	10	8	5	3
290	300	34	30	27	24	21	18	15	12	9	7	4
300	310	35	32	28	25	22	19	16	13	10	8	5
310	320	37	33	30	27	23	20	18	15	12	9	6

Exhibit 3–57

Weekly Pay Slip

Weekly Pay Slip		
Name of employee: John Peters	Department:	Production
Employee No.: 12	For period ended:	8.15.1989

Gross weekly wages	**$297.50**
Less deductions:	
FICA tax	22.34
Federal income tax	24.00
State income tax	10.00
Pension payment	7.00
Medical insurance premium	12.00
Life insurance premium	8.00
Union dues	2.00
Charitable contribution	1.00
Total withheld	86.34
Net earnings	**$211.16**

insurance premiums, union dues, charitable contributions, and other deductions. Some of these deductions are compulsory, while others are made at the employees' requests. Irrespective of the reason for a particular withholding, the employer is liable to account for each deduction and to maintain accurate accounting records.

Once all deductions are determined, the final amount paid to employees, or **net earnings**, can be calculated. Continuing with the previous example and assuming specific amounts of deductions withheld from John Peters' gross weekly wages, the final amount of net earnings can be summarized on a **weekly pay slip**. An illustration of a typical weekly pay slip is presented in Exhibit 3–57.

An effective payroll accounting system entails maintaining accurate and updated records pertaining to the earnings of each employee. An illustration of a typical manual form of **employee earnings record** is presented in Exhibit 3–58.

The employee earning record reflects all details pertaining to weekly gross earnings, deductions, and subsequent net payments. The cumulative gross earn-

Exhibit 3–58

Employee Earnings Record

Employee Earnings Record													
Name of employee: John Peters				Social security number 123-45-6789									
Address:				Employee No. 12 Hourly rate: $5.00									
				Exemptions (W-4): 3									
Phone:				Position: Machine operator									
Date of birth: 12.15.1949 Sex: M				Date of employment: 1.1.89									
Marital status: Married + one child				Date of employment ended:									

		Earnings			Deductions							Payments		
						Income Tax			Insurance					Cumulative
Period ended	Tot. hrs	Regular	Over time	Gross	FICA Tax	Fed.	State	Pension payment	Med.	Life	Other	Net	Check no.	Gross earnings
8.15.89	53	200.00	97.50	297.50	22.34	24.00	10.00	7.00	12.00	8.00	3.00	211.16	123	297.50

ings must also be reflected in this record and summarized at the end of the fiscal year. This helps the employer to comply with the rule of applying FICA taxes only up to the maximum wage level (i.e., $50,400 per year). Moreover, at the end of the year, the employer must complete a **Wage and Tax Statement (Form W-2)** summarizing the total gross earnings and deductions for each employee. This will enable each employee to prepare his individual tax return at the end of the period prescribed by the IRS. The employer must also submit a copy of the W-2 to the IRS to enable the latter to verify information submitted by employees.

All transactions pertaining to payroll accounting must also be entered into a **payroll journal**, or **payroll register**, on a weekly basis. The information contained in the payroll journal reflects all details pertaining to weekly gross earnings, deductions, and subsequent net payments to employees. An illustration of a typical payroll journal entry was presented earlier in Exhibit 3–8.

Liabilities for employer payroll taxes represent the final element of an ordinary payroll accounting system. These liabilities include all **contributions** that, by law, must be paid by the employer and sent directly to the appropriate government agencies. This group of liabilities includes the following:

- FICA tax
- Federal unemployment insurance tax
- State unemployment insurance tax

FICA tax must be paid by the employer in accordance with the Federal Insurance Contribution Act. The total amount of FICA tax payable by the employer equals the total amount of FICA tax deducted from all employees. For example, if total FICA tax deductions from all employees during one week equal $100, the employer must add another $100 and send a check for $200 to the government. The FICA tax checks must be paid at least once every three months or more frequently, depending upon the amount of tax involved.

Federal unemployment insurance tax must be paid by the employer in accordance with the Federal Unemployment Tax Act (FUTA). This is another part of the U. S. Social Security program aimed at providing financial help to unemployed workers. Unlike FICA taxes, which are imposed on both employers and employees, FUTA tax is levied only on employers. The amount of FUTA tax may vary, although 6.2 percent of the first $7,000 earned by each employee is generally imposed on the employer. Moreover, the employer may receive credit against FUTA tax for unemployment taxes paid to the state. The maximum credit amounts to 5.4 percent of the first $7,000 of each employee's gross earnings. Since most states set their unemployment insurance taxes at this maximum rate, the employer's liability for FUTA tax is 0.8 percent (6.2 − 5.4) of the taxable wages. FUTA tax must be paid once a year if the amount of tax is less than $100. Larger amounts of FUTA tax are paid quarterly.

State unemployment insurance tax must be paid by the employer if it is prescribed by the legislation of a particular state. This tax is levied on the employer in a manner similar to FUTA tax, and it is used for the same purposes. The maximum rate of state unemployment insurance tax, as mentioned earlier, is 5.4 percent of the first $7,000 earned by each employee. In some states, however, employers with good employment records are levied less than 5.4 percent. If, for example, the gross weekly payroll for all employees equals $1,000, FUTA tax is $1,000 × 0.008 = $8, and state unemployment insurance tax is $1,000 × 0.054 = $54. The payment dates for state unemployment insurance taxes vary from one state to another.

3.17 Cost Accounting System

One of the prime responsibilities of the financial manager is to develop, implement, and maintain an effective **cost accounting system.** The main purpose of this system is to facilitate practical methods of identifying and measuring costs of goods and services supplied by the company. Hence, the central question of cost accounting is: "How much does it cost?" Cost accounting deals with four important tasks:

1. Classification of costs
2. Development of a costing system
3. Determination of cost recovery rates
4. Implementation of the costing system

All costs incurred by a company during the process of supplying goods and services to customers are classified as follows:

- Direct costs
- Indirect costs

Direct costs are all operating expenses incurred by the company that can be physically traced to a particular product or service. **Indirect costs**, conversely,

Exhibit 3–59

Classification of Costs

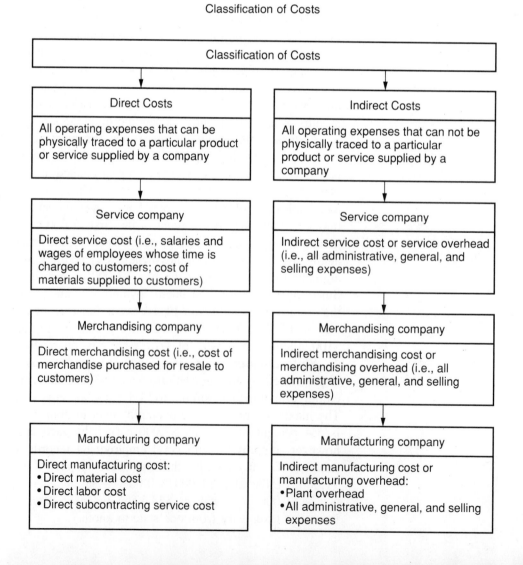

Classification of Costs	
Direct Costs	**Indirect Costs**
All operating expenses that can be physically traced to a particular product or service supplied by a company	All operating expenses that can not be physically traced to a particular product or service supplied by a company
Service company	**Service company**
Direct service cost (i.e., salaries and wages of employees whose time is charged to customers; cost of materials supplied to customers)	Indirect service cost or service overhead (i.e., all administrative, general, and selling expenses)
Merchandising company	**Merchandising company**
Direct merchandising cost (i.e., cost of merchandise purchased for resale to customers)	Indirect merchandising cost or merchandising overhead (i.e., all administrative, general, and selling expenses)
Manufacturing company	**Manufacturing company**
Direct manufacturing cost: • Direct material cost • Direct labor cost • Direct subcontracting service cost	Indirect manufacturing cost or manufacturing overhead: • Plant overhead • All administrative, general, and selling expenses

are all operating expenses that cannot be physically traced to a particular product or service. Both direct and indirect costs differ, depending upon the nature of company activities (service, merchandising, or manufacturing). A typical classification of such costs is summarized in Exhibit 3–59

Service companies provide custom and standard services to customers. A *custom service* is characterized by a nonrepetitive operation to a special customer's order (e.g., accounting, legal, health care, or plumbing). A *standard service*, on the other hand, is characterized by rendering a repetitive service to several customers on a continuous flow basis (e.g., banking, entertainment, or communication). Service companies usually do not carry inventory except for consumable items or spare parts used in the actual service process. All costs incurred by service companies during a specific accounting period are classified as follows:

- **Direct service costs.** These relate to all operating expenses that can be physically traced to a particular service. These costs include salaries and wages of all employees who are directly involved in rendering a particular service (i.e., their time is charged to a customer account).
- **Indirect service costs** or **service overheads.** These relate to all expenses that cannot be directly traced to a particular service. These costs include all administrative, general, and selling expenses incurred by service companies.

Merchandising companies specialize in purchasing and selling various products, or merchandise, to customers at a profit. There are two types of merchandising companies: wholesalers and retailers. *Wholesalers* usually purchase a limited range of goods in large quantities from manufacturers and sell them to retailers. *Retailers*, on the other hand, normally purchase a broad range of goods in smaller quantities from wholesalers, distributors, and even manufacturers and sell such goods to the general public. All costs incurred by merchandising companies during a specific accounting period are classified as follows:

- **Direct merchandising costs.** These include the net cost of all merchandise purchased for resale to customers (i.e., gross cost less discounts and allowances received from suppliers). The final value of the direct merchandising cost, or cost of goods sold, must be adjusted by values of merchandise inventory at the start and at the end of a specific accounting period.
- **Indirect merchandising costs** or **merchandising overheads.** These relate to all operating expenses that cannot be directly traced to the cost of merchandise. These costs include all administrative, general, and selling expenses incurred by merchandising companies.

Manufacturing companies specialize in converting raw materials into a range of finished goods through the use of labor, production facilities, and subcontracting services. There are three basic types of production methods widely employed by manufacturing companies: *job shop production*, *batch production*, and *flow production*. The first two methods are used to produce a limited volume of products and have definite starting and finishing points. Examples include the manufacturing of a product to a special order (job shop production) and the manufacturing of several identical products on a repetitive basis (batch production). The third method, flow production, represents a continuous process of manufacturing a standard range of products in large quantities (e.g., brewery, textile mill, or conveyor line). Additional information concerning various types of operational processes is provided in Part 4 (Volume II) and described in Exhibit 4–3.

All costs incurred by manufacturing companies during a specific accounting period are classified as follows:

- **Direct manufacturing costs.** These relate to all manufacturing expenses that can be physically traced to a particular product. These costs include the net costs of all direct materials, direct labor, and direct subcontracting services.
- **Indirect manufacturing costs or manufacturing overheads.** These relate to all manufacturing and operating expenses that cannot be physically traced to a particular product. These costs include total plant overhead and all administrative, general, and selling expenses.

Direct materials costs include the net costs of all direct materials that are used in the manufacturing process and become part of the finished goods. These materials can be easily identified and allocated to specific products (e.g., timber used in furniture or fabrics used in clothing). The final value of direct materials costs, or **cost of direct materials used**, must be adjusted by the value of direct materials inventory at the start and at the end of a specific accounting period. Materials costs that cannot be easily identified and allocated to finished products are known as **indirect materials costs** (e.g., cost of glue used in furniture or cotton thread used in clothing). The cost of these materials is allocated to indirect materials costs and becomes part of plant overhead.

Direct labor costs include the cost of all direct labor that is used in the manufacturing process and becomes part of the finished goods. These costs can be easily identified and allocated to specific products (e.g., wages of machine operators). All other labor costs that cannot be directly traced to finished products are known as **indirect labor and supervision costs**. For example, wages of production supervisors, planners, designers, assembly workers, maintenance, and other support personnel costs become part of plant overhead.

Direct subcontracting service costs are the costs of all direct subcontracted services purchased from other companies. These services are used in the manufacturing process, become part of the finished goods, and can be easily identified with and allocated to specific products. For example, a steel products manufacturer may subcontract the metal plating process. Subcontracting service costs that cannot be directly traced to finished products are known as **indirect subcontracting service costs** (e.g., cost of equipment insurance). These costs become part of plant overhead.

Plant overhead costs, also known as **factory burden**, include all manufacturing expenses that cannot be directly traced to finished products. These include the cost of indirect materials, indirect labor and supervision, and indirect subcontracting services. Plant overhead costs also include depreciation, property taxes, and rental expense of production equipment, rent and utilities. Finally, **operating expenses** include all administrative, general, and selling expenses incurred by the manufacturing company.

The sum of direct manufacturing costs and plant overhead costs must be added to the net change in work-in-process inventory to determine the **cost of goods manufactured**. Thereafter, this cost must be adjusted by the values of finished goods inventory at the start and at the end of a specific accounting period to determine the **cost of goods sold**.

Once all operating costs of the company's activities are identified, a suitable cost accounting system needs to be developed. Development of a sound cost accounting system aims at recording and recovering all operating costs incurred by the company. The costing of services and products in nonmanufacturing companies is relatively simple since all costs can be easily determined.

Unfortunately, this is not the case in manufacturing firms, where different production processes may be employed (i.e., job shop, batch, or flow production).

Cost accountants generally use one of the two basic **cost accounting methods**. These methods, illustrated in Exhibit 3–60, are as follows:

- Job order costing
- Process costing

Job order costing is used to determine cost of custom service rendered by service companies in which each customer order represents a separate task. Job order costing is also used by wholesalers and retailers to determine the ultimate cost of merchandise supplied to customers. Finally, job order costing is used to determine the cost of products manufactured in job shop or batch production environments.

Process costing, on the other hand, is used to determine cost of standard services rendered by service companies to customers on a continuous flow basis. Process costing is also used to determine cost of products manufactured in a flow production environment.

Irrespective of the type of costing method used, its purpose is to ensure accurate recording and recovery of all operating expenses incurred by the company. One of the basic problems of cost accounting is that the cost of products and services needs to be established immediately, while many operating expenses related to manufacture and supply of final products or rendering of services will occur in the future. For this reason, *the cost accounting system must aim at recovering the company's planned or budgeted expenses.*

In order to ensure effective recovery of all budgeted operating costs, accurate overhead recovery rates need to be determined in advance. An **overhead**

Exhibit 3–60

Costing Methods

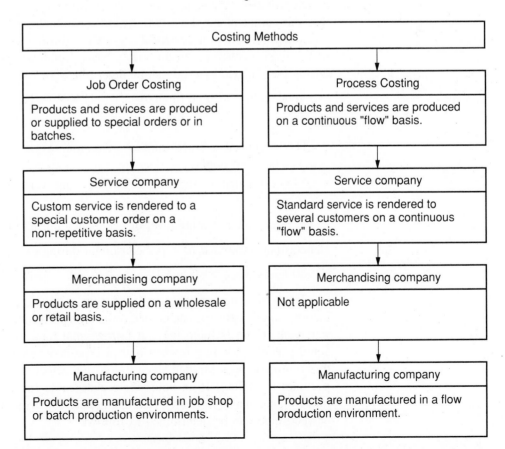

recovery rate, or **overhead rate**, is applied to a specific direct cost in order to determine the ultimate total cost of product or service. Overhead rates can be expressed in different terms, depending upon the nature of company activities and types of products or services supplied to customers. Typical examples of overhead rates are as follows:

- In a custom or standard service company: value per service time (dollars/hour) or value per service operation (dollars/operation)
- In a wholesale or retail merchandising company: value per unit cost of a product or cost markup percentage (%)
- In a manufacturing company (job shop, batch, and flow production environments): value per man-hour (dollars/labor–hour) and value per machine-hour (dollars/machine-hour)

The general process of setting overhead rates for service, merchandising, and manufacturing companies entails the following three steps:

1. Estimate the total output of the company, or per department, or section for the budgeted period. The total output must be expressed in units of the selected activity (e.g., labor-hour, machine-hour, number of operations, types of operations, or quantity of finished products).
2. Examine the budgeted income statement and determine the total estimated cost for the budgeted period, including interest and income taxes expenses.
3. Divide the total estimated cost by the total estimated output expressed in units of the selected activity for the budgeted period.

Determination of overhead rates for service, merchandising, and manufacturing companies is illustrated below. First, consider ABC Service Company, which provides a consulting service to customers (i.e., custom service). Assume that the company employs two senior consultants and two junior ones. Each consultant renders a professional service to customers on a regular basis and his or her work is charged on an hourly basis. Total estimated time per consultant during the budgeted period can be determined as follows:

Total estimated time (hours/year) = H × W × P

Key:

H = estimated average number of regular working hours during one week (say, 40 hours)

W = estimated average number of working weeks during one year (say, 48 weeks)

P = estimated average level of occupancy during one year (say, 70 percent)

Hence, total estimated time per consultant during one year:

40 hours/week × 48 weeks/year × 0.7 = 1,344 hours per year

Total estimated cost of ABC Service Company, including interest and income taxes expenses, can be determined from the company's budgeted income statement. From Exhibit 3–17, it follows that total estimated cost for the budgeted period, including interest and income taxes expenses, is $252,000. Note that profit has been omitted since it does not affect cost but will be added when it comes to pricing. If an hourly rate chargeable for a senior consultant is 1.5 times higher than the hourly rate chargeable for a junior one, then the cost to be recovered can be determined as follows:

1. Total number of unit service hours per year $= (2 \times 1.5 + 2) \times 1,344 = 6,720$ hours per year
2. Cost of a unit service hour $= (\$252,000/\text{year}) \div (6,720 \text{ hr/year}) = \$37.50$ per hour or \$38 per hour
3. Hourly cost per junior consultant is \$38 per hour.
4. Hourly cost per senior consultant is $1.5 \times \$38$ per hour $= \$57$ per hour.

If ABC Service Company provides a standard service to customers on a continuous flow basis, the total service cost can be determined in a similar manner. Assuming that the company renders such a service for 40 hours per week during 48 weeks in a year at 70 percent capacity utilization, the total cost to be recovered on a daily basis is as follows:

$$\frac{\text{Total service}}{\text{cost per hour}} = \frac{\text{Total estimated budgeted cost per year}}{\text{Total estimated service hours per year}} = \frac{\$252,000}{40 \times 48 \times 0.7}$$
$$= \$187.50 \text{ per hour or } \$188 \text{ per hour}$$

Determination of costs in a wholesale or retail merchandising company can also be carried out in a relatively simple manner. Consider, for example, ABC Merchandising Company, which sells a particular range of merchandise to customers on a wholesale or retail basis. From Exhibit 3–18, it follows that the total estimated cost of goods sold during the budgeted period is \$708,000 and the total merchandising overhead (i.e., total operating expenses, interest, and income taxes expenses) is:

$$\$160,800 + \$12,000 + \$110,400 = \$283,200 \text{ per year}$$

The cost markup percentage required to recover the merchandising overhead can be determined as follows:

$$\text{Cost markup percentage} = \frac{\text{Cost of goods sold} + \text{Merchandising overhead}}{\text{Cost of goods sold}}$$
$$= \frac{\$708,000 + \$283,200}{\$708,000} = 140.0\%$$

The cost markup percentage signifies that the actual cost of merchandise (100 percent) must be increased by 40 percent to recover the merchandising overhead. Hence, the ultimate cost of merchandise should include the total cost of doing business and not just the cost of merchandise. Furthermore, the specific method of merchandise inventory valuation should also be considered. For example, if an item costs \$100, its real cost to the merchandising company should be increased by 40 percent, or \$40, thereby reaching \$140.

Costing of products in a manufacturing company represents a more complicated task in comparison with the aforementioned methods. The costing process is based on **standard overhead rates,** which must be determined in advance. Determination of standard overhead rates in a manufacturing company is based on the **Shetzen's costing method** and entails the following seven steps:

1. Examine the production budget and summarize all estimated expenses for each work center (section or shop), excluding the cost of direct materials used and direct subcontracting service costs.
2. Classify budgeted expenses for each work center and determine total costs as follows:
   2.1 **Direct Manufacturing Cost (DMC).**   This cost relates to each *DMC-type work center* for which an hourly rate chargeable to customers can

be established (e.g., toolroom, machine shop, or welding shop).

2.2 Indirect Manufacturing Cost (IMC). This cost relates to each work center for which no hourly rate chargeable to customers is established (e.g., drafting office, production administration and planning, cost estimating, assembly, quality control, maintenance, inventory control, and dispatch).

3. Examine the budgeted income statement and determine **Total Indirect Cost (TIC)**. This cost includes cost of goods sold, total operating expenses, interest, and income taxes expenses, less cost of direct materials used, direct subcontracting service costs, and total DMC.

4. Determine **Total Budgeted Cost (TBC)** to be recovered by the company. This cost is the sum of DMC and TIC (i.e., TBC = DMC + TIC).

    4.1 Enter the individual values of DMC per each DMC-type work center, as specified in step 2, and compute individual percentages of such costs in relation to the total value of same.

    4.2 Enter the value of TIC, as specified in step 3, and compute individual portions of TIC to be recovered by each DMC-type work center. The individual portions of TIC are determined by applying percentages specified in step 4.1 to the value of TIC.

5. Select a suitable **cost recovery method** (1, 2, or 3) for each DMC-type work center as follows:

    5.1 *Method 1.* All costs are recovered solely through machine-hour rates. This is applicable to batch and flow production processes and highly priced pieces of machinery.

    5.2 *Method 2.* All costs are recovered solely through labor-hour rates. This is applicable to job shop and batch production processes for which the labor input can be easily measured and directly allocated to a particular job.

    5.3 *Method 3.* All costs are recovered through machine-hour or labor-hour rates (i.e., combination of methods 1 and 2).

6. Summarize estimated **cost recovery factors** for each DMC-type work center as follows:

    H = estimated average number of regular working hours per shift during one week (normally 40 hours)

    S = estimated average number of working shifts during one week (1 to 3 shifts)

    W = estimated average number of working weeks during one year (48 to 52 weeks)

    U = estimated required level of plant utilization during one year (60 to 80 percent)

    P = estimated required level of labor productivity during one year (60 to 80 percent)

    N = Number of machines or machine operators whose time is charged to various tasks (this number varies from one company to another)

7. Determine standard overhead rates for each DMC-type work center in accordance with the selected cost recovery method (1, 2, or 3), as follows:

$$\frac{\text{Standard overhead rate}}{\text{per machine-hour}} = \frac{\text{Total budgeted cost (TBC) per year}}{\text{Total estimated machine-hours per year}}$$

$$= \frac{\text{TBC}}{\text{H} \times \text{S} \times \text{W} \times \text{U} \times \text{N}}$$

$$\frac{\text{Standard overhead rate}}{\text{per labor-hour}} = \frac{\text{Total budgeted cost (TBC) per year}}{\text{Total estimated labor-hours per year}}$$

$$= \frac{\text{TBC}}{\text{H} \times \text{S} \times \text{W} \times \text{P} \times \text{N}}$$

Consider ABC Manufacturing Company, which is involved in the design, manufacture, assembly, and supply of specific products. Assume that the company has 15 employees in the following departments:

1. Administration, accounting, marketing, and sales — 5 people
2. Production
   - Drafting office — 1 draftsman designer
   - Machine shop — 3 machine operators
   - Welding shop — 2 welders
   - Assembly shop — 2 assembly workers
   - Production administration and maintenance — 2 people

Determination of standard overhead rates in ABC Manufacturing Company entails seven steps, as illustrated in Exhibit 3–61. These steps incorporate information specified in the company's production budget and budgeted income statement, as presented in Exhibits 3-19 and 3-20.

As a result of several calculations, company standard overhead rates are determined as follows:

- Machine shop — $87 per machine-hour
- Welding shop — $68 per labor-hour

Once standard overhead rates are determined, the actual costing process in a manufacturing company may begin. As mentioned earlier, there are two basic costing methods frequently used. These methods are as follows:

- **Job order costing.** This method is used in a job shop or batch production environment.
- **Process costing.** This method is used in a flow production environment.

Although both methods differ in their application, they are based on similar information. Three basic elements need to be established for costing of products in a manufacturing environment. These are the following:

1. **Cost of direct materials used.** This is the total cost of all direct materials and work-in-process used during a specific manufacturing process.
2. **Cost of direct labor or machine time used.** This is the total cost of all labor-hours or machine-hours used during a specific manufacturing process.
3. **Cost of direct subcontracting service used.** This is the total cost of all subcontracting services used during a specific manufacturing process.

All manufacturing costs must be entered into a **job cost sheet** (used in a job shop and batch production environments) or **work cost sheet** (used in a flow production environment). A typical job cost sheet is illustrated in Exhibit 3–62.

All information related to the cost of direct materials, work-in-process, and direct subcontracting services used in a particular manufacturing process is obtained from relevant requisition notes. The labor- or machine-time spent on a particular job is obtained from the **production timecards**, which should

Exhibit 3–61

Determination of Standard Overhead Rates for a Manufacturing Company

Step 1: Summarize budgeted manufacturing expenses per work center in the production department using data in Exhibit 3–19						
+/−	Expense Description	Expense per Work Center (in $)				Total Expense ($)
		Drafting Office	Machine Shop	Welding Shop	Assembly Shop	
+	Direct labor costs	—	76,000	45,000	35,000	156,000
+	Depreciation, production equip.	—	11,400	3,000	—	14,400
+	Indirect labor and supervision costs	20,000	18,000	18,000	8,800	64,800
+	Indirect materials purchases (net)	700	1,200	1,000	700	3,600
+	Insurance, production equip.	—	2,300	1,300	—	3,600
+	Maintenance, production equip.	—	2,800	2,000	—	4,800
+	Property taxes	—	800	400	—	1,200
+	Rent	2,800	9,200	5,600	11,200	28,800
+	Rental expense, production equipment	—	1,200	—	—	1,200
+	Utilities	500	3,700	2,700	1,500	8,400
+	Work-in-process inventory (beginning)	—	—	—	70,000	70,000
−	Work-in-process inventory (ending)	—	—	—	(88,000)	(88,000)
=	Total expense	24,000	126,600	79,000	39,200	268,800
Step 2: Classify budgeted expenses for each work center and determine Direct Manufacturing Cost (DMC) and Indirect Manufacturing Cost (IMC)						
→	Direct manufacturing cost (DMC)	—	126,600	79,000	—	205,600
→	Indirect manufacturing cost (IMC)	24,000	—	—	39,200	63,200

Step 3: Determine Total Indirect Cost (TIC) using data in Exhibits 3–19 and 3–20		
+/−	Expense description	Total Expense
+	Cost of goods sold	615,600
+	Total operating expenses	127,200
+	Interest expense	18,000
+	Income taxes expense	144,000
−	Cost of direct materials used	(330,000)
−	Direct subcontracting service cost	(4,800)
−	Total direct manufacturing cost (DMC)	(205,600)
=	Total indirect cost (TIC)	364,400

Exhibit 3–61

(Concluded)

Step 4: Determine Total Budgeted Cost (TBC) to be recovered by DMC-type work centers, where: TBC = DMC + TIC					
+/−	DMC-Type Work Center	DMC		TIC	TBC
		$	%	$	$
+	Machine shop	126,000	61.6	224,470	351,070
+	Welding shop	79,000	38.4	139,930	218,930
=	Total	205,600	100.0	364,400	570,000

Step 5: Select a suitable cost recovery method (1, 2, or 3)				
	DMC-Type Work Center	Cost Recovery Method		
		1. Machine-hour	2. Labor-hour	3. Combined
→	Machine shop	✔	—	—
→	Welding shop	—	✔	—

Step 6: Summarize estimated cost recovery factors for each DMC-type work center			
→	Cost Recovery Factor Description	Machine Shop	Welding Shop
H	Estimated average number of regular working hours per shift during one week	40 hours	40 hours
S	Estimated average number of working shifts during one year	1 shift	1.2 shift
W	Estimated average number of working weeks during one year	48 weeks	48 weeks
U	Estimated required level of plant utilization during one year	70%	— —
P	Estimated required level of labor productivity during one year	— —	70%
N	Number of machines or machine operators whose time is charged to various tasks	3 machines	2 welders

Step 7: Determine standard overhead rates for each DMC-type work center (hourly rates are rounded to the nearest dollar amount)			
→ DMC-type work center	Formula	Calculation	Overhead Rate
→ Machine shop	$\dfrac{TBC}{H \times S \times W \times U \times N}$	$\dfrac{\$351,070}{(40 \times 1 \times 48 \times 0.7 \times 3)\,hr}$	$87 per machine-hour
→ Welding shop	$\dfrac{TBC}{H \times S \times W \times P \times N}$	$\dfrac{\$218,930}{(40 \times 1.2 \times 48 \times 0.7 \times 2)\,hr}$	$68 per labor-hour

be completed by employees on a daily basis. These timecards are used only in DMC-type work centers in which direct labor or machine-time input is measured and allocated to various jobs. A typical production timecard is illustrated in Exhibit 3–63.

The basic procedures related to the process costing method are very similar to the job order costing procedures. One of the major differences between these costing methods is that, in process costing, all costs are collected on a time basis (say once a week or once a month), using similar sources of information. Once all costs are summarized, the total manufacturing cost is divided into the total number of standard units produced to determine the cost per product unit:

Exhibit 3–62

Job Cost Sheet

ABC Manufacturing Company Job Cost Sheet				
Job No./Batch No.: 123		Product description: Metal boxes		
Product No.: 1000		Quantity: 40 units		
1. *Cost of direct materials used*				
Date	**Material description**		**Requisition No.**	**Total cost**
9.1.89 9.3.89 9.4.89	Steel sheets Handles Locks and hinges		201 210 215	$130 15 20
2. *Cost of direct labor- or machine-time used*				
Date	**Work center**	**Time**	**Hourly rate**	**Total cost**
9.3.89 9.4.89	Machine shop Welding shop	5 hr 2 hr	$87/hr $68/hr	$435 136
3. *Cost of direct subcontracting service used*				
Date	**Service description**		**Requisition No.**	**Total cost**
9.8.89	Metal plating		234	$64
Total manufacturing cost (1 + 2 + 3)				$800
Units produced: 40 units		Cost per unit: $20		
Prepared:		Approved:		Date: 9.15.1989

Exhibit 3–63

Production Timecard

ABC Manufacturing Company Production Timecard					
Name of employee: John Peters		Work center: Machine shop		Date: 9.15.1989	
1st shift	**Job No.**	**2nd shift**	**Job No.**	**3rd shift**	**Job No.**
8:00- 9:00	123	16:00 - 17:00		24:00 - 1:00	
9:00-10:00	123	17:00 - 18:00		01:00 - 2:00	
10:00-11:00	123	18:00 - 19:00		02:00 - 3:00	
11:00-12:00	123	19:00 - 20:00		03:00 - 4:00	
12:00-13:00	—	20:00 - 21:00		04:00 - 5:00	
13:00-14:00	123	21:00 - 22:00		05:00 - 6:00	
14:00-15:00	345	22:00 - 23:00		06:00 - 7:00	
15:00-16:00	345	23:00 - 24:00		07:00 - 8:00	

$$\text{Cost per product unit} = \frac{\text{Total manufacturing cost during the period}}{\text{Total number of units produced during the period}}$$

Once the costs of products or services are determined, the pricing procedures may begin. These procedures are based on standard pricing methods and are discussed next in this part.

3.18 Pricing Methods

There is a certain amount of confusion about the costing and pricing of products or services by managers in various companies. It is important, therefore, to understand the meaning of each concept to ensure effective implementation of the cost accounting system. These concepts can be defined as follows:

- **Cost.** This is the total operating and financing expenses incurred by a company in producing and supplying a product or a service to a customer.
- **Price.** This is the total cost of a product or service supplied to a customer, plus profit generated by the company. Hence:

    Price = Cost + Profit

One of the prime responsibilities of the financial manager is to develop and constantly use sound **pricing methods.** Current pricing of products and services is essential to any profit-oriented organization. Setting of appropriate prices, however, often represents a difficult task for managers. The prime objective of an effective pricing procedure is to ensure that:

- Products and services are offered at competitive prices in the marketplace.
- The price is acceptable to customers
- All costs incurred in supply of products and services to customers are recovered by the company.
- The company produces an income in accordance with a predetermined level of profitability.
- The company maintains its share in the marketplace while maximizing profits.
- The company produces an acceptable level of return on investments by shareholders and outside investors.

The price-setting process is often described as more of an art than a science. Managers frequently price products and services on the basis of "what the market can bear," or "what they (the managers) can get away with." Many factors, however, may influence price-setting decisions. Some of these factors are external to the company, while others are internal.

External factors influencing pricing decisions include the following:

- Overall demand for a particular product or service in the marketplace
- Variety, quality, and price of products and services offered by competitors
- Specific preference by customers for quality versus price
- Seasonal or continuous demand for a product or service
- Stage of life cycle of the product or service

Internal factors influencing pricing decisions include the following:

- Actual cost of product or service
- Required level of return on investment

- Required level of quality of products or services
- Productivity level (for labor intensive products and services)
- Plant utilization level (for automated processes)
- Company's position in the marketplace

Appropriate prices are usually set in accordance with specific pricing strategies adopted by the company's marketing executive, as discussed in Part 5 (Volume II). These strategies include the following:

- **Penetration pricing strategy.** This strategy prescribes entering into the market with new products at reasonably low prices. This enables the company to penetrate the existing market and to attract additional customers.
- **Meet the competition strategy.** The name implies entering into the market with new products at an existing price level established by competitors. This may require that the company offers additional advantages, such as improved quality of the product, to stimulate additional business from customers.
- **Price skimming strategy.** The name suggests entering into the market with new products at reasonably high prices. This strategy is often used when brand new and unique products are introduced to customers.

The central question that relates to the pricing procedure is: "At what price should the product or service be offered to the customer?" There are several pricing methods used by managers for determining prices of products and services. One of the most popular methods is profit margin pricing. The **profit margin pricing method** entails computation of profit margin markup percentage and determination of a profit margin-based price per product or service unit as follows:

$$\text{Profit margin markup percentage} = \frac{\text{Desired income from operations}}{\text{Cost of goods sold} + \text{Total operating expenses}}$$

and

$$\text{Profit margin-based price} = \left(\frac{\text{Total cost}}{\text{per unit}}\right) \times (1 + \text{Profit margin markup percentage})$$

Profit margin pricing method can be used by service, merchandising, and manufacturing companies alike. Consider, for example, ABC Service Company discussed earlier. From the company's budgeted income statement, presented in Exhibit 3–17, the profit margin markup percentage is determined as follows:

$$\text{Profit margin markup percentage} = \frac{\$78,000}{\$222,000} = 35.2\%$$

If the cost per unit of service is $38 per hour as determined in the previous example for ABC Service Company, then:

Profit margin-based price = $38 per hour $\times (1 + 0.352) = $52 per hour

Hence, ABC Service Company should charge its clients the following:

- Hourly rate per junior consultant is $52 per hour.
- Hourly rate per senior consultant is 1.5 × $52 = $78 per hour.

Most service companies price their services on a time-per-hour basis to recover all operating expenses and to produce a desired level of profitability.

Sometimes, however, the service-rendering process entails the supplying of materials or spare parts to customers in conjunction with the providing of specialized labor input. Consider, for example, auto repair shop, plumbing, electrical, or general maintenance specialists. In each case, various materials or spare parts are used as an integral part of rendering service. In order to simplify the pricing procedure in this instance, the cost of all materials and spare parts should be marked up by 10 percent to 50 percent or more. At the same time the company's competitiveness needs to be maintained. Regardless of the quantity of materials or spare parts sold to customers, the total service overhead should be recovered solely through the labor input (i.e., hourly rates chargeable for the work of auto mechanics, plumbers, electricians or general maintenance specialists). Subsequently, additional profit generated through the sale of materials or spare parts should be treated as a bonus.

Determination of the profit margin-based price for merchandising companies can be determined in a similar manner. From ABC Merchandising Company's budgeted income statement, presented in Exhibit 3–18, the profit margin markup percentage is determined as follows:

$$\text{Profit margin markup percentage} = \frac{\$331,200}{\$708,000 + \$160,800} = 38.1\%$$

If the total cost per unit of merchandise (purchase price plus cost markup percentage) is 1.4 times higher then its original cost, as determined in the previous example for ABC Merchandising Company, then:

$$\text{Profit margin-based price} = \text{Original purchase price} \times 1.4 \times (1 + 0.381)$$
$$= \text{Original purchase price} \times 1.9334$$

This means that if ABC Merchandising Company purchased a specific product for resale for $100.00 then:

- The cost markup required to recover all merchandising expenses is $40.00 (i.e., the product actually costs the company: $100 \times 1.4 = \$140.00$).
- Profit margin-markup required to recover all merchandising expenses and generate a desired level of profit is $93.34 (i.e., the product should be sold to a customer at: $100 \times 1.4 \times (1+0.381) = \$100 \times 1.9334 = \$193.34$).

Determination of the profit margin-based price for manufacturing companies can also be determined in the manner described above. From ABC Manufacturing Company's budgeted income statement, presented in Exhibit 3–20, the profit margin markup percentage is determined as follows:

$$\text{Profit margin markup percentage} = \frac{\$457,200}{\$615,600 + \$127,200} = 61.6\%$$

Thus, for example, if the cost per product unit is $20, as illustrated in Exhibit 3–62, then:

$$\text{Profit margin-based price} = \$20 \times (1 + 0.616) = \$32.32$$

Once the selling price for products or services is determined, it is necessary to develop a suitable discount structure to accommodate various situations in a competitive business environment. There are several types of discounts, which are usually considered by the financial manager in collaboration with the marketing executive. These discounts are described in detail in Part 5 (Volume II) and include the following:

- **Trade discount.** This is a reduction in the nominal list price offered to regular customers. A *list price* or *suggested retail price* is the final price attached to a particular product or service.
- **Quantity discount.** This is a reduction in the purchase price based on the quantity of purchased products (expressed either in units or dollars). Quantity discount can be applied on a *cumulative* or *noncumulative* basis.
- **Cash discount.** This is a reduction in the purchase price when a bill is paid on time. Cash discount is usually offered to customers in addition to trade or quantity discounts.
- **Promotional discount.** This is an allowance offered to customers for promoting new products or services in the marketplace. This allowance can be offered in the form of a price reduction, free samples, or display materials.

Since pricing of products and services aims at recovering all costs incurred by the organization and at producing a desired level of profitability in a competitive market environment, it should remain the continuous responsibility of the financial and marketing executives. Only by combining their efforts will both executives be in a position to secure the profitability of their organization and customer satisfaction.

3.19 Management Accounting System

All business managers require accurate and timely information for planning, decision-making, pricing, and controlling purposes. This information, known as **management accounting information**, must be prepared in the financial department on a regular basis. In order to provide an effective method of handling such an important task, the company must develop, implement, and maintain a comprehensive **management accounting system**. The National Association of Accountants defines **management accounting** as:

> the process of identification, measurement, accumulation, analysis, preparation, and communication of financial information used by management to plan, evaluate, and control within the organization and to assure appropriate use and accountability for its resources.[16]

Managers sometimes confuse management accounting information with financial accounting. Some of the basic differences between these types of information have been described earlier in Exhibit 3–3. Additional differences between financial and management accounting are summarized in Exhibit 3–64.

Management accounting provides the basis for the information system known as **responsibility accounting**. The prime purposes of the responsibility accounting system are:

- To classify financial information in accordance with a specific area of responsibility within a company
- To report the performance of individual expense (or cost) center, revenue center, profit center, and investment center

Not all managers have the same degree of financial responsibility within the organization. Some, for example, control various aspects of the company's expenditure, while others control revenues, profits, and investment performance.

Exhibit 3–64

Comparison of Financial and Management Accounting

	Areas of Comparison	Financial Accounting	Management Accounting
1.	Primary users of information	Persons and organizations outside the business entity	Various levels of internal management
2.	Types of accounting systems	Double-entry systems	Not restricted to double-entry system; any useful system
3.	Restrictive guidelines	Adherence to generally accepted accounting principles	No guides or restrictions; only criterion is usefulness
4.	Units of measurement	Historical dollar	Any useful monetary or physical measurement such as labor-hour or machine-hour; if dollars are used, may be historical or future dollars
5.	Focal point for analysis	Business entity as a whole	Various segments of the business entity
6.	Frequency of reporting	Periodically on a regular basis	Whenever needed; may not be on a regular basis
7.	Degree of reliability	Demands objectivity; historical in nature	Heavily subjective for planning purposes, but objective data is used when relevant; futuristic in nature

SOURCE: B. E. Needles, Jr., H. R. Anderson, and J. C. Caldwell, *Financial & Managerial Accounting*, (Boston, MA: Houghton Mifflin, 1988), p. 557. Reprinted with permission.

For this reason, financial responsibility within the organization falls into four major categories:

- Expense center
- Revenue center
- Profit center
- Investment center

Every manager who has authority to spend certain amounts of money on the company's behalf to meet its operational objectives is responsible for an **expense center** or **cost center**. Thus, for example, the production executive is in charge of the production department's expense center. This means that the production executive is responsible for maintaining expenditure in his or her department within the limits prescribed by the annual production budget.

Some managers maintain the responsibility for selling sufficient volume of products or services to meet revenue projections imposed by the company's annual sales budget. These managers are responsible for **revenue centers** within the organization. A sales executive, for example, is responsible for the overall performance of the sales department in terms of meeting annual sales objectives. Moreover, each salesperson carries personal responsibility for meeting individual sales quotas in assigned geographic areas.

Every executive manager, in addition to routine functions, must be responsible for a specific **profit center** within a profit-oriented organization. The number of profit centers depends upon the size of the organization and range of products or services offered to customers. Thus, for example, small companies normally have only one profit center, which is the company itself. Therefore, the overall responsibility for the profit center in a small company is carried by the chief executive officer. Medium-sized and large organizations, on the other hand, usually have separate profit centers for various product and service lines or for various divisions, depending upon their organizational structure. The responsibility for each profit center in these companies is carried by individual product, service, or divisional managers.

The ultimate responsibility of executive managers in an organization is to secure an acceptable level of return on investment (ROI) for shareholders and outside creditors. For this reason, executive managers are responsible for a specific **investment center** within a profit-oriented organization. In financial terms, a return on investment is the ratio between net earnings and average investment value within a particular center. The number of investment centers also depends upon the size of the organization. For example, in small companies the investment center is the company itself. The overall responsibility for the investment center in a small company then is carried by the chief executive officer. Medium-sized and larger organizations usually have several investment centers in accordance with their specific organizational structures.

The main criteria of management accounting reports is their usefulness for day-to-day management control. Hence, the format of such reports may vary from one company to another, depending upon the size, type, and particular requirements of the organization. Most management accounting reports must be prepared on a regular basis to facilitate comprehensive evaluation of the company's performance. An operational guideline for an effective performance evaluation includes the following principles:

- Provision of accurate and suitable measures of performance through a budgeting procedure
- Identification of individual managerial responsibilities based on relevant budget projections
- Comparison of actual performance results with the corresponding budget projections
- Preparation of performance reports, which include the variance between the planned and actual results
- Analysis of performance results and identification of possible causes for variances and areas of concern

An isolated assessment of actual operating results usually does not provide management with the opportunity to judge the performance of the company objectively. For this reason actual levels of revenue, expenses, and income are compared with corresponding budget projection. Such projections constitute an integral part of the budgeting process and should be formulated prior to the commencement of a particular fiscal period.

Management accounting reports concerning the company's operating results should be prepared at least once a month. This will enable management to compare budgeted and actual values on a *monthly* and a *year-to-date basis*. As a result of such a comparison the *variance* between the *planned* and *actual results* can be identified and overall *trends* of the company's performance on a month-to-month basis can be established.

The variance between the planned and actual results must be identified and classified as follows:

- Favorable variance
- Unfavorable variance

Favorable variance is a variance between planned and actual results that provides a positive contribution to the company's actual net income. **Unfavorable variance**, conversely, provides a negative contribution to the company's actual net income. The classification of both types of variances is summarized in Exhibit 3–65.

Exhibit 3–65

Variance Analysis

	Variance Analysis	
Account Description	Favorable (F)	Unfavorable (U)
• Service fees earned • Gross sales • Net sales • Gross margin from sales • Income from operations • Net miscellaneous revenue • Income before taxes • Net income • Inventory (ending)	The actual value exceeds the corresponding budgeted value	The actual value is below the corresponding budgeted value
• Any cost or expense • Inventory (beginning)	The actual value is below the corresponding budgeted value	The actual value exceeds the corresponding budgeted value

Consider ABC Service Company, whose budgeted income statement for the 1990 fiscal year was presented earlier in Exhibit 3–17. Assume that the company is half way through its budgeted period (i.e., six months from the beginning of the 1990 fiscal period). The management accounting report summarizing the first six months of ABC Service Company's performance is presented in Exhibit 3–66.

It appears from Exhibit 3–66 that, although the company exceeded its monthly revenue plan by $2,000, it is still behind on a year-to-date basis by $2,000. Examination of the company's expenditure reveals mixed results and indicates that some variances are favorable on a monthly basis and unfavorable on year-to-date basis, or vice versa. Thus, for example, the company exceeded its monthly budget by $400 on advertising, by $300 on traveling and entertainment, by $100 on utilities, and by $100 on interest expense during June 1990. All other expenses incurred during the same period were well within the limit imposed by the company's monthly budget. As a result, the company produced net income of $6,100, which exceeds the budgeted net income by $2,100.

Although examination of monthly results is essential in evaluating the company's most recent performance, prime attention should be paid to the year-to-date results. These results help management to evaluate overall company performance from the beginning of a particular fiscal period, thereby providing one of the most effective tools of control. Hence, particular care should be exercised in identifying favorable and unfavorable year-to-date variances pertaining to the company's revenues, expenditures, and income.

In the case of ABC Service Company, it overspent $100 on audit and secretarial fees, $500 on communication, $700 on office supplies and expenses, $600 on salaries and wages, and subsequently $300 on total operating expenses. However, since other expenses compare favorably with corresponding budget estimates, the company almost achieved its year-to-date net income projection of $24,000.

In addition to the dollar-to-dollar comparison between budgeted and actual results, examination of monthly management reports should also include comparison of planned and actual percentages of revenues, expenditures, and income against corresponding year-to-date net sales. This enables management to interpret the significance of each year-to-date variance in terms of actual net sales achieved so far. Such a comparison is of particular importance if there is a substantial variation between budgeted and actual net sales.

Exhibit 3–66

Monthly Management Report for a Service Company

			Month: June 1990				Year-to-Date: 1990				Percentage of Actual
		ABC Service Company **Monthly Management Report**									
		Account **Description**	**Budget** **($)**	**Actual** **($)**	**Variance** **($) ÷ (F/U)**		**Budget** **($)**	**Actual** **($)**	**Variance** **($) ÷ (F/U)**		**Year-to-Date** **Net Sales**
+		Service fees earned	25,000	27,000	2,000	F	150,000	148,000	2,000	U	100.00
	+	Advertising expenses	1,800	2,200	400	U	10,800	10,000	800	F	6.8
	+	Audit and secretarial fees	200	—	200	F	1,200	1,300	100	U	0.9
		Communication expenses	1,100	800	300	F	6,600	7,100	500	U	4.8
	+	Depreciation, capital assets	700	700	—	F	4,200	4,200	—	F	2.8
	+	Insurance expenses	600	600	—	F	3,600	3,400	200	F	2.3
	+	Office supplies and expenses	1,600	1,200	400	F	9,600	10,300	700	U	7.0
	+	Rent	1,800	1,800	—	F	10,800	10,800	—	F	7.3
	+	Salaries and wages	9,600	9,500	100	F	57,600	58,200	600	U	39.3
	+	Traveling and entertainment	800	1,100	300	U	4,800	4,300	500	F	2.9
	+	Utilities	300	400	100	U	1,800	1,700	100	F	1.1
−	=	Total operating expenses	18,500	18,300	200	F	111,000	111,300	300	U	75.2
=		Income from operations	6,500	8,700	2,200	F	39,000	36,700	2,300	U	24.8
−		Interest expense	500	600	100	U	3,000	2,800	200	F	1.9
=		Income before taxes	6,000	8,100	2,100	F	36,000	33,900	2,100	U	22.9
−		Income taxes expense	2,000	2,000	—	F	12,000	10,000	2,000	F	6.8
=		Net income	4,000	6,100	2,100	F	24,000	23,900	100	U	16.1

Evaluation of monthly management reports in a merchandising company is carried out in a similar manner. Consider ABC Merchandising Company, whose budgeted income statement for the 1990 fiscal year was presented earlier in Exhibit 3–18. Assume that the company is half way through its budgeted period (i.e., six months from the beginning of the 1990 fiscal period). The management accounting report summarizing the first six months of ABC Merchandising Company's performance is presented in Exhibit 3–67.

The examination of Exhibit 3–67 helps to evaluate the company's monthly and year-to-date performance and compares corresponding budgeted and actual values of revenues, expenditures, and income. For example, the company generated net sales in June 1990 in excess of $1,900 in comparison with the budget. However, on the year-to-date basis the company's actual net sales are still behind

Exhibit 3–67

Monthly Management Report for a Merchandising Company

		Account Description	Month: June 1990				Year-to-Date: 1990				Percentage of Actual Year-to-Date Net Sales
			Budget ($)	Actual ($)	Variance ($) ÷ (F/U)		Budget ($)	Actual ($)	Variance ($) ÷ (F/U)		
	+	Gross sales	103,000	105,000	2,000	F	618,000	608,000	10,000	U	102.9
	−	Sales returns allowances	2,000	1,800	200	F	12,000	11,000	1,000	F	1.9
	−	Sales discounts	1,000	1,300	300	U	6,000	6,200	200	U	1.0
+	=	Net sales	100,000	101,900	1,900	F	600,000	590,800	9,200	U	100.0
	+	Merchandise inventory (beginning)	155,000	160,000	5,000	U	150,000	152,000	2,000	U	25.7
	+	Net purchases	60,000	62,000	2,000	U	360,000	352,000	8,000	F	59.9
	=	Cost of goods available for sale	215,000	222,000	7,000	U	510,000	504,000	6,000	F	85.3
	−	Merchandise inventory (ending)	156,000	158,000	2,000	F	156,000	158,000	2,000	F	26.7
−	=	Cost of goods sold	59,000	64,000	5,000	U	354,000	346,000	8,000	F	58.6
=		Gross margin from sales	41,000	37,900	3,100	U	246,000	244,800	1,200	U	41.4
	+	Advertising expenses	400	500	100	U	2,400	2,800	400	U	0.5
	+	Audit and secretarial fees	300	—	300	F	1,800	1,600	200	F	0.3
	+	Communication expenses	600	700	100	U	3,600	3,700	100	U	0.6
	+	Depreciation, capital assets	500	500	—	F	3,000	3,000	—	F	0.5
	+	Freight out expenses	600	500	100	F	3,600	3,200	400	F	0.5
	+	Insurance expenses	500	500	—	F	3,000	3,200	200	U	0.5
	+	Office supplies and expenses	400	600	200	U	2,400	2,600	200	U	0.4
	+	Property taxes	200	200	—	F	1,200	1,200	—	F	0.2
	+	Rent	2,400	2,400	—	F	14,400	14,400	—	F	2.4
	+	Salaries and wages	6,600	6,300	300	F	39,600	38,500	1,100	F	6.5
	+	Traveling and entertainment	400	300	100	F	2,400	2,000	400	F	0.3
	+	Utilities	500	400	100	F	3,000	2,600	400	F	0.4
−	=	Total operating expenses	13,400	12,900	500	F	80,400	78,800	1,600	F	13.3
=		Income from operations	27,600	25,000	2,600	U	165,600	166,000	400	F	28.1
−		Interest expense	1,000	800	200	F	6,000	5,100	900	F	0.9
+		Net miscellaneous revenue	400	200	200	U	2,400	1,800	600	U	0.3
=		Income before taxes	27,000	24,400	2,600	U	162,000	162,700	700	F	27.5
−		Income taxes expense	9,200	9,000	200	F	55,200	55,000	200	F	9.3
=		Net income	17,800	15,400	2,400	U	106,800	107,700	900	F	18.2

ABC Merchandising Company
Monthly Management Report (Page 1)

the budget by $9,200. This means that the company's sales department should improve its performance.

The cost of goods sold by the company during June 1990 reflects an over-expenditure of $5,000 in comparison with the corresponding budget projection. However, on the year-to-date basis, the company is still doing very well by spending $8,000 below the corresponding budget projection. Both variances are heavily influenced by the availability of inventory at the start and at the end of a particular period as well as the value of net purchases during the same period.

An unfavorable year-to-date net sales variance of $9,200 is dramatically "softened" by a favorable year-to-date cost of goods sold variance of $8,000. This, in turn, helps to reduce the unfavorable variance of gross margin from sales from $3,100 for June 1990 to $1,200 for the year-to-date period. Moreover, it appears that management succeeded in keeping the company's operating expenses below the budget allowances, thereby contributing to favorable total operating expenses variances of $500 during June 1990 and at $1,600 for the year-to-date period.

The "bottom line" parameter of the monthly management report is the value of the year-to-date net income. The company's net income for the first six months of 1990 is $107,700. This represents a very favorable reflection of the company's overall performance, even if its monthly net income is $2,400 below the budget. This is another illustration why the company's performance must be measured against corresponding budget projections not only for every month but on a year-to-date basis too.

Evaluation of monthly management reports in a manufacturing company is carried out in a similar manner. Consider ABC Manufacturing Company, whose production budget and budgeted income statement were presented in Exhibit 3–19 and Exhibit 3–20 respectively. Assume that the company is half way through its budgeted period (i.e., six months from the beginning of the 1990 fiscal period). The management accounting report summarizing the first six months of ABC Manufacturing Company's performance is presented in Exhibit 3–68.

The examination of the monthly management report helps management to control the company's performance on a monthly and year-to-date basis. The first page highlights budgeted and actual expenses incurred by the production department. It appears that the company exceeded its monthly budget by $1,000 on direct materials purchases, by $200 on direct subcontracting service costs, by $100 on indirect materials purchases, and by $500 on production equipment maintenance. This, in turn, contributed to an unfavorable total manufacturing cost variance of $1,100 for June 1990. An unfavorable work-in-process inventory variable caused further excess of the actual cost of goods manufactured in comparison with the budgeted value during June 1990.

Despite generally unfavorable monthly results, the production department appears to perform reasonably well on a year-to-date basis. This is reflected in favorable variances of cost of direct materials used ($4,000), direct labor costs ($1,000), direct subcontracting service costs ($200), total plant overhead costs ($200), total manufacturing costs ($5,400), and cost of goods manufactured ($4,400).

The next step in evaluating the performance of a manufacturing company entails examination of monthly and year-to-date variances pertaining to sales, cost of goods sold, gross margin from sales, operating expenses, income from operations, interest and taxes expenses, and net income. It appears that the company did not meet its sales target during June 1990; however, it is well ahead on a year-to-date basis by $3,000. The cost of goods sold and gross profit

Exhibit 3–68

Monthly Management Report for a Manufacturing Company

			Account Description	Month: June 1990 Budget ($)	Actual ($)	Variance ($) ÷	(F/U)	Year-to-Date: 1990 Budget ($)	Actual ($)	Variance ($) ÷	(F/U)	Percentage of Actual Year-to-Date Net Sales
		+	Direct materials inventory (beginning)	67,500	67,000	500	F	60,000	60,000	—	F	10.0
		+	Direct materials purchases (net)	29,000	30,000	1,000	U	174,000	169,000	5,000	F	28.0
		=	Cost of direct materials available for use	96,500	97,000	500	U	234,000	229,000	5,000	F	38.0
		−	Direct materials inventory (ending)	69,000	68,000	1,000	U	69,000	68,000	1,000	U	11.3
+		=	Cost of direct materials used	27,500	29,000	1,500	U	165,000	161,000	4,000	F	26.7
+			Direct labor costs	13,000	12,400	600	F	78,000	77,000	1,000	F	12.8
+			Direct subcontracting service costs	400	600	200	U	2,400	2,200	200	F	0.4
		+	Depreciation, production equipment	1,200	1,200	—	F	7,200	7,200	—	F	1.2
		+	Indirect labor and supervision costs	5,400	5,000	400	F	32,400	32,200	200	F	5.3
		+	Indirect materials purchases (net)	300	400	100	U	1,800	2,500	700	U	0.4
		+	Insurance, production equipment	300	300	—	F	1,800	1,700	100	F	0.3
		+	Maintenance, production equipment	400	900	500	U	2,400	2,300	100	F	0.4
		+	Property taxes	100	100	—	F	600	600	—	F	0.1
		+	Rent	2,400	2,400	—	F	14,400	14,400	—	F	2.4
		+	Rental expense, production equipment	100	—	100	F	600	—	600	F	—
		+	Utilities	700	600	100	F	4,200	4,300	100	U	0.7
+		=	Total plant overhead costs	10,900	10,900	—	F	65,400	65,200	200	F	10.8
=			Total manufacturing costs	51,800	52,900	1,100	U	310,800	305,400	5,400	F	50.6
+			Work-in-process inventory (beginning)	77,500	77,000	500	F	70,000	70,000	—	F	11.6
=			Total cost of work-in-process	129,300	129,900	600	U	380,800	375,400	5,400	F	62.3
−			Work-in-process inventory (ending)	79,000	78,000	1,000	U	79,000	78,000	1,000	U	12.9
=			Cost of goods manufactured*	50,300	51,900	1,600	U	301,800	297,400	4,400	F	49.3

ABC Manufacturing Company — Monthly Management Report (Page 1)

* Note: Transfer this cost to Page 2 of Monthly Management Report.

Exhibit 3–68

Monthly Management Report for a Manufacturing Company (Concluded)

			Month: June 1990				Year-to-Date: 1990				Percentage of Actual Year-to-Date Net Sales
		ABC Manufacturing Company Monthly Management Report (Page 2)									
		Account Description	**Budget ($)**	**Actual ($)**	**Variance ($) ÷ (F/U)**		**Budget ($)**	**Actual ($)**	**Variance ($) ÷ (F/U)**		
	+	Gross sales	103,000	101,000	2,000	U	618,000	621,000	3,000	F	103.0
	−	Sales returns and allowances	2,000	1,500	500	F	12,000	13,000	1,000	U	2.2
	−	Sales discounts	1,000	500	500	F	6,000	5,000	1,000	F	0.8
+	=	Net Sales	100,000	99,000	1,000	U	600,000	603,000	3,000	F	100.00
	+	Finished goods inventory (beginning)	75,000	76,000	1,000	U	80,000	80,000	—	F	13.3
	+	Cost of goods manufactured (from page 1)	50,300	51,900	1,600	U	301,800	297,400	4,400	F	49.3
	=	Cost of goods available for sale	125,300	127,900	2,600	U	381,800	377,400	4,400	F	62.6
	−	Finished goods inventory (ending)	74,000	75,000	1,000	F	74,000	75,000	1,000	F	12.4
−	=	Cost of goods sold	51,300	52,900	1,600	U	307,800	302,400	5,400	F	50.1
=		Gross margin from sales	48,700	46,100	2,600	U	292,200	300,600	8,400	F	49.9
	+	Advertising expenses	200	400	200	U	1,200	1,600	400	U	0.3
	+	Audit and secretarial fees	300	—	300	F	1,800	1,600	200	F	0.3
	+	Communication expenses	600	700	100	U	3,600	3,800	200	U	0.6
	+	Depreciation, office equipment and vehicles	200	200	—	F	1,200	1,200	—	F	0.2
	+	Freight out expenses	600	500	100	F	3,600	3,500	100	F	0.6
	+	Insurance, vehicles	400	400	—	F	2,400	2,500	100	U	0.4
	+	Office supplies and expenses	400	200	200	F	2,400	2,300	100	F	0.4
	+	Salaries and wages, administration and sales	2,500	2,100	400	F	15,000	14,600	400	F	2.4
	+	Salaries, officers	5,000	4,200	800	F	30,000	30,000	—	F	5.0
	+	Traveling and entertainment	400	600	200	U	2,400	2,900	500	U	0.5
−	=	Total operating expenses	10,600	9,300	1,300	F	63,600	64,000	400	U	10.6
=		Income from operations	38,100	36,800	1,300	U	228,600	236,600	8,000	F	39.2
−		Interest expense	1,500	1,400	100	F	9,000	10,500	1,500	U	1.7
+		Net miscellaneous revenue	400	200	200	U	2,400	1,600	800	U	0.3
=		Income before taxes	37,000	35,600	1,400	U	222,000	227,700	5,700	F	37.8
−		Income taxes expense	12,000	12,000	—	F	72,000	73,000	1,000	U	12.1
=		Net income	25,000	23,600	1,400	U	150,000	154,700	4,700	F	25.7

margin variances also appear to be unfavorable for the monthly period. However, on the year-to-date basis both variances reflect a healthy excess over the budget ($5,400 and $8,400 respectively).

Examination of the monthly management report further indicates that the company's operating expenses are controlled reasonably well despite an insignificantly unfavorable total operating expenses variable of $400 for the six month period. On the other hand, the report notes an excessive interest expense on a year-to-date basis ($1,500) and insufficient net miscellaneous revenue ($800). On the whole, however, this report reflects favorable performance because the company generated a net income of $154,700 during the first six months of 1990. This represents a $4,700 excess against the budget, despite an unfavorable variance of $1,400 during June 1990.

The ability to monitor monthly and year-to-date variations provides management with sufficient insight into the company's operating activities and allows timely identification of problematic areas. Management accounting reports also play an important role in the process of *participative budgeting,* allowing for more active involvement of lower-level managers in the routine control of the organization.

3.20 Computerized Systems

Once a company's operations reach a certain volume, management should consider introducing **computerized systems** to speed up the data collection process. Technological progress in the area of micro and minicomputers and attractive prices further enhance the usefulness of computerized systems. These systems offer a number of important features such as:

- Accurate and fast computation of repetitive accounting tasks
- Storage of large amounts of accounting information
- Easy access to accounting information for evaluation and processing purposes
- Effective transfer of information to other computerized systems
- Possible reduction of administrative staff

There are a variety of micro and minicomputers in the marketplace that may be suitable for small and medium-sized organizations. It is essential, therefore, to identify specific computer requirements and to establish whether a company should invest funds in a computerization process.

Prior to detailed evaluation of computer requirements, it is essential to establish high priority areas in accordance with overall business objectives and to set appropriate cost parameters. The preliminary evaluation of computer needs will indicate:

- The reasons for and against computerization
- The specific objectives and the anticipated benefits as a result of computerization
- The cost justification for a computerized system

Computers are frequently used in a variety of accounting procedures, such as preparing salaries and wages, printing of sales invoices, recording of data into the general ledger, and maintaining inventory control records. It is suggested, however, that an existing set of procedures within the accounting department not be replaced without a comprehensive investigation. It should be remembered that the introduction of a computerized system into the company may require additional training for current personnel, engagement of new employees, and redesign of certain accounting procedures and forms. Thus, the computerization process could present certain difficulties during its integration with other operational activities.

There are several types of computerized systems available to small and medium-sized organizations. In general, these systems are classified as:

- **Microcomputer.** This system includes a single terminal, hard disk storage (or diskette), monitor, and a printer. A microcomputer can be used independently or as a terminal to a larger computer network.
- **Multi-work station system.** This system includes a number of interconnected terminals, which represent a computerized network. Such a network includes several monitors, printers, and storage devices.
- **Computer service bureau** This system does not require computer installation within a company. It merely provides access to an outside computer network either by means of manually generated forms or by means of a terminal or a telephone link-up.

It may be advisable at the initial stage to utilize facilities offered by a reputable computer service bureau, particularly for payroll accounting. Upon the further growth of the company's operations, it may become appropriate to investigate the possible purchase and installation of a microcomputer or, alternatively, of a multi-work station system. The cost of microcomputers has fallen dramatically during recent years, and their average price varies between $1,500 and $5,000 per unit.

Regardless of size, a computerized system is made up of three major components:

- Software
- Hardware
- Computer operators

Software is a special program that is comprised of a set of instructions for the computer to perform routine procedures. There are various software packages in the marketplace designed to serve the needs of small and medium-sized companies. These packages are available in such areas as general accounting and payroll systems, inventory and capital assets management, product design, manufacturing, and sales planning. The price of these packages may vary between $500 and $5,000, depending upon their function and the degree of sophistication.

Hardware consists of input devices, a central processing unit, and output devices. Initial information is entered into the computerized system through appropriate *input devices* such as keyboard terminal, magnetic tapes, card and tape readers, light pens, magnetic ink readers, audio units, numeric pads, mice, and optical scanners.

Once the data is entered into the computerized system, it is directed to the **central processing unit (CPU)**. The CPU consists of a control unit, an arithmetic-logic unit, and a memory section. The prime function of the *control unit* is to interpret instructions from a particular computer program or software package. The *arithmetic-logic unit* is designed to execute various instructions prescribed by the computer program and to perform appropriate calculations. The prime function of the *memory section* in the CPU is to store data. **Read**

Exhibit 3–69

Electronic Computer System

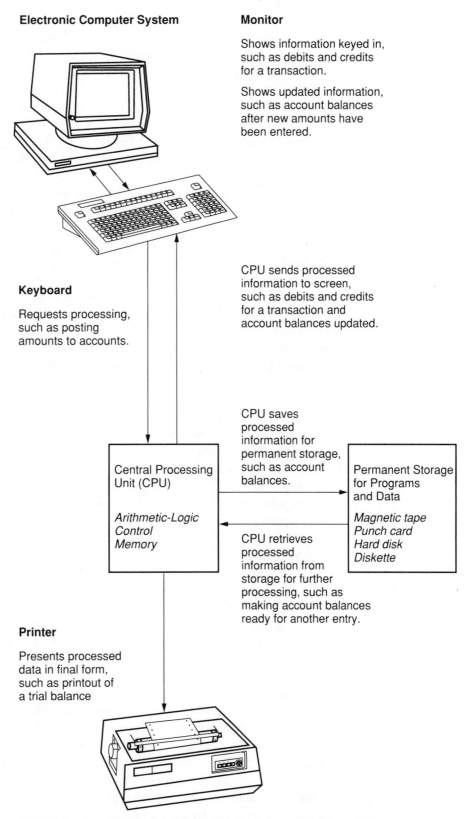

Electronic Computer System

Monitor

Shows information keyed in, such as debits and credits for a transaction.

Shows updated information, such as account balances after new amounts have been entered.

Keyboard

Requests processing, such as posting amounts to accounts.

CPU sends processed information to screen, such as debits and credits for a transaction and account balances updated.

CPU saves processed information for permanent storage, such as account balances.

Central Processing Unit (CPU)

*Arithmetic-Logic
Control
Memory*

Permanent Storage for Programs and Data

*Magnetic tape
Punch card
Hard disk
Diskette*

CPU retrieves processed information from storage for further processing, such as making account balances ready for another entry.

Printer

Presents processed data in final form, such as printout of a trial balance

SOURCE: Douglas J. McQuaig, *College Accounting*, 4th ed. (Boston, MA.: Hougton Mifflin, 1989), p. 71. Reprinted with permission.

Only Memory (ROM), for example, is designed to store programs built into the computer by the manufacturer. **Random Access Memory (RAM)**, on the other hand, enables the computer to receive information through input media and to store it efficiently. A computer's memory is measured in **kilobytes**; one kilobyte has the capacity to store 1,024 characters.

The third element of computer hardware, the *output device*, is designed to provide temporary or permanent storage of data and display of requested information to computer operators or to other computers. The output devices consist of hard or floppy disks, printers, monitors, and card punchers. **Floppy disks,** for example, can be easily stored and moved from one computer to another, thereby providing high flexibility in application. **Hard disks,** on the other hand, are an integral part of the memory section and are usually built into the computer itself.

The critical element in a computerized system is the **computer operator**. The prime functions of a computer operator are to activate and to operate the computerized system continuously. This entails feeding the input data into the system, monitoring the computer's performance, collecting results, and preparing reports. Since the computer is only an electronic machine, the human factor plays a highly significant role in its performance. A computerized system, therefore, is only as effective as the human link involved in its operation. A typical electronic computerized system is presented in Exhibit 3–69.

Correct selection of a computerized system may provide several important advantages and may improve overall efficiency of work within the financial department. Several small and medium-sized companies have already replaced their manual systems with computerized ones for such purposes as:

- Journalizing accounts
- Posting accounts into the ledger
- Preparing trial balances
- Producing financial statements
- Preparing monthly age analysis reports
- Preparing monthly management reports
- Preparing inventory status reports
- Maintaining capital assets status reports
- Printing invoices and statements
- Maintaining a payroll accounting system

The process of switching from a manual accounting system to a computerized one requires additional investment in computer hardware, software, and training of operators. The final decision in switching to the computerized system, therefore, is based on the economic viability of the computerization process. Managers need to remember that even when a computerized system is installed within the financial department, the manual system must remain operative until the new system becomes reliable. The switching process can be a lengthy one and may take several months before the new system is fully operational. Managers also need to remember that any computerized system is only as effective as the people who operate it. Thus, if computer operators are not sufficiently trained, unsuitable software packages are used, or both, the result may be very disappointing. Many companies that have purchased computerized systems failed to implement such systems correctly and subsequently reverted to the "old-fashioned" manual accounting. Hence, in order to succeed in the computerization process, it is vitally important to have reliable hardware, suitable software, and skilled computer operators.

3.21 Working Instructions and Forms

All information related to financial management principles has been presented in Sections 3.01–3.20. It is essential to understand this information and to proceed with the compilation of forms provided at the end of Part 3. Working instructions for completing these forms follow immediately. These instructions require that management rates its knowledge of financial management principles and evaluates company performance in the area of financial management. Aggregate scores will help to identify possible problems and to assign priorities for implementing the most effective solutions. The sequence of activities pertinent to completion of working forms is presented in Exhibit 3–70.

Exhibit 3–70

Summary of Forms for Part 3

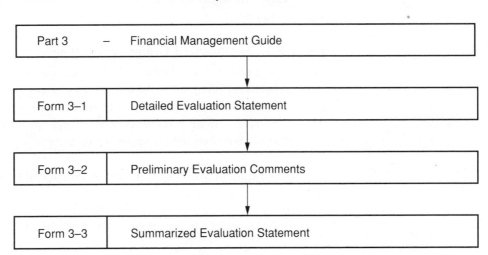

| Part 3 | – | Financial Management Guide |

| Form 3–1 | Detailed Evaluation Statement |

| Form 3–2 | Preliminary Evaluation Comments |

| Form 3–3 | Summarized Evaluation Statement |

Form 3–1   Detailed Evaluation Statement

15. Study the description of all checkpoints related to *financial management principles* as outlined in Part 3.

16. Evaluate your personal knowledge in the area of financial management and score your *personal knowledge level* of each checkpoint. Scores should be based on the scale shown below:

> 0–20(%)   Very poor level of knowledge
> 21–40(%)   Poor level of knowledge
> 41–60(%)   Fair level of knowledge
> 61–80(%)   Good level of knowledge
> 81–100(%) Very good level of knowledge

17. Evaluate your company's performance in the area of financial management and score your *company's performance level* on each checkpoint. Scores should be based on the scale shown below:

> 0–20(%)   Very poor level of performance (the checkpoint has never been implemented)
> 21–40(%)   Poor level of performance (the checkpoint is implemented sometimes)

41–60(%)   Fair level of performance (the checkpoint is implemented but not managed well)

61–80(%)   Good level of performance (the checkpoint is implemented and managed well)

81–100(%)   Very good level of performance (the checkpoint is constantly implemented and managed very well)

18.   Determine the *average evaluation level* pertaining to your personal knowledge and the company's performance within each area of financial management as follows:

$$\text{Average Evaluation Level}(\%) = \frac{\text{Total Score}}{\text{Number of Applicable Checkpoints}}$$

Form 3–2   Preliminary Evaluation Comments

19.   State your personal opinion related to financial management principles currently employed by your company and summarize *preliminary evaluation comments*.

Form 3–3   Summarized Evaluation Statement

20.   Issue Form 3–1 and Form 3–2 to key executives within your company who are actively involved in the *financial management activities* and ensure that both forms are completed in accordance with instructions.

21.   Designate a *final evaluation level*[a] for each checkpoint as a result of a meeting between the company's executives.

See continuation of working instructions on page 100 (Part 4, Volume II)

----

[a] The final evaluation level may not represent an average value of the individual results and should be determined by mutual consent.

NAME OF COMPANY:

FINANCIAL MANAGEMENT ANALYSIS
DETAILED EVALUATION STATEMENT

No.	DESCRIPTION	PERSONAL KNOWLEDGE LEVEL (%)	COMPANY'S PERFORMANCE LEVEL (%)				
			VERY POOR	POOR	FAIR	GOOD	VERY GOOD
		0 - 100	0 - 20	21 - 40	41 - 60	61 - 80	81 - 100
3.01	The Financial Management Process						
3.02	Accounting Information						
3.03	Bookkeeping System						
3.04	Financial Statements						
3.05	Financial Performance Evaluation						
3.06	Operating Budget						
3.07	Capital Expenditure Budget						
3.08	Cash Budget						
3.09	Tax Strategies						
3.10	Sources of Finance						
3.11	Internal Control and Cash Management						
3.12	Control of Purchases and Disbursements						
3.13	Credit Control						
3.14	Inventory Management						
3.15	Capital Assets Management						
3.16	Payroll Accounting System						
3.17	Cost Accounting System						
3.18	Pricing Methods						
3.19	Management Accounting System						
3.20	Computerized System						
→	AVERAGE EVALUATION LEVEL						

NAME: POSITION: DATE:

FINANCIAL MANAGEMENT ANALYSIS
PRELIMINARY EVALUATION COMMENTS

No.	DESCRIPTION	PRELIMINARY EVALUATION COMMENTS
3.01	The Financial Management Process	
3.02	Accounting Information	
3.03	Bookkeeping System	
3.04	Financial Statements	
3.05	Financial Performance Evaluation	
3.06	Operating Budget	
3.07	Capital Expenditure Budget	
3.08	Cash Budget	
3.09	Tax Strategies	
3.10	Sources of Finance	
3.11	Internal Control and Cash Management	
3.12	Control of Purchases and Disbursements	
3.13	Credit Control	
3.14	Inventory Management	
3.15	Capital Assets Management	
3.16	Payroll Accounting System	
3.17	Cost Accounting System	
3.18	Pricing Methods	
3.19	Management Accounting System	
3.20	Computerized System	

NAME:	POSITION:	DATE:

NAME OF COMPANY:

FINANCIAL MANAGEMENT ANALYSIS
SUMMARIZED EVALUATION STATEMENT

No.	DESCRIPTION	COMPANY'S PERFORMANCE LEVEL (%)				
		ASSESSED BY PRESIDENT	ASSESSED BY FINANCIAL EXECUTIVE	ASSESSED BY	ASSESSED BY	FINAL EVALUATION LEVEL
3.01	The Financial Management Process					
3.02	Accounting Information					
3.03	Bookkeeping System					
3.04	Financial Statements					
3.05	Financial Performance Evaluation					
3.06	Operating Budget					
3.07	Capital Expenditure Budget					
3.08	Cash Budget					
3.09	Tax Strategies					
3.10	Sources of Finance					
3.11	Internal Control and Cash Management					
3.12	Control of Purchases and Disbursements					
3.13	Credit Control					
3.14	Inventory Management					
3.15	Capital Assets Management					
3.16	Payroll Accounting System					
3.17	Cost Accounting System					
3.18	Pricing Methods					
3.19	Management Accounting System					
3.20	Computerized System					
→	AVERAGE EVALUATION LEVEL					

NAME:	POSITION:	DATE:

3.22 Appendix A: Compound Interest and Present Value Tables

Exhibit A–1

Future Value of $1 After a Given Number of Time Periods

Periods	1%	2%	3%	4%	5%	6%	7%	8%	9%	10%	12%	14%	15%
1	1.010	1.020	0.030	1.040	1.050	1.060	1.070	1.080	1.090	1.100	1.120	1.140	1.150
2	1.020	1.040	1.061	1.082	1.103	1.124	1.145	1.166	1.188	1.210	1.254	1.300	1.323
3	1.030	1.061	1.093	1.125	1.158	1.191	1.225	1.260	1.295	1.331	1.405	1.482	1.521
4	1.041	1.082	1.126	1.170	1.216	1.262	1.311	1.360	1.412	1.464	1.574	1.689	1.749
5	1.051	1.104	1.159	1.217	1.276	1.338	1.403	1.469	1.539	1.611	1.762	1.925	2.011
6	1.062	1.126	1.194	1.265	1.340	1.419	1.501	1.587	1.677	1.772	1.974	2.195	2.313
7	1.072	1.149	1.230	1.316	1.407	1.504	1.606	1.714	1.828	1.949	2.211	2.502	2.660
8	1.083	1.172	1.267	1.369	1.477	1.594	1.718	1.851	1.993	2.144	2.476	2.853	3.059
9	1.094	1.195	1.305	1.423	1.551	1.689	1.838	1.999	2.172	2.358	2.773	3.252	3.518
10	1.105	1.219	1.344	1.480	1.629	1.791	1.967	2.159	2.367	2.594	3.106	3.707	4.046
11	1.116	1.243	1.384	1.539	1.710	1.898	2.105	2.332	2.580	2.853	3.479	4.226	4.652
12	1.127	1.268	1.426	1.601	1.796	2.012	2.252	2.518	2.813	3.138	3.896	4.818	5.350
13	1.138	1.294	1.469	1.665	1.886	2.133	2.410	2.720	3.066	3.452	4.363	5.492	6.153
14	1.149	1.319	1.513	1.732	1.980	2.261	2.579	2.937	3.342	3.798	4.887	6.261	7.076
15	1.161	1.346	1.558	1.801	2.079	2.397	2.759	3.172	3.642	4.177	5.474	7.138	8.137
16	1.173	1.373	1.605	1.873	2.183	2.540	2.952	3.426	3.970	4.595	6.130	8.137	9.358
17	1.184	1.400	1.653	1.948	2.292	2.693	3.159	3.700	4.328	5.054	6.866	9.276	10.76
18	1.196	1.428	1.702	2.026	2.407	2.854	3.380	3.996	4.717	5.560	7.690	10.58	12.38
19	1.208	1.457	1.754	2.107	2.527	3.206	3.617	4.316	5.142	6.116	8.613	12.06	14.23
20	1.220	1.486	1.806	2.191	2.653	3.207	3.870	4.661	5.604	6.728	9.646	13.74	16.37
21	1.232	1.516	1.860	2.279	2.786	3.400	4.141	5.034	6.109	7.400	10.80	15.67	18.82
22	1.245	1.546	1.916	2.370	2.925	3.604	4.430	5.437	6.659	8.140	12.10	17.86	21.64
23	1.257	1.577	1.974	2.465	3.072	3.820	4.741	5.871	7.258	8.954	13.55	20.36	24.89
24	1.270	1.608	2.033	2.563	3.225	4.049	5.072	6.341	7.911	9.850	15.18	23.21	28.63
25	1.282	1.641	2.094	2.666	3.386	4.292	5.427	6.848	8.623	10.83	17.00	26.46	32.92
26	1.295	1.673	2.157	2.772	3.556	4.549	5.807	7.396	9.399	11.92	19.04	30.17	37.86
27	1.308	1.707	2.221	2.883	3.733	4.822	6.214	7.988	10.25	13.11	21.32	34.39	43.54
28	1.321	1.741	2.288	2.999	3.920	5.112	6.649	8.627	11.17	14.42	23.88	39.20	50.07
29	1.335	1.776	2.357	3.119	4.116	5.418	7.114	9.317	12.17	15.86	26.75	44.69	57.58
30	1.348	1.811	2.427	3.243	4.322	5.743	7.612	10.06	13.27	17.45	29.96	50.95	66.21
40	1.489	2.208	3.262	4.801	7.040	10.29	14.97	21.72	31.41	45.26	93.05	188.9	267.9
50	1.645	2.692	4.384	7.107	11.47	18.42	29.46	46.90	74.36	117.4	289.0	700.2	1,084

SOURCE: All tables in Appendix A are from Henry R. Anderson and Mitchell H. Raiborn, *Basic Cost Accounting Concepts* (Boston, MA: Houghton Mifflin, 1977), pp. 552–557. Reprinted with permission.

Exhibit A–2

Future Value of $1 Paid in Each Period for a Given Number of Time Periods

Periods	1%	2%	3%	4%	5%	6%	7%	8%	9%	10%	12%	14%	15%
1	1.000	1.000	1.000	1.000	1.000	1.000	1.000	1.000	1.000	1.000	1.000	1.000	1.000
2	2.010	2.020	2.030	2.040	2.050	2.060	2.070	2.080	2.090	2.100	2.120	2.140	2.150
3	3.030	3.060	3.091	3.122	3.153	3.184	3.215	3.246	3.278	3.310	3.374	3.440	3.473
4	4.606	4.122	4.184	4.246	4.310	4.375	4.440	4.506	4.573	4.641	4.779	4.921	4.993
5	5.101	5.240	5.309	5.419	5.526	5.637	5.751	5.867	5.985	6.105	6.353	6.610	6.742
6	6.152	6.308	6.468	6.633	6.802	6.975	7.153	7.336	7.523	7.716	8.115	8.536	8.754
7	7.214	7.434	7.662	7.898	8.142	8.394	8.654	8.923	9.200	9.487	10.09	10.73	11.07
8	8.286	8.583	8.892	9.214	9.549	9.897	10.26	10.64	11.03	11.44	12.30	13.23	13.73
9	9.369	9.755	10.16	10.58	11.03	11.49	11.98	12.49	13.02	13.58	14.78	16.09	16.79
10	10.46	10.95	11.46	12.01	12.58	13.18	13.82	14.49	15.19	15.94	17.55	19.34	20.30
11	11.57	12.17	12.81	13.49	14.21	14.97	15.78	16.65	17.56	18.53	20.65	23.04	24.35
12	12.68	13.41	14.19	15.03	15.92	16.87	17.89	18.98	20.14	21.38	24.13	27.27	29.00
13	13.81	14.68	15.62	16.63	17.71	18.88	20.14	21.50	22.95	24.52	28.03	32.09	34.35
14	14.95	15.97	17.09	18.29	19.60	21.02	22.55	24.21	26.02	27.98	32.39	37.58	40.50
15	16.10	17.29	18.60	20.02	21.58	23.28	25.13	27.15	29.36	31.77	37.28	43.84	47.58
16	17.26	18.64	20.16	21.82	23.66	25.67	27.89	30.32	33.00	35.95	42.75	50.98	55.72
17	18.43	20.01	21.76	23.70	25.84	28.21	30.84	33.75	36.97	40.54	48.88	59.12	65.08
18	19.61	21.41	23.41	25.65	28.13	30.91	34.00	37.45	41.30	45.60	55.75	68.39	75.84
19	20.81	22.84	25.12	27.67	30.54	33.76	37.38	41.45	46.02	51.16	63.44	78.97	88.21
20	22.02	24.30	26.87	29.78	33.07	36.79	41.00	45.76	51.16	57.28	72.05	91.02	102.4
21	23.24	25.78	28.68	31.97	35.72	39.99	44.87	50.42	56.76	64.00	81.70	104.8	118.8
22	24.47	27.30	30.54	34.25	38.51	43.39	49.01	55.46	62.87	71.40	92.50	120.4	137.6
23	25.72	28.85	32.45	36.62	41.43	47.00	53.44	60.89	69.53	79.54	104.6	138.3	159.3
24	26.97	30.42	34.43	39.08	44.50	50.82	58.18	66.76	76.79	88.50	118.2	158.7	184.2
25	28.24	32.03	36.46	41.65	47.73	54.86	63.25	73.11	84.70	98.35	133.3	181.9	212.8
26	29.53	33.67	38.55	44.31	51.11	59.16	68.68	79.95	93.32	109.2	150.3	208.3	245.7
27	30.82	35.34	40.71	47.08	54.67	63.71	74.48	87.35	102.7	121.1	169.4	238.5	283.6
28	32.13	37.05	42.93	49.97	58.40	68.53	80.70	95.34	113.0	134.2	190.7	272.9	327.1
29	33.45	38.79	45.22	52.97	62.32	73.64	87.35	104.0	124.1	148.6	214.6	312.1	377.2
30	34.78	40.57	47.58	56.08	66.44	79.06	94.46	113.3	136.3	164.5	241.3	356.8	434.7
40	48.89	60.40	75.40	95.03	120.8	154.8	199.6	259.1	337.9	442.6	767.1	1,342	1,779
50	64.46	84.58	112.8	152.7	209.3	290.3	406.5	573.8	815.1	1,164	2,400	4,995	7,218

Exhibit A–3

Present Value of $1 to Be Received at the End of a Given Number of Time Periods

Periods	1%	2%	3%	4%	5%	6%	7%	8%	9%	10%	12%
1	0.990	0.980	0.971	0.962	0.952	0.943	0.935	0.926	0.917	0.909	0.893
2	0.980	0.961	0.943	0.925	0.907	0.890	0.873	0.857	0.842	0.826	0.797
3	0.971	0.942	0.915	0.889	0.864	0.840	0.816	0.794	0.772	0.751	0.712
4	0.961	0.924	0.888	0.855	0.823	0.792	0.763	0.735	0.708	0.683	0.636
5	0.951	0.906	0.863	0.822	0.784	0.747	0.713	0.681	0.650	0.621	0.567
6	0.942	0.888	0.837	0.790	0.746	0.705	0.666	0.630	0.596	0.564	0.507
7	0.933	0.871	0.813	0.760	0.711	0.665	0.623	0.583	0.547	0.513	0.452
8	0.923	0.853	0.789	0.731	0.677	0.627	0.582	0.540	0.502	0.467	0.404
9	0.914	0.837	0.766	0.703	0.645	0.592	0.544	0.500	0.460	0.424	0.361
10	0.905	0.820	0.744	0.676	0.614	0.558	0.508	0.463	0.422	0.386	0.322
11	0.896	0.804	0.722	0.650	0.585	0.527	0.475	0.429	0.388	0.350	0.287
12	0.887	0.788	0.701	0.625	0.557	0.497	0.444	0.397	0.356	0.319	0.257
13	0.879	0.773	0.681	0.601	0.530	0.469	0.415	0.368	0.326	0.290	0.229
14	0.870	0.758	0.661	0.577	0.505	0.442	0.388	0.340	0.299	0.263	0.205
15	0.861	0.743	0.642	0.555	0.481	0.417	0.362	0.315	0.275	0.239	0.183
16	0.853	0.728	0.623	0.534	0.458	0.394	0.339	0.292	0.252	0.218	0.163
17	0.844	0.714	0.605	0.513	0.436	0.371	0.317	0.270	0.231	0.198	0.146
18	0.836	0.700	0.587	0.494	0.416	0.350	0.296	0.250	0.212	0.180	0.130
19	0.828	0.686	0.570	0.475	0.396	0.331	0.277	0.232	0.194	0.164	0.116
20	0.820	0.673	0.554	0.456	0.377	0.312	0.258	0.215	0.178	0.149	0.104
21	0.811	0.660	0.538	0.439	0.359	0.294	0.242	0.199	0.164	0.135	0.093
22	0.803	0.647	0.522	0.422	0.342	0.278	0.226	0.184	0.150	0.123	0.083
23	0.795	0.634	0.507	0.406	0.326	0.262	0.211	0.170	0.138	0.112	0.074
24	0.788	0.622	0.492	0.390	0.310	0.247	0.197	0.158	0.126	0.102	0.066
25	0.780	0.610	0.478	0.375	0.295	0.233	0.184	0.146	0.116	0.092	0.059
26	0.772	0.598	0.464	0.361	0.281	0.220	0.172	0.135	0.106	0.084	0.053
27	0.764	0.586	0.450	0.347	0.268	0.207	0.161	0.125	0.098	0.076	0.047
28	0.757	0.574	0.437	0.333	0.255	0.196	0.150	0.116	0.090	0.069	0.042
29	0.749	0.563	0.424	0.321	0.243	0.185	0.141	0.107	0.082	0.063	0.037
30	0.742	0.552	0.412	0.308	0.231	0.174	0.131	0.099	0.075	0.057	0.033
40	0.672	0.453	0.307	0.208	0.142	0.097	0.067	0.046	0.032	0.022	0.011
50	0.608	0.372	0.228	0.141	0.087	0.054	0.034	0.021	0.013	0.009	0.003

Exhibit A–3

(continued)

14%	15%	16%	18%	20%	25%	30%	35%	40%	45%	50%	Periods
0.877	0.870	0.862	0.847	0.833	0.800	0.769	0.741	0.714	0.690	0.667	1
0.769	0.756	0.743	0.718	0.694	0.640	0.592	0.549	0.510	0.476	0.444	2
0.675	0.658	0.641	0.609	0.579	0.512	0.455	0.406	0.364	0.328	0.296	3
0.592	0.572	0.552	0.516	0.482	0.410	0.350	0.301	0.260	0.226	0.198	4
0.519	0.497	0.476	0.437	0.402	0.320	0.269	0.223	0.186	0.156	0.132	5
0.456	0.432	0.410	0.370	0.335	0.262	0.207	0.165	0.133	0.108	0.088	6
0.400	0.376	0.354	0.314	0.279	0.210	0.159	0.122	0.095	0.074	0.059	7
0.351	0.327	0.305	0.266	0.233	0.168	0.123	0.091	0.068	0.051	0.039	8
0.300	0.284	0.263	0.225	0.194	0.134	0.094	0.067	0.048	0.035	0.026	9
0.270	0.247	0.227	0.191	0.162	0.107	0.073	0.050	0.035	0.024	0.017	10
0.237	0.215	0.195	0.162	0.135	0.086	0.056	0.037	0.025	0.017	0.012	11
0.208	0.187	0.168	0.137	0.112	0.069	0.043	0.027	0.018	0.012	0.008	12
0.182	0.163	0.145	0.116	0.093	0.055	0.033	0.020	0.013	0.008	0.005	13
0.160	0.141	0.125	0.099	0.078	0.044	0.025	0.015	0.009	0.006	0.003	14
0.140	0.123	0.108	0.084	0.065	0.035	0.020	0.011	0.006	0.004	0.002	15
0.123	0.107	0.093	0.071	0.054	0.028	0.015	0.008	0.005	0.003	0.002	16
0.108	0.093	0.080	0.060	0.045	0.023	0.012	0.006	0.003	0.002	0.001	17
0.095	0.081	0.069	0.051	0.038	0.018	0.009	0.005	0.002	0.001	0.001	18
0.083	0.070	0.060	0.043	0.031	0.014	0.007	0.003	0.002	0.001		19
0.073	0.061	0.051	0.037	0.026	0.012	0.005	0.002	0.001	0.001		20
0.064	0.053	0.044	0.031	0.022	0.009	0.004	0.002	0.001			21
0.056	0.046	0.038	0.026	0.018	0.007	0.003	0.001	0.001			22
0.049	0.040	0.033	0.022	0.015	0.006	0.002	0.001				23
0.043	0.035	0.028	0.019	0.013	0.005	0.002	0.001				24
0.038	0.030	0.024	0.016	0.010	0.004	0.001	0.001				25
0.033	0.026	0.021	0.014	0.009	0.003	0.001					26
0.029	0.023	0.018	0.011	0.007	0.002	0.001					27
0.026	0.020	0.016	0.010	0.006	0.002	0.001					28
0.022	0.017	0.014	0.008	0.005	0.002						29
0.020	0.015	0.012	0.007	0.004	0.001						30
0.005	0.004	0.003	0.001	0.001							40
0.001	0.001	0.001									50

Exhibit A–4

Present Value of $1 Received Each Period for a Given Number of Time Periods

Periods	1%	2%	3%	4%	5%	6%	7%	8%	9%	10%	12%
1	0.990	0.980	0.971	0.962	0.952	0.943	0.935	0.926	0.917	0.909	0.893
2	1.970	1.942	1.913	1.886	1.859	1.833	1.808	1.783	1.759	1.736	1.690
3	2.941	2.884	2.829	2.775	2.723	2.673	2.624	2.577	2.531	2.487	2.402
4	3.902	3.808	3.717	3.630	3.546	3.465	3.387	3.312	3.240	3.170	3.037
5	4.853	4.713	4.580	4.452	4.329	4.212	4.100	3.993	3.890	3.791	3.605
6	5.795	5.601	5.417	5.242	5.076	4.917	4.767	4.623	4.486	4.355	4.111
7	6.728	6.472	6.230	6.002	5.786	5.582	5.389	5.206	5.033	4.868	4.564
8	7.652	7.325	7.020	6.733	6.463	6.210	5.971	5.747	5.535	5.335	4.968
9	8.566	8.162	7.786	7.435	7.108	6.802	6.515	6.247	5.995	5.759	5.328
10	9.471	8.983	8.530	8.111	7.722	7.360	7.024	6.710	6.418	6.145	5.650
11	10.368	9.787	9.253	8.760	8.306	7.887	7.499	7.139	6.805	6.495	5.938
12	11.255	10.575	9.954	9.385	8.863	8.384	7.943	7.536	7.161	6.814	6.194
13	12.134	11.348	10.635	9.986	9.394	8.853	8.358	7.904	7.487	7.103	6.424
14	13.004	12.106	11.296	10.563	9.899	9.295	8.745	8.244	7.786	7.367	6.628
15	13.865	12.849	11.938	11.118	10.380	9.712	9.108	8.559	8.061	7.606	6.811
16	14.718	13.578	12.561	11.652	10.838	10.106	9.447	8.851	8.313	7.824	6.974
17	15.562	14.292	13.166	12.166	11.274	10.477	9.763	9.122	8.544	8.022	7.102
18	16.398	14.992	13.754	12.659	11.690	10.828	10.059	9.372	8.756	8.201	7.250
19	17.226	15.678	14.324	13.134	12.085	11.158	10.336	9.604	8.950	8.365	7.366
20	18.046	16.351	14.878	13.590	12.462	11.470	10.594	9.818	9.129	8.514	7.469
21	18.857	17.011	15.415	14.029	12.821	11.764	10.836	10.017	9.292	8.649	7.562
22	19.660	17.658	15.937	14.451	13.163	12.042	11.061	10.201	9.442	8.772	7.645
23	20.456	18.292	16.444	14.857	13.489	12.303	11.272	10.371	9.580	8.883	7.718
24	21.243	18.914	16.936	15.247	13.799	12.550	11.469	10.529	9.707	8.985	7.784
25	22.023	19.523	17.413	15.622	14.094	12.783	11.654	10.675	9.823	9.077	7.843
26	22.795	20.121	17.877	15.983	14.375	13.003	11.826	10.810	9.929	9.161	7.896
27	23.560	20.707	18.327	16.330	14.643	13.211	11.987	10.935	10.027	9.237	7.943
28	24.316	21.281	18.764	16.663	14.898	13.406	12.137	11.051	10.116	9.307	7.984
29	25.066	21.844	19.189	16.984	15.141	13.591	12.278	11.158	10.198	9.370	8.022
30	25.808	22.396	19.600	17.292	15.373	13.765	12.409	11.258	10.274	9.427	8.055
40	32.835	27.355	23.115	19.793	17.159	15.046	13.332	11.925	10.757	9.779	8.244
50	39.196	31.424	25.730	21.482	18.256	15.762	13.801	12.234	10.962	9.915	8.305

Exhibit A–4

(continued)

14%	15%	16%	18%	20%	25%	30%	35%	40%	45%	50%	Periods
0.877	0.870	0.862	0.847	0.833	0.800	0.769	0.741	0.714	0.690	0.667	1
1.647	1.626	1.605	1.566	1.528	1.440	1.361	1.289	1.224	1.165	1.111	2
2.322	2.283	2.246	2.174	2.106	1.952	1.816	1.696	1.589	1.493	1.407	3
2.914	2.855	2.798	2.690	2.589	2.362	2.166	1.997	1.849	1.720	1.650	4
3.433	3.352	3.274	3.127	2.991	2.689	2.436	2.220	2.035	1.876	1.737	5
3.889	3.784	3.685	3.498	3.326	2.951	2.643	2.385	2.168	1.983	1.824	6
4.288	4.160	4.039	3.812	3.605	3.161	2.802	2.508	2.263	2.057	1.883	7
4.639	4.487	4.344	4.078	3.837	3.329	2.925	2.598	2.331	2.109	1.922	8
4.946	4.772	4.607	4.303	4.031	3.463	3.019	2.665	2.379	2.144	1.948	9
5.216	5.019	4.833	4.494	4.192	3.571	3.092	2.715	2.414	2.168	1.965	10
5.453	5.234	5.029	4.656	4.327	3.656	3.147	2.752	2.438	2.185	1.977	11
5.660	5.421	5.197	4.793	4.439	3.725	3.190	2.779	2.456	2.197	1.985	12
5.842	5.583	5.342	4.910	4.533	3.780	3.223	2.799	2.469	2.204	1.990	13
6.002	5.724	5.468	5.008	4.611	3.824	3.249	2.814	2.478	2.210	1.993	14
6.142	5.847	5.575	5.092	4.675	3.859	3.268	2.825	2.484	2.214	1.995	15
6.265	5.954	5.669	5.162	4.730	3.887	3.283	2.834	2.489	2.216	1.997	16
6.373	6.047	5.749	5.222	4.775	3.910	3.295	2.840	2.492	2.218	1.998	17
6.467	6.128	5.818	5.273	4.812	3.928	3.304	2.844	2.494	2.219	1.999	18
6.550	6.198	5.877	5.316	4.844	3.942	3.311	2.848	2.496	2.220	1.999	19
6.623	6.259	5.929	5.353	4.870	3.954	3.316	2.850	2.497	2.221	1.999	20
6.687	6.312	5.973	5.384	4.891	3.963	3.320	2.852	2.498	2.221	2.000	21
6.743	6.359	6.011	5.410	4.909	3.970	3.323	2.853	2.498	2.222	2.000	22
6.792	6.399	6.044	5.432	4.925	3.976	3.325	2.854	2.499	2.222	2.000	23
6.835	6.434	6.073	5.451	4.937	3.981	3.327	2.855	2.499	2.222	2.000	24
6.873	6.464	6.097	5.467	4.948	3.985	3.329	2.856	2.499	2.222	2.000	25
6.906	6.491	6.118	5.480	4.956	3.988	3.330	2.856	2.500	2.222	2.000	26
6.935	6.514	6.136	5.492	4.964	3.990	3.331	2.856	2.500	2.222	2.000	27
6.961	6.534	6.152	5.502	4.970	3.992	3.331	2.857	2.500	2.222	2.000	28
6.938	6.551	6.166	5.510	4.975	3.994	3.332	2.857	2.500	2.222	2.000	29
7.003	6.566	6.177	5.517	4.979	3.995	3.332	2.857	2.500	2.222	2.000	30
7.105	6.642	6.234	5.548	4.997	3.999	3.333	2.857	2.500	2.222	2.000	40
7.133	6.661	6.246	5.554	4.999	4.000	3.333	2.857	2.500	2.222	2.000	50

3.23 References

1. Don Ricketts and Jack Gray, *Managerial Accounting*, (Boston, MA: Houghton Mifflin, 1988), pp. 8 and 10.

2. "Basic Concepts and Accounting Principles Underlying Financial Statements of Business Enterprises," *Statement of the Accounting Principles Board, no. 4* American Institute of Certified Public Accountants, (New York: American Institute of Certified Public Accountants, 1970), par.40.

3. "Objectives of Financial Reporting by Business Enterprises," *Statement of Financial Accounting Concepts, no.1* Financial Accounting Standards Board, (Stamford, CT: Financial Accounting Standards Board, 1978), p.17.

4. "Basic Concepts," par.138.

5. Henry R. Anderson and Rickard P. Schwartz, "The Capital Facility Decision," *Management Accounting* (National Association of Accountants, February 1971).

6. Belverd E. Needles Jr., Henry R. Anderson, and James C. Caldwell, *Financial & Managerial Accounting* (Boston, MA: Houghton Mifflin, 1988), pp.985–994.

7. Seymour Jones, M. Bruce Cohen, and Victor V. Coppola, *The Coopers & Lybrand Guide to Growing Your Business* (New York: John Wiley & Sons, 1988), pp. 47–75.

8. American Institute of Certified Public Accountants, *Professional Standards* Vol. I (New York: AICPA, 1 June 1982), sec. AU 320.09.

9. Ibid., Sec.AU 320.28.

10. American Institute of Certified Public Accountants, *Accounting Research Bulletins*, no.43 (New York: AICPA, 1968), ch.4.

11. Ibid.

12. Financial Accounting Standards Board, *Financial Accounting Standards: Original Pronouncements* (Stamford, CT: 1977), ARB No. 43, chap. 9, sec. C, par. 5.

13. Needles, p. 377.

14. Adapted from Accounting Principles Board, "Intangible Assets" *Opinion No. 17* (New York: AICPA, 1970), par. 2.

15. Needles, pp. 341–348.

16. National Association of Accountants, *Statement, no. IA* (New York: NAA, 1982).

Index